The Translator and Editors

Marie Borroff is Sterling Professor of English, Emeritus, at Yale University. Her verse translation of *Sir Gawain and the Green Knight* was first published in 1967; it appeared together with her translations of *Patience* and *Pearl* in 2001. *The Gawain-Poet: Complete Works*, including her translations of *Cleanness* and *St. Erkenwald*, is scheduled for publication in 2010. She is the author of *Sir Gawain and the Green Knight: A Stylistic and Metrical Study* and of *Traditions and Renewals: Chaucer, the Gawain-Poet, and Beyond* (Yale University Press, 1962, 2003).

Laura L. Howes is Associate Professor of English at the University of Tennessee. She is the author of *Chaucer's Gardens and the Language of Convention* (1997) and editor of *Place, Space, and Landscape in Medieval Narrative* (2007).

W. W. NORTON & COMPANY, INC.
Also Publishes

ENGLISH RENAISSANCE DRAMA: A NORTON ANTHOLOGY
edited by David Bevington et al.

THE NORTON ANTHOLOGY OF AFRICAN AMERICAN LITERATURE
edited by Henry Louis Gates Jr. and Nellie Y. McKay et al.

THE NORTON ANTHOLOGY OF AMERICAN LITERATURE
edited by Nina Baym et al.

THE NORTON ANTHOLOGY OF CHILDREN'S LITERATURE
edited by Jack Zipes et al.

THE NORTON ANTHOLOGY OF DRAMA
edited by J. Ellen Gainor, Stanton B. Garner Jr., and Martin Puchner

THE NORTON ANTHOLOGY OF ENGLISH LITERATURE
edited by M. H. Abrams and Stephen Greenblatt et al.

THE NORTON ANTHOLOGY OF LITERATURE BY WOMEN
edited by Sandra M. Gilbert and Susan Gubar

THE NORTON ANTHOLOGY OF MODERN AND CONTEMPORARY POETRY
edited by Jahan Ramazani, Richard Ellmann, and Robert O'Clair

THE NORTON ANTHOLOGY OF POETRY
edited by Margaret Ferguson, Mary Jo Salter, and Jon Stallworthy

THE NORTON ANTHOLOGY OF SHORT FICTION
edited by R. V. Cassill and Richard Bausch

THE NORTON ANTHOLOGY OF THEORY AND CRITICISM
edited by Vincent B. Leitch et al.

THE NORTON ANTHOLOGY OF WORLD LITERATURE
edited by Sarah Lawall et al.

THE NORTON FACSIMILE OF THE FIRST FOLIO OF SHAKESPEARE
prepared by Charlton Hinman

THE NORTON INTRODUCTION TO LITERATURE
edited by Alison Booth and Kelly J. Mays

THE NORTON READER
edited by Linda H. Peterson and John C. Brereton

THE NORTON SAMPLER
edited by Thomas Cooley

THE NORTON SHAKESPEARE, BASED ON THE OXFORD EDITION
edited by Stephen Greenblatt et al.

For a complete list of Norton Critical Editions, visit
www.wwnorton.com/college/English/nce_home.htm

A NORTON CRITICAL EDITION

SIR GAWAIN AND THE GREEN KNIGHT

AN AUTHORITATIVE TRANSLATION
CONTEXTS
CRITICISM

Translation by

MARIE BORROFF
YALE UNIVERSITY

Edited by

MARIE BORROFF

and

LAURA L. HOWES
UNIVERSITY OF TENNESSEE

W • W • NORTON & COMPANY • *New York* • *London*

W. W. Norton & Company has been independent since its founding in 1923, when William Warder Norton and Mary D. Herter Norton first published lectures delivered at the People's Institute, the adult education division of New York City's Cooper Union. The firm soon expanded its program beyond the Institute, publishing books by celebrated academics from America and abroad. By mid-century, the two major pillars of Norton's publishing program—trade books and college texts—were firmly established. In the 1950s, the Norton family transferred control of the company to its employees, and today—with a staff of four hundred and a comparable number of trade, college, and professional titles published each year—W. W. Norton & Company stands as the largest and oldest publishing house owned wholly by its employees.

The text of this book is composed in Fairfield Medium with the display set in Bernhard Modern.
Manufacturing by the Courier Companies—Westford division.
Book design by Antonina Krass.
Composition by Binghamton Valley Composition.
Production manager: Eric Pier-Hocking

Library of Congress Cataloging-in-Publication Data

Gawain and the Grene Knight.
    Sir Gawain and the Green Knight : an authoritative translation, contexts, criticism / translation by Marie Borroff ; edited by Marie Borroff and Laura L. Howes.—1st ed.
        p. cm. — (A Norton critical edition)
    Includes bibliographical references.
    ISBN 978-0-393-93025-2 (pbk.)
    1. Gawain (Legendary character)—Romances. 2. Knights and knighthood—Poetry. 3. Arthurian romances. 4. Gawain and the Grene Knight. I. Borroff, Marie. II. Howes, Laura L. III. Title.
    PR2065.G3A333 2010
    821'.1—dc22

                                                            2009041535

W. W. Norton & Company, Inc., 500 Fifth Avenue, New York, N.Y. 10110
www.wwnorton.com

W. W. Norton & Company Ltd., Castle House, 75/76 Wells Street,
London W1T 3QT

1 2 3 4 5 6 7 8 9 0

Contents

Introduction   vii
The Metrical Forms   xv
Translator's Note   xxvii

The Translated Text of *Sir Gawain and the Green Knight*   1

Contexts

Sir Gawain in Middle English   67
    The Green Knight Enters, lines 130–50   67
    Sir Gawain's Shield, lines 619–39   67
    The Gift of the Green Girdle, lines 1846–69   68
Two Old French *Gauvain* Romances   69
    The Knight of the Sword   71
    The Mule without a Bridle   78
From The *Alliterative Morte Arthure*   81
    Feast at Christmas   81

Criticism

Alain Renoir • Descriptive Technique in *Sir Gawain and the Green Knight*   87
Marie Borroff • [The Challenge Episode: A Stylistic Interpretation]   93
J. A. Burrow • [Recognition and Confession at the Green Chapel]   104
A. Kent Hieatt • *Sir Gawain*: Pentangle, *Luf-Lace*, Numerical Structure   113
W. A. Davenport • [The Hero and His Adventure]   131
Ralph Hanna III • Unlocking What's Locked: Gawain's Green Girdle   144
Lynn Staley Johnson • [Regenerative Time in *Sir Gawain and the Green Knight*]   158
Jonathan Nicholls • [The Testing of Courtesy at Camelot and Hautdesert]   173

Geraldine Heng • Feminine Knots and the Other
   Sir Gawain and the Green Knight   194
Leo Carruthers • The Duke of Clarence and the
   Earls of March: Garter Knights and *Sir Gawain*
   and the Green Knight   217

Chronology   233
Selected Bibliography   235

Introduction

The poem now known as *Sir Gawain and the Green Knight* lay hidden in a fourteenth-century manuscript for over four hundred years. When Sir Frederic Madden of the British Museum recognized the poem as one worth reading, he and a colleague painstakingly transcribed the poem for publication. The first printed edition appeared in 1839 in London, and subsequent editions have followed at regular intervals, including one by the medieval scholar J. R. R. Tolkien a dozen years before he published *The Hobbit*.[1]

The poem might still have languished in scholarly seclusion, because of its relatively difficult dialect of Middle English, had modern translations not followed its discovery, beginning in 1898 with a prose translation by Jessie L. Weston, the same scholar whose work on medieval romance was cited by T. S. Eliot in his notes to *The Wasteland*.[2] The current volume centers on a newly revised verse translation by the scholar and poet Marie Borroff, which first appeared in 1967.

Early in its modern reception, the poem was recognized as an exemplary Arthurian romance, the best in English, a masterpiece of alliterative verse. Appreciation of its poetic artistry—including its style, its surprise ending, the care with which its plot is structured, its descriptive techniques, the development of its hero, its symbolism, and its relation to Christian truth and chivalric mores—contributed to a chorus of critical acclaim that shows no signs of abating. The poem that emerges from these examinations more than holds it own and is often compared with the work of the poet's more famous contemporary, Geoffrey Chaucer.

The Story

In its simplest form, the story of *Sir Gawain and the Green Knight* follows Gawain from Arthur's court, where he steps in for Arthur

1. J. R. R. Tolkien and E. V. Gordon, eds., *Sir Gawain and the Green Knight* (Oxford: Clarendon Press, 1925).
2. Jessie L. Weston, trans., *Sir Gawain and the Green Knight: A Middle English Arthurian Romance Retold in Modern Prose*, (London: D. Nutt, 1898; rpt. 1907).

when the king is challenged by the green intruder; to a remote castle almost a year later, where Gawain is lavishly entertained—and tempted—by a gracious host and his wife; and finally to a prearranged second meeting with the Green Knight, solo, in a wild, wooded valley. The poem's end finds Gawain reunited with his cohorts at Camelot, but with a difference, as he has been tested and, by his own reckoning, has come up short.

The nature of Gawain's test spurs much debate, even within the poem itself, but again the narrative events are clear: the host's wife enters Gawain's bedroom on three successive mornings during his stay, while her husband hunts wild game with his own men. Gawain has agreed to exchange whatever he "wins" during those mornings in bed with whatever his host "wins" while hunting. And so Gawain receives several deer from the host on the first day, a wild boar on the second, and a fox on the third. In return, Gawain presents to his host a series of one, two, and three kisses he has gotten while in bed, although he refuses to tell his host the source of those kisses.

On the third morning, the lady of the castle offers Gawain something else as well: a magic girdle, an embroidered silk sash, that she claims can save his life. This is of great interest to Gawain, who knows he must meet the mysterious and apparently magical Green Knight for a second time at the so-called Green Chapel. At their first meeting, at Arthur's court, the Green Knight had proposed a "game" for any one brave enough to undertake it: a chance to behead the Green Knight, using the intruder's large ax, but with the caveat that he must then submit to the same treatment from the Green Knight in one year's time. At the poem's start, Sir Gawain successfully separates the Green Knight's head from his body, but, to the court's amazement, the Green Knight simply retrieves his head and exits the court, with a reminder to Gawain—delivered from his severed head—to keep his promise. The alleged magic of the lady's green girdle could serve as a forceful secret weapon in Gawain's next encounter with the Green Knight. And Gawain does not exchange this gift, "won" on the third day, with his host, as he should according to the terms of their agreement, but keeps it for himself.

All of these narrative threads are neatly knotted up at the end of the tale, when two of the characters coalesce into one, and the magic of Morgan la Fay is revealed as a source of underlying enchantment. While the poem's resolution may come as a complete surprise to the first-time reader, clues to its denouement in fact are scattered in the poem like bread crumbs, and the repeat reader will enjoy following their trail of discovery.

Sources and Influences

A poem as well designed and as beautifully executed as *Sir Gawain and the Green Knight* was considered an anomaly in English by early scholars, and much effort went into searching for a French poem, from which the *Gawain*-author could have translated in creating *Sir Gawain*. In fact, several other poems contain narrative elements found in *Sir Gawain*, but no single source has been located and the skill of the *Gawain*-poet, now widely recognized, suggests that the poem is original to this poet.

Nevertheless, all writers feel the influence of previous authors, medieval writers gesture especially forthrightly to earlier works, and the *Gawain*-poet clearly knew his French. Echoes from the romances of Chrétien de Troyes include a variety of literary conventions, such as the descriptions of hospitality and a chivalric sensibility.[3] Several, more specific plot echoes can be found in post-Chrétien French romances, two of which are translated for this volume. *La Chevalier à l'Epée* (The Knight of the Sword) depicts a Gauvain renowned for his elegant manners and military prowess, who visits a stranger's castle where he is tempted sexually by the lord's beautiful daughter. In this poem, Gauvain escapes with his life from two surprise attacks by a magic sword that hangs in the daughter's bedroom. In *La Mule sans Frein* (The Mule without a Bridle), Gauvain similarly stays in a stranger's castle, but this time he engages in a game of exchanging blows to the neck with his host. Gauvain emerges unscathed from this adventure as well, for demonstrating loyalty and "trawth," the ability to keep his word.

In addition to these examples, instances of similar beheading games, found in Old Irish and in medieval French versions, suggest that underlying all of these tales is a fluid layer of oral folk tale. Indeed, another path taken by source scholarship involves following folk motifs through various narrative traditions. The Beheading Bargain, identified as folk motif type M221 by Thompson,[4] also figures in the eighth-century Irish tale *Fled Bricrend* (Bricriu's Feast) in which the hero, Cuchulainn, meets a supernatural challenger, as well as in later French romances, including the *Livre de Caradoc* and *La Mule sans Frein*, both of which feature Sir Gawain. The Exchange of

---

3. Ad Putter, *Sir Gawain and the Green Knight and French Arthurian Romance* (Oxford: Clarenden Press, 1995).
4. Stith Thompson, *Motif-Index of Folk-Literature: A Classification of Narrative Elements in Folktales, Ballads, Myths, Fables, Mediaeval Romances, Exempla, Fabliaux, Jest-Books, and Local Legends* (Bloomington: Indiana University Press, 1957). See also Carl Lindahl, John McNamara, and John Lindow, eds., *Medieval Folklore: An Encyclopedia of Myths, Legends, Tales, Beliefs, and Customs,* (Santa Barbara, Calif.: ABC-CLIO, 2000).

Winnings motif itself conforms to another type (M241.2) but is harder to trace in French romances that predate *Sir Gawain*. Several French romances, including *Le Chevalier a l'Epee*, test heroes through sexual temptation, but none weaves the hero's temptation so tightly with the two games.

Tracing the threads of folk narrative should be distinguished from a search for underlying mythic structure. As Carl Lindahl notes, "whatever myth lives in *Gawain*, it is clearly not a timeless, pagan Celtic construct but rather a synthesis of fourteenth-century folk beliefs and ritual patterns."[5] Studies that seek to establish the persistence of a pre-Christian "green man" myth, for example, must note that greenness is also associated with the devil in medieval literature;[6] such symbolic meaning does not remain static over time and across continents. Indeed, the fluidity of such beliefs and patterns allows poets to mold their inherited narrative motifs into their own particular design.

The Manuscript

The original manuscript of *Sir Gawain* is small, its vellum pages measuring roughly five inches across and less than seven inches high. Written in a neat, angular, scribal hand, with thirty-six lines to each page, the manuscript contains three other poems, now widely considered the work of the same poet who composed *Sir Gawain*. The group begins with a dream-vision, titled *Pearl* by modern editors, in which the poem's speaker mourns the death of his infant daughter, figured as a "precious pearl," and engages in dialogue with a Heavenly Maiden, thereby transforming his understanding of death and human loss. Two other poems, *Cleannesse* (or *Purity*) and *Patience* use biblical tales to teach moral and theological lessons, in the manner of an extended sermon or homily.[7] A fifth poem in a separate manuscript, *St. Erkenwald,* may also have been composed by the *Gawain*-poet.[8]

Twelve illustrations and several large decorated capital letters adorn the *Gawain* manuscript. In *Sir Gawain and the Green Knight*, four of

5. "*Sir Gawain and the Green Knight* and Myth in Its Time," in *Telling Tales: Medieval Narratives and the Folk Tradition*, ed. F. C. Sautman, D. Conchoda, and G. C. DiScipio (New York: St. Martin's Press, 1998); but see also Christopher Wrigley, "*Sir Gawain and the Green Knight*: The Underlying Myth" in *Studies in Medieval English Romance: Same New Approaches*, ed. Elizabeth Brewer, (Cambridge: D. S. Brewer, 1988), pp. 113–128, who argues that the beheading game and the temptation scenes were "related episodes of the same immemorial myth" (p. 116).

6. See, for example, Claude Luttrell, "The Folk-Tale Element in *Sir Gawain and the Green Knight*," in Brewer, pp. 92–112.

7. Marie Borroff, trans., *The Gawain-Poet: Complete Works* (New York: Norton, forthcoming).

8. Marie Borroff, "Narrative Artistry in *St. Erkenwald* and the *Gawain*-Group: The Case for Common Authorship Reconsidered," *Studies in the Age of Chaucer* 28 (2006): 41–76.

the large capital letters (each stretching over five to ten lines) mark the start of four distinct sections of the poem, referred to as *fitts* by scholars, from the Middle English word for "section."[9] And even though the illustrations have been pronounced substandard by critics and in places misrepresent the text, they reveal a lively interest in narrative action. Four of the illustrations depict scenes from *Gawain*: the moments after Sir Gawain has cut off the Green Knight's head, and it speaks; the attempted seduction of Gawain by the host's wife, Lady Bertilak (see front cover); Sir Gawain's arrival at the Green Knight's outdoor "chapel"; and Sir Gawain's return to Arthur's court

Unlike several other known fourteenth-century works such as Chaucer's *Canterbury Tales* and William Langland's *Piers Plowman*, *Sir Gawain and the Green Knight* descends to us in this single manuscript, its preservation thanks to the antiquarian collector Sir Robert Cotton (1571–1631), whose seventeenth-century library also preserved for the modern era the unique copy of the epic poem *Beowulf*. The manuscript's official name, Cotton Nero A.x, Art. 3, designates its location in Sir Robert's library, which was arranged in shelves beneath the busts of Roman emperors. Before Cotton's possession of it, the *Sir Gawain* manuscript was owned by Henry Savile of Bank (1568–1617), in Yorkshire, but where it was during the two hundred years between its creation, around 1400, and its first recorded owner, no one knows.

Evidence debated by scholars since the mid-1800s indicates that Cotton Nero A.x is a copy of a lost original. This copy may itself have been made from an earlier copy, perhaps even a lavish presentation copy,[1] but we do know that it was completed around 1400, about the time that Geoffrey Chaucer died and King Richard II of England was deposed by his popular cousin Henry of Bolingbroke, who, in 1399, became King Henry IV. Some scholars date the composition of the four poems in Cotton Nero A.x to King Richard's reign (1377–99), thus naming a literary cluster of remarkable Middle English poems from this period "Ricardian poetry."[2] But others argue that the *Gawain*-poet could have been active before Richard's reign,[3] and so his poems may pre-date the mature works of Chaucer, Langland, and John Gower. It

---

9. For a discussion of the manuscript's capitals, see Donald Howard, "Structure and Symmetry in *Sir Gawain and the Green Knight*," *Speculum* 39 (1964): 425–433; and Tolkien and Gordon, *Sir Gawain and the Green Knight*, pp. xi–xiv.
1. Gervase Matthews, *The Court of Richard II* (London: John Murray, 1968), p. 117.
2. J. A. Burrow, *Ricardian Poetry: Chaucer, Gower, Langland and the "Gawain" Poet*, (New Haven, Conn.: Yale University Press, 1971); M.J. Bennett, "The Historical Background, in *A Companion to the Gawain-Poet*, ed. Derek Brewer and Jonathon Gibson (Cambridge: D. S. Brewer, 1997), pp. 71–90, presents a useful overview of dating scholarship.
3. See, for example, W. G. Cooke, "*Sir Gawain and the Green Knight*: A Restored Dating," *Medium Ævum* 58 (1989): 34–48; and Francis Ingledew, *Sir Gawain and the Green Knight and the Order of the Garter* (Notre Dame, Ind., University of Notre Dame Press, 2006), pp. 93–104.

seems safe to say that *Sir Gawain and the Green Knight* was composed in the latter half of the fourteenth century and that the copy in the British Museum was made in the latter years of that century.

Where these poems were written may be discussed with more certainty, as their dialect of Middle English directs us to the northwest Midlands of England. Before English spelling was standardized, beginning with the advent of the printing press in the fifteenth century, poets and their scribes spelled words as they spoke them. Thus linguistic differences within spoken English were preserved, and texts from this period can be placed fairly accurately, at times within the space of a few miles. For the poems of Cotton Nero A.x, and the manuscript that contains *St. Erkenwald,* linguists can locate their geographic provenance to an area in east Cheshire, just south of present-day Manchester and not far from the border with northern Wales. The poem in fact names two actual places: the "iles of Anglesay" (line 698) and the "wyldrenesse of Wyral" (line 701), during Sir Gawain's journey in Part II. Both places are located along the northern coast of Wales, a geographical specificity that contrasts with the general romance descriptions of other places in the poem.[4]

The Author

Because of the relatively remote location of the poet's dialect area, scholars for some time assumed that the *Gawain*-poet wrote for a provincial court, with little contact with the wider international culture known to his contemporaries in London. But more recently, the author's possible connections with the king (either Edward III or Richard II, depending on the poem's date), or other members of the royal court, and even his acquaintance with London have been the subject of speculation.[5] This Cheshire poet may well have written for a community of his fellow expatriates, all living in London. That he was a learned man, most likely a secular cleric but possibly a priest, that he knew chivalric life and customs well, that he elected to compose not only in his native language but also using a native verse form can all be deduced from the poems themselves. Alliterative verse, which Borroff's translation seeks to emulate, is also the verse form of Old English poetry in which the initial sounds of important words— not their endings, as when rhyme is used—is what counts. The *Gawain*-poet wrote in a very English alliterative line, which appears to

---

4. See Ralph Elliott, "Landscape and Geography," in *A Companion to the Gawain-Poet,* ed. Derek Brewer and Jonathon Gibson, (Cambridge: D. S. Brewer, 1997), pp. 105–117.
5. Leo Carruthers, "The Duke of Clarence and the Earls of March: Garter Knights and *Sir Gawain and the Green Knight,*" *Medium Ævum* 70, no. 1 (2001): 66–79; Ad Putter, *An Introduction to the Gawain-Poet* (London: Longman Press, 1996).

have been in continuous use from Anglo-Saxon times, with sporadic written records testifying to its development.[6]

Modern scholars of *Sir Gawain and the Green Knight* continue to debate and explore a wide array of topics: How Christian is this poem? Does it conform to generic expectations for medieval romance or does it thwart them? Can we discern a specific historical reference in the poem that would enable us to date its composition more accurately? How are we to interpret Sir Gawain's shield? How are we to understand the Green Girdle? What does the Green Knight himself represent? Is Morgan la Fay a major player in this poem, or just a marginal character? How do the intertwined hunt and bedroom scenes, in Part III, comment on each other? And when Sir Gawain "confesses" his fault to the Green Knight, are we meant to take it as a Christian act or as an act that simply mimics Roman Catholic practice? The essays that appear in this edition address these, and many other, issues. The Selected Bibliography will lead the reader more deeply into the midst of a scholarly conversation that has been going on for over a century. Indeed, for a six-hundred-year-old poem to enthrall and engage several generations of modern readers suggests just how potent its poetic power remains.

LAURA L. HOWES

6. Derek Pearsall, "The Alliterative Revival: Origins and Social Backgrounds," in *Middle English Alliterative Poetry and its Literary Background: Seven Essays*, ed. David Lawton (Cambridge: Cambridge University Press, 1982), pp. 34–53. Ralph Hanna, "Alliterative Poetry," in *The Cambridge History of Medieval English Literature*, ed. David Wallace (Cambridge: Cambridge University Press, 1999), pp. 488–512.

The Metrical Forms

We cannot understand fully the metrical patterns of the *Gawain*-poet's verse unless we know something about how the English language was pronounced in the late fourteenth century in the northwest midland dialect area where he lived. A feature of crucial importance in this connection is the syllabic "final -*e*" that is often sounded between the stressed syllables of Chaucer's iambic verse and always, when the word in question contains it, at the end of the line. In Chaucer's London English, this -*e* was probably pronounced in speech as well as in verse, at least in words pronounced with some degree of emphasis. It is my contention that in the spoken language of the *Gawain*-poet -*e* had wholly died out, though it continued to be reproduced in spelling (as it still is in modern words with "long vowels" like *came, hope*).[1] Accordingly, I believe that the alliterating lines of *Gawain* and *Patience* were read in the original with no sounding of -*e* within the line. Noun–adjective phrases preceded by the definite article, like "the good knight" and "the good man," which would have had four syllables in Chaucer's verse ("the goodë knight," "the goodë man") would have had three in the *Gawain*-poet's verse, as they do today, whether or not an *e* was appended to the adjective by the scribe who copied the manuscript. (In the manuscript original, we find "the gode knyght" in line 482, but "the god mon" in line 1179.) I concede the possibility that at the end of the alliterating line, -*e* was sounded where present—for example, in *Troyë* at the end of line 1. Such an archaizing mode of recitation would have been handed down from earlier times, along with the formulaic phrases that were part of the inherited tradition.

If final -*e* is silent within the long alliterating line, it follows that modern translations can reproduce, and not merely approximate, the metrical patterns of the original, as I believe I have done. My line, "There was meat, there was mirth, there was much joy" (*Gawain*, line 1007), for example, has exactly the same wording as the line in the original poem and the same metrical pattern, except for the

---

1. I present these views at length in "The Phonological Evidence" and "The Metrical Evidence" in my *Sir Gawain and the Green Knight: A Stylistic and Metrical Study* (New Haven, Conn.: Yale University Press, 1962).

above-mentioned possibility of a sounded final *-e* in *joy* (Chaucer's *joyë*). In Chaucer's verse, *meat* and *mirth*, as well as *joy*, had an *-e* that was sounded when not elided before a vowel. Because the patterns of the original are reproduced in my own verse, I see no reason to quote the Middle English version in illustrating them.

Alliterative verse as composed in the *Gawain*-poet's time had descended, with modifications reflecting changes in the language itself, from alliterative verse in Old English, which in turn was a Germanic inheritance. The tradition retained its vitality in the midland and northern regions of England in the second half of the fourteenth century but had fallen into disuse by the end of the fifteenth. Chaucer knew of it but did not compose in it himself. His Parson, in the prologue to the last of the *Canterbury Tales*, says "I am a southren man; I can nat geste [compose poetry] rum, ram, ruf, bi lettre."

Alliterative Verse

The Basic Form

The so-called alliterative long line, as we find in *Sir Gawain and the Green Knight*, is best described in terms of a basic form that serves as a point of departure for a number of variations. The fact that this same basic form and these same variations also appear in *Patience*, *Purity*, and *St. Erkenwald* is one kind of evidence for what I believe to be the common authorship of the four poems.

The rhythm of the lines that recurrently exemplify the basic form is easy to sense, as is the formal relationship between alliteration and stress. The line is divided into two half lines; this division, called the caesura, is marked by a syntactic break of at least minor importance. Each half line contains two stressed syllables, or, as I call them, chief syllables, for a total of four per line. Chief syllables are spaced temporally as the downbeats of successive measures are spaced in a musical piece played freely rather than metronomically. That is, we perceive them as recurring in a time continuum at regular, though not at exactly equal, intervals. The line can thus be described as having four "measures," in the musical sense of that word. Alliteration is not ornamental, as it is in most of the verse modern readers are familiar with, but a requirement of the form: the two chief syllables in most first half lines alliterate with each other and with the first chief syllable of the second, for a total three alliterating syllables per line. There must be at least one alliterative link between half lines. The chief syllable at the end of the line normally does not alliterate.

Some examples should make all this clearer. (I mark the vowels of stressed, or chief, syllables with a capital C above the line, and the first letters of stressed alliterating words with lower-case *a* below the line. The first letters of stressed nonalliterating syllables are marked *x*. The caesura in mid-line is marked /.) In the first pair of examples only, I indicate with vertical bars downbeats such as are heard, with slight variations of tempo, in freely played music.

<pre>
               C   C   C   C
With all the |meat and the |mirth that |men could de|vise,
            a   a / a   x
</pre>

<pre>
      C   C   C   C
Such |gaiety and |glee, |glorious to |hear.
     a   a /a   x
</pre>
(lines 45–46)

<pre>
  C   C   C   C
|Readily from his |rest he |rose before |dawn,
 a   a / a   x
</pre>

<pre>
        C   C   C   C
For a |lamp had been |left him, that |lighted his |chamber.
      a   a   /   a   x
</pre>
(lines 2009–10)

As the above examples show, chief syllables may be separated by one, two, or three "intermediate" syllables, most frequently by one or two. It is natural to read measures containing two and three intermediate syllables more rapidly than those containing only one.

Occasionally, chief syllables are juxtaposed, usually in the second half line:

<pre>
     C   C   C   C
All the onlookers eyed him and edged nearer
    a   a   /   a   x
</pre>
(line 237)

In the above example, as is permissible, several different vowels alliterate with one another.

Occasionally, the first half line contains only one alliterating chief syllable:

<pre>
    C   C   C   C
The stranger before him stood there erect.
    a   x   /a   x
</pre>
(line 332)

Sometimes the line contains two different alliterating letters; I mark these *a* and *b*. The pattern may be either *ab/ba* or *ab/ab*:

        C   C   C   C
And with undaunted countenance drew down his coat,
      a   b   /a   b

                                  (line 335)

          C   C   C   C
And they set about briskly to bind on saddles,
        a   (b)   b   /   b   a

                                (line 1128)

I have put the *b* of *about* in parenthesis because it is superfluous to the formal requirements of the line; in addition, it is brought in not by the poet's choice among descriptive alternatives but inadvertently, so to speak, by his use of an idiom requiring that adverb.

    Rarely, all four chief syllables alliterate:

       C   C   C   C
Sir Bors and Sir Bedivere, big men both,
  a   a   /a   a

                                (line 554)

    All the examples I have given so far can easily be read as having four chief syllables, and these syllables alone participate in the alliterative pattern. But two related variant forms occur in which alliteration and chief stress do not coincide, and the frequency of their appearance in the alliterative verse of the *Gawain*-poet sets him apart from other poets. In one of these variants, at least one alliterating syllable, often the single one that is required in the second half line, is an unstressed prefix:

          C   C   C   C
And that is best, I believe, and behooves me now."
       a   a   /   a   x

                                (line 1216)

In the other variant, the single alliterating syllable required in the second half line is a word normally read with less stress than are neighboring words in the sentence:

       C   C   C   C
The terms of this task too well you know—
  a   a /a   x

                                (line 546)

Variants of this sort seem to appear more frequently in quoted speech than in the language of the narrator.

The Heavy Lines

A number of lines and groups of lines in *Gawain* exemplify a variant form of a different, and more important, sort. Its frequent and conspicuous presence, as with the variants just discussed, distinguishes the *Gawain*-poet from other poets of the alliterative tradition. In lines having this form, the count of stressed syllables exceeds in number the basic four. The first half line, for example, may contain three such syllables. The metrical analysis of these heavy lines has been subject to debate, the main question being whether they should be read as having five stressed syllables of equal rank rather than four and thus as divided into five stressed syllables of equal rank rather than four and thus as divided into five measures, rather than four, in the musical sense. Consider, for example, the second line of each of the following passages:

> And since this Britain was built by this baron great,
> Bold boys bred there, in broils delighting,
>
> > (lines 1971–72)

> He assigns him a servant to set him on the path,
> To see him safe and sound over the snowy hills,
>
> > (lines 20–21)

If equal rank were assigned to *bold, boys*, and *bred* in *Gawain* line 21, the measure-bars preceding syllables perceived as occurring at temporally regular intervals would be placed thus:

  |Bold |boys |bred there, in |broils de|lighting

  To |see him |safe and |sound over the |snowy |hills,

I contend, however, and have argued at length elsewhere,[2] that one of the three stressed syllables in these and other heavy first half lines is subordinated to the other two; in linguistic terms, two syllables bear primary stress, and one secondary stress. I call syllables bearing primary stress "major chief," and those bearing secondary stress "minor chief," marking minor chief syllables with a lower-case *c*. I call unstressed syllables "intermediate" and leave them unmarked. The resultant patterns appear in metrical notation as follows (I have again added measure-bars to indicate the placement of the downbeats):

```
      C    c    C           C      C
     |Bold boys |bred there, in |broils de|lighting
      a    a    a        /     a      x
```

2. See "The Alliterative Long Line: The Extended Form" in *Sir Gawain and the Green Knight: A Stylistic and Metrical Study*.

"The first measures or units of these lines exemplify what I term "compound meter,"—that is, the pattern includes two grades of stress, major and minor, as well as intermediate syllables such as "And since this" and "over the.""

An alternative reading of *Gawain* line 21 might give *there* more emphasis than it receives in my scansion above, raising it, along with *boys*, to minor chief rank; the second measure as well as the first thus becomes compound. Such an alternative reflects differences of expressive emphasis rather than of metrical form; in both, the half lines are divided into two measures, and compounding occurs.

The patterns I am describing are in fact familiar to us from nursery rhymes, jump-rope chants, and other popular forms of verse. The half line "Bold boys bred there," read with minor chief as well as major chief syllables, is similar in pattern to the first half line of "Baa baa black sheep, have you any wool?" Such popular verse exemplifies compound meter; if we tap with a finger while reciting it at a normal pace, the taps will fall on the downbeats indicated below:

```
        C   c   C    c     C    c    C
    |"Baa baa |black sheep, |have you any |wool?"
```

```
        C   c   C   c    C   c    C
    |"Yes, sir, |yes, sir, |three bags |full."
```

This kinship is one aspect of the affinity between the long alliterative line and the language and poetry of everyday.[3]

I am arguing that the triply stressed first half lines that appear in the *Gawain*-poet's alliterative verse should be scanned as consisting not of three but of two measures, one or both of these being compound, with a demotion of one primary stress to secondary. But I am not arguing, be it noted, that the metrical patterns of *Sir Gawain* are compound throughout. There is a crucial difference between the alliterative verse of the *Gawain*-poet and the kind of verse we find in such nursery rhymes as "Baa, baa, black sheep"—a difference that in fact provides additional evidence for the scansion I am proposing. The difference is that compound measures in the *Gawain*-poet's lines are read in a context in which the basic form I described at the outset predominates, creating a rhythmical momentum, an ongoing "swing," of four simple

---

3. The subordination of *boys* to *bold* accords also with a linguistic rule. In English, adjacent words of the four "open classes" (nouns, verbs, descriptive adjectives, and descriptive adverbs) do not both bear primary stress within a phrase; the stress given one of them is demoted to secondary. In sequences of adjective plus noun, for example, either the adjective or the noun will be subordinated, depending on whether the adjective has contrastive or emphatic as well as descriptive force. Thus in the isolated clause "She lives in a white house," *house* receives primary stress and *white* secondary; in the sentence "She lives in a white house, but his house is gray," the order is reversed. In line 21 of *Gawain* the adjective *bold* is rhetorically emphatic, as it might be in the spoken language in "He's a bold boy, that one."

measures per line to which the reader instinctively accommodates compound measures by accelerating them a little. If I were to rewrite *Gawain* line 21 as "Bold boys bred there, that braved fierce foes," its meter would become compound in its entirety, like that of "Sing a song of sixpence, a pocket full of rye," and it has in fact been argued that the meter of these poems is of this sort. But a large majority of measures contain too few stressed syllables to permit us to read them as compound without distortion. In the second half line of *Gawain* 21— "in broils delighting"—compound meter relaxes into simple combinations of stressed and unstressed syllables, in accordance with the prevailing norm. The same effect would be achieved by rewriting the nursery rhymes I have been quoting as "Sing a song of sixpence, pockets of rye," and "Baa baa black sheep, have you some wool?"

Variant Combinations of Alliteration and Stress in the Heavy Lines

In the lines I have used as examples thus far, it is the first half line in which compounding occurs, and all three stressed syllables alliterate. But compounding sometimes occurs in the second half line; and the relation between alliteration, on the one hand, and major and minor (chief) rank, on the other hand, is variable. The examples that follow by no means illustrate all the possible permutations and combinations of the two aspects of the form.

Compounding in one or both halves of the line; alliteration on major chief syllables only:

$$\begin{array}{ccccccc} C & & C & c & C & c & C \\ \text{And Gawain the good man in gay bed lies} \\ a & & a & & x & / & a & x & x \end{array}$$

(line 1179)

Compounding, with alliteration lacking on minor or major chief syllables:

$$\begin{array}{cccccc} C & c & & C & C & & C \\ \text{Gawain gazed on the host that greeted him there} \\ a & a & & x & / & a & & x \end{array}$$

(line 542)

$$\begin{array}{ccccc} C & c & C & C & C \\ \text{Sleet showered aslant upon shivering beasts;} \\ x & a & x & / & a & x \end{array}$$

(line 2003)

In this last example, I have counted the alliteration of *sleet* with *aslant* as ornamental rather than as part of the formal pattern, because it does not link the two halves of the line.

<pre>
      C   C   c   C   C
And so he leads them a merry chase, the lord and his men,
      a   b   x   /   a   b
</pre>

(line 1729)

Specimen Scansions

I have chosen two passages from *Gawain,* presenting them first in the
original, then in my translation. I quote the Middle English text in the
second edition, revised by Norman Davis, of the 1925 edition by J. R.
R. Tolkien and E. V. Gordon (Clarendon Press, 1967). I have substituted *i* for *j*, *v* for *u*, and *u* for *v*, in accordance with modern spelling,
and *th* for the Middle English letter *thorn*. For the Middle English letter *yogh*, I have substituted *y* at the beginnings of words and *gh* or *s*/*z*
at the ends of words, depending on the sound represented.

Passage 1 and Passage 2 illustrate two different kinds of metrical
effect. This difference in turn correlates with two differences that can
be described statistically, in factual terms. The first passage, a description of Lord Bertilak's castle as Sir Gawain first sees it, contains, in
the original poem, a sequence of five lines (785–89) in which a minor
chief syllable is present in addition to the two major chief syllables of
the first half line. In my translation, there is a sequence of four such
first half lines (786–89). The second passage, taken from the conversation of the first bedroom scene, contains, in the original, no such
half lines. In my translation, there is one. In addition, the second passage contains, in the original, four sequences of three (or in one case,
four) intermediate syllables between major chief syllables; there are
five in my translation. The first passage contains only two such
sequences (assuming that the *-ez* of *garytez* is not syllabic); there are
two in my translation. The first passage is thus metrically heavier than
the second; it contains a greater proportion of stressed to unstressed
syllables and, as a result, is slower in pace.

   "Clusters" of heavy lines appear in descriptive passages such as passage 1 and the description of the Green Knight when he first appears;
sequences of lines that are comparatively light appear in passages of
direct discourse, especially in conversations between Sir Gawain and
the lady. The first effect seems to express the sustained impact of
a remarkable sight on the beholder; the second, the fluency of casual
repartee.

1. *Lines 785–93*

```
    C    c      C              C    C
The burne bode on bonk, that on blonk hoved,
    a      a       a    /      a    x
```

```
      C    c     C      C        C
Of the depe double dich that drof to the place;
      a    a      a   /  a           x
```

```
    C   c          C    C        C
The walle wod in the water wonderly depe,
    a     a         a   /a       x
```

```
    C      C    c      C          C
And eft a ful huge heght hit haled up on lofte,
    a      a    a    /   a           x
```

```
    C   c     C  C          C
Of harde hewen ston up to the tablez,
    a      a    x  /a        x
```

```
    C                C                 C   C
Enbaned under the abataylment in the best lawe;
    a                a          /      a   x
```

```
          C         C   C       C
And sythen garytez ful gaye gered bitwene,
          a         a   /a      x
```

```
        C    C        C           C
Wyth mony luflych loupe that louked ful clene:
        a    a    /   a           x
```

```
    C    c           C    C             C
A better barbican that burne blusched upon never.
    a    a           a   /a             x
```

```
       C         C      C            C
The man on his mount remained on the bank
       a         a   /  a           x
```

```
        C    c     C          C         C
Of the deep double moat that defended the place.
        a    a      x   /     a         x
```

```
      C   c        C    C       C
The wall went in the water wondrous deep,
      a   a         a    /a      x
```

     C   c   C   C   C
And a long way aloft it loomed overhead.
      a   x   a   /a   x

       C   c   C   C   C
It was built of stone blocks to the battlements' height,
      a   x   a   /   a   x

     C   C   C   C
With corbels under cornices in comeliest style;
       a   a   / a   x

  C   c   C   C   C
Watch-towers trusty protected the gate,
x   a   a   / a   x

       C   c   C   C   C
With many a lean loophole, to look from within:
      x   a   a   / a   x

  C   c   C   C   c   C
A better-made barbican the knight beheld never.
  a   x   a   /   b   a   b

2. Lines 1208–17

      C   C   C C
"God moroun, Sir Gawayn," sayde that gay lady,
a   a   /   a x

       C   C   C   C
"Ye ar a sleper unslyghe, that mon may slyde hider;
       a   a   /   a x

        C C   C   C
Now ar ye tan astyt! Bot true uus may schape,
        a   a / a   x

     C   C   C c   C
I schal bynde you in your bedde, that be ye trayst!"
       a   a /x a   x

  C   C C   C
Al laghande the lady lanced tho bourdez.
a   a /a   x

      C   C   C   C
"Goud moroun, gay," quoth Gawayn the blythe,
a   a /   a   x

    C   C   C c C
"Me schal worthe at your wille, and that me wel lykez,
     a   a / x   a x

   C   C   C   C
For I yelde me yederly, and yeghe after grace,
  a   a   / a   x

      C   C   C C
And that is the best, be my dome, for my byhovez nede!"
       a a x /   a   x

     C   C   C   c C
And thus he bourded ayayn with mony a blythe laghter.
       a   x / x   a x

    C   C   C C
"Good morning, Sir Gawain," said that gay lady,
  a   a   /   a x

   C c   C   C   C
"A slack sleeper you are, to let one slip in!
   a   a   x / x   a x

     C   C   C   C
Now you are taken in a trice—a truce we must make,
       a   a / a   x

    C   C   C   C
Or I shall bind you in your bed, of that be assured."
      a   a / x a   x

   C   C   C C
Thus laughing lightly that lady jested.
     a   a / a x

    C   C   C   C
"Good morning, gay lady," said Gawain the blithe,
  a   a   / a   x

    C   C   C   C
"Be it with me as you will; I am well content!
    a   a / a   x

     C   C   C   C
For I surrender myself, and sue for your grace,
      a   a / a   x

        C   C   C   C
And that is best, I believe, and behooves me now."
        a   a   /   a   x

    C   C   C   C
Thus jested in answer that gentle knight.
    a   x   /   a   x

MARIE BORROFF

Translator's Note

In "The Metrical Forms," I explain how the *Gawain*-poet's late Middle English resembles present-day English, and differs from the language of Chaucer, in such a way that it is possible to reproduce the patterns of his alliterative verse in a modern translation. I also present an analysis of those patterns in technical terms. Regardless of any particular analysis and terminology, the rhythms of the verse, when read aloud or heard in the responsive reader's imagination, are easy to feel. The poem sweeps along in series of lines variable in syllable count but uniformly marked by four syllables bearing major stresses comparable to the downbeats of musical measures, with an occasional minor stress tucked in between them. Two or more of these syllables must begin with the same letter—that is, they must alliterate with each other.

Every translator who chooses to express in detail the content of an original in another language, while simultaneously imposing a metrical form on the new version, faces a unique set of difficulties. These depend not only on the differences between the two languages involved but on the differences between the two cultures. Fortunately, to translate *Sir Gawain*, despite the fact that it was composed over six hundred years ago, is to translate from English to English. Though there has been much change in vocabulary, the "little words" providing the grammatical frames of our English sentences and much of the basic vocabulary itself have stayed the same. As a result, many lines in the original poem can be carried over into modern English virtually without change of wording, with rhythmic, alliterative, and intonation patterns remaining intact. Examples in my translation include "This king lay at Camelot at Christmastide" (line 37), "Near slain with the sleet he sleeps in his irons" (line 729); "And soberly your servant, my sovereign I hold you" (line 1278); "And blithely brought to his bed, to be at his rest" (line 1990); and "Hit his horse with his heels as hard as he might" (line 2153). Parts of almost all of the other lines pass with similar ease into modern English.

The chief technical problem facing the translator of late Middle English alliterative verse, of course, is to substitute new alliterating words with relevant meanings for those words that have become obsolete since the poet's day. As was stated earlier, at least two words in each line must alliterate with each other. Usually, in fact, the lines contain three such words. The task is made easier by the fact that in alliterative verse as composed by the *Gawain*-poet, there is flexibility in the choice of the one required alliterating syllable in the second half line. Words of less than major importance, and even unstressed syllables, as well as stressed words, can fulfill the requirement. In the second half of the line "I have been much to blame, if your story be true" (line 1488), for example, the single alliterating word *be* receives less stress than *story*. In "Bishop Baldwin above *begins* the table" (line 112), alliteration falls on the unstressed prefix *be-* and in "And lined warmly and well with furs of the best" (line 2029), it falls on the unstressed preposition *with*.

A major problem is presented by the presence in traditional alliterative verse of a number of groups of synonymous words expressing important ideas, including nouns meaning "knight," and "sword," and verbs meaning "to go" and "to speak." These were already restricted to poetry in the *Gawain*-poet's time and have disappeared altogether from the language since then. Because they began with a variety of first letters, they were a technical aid. Suppose, for example, that the poet wanted to say that a knight went over a bridge. He could combine the word *bridge,* which existed in his language, with the archaic synonymous word for "knight" beginning with *b*—namely, *burne.* Similarly, if he wanted to say that a knight came into the hall, he could combine the word *hall* with the archaic word for "knight" that began with *h*—namely, *hathel.* In translating the many lines containing such words, I have regretfully had to forego the literary associations with which they embellished the original language and substitute ordinary words beginning with the requisite letters, combining *bridge,* for example, with *bold knight, hall* with *horseman,* and so on.

Obviously there is more to writing a good translation than solving the technical problems I have described. What must also be conveyed, so far as possible, are the qualities and effects of the original language. Two aspects of the *Gawain*-poet's artistry come into play here. The first is a feature of the language of alliterative verse generally: its affinities in rhythm and diction with the spoken language. Present-day English contains countless stock phrases inherited from the past, phrases that form part of the shared repertoire of speech and turn up now and again as we speak. Many of them contain alliterating combinations, as in "up and at 'em," "common cause," and "left in the lurch." Others, equally traditional, do not: "cut and dried," "don't give a hoot," "out like a light." I have done my best to season the language of my translation with such phrases—for example, "tried and true" (line 36), "they welcome him warmly" (line 975). "I shall while the time away" (line 1235), "he leads them a merry chase" (line 1729), "off like the wind" (line 2154), and "echoed loud and long" (line 2204).

At times, the poet's language works to reinforce one of his themes by blurring the distinction between reputation, as conveyed by traditional stories, and real life. The Green Knight's words to King Arthur in the first episode indicate that he has come to Camelot to find out whether the "praises" of the court that he has heard (line 258) are justified in fact. And in the second bedroom scene at Hautdesert, the wife of Lord Bertilak questions Sir Gawain's identity: in an actual situation, he apparently isn't going to act in accordance with his renowned prowess as a lover. In passages like these, I have tried to retain the associations with storytelling in the original language. The visiting lady says that knights are "noblest esteemed / For loyal faith in love, in life as in story" (line 1512–13); the last phrase of the second line of the original reads "the lore of arms." She adds that these "bold knights" have "made happy ever after the hearts of their ladies" (lines 1516, 1519). Here I have substituted a phrase specifically associated with fiction, "happy ever after," for the poet's less specifically allusive "brought bliss into bower."

In revising my translation for this Norton Critical Edition, I have substituted current words for some archaisms that in retrospect seemed pointless and corrected a few mistakes. I have also provided marginal glosses for words that may be unfamiliar to students reading the poem for the first time. My aim, as when I first published it, has been to enable a modern audience to experience at firsthand a superb poetic drama, crafted by an author whose vision of the human comedy we can still share and savor after a time interval of over six hundred years.

Marie Borroff

The Translated Text of
SIR GAWAIN AND THE GREEN KNIGHT

Sir Gawain and the Green Knight

Part I

Since the siege and the assault was ceased at Troy,[1]
The walls breached and burnt down to brands
    and ashes,
The knight that had knotted the nets of deceit
Was impeached for his perfidy,° proven most true,[2]   *treachery*
5 It was high-born Aeneas and his haughty race
That since prevailed over provinces, and proudly reigned
Over well-nigh all the wealth of the West Isles.
Great Romulus to Rome repairs in haste;
With boast and with bravery builds he that city
10 And names it with his own name, that it now bears.
Ticius to Tuscany, and towers raises.
Langobard in Lombardy lays out homes,
And far over the French Sea, Felix Brutus[3]
On many broad hills and high Britain he sets,
15   most fair,
        Where war and wrack and wonder
        By shifts have sojourned there,
        And bliss by turns with blunder
        In that land's lot had share.

20 And since this Britain was built by this baron great,
Bold boys bred there, in broils° delighting,   *fights*
That did in their day many a deed most dire.
More marvels have happened in this merry land

---

1. line 1: **Since the siege . . . ceased at Troy.** The poet begins his story, as he later ends it, by placing the reign of King Arthur in a broad historical perspective, which includes the fall of Troy. In accordance with medieval notions of history (though not all of his details can be found in the early chronicles), he visualizes Aeneas, son of the king of Troy, and his descendants as founding a series of western kingdoms to which each gives his name.
2. lines 3–4: **The knight that had knotted . . . proven most true.** This deceitful knight is evidently Antenor, who in Virgil's *Aeneid* is a trusted counselor but who appears as a traitor in later versions of the Troy story.
3. line 13: **And far over the French Sea, Felix Brutus.** The westward movement ends with the crossing of the "French Sea," or English Channel, by Brutus, great-grandson of Aeneas, legendary founder of the kingdom of Britain. This Brutus, whom the poet calls *Felix*, or fortunate, is not to be confused with the Marcus Brutus of Roman history.

Than in any other I know, since that olden time,
25 But of those that here built, of British kings,
King Arthur was counted most courteous of all,
Wherefore an adventure I aim to unfold,
That a marvel of might some men think it,
And one unmatched among Arthur's wonders.
30 If you will listen to my lay° but a little while,   *narrative poem*
As I heard it in hall, I shall hasten to tell
anew
As it was fashioned featly°   *skillfully*
In tale of derring-do,
35   And linked in measures meetly°   *suitably*
By letters tried and true.

This king lay at Camelot at Christmastide;
Many good knights and gay his guests were there,
Arrayed of the Round Table rightful brothers,
40 With feasting and fellowship and carefree mirth.
There true men contended in tournaments many,
Joined there in jousting these gentle knights,
Then came to the court for carol-dancing,[4]
For the feast was in force full fifteen days,
45 With all the meat and the mirth that men could devise,
Such gaiety and glee, glorious to hear,
Brave din by day, dancing by night.
High were their hearts in halls and chambers,
These lords and these ladies, for life was sweet.
50 In peerless pleasures passed they their days,
The most noble knights known under Christ,
And the loveliest ladies that lived on earth ever,
And he the comeliest king, that that court holds,
For all this fair folk in their first age
55   were still.
Happiest of mortal kind,
King noblest famed of will;
You would now go far to find
So hardy a host on hill.

60 While the New Year was new, but yesternight come,
This fair folk at feast two-fold was served,
When the king and his company were come in together,
The chanting in chapel achieved and ended.

---

4. line 43: **Then came to the court for carol-dancing.** In the original, the poet simply says
that lords and ladies came to Arthur's court "to make carols"; there was no need in late
Middle English to add the word *dancing*. Caroling, in this context, means singing while
dancing in a circle. Such carols were not necessarily religious, though at a Christmas feast
some of them were probably what we think of as Christmas carols today.

Clergy and all the court acclaimed the glad season,
65 Cried Noel anew, good news to men;
Then gallants gather gaily, hand-gifts to make,[5]
Called them out clearly, claimed them by hand,
Bickered long and busily about those gifts.
Ladies laughed aloud, though losers they were,
70 And he that won was not angered, as well you will know.
All this mirth they made until meat was served;
When they had washed them worthily, they went to their seats,
The best seated above, as best it beseemed,
Guenevere the goodly queen gay in the midst
75 On a dais° well-decked and duly arrayed   *platform*
With costly silk curtains, a canopy over,
Of Toulouse and Turkestan tapestries rich,
All broidered and bordered with the best gems
Ever brought into Britain, with bright pennies
80   to pay.
          Fair queen, without a flaw,
          She glanced with eyes of grey.
          A seemlier that once he saw,
          In truth, no man could say.

85 But Arthur would not eat till all were served;
So light was his lordly heart, and a little boyish;
His life he liked lively—the less he cared
To be lying for long, or long to sit,
So busy his young blood, his brain so wild.
90 And also a point of pride pricked him in heart,
For he nobly had willed, he would never eat
On so high a holiday, till he had heard first
Of some fair feat or fray° some far-borne tale,   *battle*
Of some marvel of might, that he might trust,
95 By champions of chivalry achieved in arms,
Or some suppliant° came seeking some single knight   *seeker of help*
To join with him in jousting, in jeopardy° each   *danger*
To lay life for life, and leave it to fortune
To afford him on field fair hap or other.
100 Such is the king's custom, when his court he holds
At each far-famed feast amid his fair host
               so dear.
          The stout king stands in state
          Till a wonder shall appear;

5. line 66: . . . **hand-gifts to make.** In the original, the poet says that the participants offered *hondeselle*, literally "hand" + "give," to each other. What seems to be meant is a game in which men concealed gifts in their outstretched hands, offering them to ladies who had to guess what the gift was or perhaps which hand held it (line 67). The forfeit for guessing wrong was a kiss.

105   He leads, with heart elate,
                      High mirth in the New Year.

              So he stands there in state, the stout young king,
              Talking before the high table of trifles fair.
              There Gawain the good knight by Guenevere sits,
110   With Agravain à la dure main° on his other side,   *of the hard hand*
              Both knights of renown, and nephews of the king.
              Bishop Baldwin above begins the table,
              And Yvain, son of Urien, ate with him there.
              These few with the fair queen were fittingly served;
115   At the side-tables sat many stalwart knights.[6]
              Then the first course comes, with clamor of trumpets
              That were bravely bedecked with bannerets bright,
              With new sounding of drums and the noble pipes.
              Wild were the warbles that wakened that day
120   In strains that stirred many strong men's hearts.
              There dainties were dealt out, dishes rare,
              Choice fare to choose, on chargers° so many   *platters*
              That scarce was there space to set before the people
              The service of silver, with sundry meats,
125   on cloth.
                      Each fair guest freely there
                      Partakes, and nothing loath;°   *not at all unwilling*
                      Twelve dishes before each pair;
                      Good beer and bright wine both.

130   Of the service itself I need say no more,
         For well you will know no title was wanting.
         Another noise and a new was well-nigh at hand,
         That the lord might have leave his life to nourish;
         For scarce were the sweet strains still in the hall,
135   And the first course come to that company fair,
         There hurtles in at the hall-door an unknown rider,
         One the greatest on ground in growth of his frame:

---

6. lines 108–15: **Talking before the high table . . . many stalwart knights.** What we are
asked to visualize here is not the "Table Round" at which no place was higher or lower than
any other, though that table is referred to later by the Green Knight (line 313). Rather, the
poet describes the kind of seating arrangement that he might have seen in a baronial hall
and indeed is still seen in the dining halls at the universities of Oxford and Cambridge. The
"high table," reserved for the most honored guests, stands on a dais opposite the entrance
through which the Green Knight will ride. Those seated there face the rest of the company,
who occupy tables ranged along either side of the hall (line 115). The middle seat is the
king's, though when the story opens it is vacant. A distinguished representative of the
church, Bishop Baldwin, occupies the place of honor at the king's right. Next to the bishop
sits Sir Yvain, who, as his partner at table, will share with him the twelve dishes served at the
feast (line 128). At the king's left sits the queen; beside her, Sir Gawain, and beside him, his
table partner, Sir Agravain.

From broad neck to buttocks so bulky and thick,
And his loins and his legs so long and so great,
140 Half a giant on earth I hold him to be,
But believe him no less than the largest of men,
And that the seemliest in his stature to see, as he rides,
For in back and in breast though his body was grim,
His waist in its width was worthily small,
145 And formed with every feature in fair accord
                                        was he.
                        Great wonder grew in hall
                        At his hue most strange to see,
                        For man and gear and all
150   Were green as green could be.

And in guise all of green, the gear and the man:
A coat cut close, that clung to his sides,
And a mantle to match, made with a lining
Of furs cut and fitted—the fabric was noble,
155 Embellished all with ermine, and his hood beside,
That was loosed from his locks, and laid on his shoulders.
With trim hose and tight, the same tint of green,
His great calves were girt,° and gold spurs under   *encircled*
He bore on silk bands that embellished his heels,
160 And footgear well-fashioned, for riding most fit.
And all his vesture° verily was verdant green;   *clothing*
Both the bosses° on his belt and other bright gems   *circular ornaments*
That were richly ranged on his raiment noble
About himself and his saddle, set upon silk,
165 That to tell half the trifles would tax my wits,
The butterflies and birds embroidered thereon
In green of the gayest, with many a gold thread.
The pendants of the breast-band, the princely
            crupper,°   *strap around rump*
And the bars of the bit were brightly enameled;
170 The stout stirrups were green, that steadied his feet,
And the bows of the saddle and the side-panels both,
That gleamed all and glinted with green gems about.
The steed he bestrides of that same green
                        so bright.
175   A green horse great and thick;
                        A headstrong steed of might;
                        In broidered bridle quick,
                        Mount matched man aright.

Gay was this goodly man in guise all of green,
180 And the hair of his head to his horse suited;

Fair flowing tresses enfold his shoulders;
A beard big as a bush on his breast hangs,[7]
That with his heavy hair, that from his head falls,
Was evened all about above both his elbows,
185 That half his arms thereunder were hid in the fashion
Of a king's cap-à-dos,[8] that covers his throat.
The mane of that mighty horse much to it like,
Well curled and becombed, and cunningly knotted
With filaments° of fine gold amid the fair green,   *threads*
190 Here a strand of the hair, here one of gold;
His tail and his foretop° twin in their hue,   *lock of hair on brow*
And bound both with a band of a bright green
That was decked adown the dock° with dazzling stones   *clipped tail*
And tied tight at the top with a triple knot
195 Where many bells well burnished rang bright and clear.
Such a mount in his might, nor man on him riding,
None had seen, I dare swear, with sight in that hall
           so grand.
        As lightning quick and light
200   He looked to all at hand;
        It seemed that no man might
        His deadly blows withstand.

Yet had he no helm, nor hauberk° neither,   *tunic of chain mail*
Nor plate, nor appurtenance° appending to arms,   *item of equipment*
205 Nor shaft pointed sharp, nor shield for defense,
But in his one hand he had a holly bob
That is goodliest in green when groves are bare,
And an ax in his other, a huge and immense,
A wicked piece of work in words to expound:
210 The head on its haft was an ell° long;   *forty-five inches*
The spike of green steel, resplendent with gold;
The blade burnished bright, with a broad edge,
As well shaped to shear as a sharp razor;
Stout was the stave in the strong man's gripe,
215 That was wound all with iron to the weapon's end,
With engravings in green of goodliest work.

---

7. line 182: **A beard big as a bush on his breast hangs.** This detail is one sign of a generation
gap evidently envisaged by the poet between the Green Knight and the company at King
Arthur's court. Abundance of beard and hair bespeak a man past his first youth, as do
"bristling" eyebrows (line 305) such as the Green Knight is said to possess. Our attention is
again drawn to the beard in line 306, when the knight wags it as he looks around, and in line
334, when he strokes it while awaiting a blow from the ax in the king's hands. His belittling
reference to Arthur's knights as "beardless children" (line 280) further signifies this distance
in age between them. Cf. also line 2228.
8. line 186: **Of a king's cap-à-dos . . .** The word *capados* occurs in this form in Middle English only in *Gawain*, here and in line 572. I have interpreted it, as the poet apparently did
also, as *cap-à-dos*—i.e., a garment covering its wearer "from head to back," on the model of
cap-à-pie, "from head to foot," referring to armor.

A lace lightly about, that led to a knot,
Was looped in by lengths along the fair haft,
And tassels thereto attached in a row,
220 With buttons of bright green, brave to behold.
This horseman hurtles in, and the hall enters;
Riding to the high dais, recked he no danger;
Not a greeting he gave as the guests he o'erlooked,
Nor wasted his words, but "Where is," he said,
225 "The captain of this crowd?⁹ Keenly I wish
To see that sire with sight, and to himself say
                    my say."
            He swaggered all about
            To scan the host so gay;
230   He halted, as if in doubt
            Who in that hall held sway.

There were stares on all sides as the stranger spoke,
For much did they marvel what it might mean
That a horseman and a horse should have such a hue,¹
235 Grow green as the grass, and greener, it seemed,
Than green fused on gold more glorious by far.
All the onlookers eyed him, and edged nearer,
And awaited in wonder what he would do,
For many sights had they seen, but such a one never,
240 So that phantom and faerie the folk there deemed it,
Therefore chary° of answer was many a champion bold,   *cautious*
And stunned at his strong words stone-still they sat
In a swooning silence in the stately hall.
As all were slipped into sleep, so slackened their speech
245   apace.
            Not all, I think, for dread,
            But some of courteous grace

9. lines 224–25: . . . **"Where is," he said, "The captain of this crowd** . . . The Green Knight's inability, or feigned inability, to tell which of the people before him is King Arthur has insulting implications; in heroic legend, a leader typically stands out in a crowd. In *Beowulf*, for example, the coast guard, greeting the band of Geats on their arrival in the land of the Danes, clearly refers to the hero when he says "I have never seen a mightier warrior on earth than is one of you. That is no retainer made to seem good by his weapons" (trans. Donaldson).

1. lines 233–34: **For much did they marvel what it might mean / That a horseman and a horse should have such a hue.** The greenness of the Green Knight is susceptible of many interpretations, none of which need preclude the others. It is, most obviously, the color of vegetation and thus symbolizes the endless vegetative cycle of death and rebirth; the spectators are amazed that a horse and his rider should "grow green as the grass" (line 235). But this image from the natural realm is immediately discarded in favor of one drawn from the realm of artifice, that of green enamel on gold. And in fact neither can compare, the poet thinks, with the "glorious" hue of the knight. Green also had associations in medieval thought with the infernal realm: a devil in Chaucer's *Friar's Tale*, for example, is dressed all in green. For the members of Arthur's court, the stranger's hue simply enhances his phantasmal and uncanny appearance (lines 239–40).

Let him who was their head
Be spokesman in that place.

250 Then Arthur before the high dais that entrance beholds,
And hailed him, as behooved, for he had no fear,
And said "Fellow, in faith you have found fair welcome;
The head of this hostelry° Arthur am I;   *inn*
Leap lightly down, and linger, I pray,
255 And the tale of your intent you shall tell us after."
"Nay, so help me," said the other, "He that on high sits,
To tarry here any time, 'twas not mine errand;
But as the praise of you, prince, is puffed up so high,
And your court and your company are counted the best,
260 Stoutest under steel-gear on steeds to ride,
Worthiest of their works the wide world over,
And peerless to prove in passages of arms,
And courtesy here is carried to its height,
And so at this season I have sought you out.
265 You may be certain by the branch that I bear in hand
That I pass here in peace, and would part friends,
For had I come to this court on combat bent,
I have a hauberk at home, and a helm beside,
A shield and a sharp spear, shining bright,
270 And other weapons as well, war-gear of the best;
But as I willed no war, I wore no metal.
But if you be so bold as all men believe,
You will graciously grant the game that I ask
                              by right."
275   Arthur answer gave
                        And said, "Sir courteous knight,
                        If contest here you crave,
                        You shall not fail to fight."

Nay, to fight, in good faith, is far from my thought;
280 There are about on these benches but beardless children,
Were I here in full arms on a haughty steed,
For measured against mine, their might is puny.°   *weak*
And so I call in this court for a Christmas game,
For 'tis Yule and New Year, and many young bloods about;
285 If any in this house such hardihood claims,
Be so bold in his blood, his brain so wild,
As stoutly to strike one stroke for another,
I shall give him as my gift this gisarme noble,
This ax, that is heavy enough, to handle as he likes,
290 And I shall bide the first blow, as bare as I sit.
If there be one so wilful my words to assay,°   *put to the test*

Let him leap hither lightly, lay hold of this weapon;
I quitclaim° it forever, keep it as his own,   *give it up*
And I shall stand him a stroke, steady on this floor,
So you grant me the guerdon° to give him another,   *reward*
              sans blame.
          In a twelvemonth and a day
          He shall have of me the same;
          Now be it seen straightway
          Who dares take up the game."

If he astonished them at first, stiller were then
All that household in hall, the high and the low;
The stranger on his green steed stirred in the saddle,
And roisterously his red eyes he rolled all about,
Bent his bristling brows, that were bright green,
Wagged his beard as he watched who would arise.
When the court kept its counsel he coughed aloud,
And cleared his throat coolly, the clearer to speak:
"What, is this Arthur's house," said that horse-man then,
"Whose fame is so fair in far realms and wide?
Where is now your arrogance and your awesome deeds,
Your valor and your victories and your vaunting° words?   *boastful*
Now are the revel and renown of the Round Table
Overwhelmed with a word of one man's speech,
For all cower and quake, and no cut felt!"
With this he laughs so loud that the lord grieved;
The blood for sheer shame shot to his face,
              and pride.
          With rage his face flushed red,
          And so did all beside.
          Then the king as bold man bred
          Toward the stranger took a stride.

And said "Sir, now we see you will say but folly,
Which whoso has sought, it suits that he find.
No guest here is aghast° of your great words.   *frightened*
Give to me your gisarme, in God's own name,
And the boon you have begged shall straight be granted."
He leaps to him lightly, lays hold of his weapon;
The green fellow on foot fiercely alights.
Now has Arthur his ax, and the haft grips,
And sternly stirs it about, on striking bent.
The stranger before him stood there erect,
Higher than any in the house by a head and more;
With stern look as he stood, he stroked his beard,
And with undaunted countenance drew down his coat,

No more moved nor dismayed for his mighty blows
Than any bold man on bench had brought him a drink
        of wine.
        Gawain by Guenevere
340   Toward the king doth now incline:
        "I beseech, before all here,
        That this melee° may be mine."   *combat*

"Would you grant me the grace," said Gawain to the king,
"To be gone from this bench and stand by you there,
345 If I without discourtesy might quit this board,
And if my liege lady° misliked it not,   *wife of a feudal lord*
I would come to your counsel before your court noble.
For I find it not fit, as in faith it is known,
When such a boon is begged before all these knights,
350 Though you be tempted thereto, to take it on yourself
While so bold men about upon benches sit,
That no host under heaven is hardier of will,
Nor better brothers-in-arms where battle is joined;
I am the weakest, well I know, and of wit feeblest;
355 And the loss of my life would be least of any;
That I have you for uncle is my only praise;
My body, but for your blood, is barren of worth;
And for that this folly befits not a king,
And it is I that have asked it, it ought to be mine,
360 And if my claim be not comely let all this court judge,
        in sight."
        The court assays the claim,
        And in counsel all unite
        To give Gawain the game
365   And release the king outright.

Then the king called the knight to come to his side,
And he rose up readily, and reached him with speed,
Bows low to his lord, lays hold of the weapon,
And he releases it lightly, and lifts up his hand,
370 And gives him God's blessing, and graciously prays
That his heart and his hand may be hardy both.
"Keep, cousin," said the king, "what you cut with this day,
And if you rule it aright, then readily, I know,
You shall stand the stroke it will strike after."
375 Gawain goes to the guest with gisarme in hand,
And boldly he bides there, abashed not a whit.
Then hails he Sir Gawain, the horseman in green:
"Recount we our contract, ere you come further.
First I ask and adjure° you, how you are called   *solemnly command*

380   That you tell me true, so that trust it I may."
"In good faith," said the good knight, "Gawain am I
Whose buffet befalls you, whate'er betide after,
And at this time twelvemonth take from you another
With what weapon you will, and with no man else
385   alive."
                The other nods assent:
                "Sir Gawain, as I may thrive,
                I am wondrous well content
                That you this dint shall drive."

390   "Sir Gawain," said the Green Knight, "By Gog, I rejoice[2]
That your fist shall fetch this favor I seek,
And you have readily rehearsed, and in right terms,
Each clause of my covenant with the king your lord,
Save that you shall assure me, sir, upon oath,
395   That you shall seek me yourself, wheresoever you think
My lodgings may lie, and look for such wages
As you have offered me here before all this host."
"What is the way there?" said Gawain, "Where do you live?
I never heard of your house, by Him that made me,
400   Nor I know you not, knight, your name nor your court.
But tell me truly thereof, and teach me your name,
And I shall fare forth to find you, so far as I may,
And this I say in good certain, and swear upon oath."
"That is enough in New Year, you need say no more,"
405   Said the knight in the green to Gawain the noble,
"If I tell you true, when I have taken your knock,
And if you handily have hit, you shall hear straightway
Of my house and my home and my own name;
Then follow in my footsteps by faithful accord.
410   And if I spend no speech, you shall speed the better:
You can feast with your friends, nor further trace
                     my tracks.
                Now hold your grim tool steady
                And show us how it hacks."
415   "Gladly, sir; all ready,"
                Says Gawain; he strokes the ax.

2. line 390: **"Sir Gawain," said the Green Knight, "by Gog, I rejoice.** In chapters 38–39 of the Old Testament Book of Ezekiel, the Lord says to the prophet "Son of man, set thy face against Gog" (38.2) and later tells him to "prophesy against Gog, and say: Thus saith the Lord God; Behold, I am against thee, O Gog. . . . Thou shalt fall upon the open field" (39.1,5). Gog is also mentioned in Revelation as a power that appears when Satan is released from his thousand years of bondage and joins forces with him (20.7–9). The Green Knight's oath thus superficially resembles such innocuous expressions as "by golly" and "by gosh" but, at the same time, carries a fleeting suggestion of a demonic supernatural realm.

The Green Knight upon ground girds him° with care;   *prepares himself*
Bows a bit with his head, and bares his flesh;
His long lovely locks he laid over his crown,
420   Let the naked nape for the need be shown.
Gawain grips to his ax and gathers it aloft—
The left foot on the floor before him he set—
Brought it down deftly upon the bare neck,
That the shock of the sharp blow shivered the bones
425   And cut the flesh cleanly and clove it in twain,
That the blade of bright steel bit into the ground.
The head fell to the floor as the ax hewed it off;
Many found it at their feet, as forth it rolled;
The blood gushed from the body, bright on the green,
430   Yet fell not the fellow, nor faltered a whit,
But stoutly he starts forth upon stiff shanks,
And as all stood staring he stretched forth his hand,
Laid hold of his head and heaved it aloft,
Then goes to the green steed, grasps the bridle,
435   Steps into the stirrup, bestrides his mount,
And his head by the hair in his hand holds,
And as steady he sits in the stately saddle
As he had met with no mishap, nor missing were
                    his head.
440   His bulk about he haled,°   *hauled*
           That fearsome body that bled;
           There were many in the court that quailed°   *cowered*
           Before all his say was said.

For the head in his hand he holds right up;
445   Toward the first on the dais directs he the face,
And it lifted up its lids, and looked with wide eyes,
And said as much with its mouth as now you may hear:
"Sir Gawain, forget not to go as agreed,
And cease not to seek till me, sir, you find,
450   As you promised in the presence of these proud knights.
To the Green Chapel come, I charge you, to take
Such a blow as you bestowed—you deserve, beyond doubt,
A knock on your neck next New Year's morn.
The Knight of the Green Chapel I am well-known to many,
455   Wherefore you cannot fail to find me at last;
Therefore come, or be counted a recreant° knight."   *faithless*
With a roisterous rush he flings round the reins,
Hurtles out at the hall-door, his head in his hand,
That the flint-fire flew from the flashing hooves.
460   Which way he went, not one of them knew

Nor whence he was come in the wide world
                    so fair.
          The king and Gawain gay
          Make game of the Green Knight there,
465   Yet all who saw it say
          'Twas a wonder past compare.

Though high-born Arthur at heart had wonder,
He let no sign be seen, but said aloud
To the comely queen, with courteous speech,
470 "Dear dame, on this day dismay you no whit;
Such crafts are becoming at Christmastide,
Laughing at interludes,° light songs and mirth,   *short farcical plays*
Amid dancing of damsels with doughty° knights.   *stout-hearted*
Nevertheless of my meat now let me partake,
475 For I have met with a marvel, I may not deny."
He glanced at Sir Gawain, and gaily he said,
"Now, sir, hang up your ax, that has hewn enough,"[3]
And over the high dais it was hung on the wall
That men in amazement might on it look,
480 And tell in true terms the tale of the wonder.
Then they turned toward the table, these two together,
The good king and Gawain, and made great feast,
With all dainties double, dishes rare,
With all manner of meat and minstrelsy both,
485 Such happiness wholly had they that day
                    in hold.
          Now take care, Sir Gawain,
          That your courage wax not cold
          When you must turn again
490   To your enterprise foretold.

Part II

This adventure had Arthur of hand-gifts first
When young was the year, for he yearned to hear tales;
Though they wanted for words when they went to sup,
Now are fierce deeds to follow, their fists stuffed full.
495 Gawain was glad to begin those games in hall,
But if the end be harsher, hold it no wonder,
For though men are merry in mind after much drink,
A year passes apace, and proves ever new:

3. line 477: **"Now, sir, hang up your ax, that has hewn enough."** The "gay" remark with
   which the king counters the tension of the moment is a witty play on words; the phrase
   "To hang up one's ax" meant, in Middle English, to stop whatever one has been doing.

First things and final conform but seldom.
500 And so this Yule to the young year yielded place,
And each season ensued at its set time;
After Christmas there came the cold cheer of Lent,
When with fish and plainer fare our flesh we reprove;
But then the world's weather with winter contends;
505 The keen cold lessens, the low clouds lift;
Fresh falls the rain in fostering showers
On the face of the fields; flowers appear.
The ground and the groves wear gowns of green;
Birds build their nests, and blithely sing
510 That solace of all sorrow with summer comes
                    ere long.
            And blossoms day by day
            Bloom rich and rife° in throng;   *numerous*
            Then every grove so gay
515   Of the greenwood rings with song.

And then the season of summer with the soft winds,
When Zephyr sighs low over seeds and shoots;[4]
Glad is the green plant growing abroad,
When the dew at dawn drops from the leaves,
520 To get a gracious glance from the golden sun.
But harvest with harsher winds follows hard after,
Warns him to ripen well ere winter comes;
Drives forth the dust in the droughty season,
From the face of the fields to fly high in air.
525 Wroth winds in the welkin° wrestle with the sun,   *sky*
The leaves launch from the linden and light on the ground,
And the grass turns to gray, that once grew green.
Then all ripens and rots that rose up at first,
And so the year moves on in yesterdays many,
530 And winter once more, by the world's law,
                    draws nigh.
            At Michaelmas° the moon   *September 29*
            Hangs wintry pale in sky;
            Sir Gawain girds him soon
535   For travails yet to try.

Till All-Saints' Day° with Arthur he stays,   *November 1*
And he held a high feast to honor that knight

---

4. line 517: **When Zephyr sighs low . . .** Latin *Zephirus* (Greek *Zephyros*) was a name for the
west wind in classical mythology. It was transmitted to the late Middle Ages in Latin works
such as Guido delle Colonne's prose *History of the Destruction of Troy*, where the blowing
of Zephyr forms part of a description of the coming of spring. Chaucer, famously, uses the
detail in a similar description in the opening of the "General Prologue" to *The Canterbury
Tales*. It appears also in *Destruction of Troy*, an adaptation of Guido's work representing the
same alliterative tradition as the long lines of *Sir Gawain and the Green Knight*.

With great revels and rich, of the Round Table.
Then lovely ladies and lords debonair
540 With sorrow for Sir Gawain were sore at heart;
Yet they covered their care with countenance glad:
Many a mournful man made mirth for his sake.
So after supper soberly he speaks to his uncle
Of the hard hour at hand, and openly says,
545 "Now, liege lord of my life, my leave I take;
The terms of this task too well you know—
To count the cost over concerns me nothing.
But I am bound forth betimes to bear a stroke
From the grim man in green, as God may direct."
550 Then the first and foremost came forth in throng:
Yvain and Eric and others of note,
Sir Dodinal le Sauvage, the Duke of Clarence,
Lionel and Lancelot and Lucan the good,
Sir Bors and Sir Bedivere, big men both,
555 And many manly knights more, with Mador de la Porte,
All this courtly company comes with the king
To counsel their comrade, with care in their hearts;
There was much secret sorrow suffered that day
That one so good as Gawain must go in this fashion
560 To bear a bitter blow, and his bright sword
            lay by.
      He said, "Why should I tarry?"
      And smiled with tranquil eye;
      "In destinies sad or merry,
565   True men can but try."

He dwelt there all that day, and dressed in the morning;
Asked early for his arms, and all were brought.
First a carpet of rare cost was cast on the floor
Where much goodly gear gleamed golden bright;
570 He takes his place promptly and picks up the steel,
Attired in a tight coat of Turkestan silk
And a kingly cap-à-dos, closed at the throat,
That was lavishly lined with a lustrous fur.
Then they set the steel shoes on his sturdy feet
575 And clad his calves about with comely greaves,°   *leg armor*
And plate well-polished protected his knees,
Affixed with fastenings of the finest gold.
Fair cuisses enclosed, that were cunningly wrought,
His thick-thewed° thighs, with thongs bound fast,   *well-muscled*
580 And massy chain-mail of many a steel ring
He bore on his body, above the best cloth,
On his arms, at his elbows, armor well wrought

Protected that prince, with plated gloves,
And all the goodly gear to grace him well
585   that tide.
          His surcoat° blazoned bold;   *cloth tunic*
          Sharp spurs to prick with pride;
          And a brave silk band to hold
          The broadsword at his side.

590 When he had on his arms, his harness was rich,
     The least latchet° or loop laden with gold;   *thong*
     So armored as he was, he heard a mass,
     Honored God humbly at the high altar.
     Then he comes to the king and his comrades-in-arms,
595 Takes his leave at last of lords and ladies,
     And they clasped and kissed him, commending him to Christ.
     By then Gringolet was girt with a great saddle
     That was gaily agleam with fine gilt fringe,
     New-furbished for the need with nail-heads bright;
600 The bridle and the bars bedecked all with gold;
     The breast-plate, the saddlebow, the side-panels both,
     The caparison° and the crupper accorded in hue,   *decorated cloth cover*
     And all ranged on the red the resplendent studs
     That glittered and glowed like the glorious sun.
605 His helm now he holds up and hastily kisses,
     Well-closed with iron clinches, and cushioned within;
     It was high on his head, with a hasp behind,
     And a covering of cloth to encase the visor,
     All bound and embroidered with the best gems
610 On broad bands of silk, and bordered with birds,
     Parrots and popinjays preening their wings,
     Lovebirds and love-knots as lavishly wrought
     As many women had worked seven winters thereon,
                         entire.
615   The diadem costlier yet
          That crowned that comely sire,
          With diamonds richly set,
          That flashed as if on fire.

     Then they showed forth the shield, that shone all red,
620 With the pentangle portrayed in purest gold.[5]

---

5. lines 619–20: **Then they showed forth his shield, that shone all red, / With the pen-tangle portrayed in purest gold.** The "pentangle" was a five-pointed star drawn in a con-tinuous line and rejoining itself without a break. In the completed design, the line weaves in and out, going alternately over and under itself. The ancient concept of the five-pointed star merged in medieval thought with that of the six-pointed star of Solomon. Both emblems had magical and religious associations.

About his broad neck by the baldric° he casts it,   *slantwise band*
That was meet° for the man, and matched him well.   *fitting*
And why the pentangle is proper to that peerless prince
I intend now to tell, though detain me it must.
625 It is a sign by Solomon sagely devised
To be a token of truth, by its title of old,
For it is a figure formed of five points,
And each line is linked and locked with the next
For ever and ever, and hence it is called
630 In all England, as I hear, the endless knot.[6]
And well may he wear it on his worthy arms,
For ever faithful five-fold in five-fold fashion
Was Gawain in good works, as gold unalloyed,°   *pure*
Devoid of all villainy, with virtues adorned
635   in sight.
              On shield and coat in view
              He bore that emblem bright,
              As to his word most true
              And in speech most courteous knight.

640 And first, he was faultless in his five senses,
Nor found ever to fail in his five fingers,
And all his fealty° was fixed upon the five wounds   *allegiance*
That Christ got on the cross, as the creed tells;
And wherever this man in melee took part,
645 His one thought was of this, past all things else,
That all his force was founded on the five joys
That the high Queen of heaven had in her child.
And therefore, as I find, he fittingly had
On the inner part of his shield her image portrayed,
650 That when his look on it lighted, he never lost heart.
The fifth of the five fives followed by this knight
Were beneficence° boundless and brotherly love   *kindness*
And pure mind and manners, that none might impeach,°   *discredit*
And compassion most precious[7]—these peerless five
655 Were forged and made fast in him, foremost of men.
Now all these five fives were confirmed in this knight,
And each linked in other, that end there was none,
And fixed to five points, whose force never failed,
Nor assembled all on a side, nor asunder either,
660 Nor anywhere at an end, but whole and entire

---

6. lines 629–30: . . . **and hence it is called / In all England, as I hear, the endless knot.**
But in fact there is no recorded instance of such a phrase.
7. lines 652–54: . . . **beneficence boundless and brotherly love / And pure mind and manners, that none might impeach, / And compassion most precious.** In the poet's Middle
English, the names of the five virtues are *franchise, fellowship, cleanness, courtesy,* and *pity.*

However the pattern proceeded or played out its course.
And so on his shining shield shaped was the knot
Royally in red gold against red gules,°   red (heraldic)
That is the peerless pentangle, prized of old
665   in lore.
                    Now armed is Gawain gay,
                    And bears his lance before,
                    And soberly said good day,
                    He thought forevermore.

670 He struck his steed with the spurs and sped on his way
So fast that the flint-fire flashed from the stones.
When they saw him set forth they were sore aggrieved,
And all sighed softly, and said to each other,
Fearing for their fellow, "Ill fortune it is
675 That you, man, must be marred, that are most worthy!
His equal on this earth can hardly be found;
To have dealt more discreetly had done less harm,
And have dubbed° him a duke, with all due honor.   appointed
A great leader and lord he was like to become,
680 And better so to have been than battered to bits,
Beheaded by an elf-man, for empty pride!
Who would credit that a king could be counseled so,
And caught in a cavil° in a Christmas game?"   trivial argument
Many were the warm tears they wept from their eyes
685 When goodly Sir Gawain was gone from the court
                        that day.
                    No longer he abode,
                    But speedily went his way
                    Over many a wandering road,
690   As I heard my author say.

Now he rides in his array through the realm of Logres,[8]
Sir Gawain, God knows, though it gave him small joy!
All alone must he lodge through many a long night
Where the food that he fancied was far from his plate;
695 He had no mate but his mount, over mountain and plain,
Nor man to say his mind to but almighty God,
Till he had wandered well-nigh into North Wales.
All the islands of Anglesey he holds on his left,
And follows, as he fares, the fords by the coast,

---

8. lines 691–701: **Now he rides in his array through the realm of Logres . . . The Wilderness of Wirral.** The poet evidently thought that Logres, King Arthur's kingdom, was in central or south Wales. Sir Gawain rides north and then turns eastward along the north coast of Wales, leaving Anglesey and its neighboring islands to his left. It was considered dangerous in the poet's time to pass through the forest of Wirral, which was a place of refuge for outlaws and other criminals.

700 Comes over at Holy Head, and enters next
The Wilderness of Wirral—few were within
That had great good will toward God or man.
And earnestly he asked of each mortal he met
If he had ever heard aught of a knight all green,
705 Or of a Green Chapel, on ground thereabouts,
And all said the same, and solemnly swore
They had seen no such knight all solely green
                              in hue.
                    Over country wild and strange
710   The knight sets off anew;
                    Often his course must change
                    Ere the Chapel comes in view.

Many a cliff must he climb in country wild;
Far off from all his friends, forlorn must he ride;
715 At each strand or stream where the stalwart one passed
'Twere a marvel if he met not some monstrous foe,
And that so fierce and forbidding that fight he must.
So many were the wonders he wandered among
That to tell but the tenth part would tax my wits.
720 Now with serpents he wars, now with savage wolves,
Now with wild men of the woods, that watched from the rocks,
Both with bulls and with bears, and with boars besides,
And giants that came gibbering° from the jagged   *shouting crazily*
      steeps.
Had he not borne himself bravely, and been on God's side,
725 He had met with many mishaps and mortal harms.
And if the wars were unwelcome, the winter was worse,
When the cold clear rains rushed from the clouds
And froze before they could fall to the frosty earth.
Near slain by the sleet he sleeps in his irons
730 More nights than enough, among naked rocks,
Where clattering from the crest the cold stream ran
And hung in hard icicles high overhead.
Thus in peril and pain and predicaments dire
He rides across country till Christmas Eve,
735   our knight.
                    And at that holy tide
                    He prays with all his might
                    That Mary may be his guide
                    Till a dwelling comes in sight.

740 By a mountain next morning he makes his way
Into a forest fastness, fearsome and wild;
High hills on either hand, with hoar° woods below,   *gray with frost*

Oaks old and huge by the hundred together,
The hazel and the hawthorn were all intertwined
745 With rough raveled moss, that raggedly hung,
With many birds unblithe upon bare twigs
That peeped most piteously for pain of the cold.
The good knight on Gringolet glides thereunder
Through many a marsh and mire, a man all alone;
750 He feared for his default, should he fail to see
The service of that Sire that on that same night
Was born of a blessèd maid, to bring us His peace.
And therefore sighing he said, "I beseech of Thee, Lord,
And Mary, thou mildest mother so dear,
755 Some harborage where haply I might hear mass
And Thy matins tomorrow—meekly I ask it,
And thereto proffer and pray my Pater,° and Ave°   *Our Father / Hail Mary*
                    and Creed."°   *statement of belief*
              He said his prayer with sighs,
760   Lamenting his misdeed;
              He crosses himself, and cries
              On Christ in his great need.

No sooner had Sir Gawain signed° himself thrice   *crossed*
Than he was ware, in the wood, of a wondrous dwelling,
765 Within a moat, on a mound, bright amid boughs
Of many a tree great of girth that grew by the water—
A castle as comely as a knight could own,
On grounds fair and green, in a goodly park
With a palisade of palings planted about
770 For two miles and more, round many a fair tree.
The stout knight stared at that stronghold great
As it shimmered and shone amid shining leaves,
Then with helmet in hand he offers his thanks
To Jesus and Saint Julian,° that are gentle both,   *travelers' protector*
775 That in courteous accord had inclined to his prayer;
"Now fair harbor," said he, "I humbly beseech!"
Then he pricks his proud steed with the plated spurs,
And by chance he has chosen the chief path
That brought the bold knight to the bridge's end
780   in haste.
              The bridge hung high in air;
              The gates were bolted fast;
              The walls well-framed to bear
              The fury of the blast.

785 The man on his mount remained on the bank
Of the deep double moat that defended the place.

The wall went in the water wondrous deep,
And a long way aloft it loomed overhead.
It was built of stone blocks to the battlements' height,
790 With corbels° under cornices°   *supporting brackets / projecting layers*
       in comeliest style;
Watch-towers trusty protected the gate,
With many a lean loophole, to look from within:
A better-made barbican° the knight beheld never.   *fortification*
And behind it he beheld a great hall and fair:
795 Turrets rising in tiers, with tines at their tops,
Spires set beside them, splendidly tall,
With finials° well-fashioned, as filigree fine.   *ornamental tops*
Chalk-white chimneys over chambers high
Gleamed in gay array upon gables and roofs;
800 The pinnacles in panoply, pointing in air,
So vied there for his view that verily it seemed
A castle cut of paper for a king's feast.
The good knight on Gringolet thought it great luck
If he could but contrive to come there within
805 To keep the Christmas feast in that castle fair
                    and bright.
          There answered to his call
          A porter most polite;
          From his station on the wall
810   He greets the errant knight.

"Good sir," said Gawain, "Would you go to inquire
If your lord would allow me to lodge here a space?"
"Peter!" said the porter, "For my part, I think
So noble a knight will not want for a welcome!"
815 Then he bustles off briskly, and comes back straight,
And many servants beside, to receive him the better.
They let down the drawbridge and duly went forth
And kneeled down on their knees on the naked earth
To welcome this warrior as best they were able.
820 They proffered him passage—the portals stood wide—
And he beckoned them to rise, and rode over the bridge.
Men steadied his saddle as he stepped to the ground,
And there stabled his steed many stalwart folk.
Now come the knights and the noble squires
825 To bring him with bliss into the bright hall.
When his high helm was off, there hastened a throng
Of attendants to take it, and see to its care;
They bore away his broad sword and blazoned shield;
Then graciously he greeted those gallants each one,

830 And many a noble drew near, to do the knight honor.
All in his armor into hall he was led,
Where fire on a fair hearth fiercely blazed.
And soon the lord himself descends from his chamber
To meet in mannerly fashion the man on his floor.
835 He said, "To this house you are heartily welcome:
What is here is wholly yours, to have in your power
                    and sway."°   *control*
            Says Gawain with a smile
            "May Christ your pains repay!"
840   They embrace in courteous style
            As men well met that day.

Gawain gazed on the host that greeted him there,
And a lusty fellow he looked, the lord of that place:
A man of massive mold, and of middle age;
845 Broad, bright was his beard, of a beaver's hue,[9]
Strong, steady his stance, upon stalwart shanks,
His face fierce as fire, fair-spoken withal,
And well-suited he seemed in Sir Gawain's sight
To be a master of men in a mighty keep.°   *strong fort*
850 They pass into a parlor, where promptly the host
Has a servant assigned him to see to his needs,
And there came upon his call many courteous folk
That brought him to a bower where bedding was noble,
With heavy silk hangings hemmed all in gold,
855 Coverlets and counterpanes° curiously wrought,   *bedspreads*
A canopy over the couch, clad all with fur,
Curtains running on cords, caught to gold rings,
Woven rugs on the walls of eastern work,
And the floor, under foot, well-furnished with the same.
860 With light talk and laughter they loosed from him then
His war-dress of weight and his worthy clothes.
Robes richly wrought they brought him right soon,
To change there in chamber and choose what he would.
865 When he had found one he fancied, and flung it about,
Well-fashioned for his frame, with flowing skirts,
His face fair and fresh as the flowers of spring,
All the good folk agreed, that gazed on him then,
His limbs arrayed royally in radiant hues,
870 That so comely a mortal never Christ made
                    as he.
            Whatever his place of birth,
            It seemed he well might be

9. line 845: **Broad, bright was his beard, of a beaver's hue.** See n. 7, p. 8 (line 182).

Without a peer on earth
875   In martial rivalry.

A couch before the fire, where fresh coals burned,
They spread for Sir Gawain splendidly now
With quilts quaintly stitched, and cushions beside,
And then a costly cloak they cast on his shoulders
880 Of bright silk, embroidered on borders and hems,
With furs of the finest well-furnished within,
And bound about with ermine, both mantle and hood;
And he sat at that fireside in sumptuous estate
And warmed himself well, and soon he waxed merry.
885 Then attendants set a table upon trestles broad,
And lustrous white linen they laid thereupon,
A saltcellar of silver, spoons of the same.
He washed himself well and went to his place,
Men set his fare before him in fashion most fit.
890 There were soups of all sorts, seasoned with skill,
Double-sized servings, and sundry fish,
Some baked, some breaded, some broiled on the coals,
Some simmered, some in stews, steaming with spices,
And with sauces to sup that suited his taste.
He confesses it a feast with free words and fair;
895 They requite° him as kindly with courteous jests,   *repay*
                    well-sped.
               "Tonight you fast and pray;
               Tomorrow we'll see you fed."[1]
               The knight grows wondrous gay
900   As the wine goes to his head.

Then at times and by turns, as at table he sat,
They questioned him quietly, with queries discreet,
And he courteously confessed that he comes from the court,
And owns him of the brotherhood of high-famed Arthur,
905 The right royal ruler of the Round Table,
And the guest by their fireside is Gawain himself,
Who has happened on their house at that holy feast.
When the name of the knight was made known to the lord,
Then loudly he laughed, so elated he was,
910 And the men in that household made haste with joy
To appear in his presence promptly that day,
That of courage ever-constant, and customs pure,

---

1. lines 897–98: **Tonight you fast and pray; / Tomorrow we'll see you fed.** Those who
   serve Sir Gawain his meal are joking. On Christmas Eve, as on Fridays and during Lent,
   Christians were supposed to abstain from meat. The elaborate fish dishes, of course,
   make the meal anything but an occasion for self-denial.

Is pattern and paragon,° and praised without end: *model of perfection*
Of all knights on earth most honored is he.
915 Each said solemnly aside to his brother,
"Now displays of deportment shall dazzle our eyes
And the polished pearls of impeccable° speech;   *flawless*
The high art of eloquence is ours to pursue
Since the father of fine manners is found in our midst.
920 Great is God's grace, and goodly indeed,
That a guest such as Gawain he guides to us here
When men sit and sing of their Savior's birth
                in view.
        With command of manners pure
925   He shall each heart imbue;°   *fill*
        Who shares his converse, sure,
        Shall learn love's language true."

When the knight had done dining and duly arose,
The dark was drawing on; the day nigh ended.
930 Chaplains in chapels and churches about
Rang the bells aright, reminding all men
Of the holy evensong° of the high feast.   *evening service*
The lord attends alone; his fair lady sits
In a comely closet, secluded from sight.
935 Gawain in gay attire goes thither soon;
The lord catches his coat, and calls him by name,
And has him sit beside him, and says in good faith
No guest on God's earth would he gladlier greet.
For that Gawain thanked him; the two then embraced
940 And sat together soberly the service through.
Then the lady, that longed to look on the knight,
Came forth from her closet with her comely maids.
The fair hues of her flesh, her face and her hair
And her body and her bearing were beyond praise,
945 And excelled the queen herself, as Sir Gawain thought.
He goes forth to greet her with gracious intent;
Another lady led her by the left hand
That was older than she—an ancient, it seemed,
And held in high honor by all men about.
950 But unlike to look upon, those ladies were,[2]
For if the one was fresh, the other was faded:
Bedecked in bright red was the body of one;
Flesh hung in folds on the face of the other;

---

2. line 950: **But unlike to look upon, those ladies were.** Underlying the double description
   is a message of religious import: mortal beauty is transitory. Such as the old lady now is,
   the desirable young lady will be.

On one a high headdress, hung all with pearls;
955 Her bright throat and bosom fair to behold,
Fresh as the first snow fallen upon hills;
A wimple° the other one wore round her throat;   *cloth wrapping*
Her swart° chin well swaddled, swathed all in white;   *dark*
Her forehead enfolded in flounces of silk
960 That framed a fair fillet,° of fashion ornate.   *headband*
And nothing bare beneath save the black brows,
The two eyes and the nose, the naked lips,
And they unsightly to see, and sorrily bleared.
A beldame,° by God, she may well be deemed,   *formidable lady*
965   of pride!
          She was short and thick of waist,
          Her buttocks round and wide;
          More toothsome, to his taste,
          Was the beauty by her side.

970 When Gawain had gazed on that gay lady,
With leave of her lord, he politely approached;
To the elder in homage he humbly bows;
The lovelier he salutes with a light embrace.
He claims a comely kiss, and courteously he speaks;
975 They welcome him warmly, and straightway he asks
To be received as their servant, if they so desire.
They take him between them; with talking they bring him
Beside a bright fire; bade then that spices
Be freely fetched forth, to refresh them the better,
980 And the good wine therewith, to warm their hearts.
The lord leaps about in light-hearted mood;
Contrives entertainments and timely sports;
Takes his hood from his head and hangs it on a spear,
And offers him openly the honor thereof
985 Who should promote the most mirth at that Christmas feast;
"And I shall try for it, trust me—contend with the best,
Ere I go without my headgear by grace of my friends!"
Thus with light talk and laughter the lord makes merry
To gladden the guest he had greeted in hall
990   that day.
          At the last he called for light
          The company to convey;
          Gawain says goodnight
          And retires to bed straightway.

995 On the morn when each man is mindful in heart
That God's son was sent down to suffer our death,
No household but is blithe for His blessed sake;

So was it there on that day, with many delights.
Both at larger meals and less they were lavishly served
1000   By doughty° lads on dais,° with delicate fare;   *capable / platform*
The old ancient lady, highest she sits;
The lord at her left hand leaned, as I hear;
Sir Gawain in the center, beside the gay lady,
Where the food was brought first to that festive board,
1005   And thence throughout the hall, as they held most fit,
To each man was offered in order of rank.
There was meat, there was mirth, there was much joy,
That to tell all the tale would tax my wits,
Though I pained me, perchance, to paint it with care;
1010   But yet I know that our knight and the noble lady
Were accorded so closely in company there,
With the seemly solace of their secret words,
With speeches well-sped, spotless and pure,
That each prince's pastime their pleasures far
1015   outshone.
                Sweet pipes beguile their cares,
                And the trumpet of martial tone;
                Each tends his affairs
                And those two tend their own.

1020   That day and all the next, their disport was noble,
And the third day, I think, pleased them no less;
The joys of St. John's Day were justly praised,[3]
And were the last of their like for those lords and ladies;
Then guests were to go in the gray morning,
1025   Wherefore they whiled the night away with wine and with mirth,
Moved to the measures of many a blithe carol;
At last, when it was late, took leave of each other,
Each one of those worthies, to wend his way.
Gawain bids goodbye to his goodly host
1030   Who brings him to his chamber, the chimney beside,
And detains him in talk, and tenders his thanks
And holds it an honor to him and his people
That he has harbored in his, house at that holy time
And embellished his abode° with his inborn grace.   *adorned his dwelling*
1035   "As long as I may live, my luck is the better
That Gawain was my guest at God's own feast!"
"Noble sir," said the knight, "I cannot but think

---

3. line 1022: **The joys of St. John's Day were justly praised.** The date of St. John's Day is
December 27, so there are four days left, not three, before New Year's morning, on which
Sir Gawain is bound to set out to meet the Green Knight. But he lies late in bed at the
lord's behest only three days. A line after 1022 may inadvertently have been omitted; in
any case, a day seems to be missing.

All the honor is your own—may the high king repay you!
And your man to command I account myself here
1040　As I am bound and beholden, and shall be, come
　　　　　　　　　　what may."
　　　　　　　　　The lord with all his might
　　　　　　　　　Entreats his guest to stay;
　　　　　　　　　Brief answer makes the knight:
1045　　　　　　　　Next morning he must away.

Then the lord of that land politely inquired
What dire affair had forced him, at that festive time,
So far from the king's court to fare forth alone
Ere the holidays wholly had ended in hall.
1050　"In good faith," said Gawain, "you have guessed the truth:
On a high errand and urgent I hastened away,
For I am summoned by myself to seek for a place—
I wish I knew whither, or where it might be!
Far rather would I find it before the New Year
1055　Than own the land of Logres, so help me our Lord!
Wherefore, sir, in friendship this favor I ask,
That you say in sober earnest, if something you know
Of the Green Chapel, on ground far or near,
Or the lone knight that lives there, of like hue of green.
1060　A certain day was set by assent of us both
To meet at that landmark, if I might last,
And from now to the New Year is nothing too long,
And I would greet the Green Knight there, would God but allow,
More gladly, by God's Son, than gain the world's wealth!
1065　And I must set forth to search, as soon as I may;
To be about the business I have but three days
And would as soon sink down dead as desist from my errand."
Then smiling said the lord, "Your search, sir, is done,
For we shall see you to that site by the set time.
1070　Let Gawain grieve no more over the Green Chapel;
You shall be in your own bed, in blissful ease,
All the forenoon, and fare forth the first of the year,
And make the goal by midmorn, to mind your affairs,
　　　　　　　　　　no fear!
1075　　　　　　　　Tarry till the fourth day
　　　　　　　　　And ride on the first of the year.
　　　　　　　　　We shall set you on your way;
　　　　　　　　　It is not two miles from here."

Then Gawain was glad, and gleefully he laughed:
1080　"Now I thank you for this, past all things else!
Now my goal is here at hand! With a glad heart I shall

Both tarry, and undertake any task you devise."
Then the host seized his arm and seated him there;
Let the ladies be brought, to delight them the better,
1085 And in fellowship fair by the fireside they sit;
So gay waxed the good host, so giddy his words,
All awaited in wonder what next he would say.
Then he stares on the stout knight, and sternly he speaks:
"You have bound yourself boldly my bidding to do—
1090 Will you stand by that boast, and obey me this once?"
"I shall do so indeed," said the doughty knight;
"While I lie in your lodging, your laws will I follow."
"As you have had," said the host, "many hardships abroad
And little sleep of late, you are lacking, I judge,
1095 Both in needful nourishment and nightly rest;
You shall lie abed late in your lofty chamber
Tomorrow until mass, and meet then to dine
When you will, with my wife, who will sit by your side
And talk with you at table, the better to cheer
1100   our guest.
                         A-hunting I will go
                         While you lie late and rest."
                         The knight, inclining low,
                         Assents to each behest.°   command

1105 "And Gawain," said the good host, "agree now to this:
Whatever I win in the woods I will give you at eve,
And all you have earned you must offer to me;
Swear now, sweet friend, to swap as I say,
Whether hands, in the end, go empty or no."
1110 "By God," said Sir Gawain, "I grant it forthwith!
If you find the game good, I shall gladly take part."
"Let the bright wine be brought, and our bargain is done,"
Said the lord of that land—the two laughed together.
Then they drank and they dallied and doffed all constraint,
1115 These lords and these ladies, as late as they chose,
And then with gaiety and gallantries and graceful adieux
They talked in low tones, and tarried at parting.
With compliments comely they kiss at the last;
There were brisk lads about with blazing torches
1120 To see them safe to bed, for soft repose
                              long due.
                         Their covenants,° yet awhile,   agreements
                         They repeat, and pledge anew;
                         That lord could well beguile
1125   Men's hearts, with mirth in view.

Part III

Long before daylight they left their beds;
Guests that wished to go gave word to their grooms,
And they set about briskly to bind on saddles,
Tend to their tackle, tie up trunks.
1130 The proud lords appear, appareled to ride.
Leap lightly astride, lay hold of their bridles,
Each one on his way to his worthy house.
The liege lord of the land was not the last
Arrayed there to ride, with retainers° many;   *attendants*
1135 He had a bite to eat when he had heard mass;
With horn to the hills he hastens betimes.°   *early*
By the dawn of that day over the dim earth,
Master and men were mounted and ready.
Then they harnessed in couples the keen-scented hounds,
1140 Cast wide the kennel-door and called them forth,
Blew upon their bugles bold blasts three;⁴
The dogs began to bay with a deafening din,
And they quieted them quickly and called them to heel,
A hundred brave huntsmen, as I have heard tell,
1145   together.
              Men at stations meet;
              From the hounds they slip the tether;°   *leash*
              The echoing horns repeat,
              Clear in the merry weather.

1150 At the clamor of the quest, the quarry trembled;
Deer dashed through the dale, dazed with dread;
Hastened to the high ground, only to be
Turned back by the beaters, who boldly shouted.
They harmed not the harts, with their high heads,
1155 Let the bucks go by, with their broad antlers,
For it was counted a crime, in the close season,
If a man of that demesne° should molest the male deer.   *kingdom*
The hinds were headed up, with "Hey!" and "Ware!"°   *Look out!*
The does with great din were driven to the valleys.
1160 Then you were ware,° as they went, of the whistling   *conscious*
              of arrows;
At each bend under boughs the bright shafts flew
That tore the tawny hide with their tapered heads.

---

4. line 1141: **Blew upon their bugles bold blasts three.** Three long notes, or *motes*, were
sounded when the hunters unleashed the hounds. The words used by the poet are *thre
bare mote*, an onomatopoeic sequence of three long syllables, which I have replicated in
my version of the line.

Ah! they bray and they bleed, on banks they die,
And ever the pack pell-mell comes panting behind;
1165 Hunters with shrill horns hot on their heels—
Like the cracking of cliffs their cries resounded.
What game got away from the gallant archers
Was promptly picked off at the posts below
When they were harried on the heights and
    herded to the streams:
1170 The watchers were so wary at the waiting-stations,
And the greyhounds so huge, that eagerly snatched,
And finished them off as fast as folk could see
        with sight.
      The lord, now here, now there,
1175   Spurs forth in sheer delight.
      And drives, with pleasures rare,
      The day to the dark night.

So the lord in the linden-wood leads the hunt
And Gawain the good man in gay bed lies,
1180 Lingered late alone, till daylight gleamed,
Under coverlet costly, curtained about.
And as he slips into slumber, slyly there comes
A little din at his door, and the latch lifted,
And he holds up his heavy head out of the clothes;
1185 A corner of the curtain he caught back a little
And kept watch warily, to see what befell.
Lo! it was the lady, loveliest to behold,
That drew the door behind her deftly and still
And was bound for his bed—abashed was the knight,
1190 And laid his head low again in likeness of sleep;
And she stepped stealthily, and stole to his bed,
Cast aside the curtain and came within,
And set herself softly on the bedside there,
And lingered at her leisure, to look on his waking.
1195 The fair knight lay feigning for a long while,
Conning in his conscience what his case might
Mean or amount to—a marvel he thought it.
But yet he said to himself, "More seemly it were
To try her intent by talking a little."
1200 So he started and stretched, as if startled from sleep,
Lifts wide his eyelids in likeness of wonder,
And signs° himself swiftly, as safer to be,   *crosses*
        with art.
      Sweetly does she speak
1205   And kindling glances dart,

Blent white and red on cheek
And laughing lips apart.

"Good morning, Sir Gawain," said that gay lady,
"A slack sleeper you are, to let one slip in!
1210 Now you are taken in a trice—a truce we must make,
Or I shall bind you in your bed, of that be assured."
Thus laughing lightly that lady jested.
"Good morning, gay lady," said Gawain the blithe,
"Be it with me as you will; I am well content!
1215 For I surrender myself, and sue for your grace,
And that is best, I believe, and behooves me now."
Thus jested in answer that gentle knight.
"But if, lovely lady, you misliked it not,
And were pleased to permit your prisoner to rise,
1220 I should quit this couch and accoutre° me better,   outfit
And be clad in more comfort for converse here."
"Nay, not so, sweet sir," said the smiling lady;
"You shall not rise from your bed; I direct you better:
I shall hem and hold you on either hand,
1225 And keep company awhile with my captive knight.
For as certain as I sit here, Sir Gawain you are,
Whom all the world worships, whereso you ride;
Your honor, your courtesy are highest acclaimed
By lords and by ladies, by all living men;
1230 And lo! we are alone here, and left to ourselves;
My lord and his liegemen are long departed,
The household asleep, my handmaids too,
The door drawn, and held by a well-driven bolt,
And since I have in this house him whom all love,
1235 I shall while the time away with mirthful speech
            at will.
        My body is here at hand,
        Your each wish to fulfill;
        Your servant to command
1240   I am, and shall be still."5

"In good faith," said Gawain, "my gain is the greater,
Though I am not he of whom you have heard;
To arrive at such reverence as you recount here
I am one all unworthy, and well do I know it.
1245 By heaven, I would hold me the happiest of men

5. lines 1239–40: **Your servant to command / I am, and shall be still.** *Servant* could have
its innocuous modern meaning ("one who would be glad to be of service") in the poet's
Middle English. But it also meant specifically "a professed lover." Sir Gawain takes advantage of this ambiguity in line 1278.

If by word or by work I once might aspire
To the prize of your praise—'twere a pure joy!"
"In good faith, Sir Gawain," said that gay lady,
"The well-proven prowess that pleases all others,
1250   Did I scant or scout it, 'twere scarce becoming.
But there are ladies, believe me, that had liefer far
Have thee here in their hold, as I have today,
To pass an hour in pastime with pleasant words,
Assuage all their sorrows and solace their hearts,
1255   Than much of the goodly gems and gold they possess.
But lauded° be the Lord of the lofty skies,   *praised*
For here in my hands all hearts' desire
                    doth lie."
            Great welcome got he there
1260   From the lady who sat him by;
            With fitting speech and fair
            The good knight makes reply.

"Madame," said the merry man, "Mary reward you!
For in good faith, I find your beneficence° noble.   *generosity*
1265   And the fame of fair deeds runs far and wide,
But the praise you report pertains not to me,
But comes of your courtesy and kindness of heart."
"By the high Queen of heaven" (said she) "I count it not so,
For were I worth all the women in this world alive,
1270   And all wealth and all worship were in my hands,
And I should hunt high and low, a husband to take,
For the nurture I have noted in you, knight, here,
The comeliness and courtesies and courtly mirth—
And so I had ever heard, and now hold it true—
1275   No other on this earth, should have me for wife."
"You are bound to a better man," the bold knight said,
"Yet I prize the praise you have proffered me here,
And soberly your servant, my sovereign I hold you,
And acknowledge me your knight, in the name of Christ."
1280   So they talked of this and that until 'twas nigh noon,
And ever the lady languishing in likeness of love.
With feat° words and fair he framed his defense,   *clever*
For were she never so winsome, the warrior had
The less will to woo, for the wound that his bane°   *doom*
1285   must be.
            He must bear the blinding blow,
            For such is fate's decree;
            The lady asks leave to go;
            He grants it full and free.

1290 Then she gaily said goodbye, and glanced at him, laughing,
And as she stood, she astonished him with a stern speech:
"Now may the Giver of all good words these glad hours repay!
But our guest is not Gawain—forgot is that thought."
"How so?" said the other, and asks in some haste,
1295 For he feared he had been at fault in the forms of his speech.
But she held up her hand, and made answer thus:
"So good a knight as Gawain is given out to be,
And the model of fair demeanor° and manners pure,   *behavior*
Had he lain so long at a lady's side,
1300 Would have claimed a kiss, by his courtesy,
Through some touch or trick of phrase at some tale's end."
Said Gawain, "Good lady, I grant it at once!
I shall kiss at your command, as becomes a knight,
And more, lest you mislike, so let be, I pray."
1305 With that she turns toward him, takes him in her arms,
Leans down her lovely head, and lo! he is kissed.
They commend each other to Christ with comely words,
He sees her forth safely, in silence they part,
And then he lies no later in his lofty bed,
1310 But calls to his chamberlain, chooses his clothes,
Goes in those garments gladly to mass,
Then takes his way to table, where attendants wait,
And made merry all day, till the moon rose
                         in view.
1315   Was never knight beset
              'Twixt worthier ladies two:
              The crone° and the coquette,°   *old lady / flirt*
              Fair pastimes they pursue.

And the lord of the land rides late and long,
1320 Hunting the barren hinds over the broad heath.
He had slain such a sum, when the sun sank low,
Of does and other deer, as would dizzy one's wits.
Then they trooped in together in triumph at last,
And the count of the quarry quickly they take.
1325 The lords lent a hand[6] with their liegemen many,
Picked out the plumpest and put them together
And duly dressed the deer, as the deed requires.
Some were assigned the assay° of the fat: *measurement*
Two fingers'-width fully they found on the leanest.
1330 Then they slit the slot open and searched out the paunch,
Trimmed it with trencher°-knives and tied it up tight.   *carving*

---

6. line 1325: **The lords lent a hand.** The skills proper to a nobleman in the poet's time
included the dressing—disemboweling and dismembering—of deer killed in the hunt.

They flayed the fair hide from the legs and trunk,
Then broke open the belly and laid bare the bowels,
Deftly detaching and drawing them forth.
1335 And next at the neck they neatly parted
The weasand° from the windpipe, and cast away the guts.   *throat*
At the shoulders with sharp blades they showed their skill,
Boning them from beneath, lest the sides be marred;
They breached the broad breast and broke it in twain,
1340 And again at the gullet they begin with their knives,
Cleave down the carcass clear to the breach;
Two tender morsels they take from the throat,
Then round the inner ribs they rid off a layer
And carve out the kidney-fat, close to the spine,
1345 Hewing down to the haunch, that all hung together,
And held it up whole, and hacked it free,
And this they named the numbles,⁷ that knew such terms
                    of art.
            They divide the crotch in two,
1350   And straightway then they start
            To cut the backbone through
            And cleave the trunk apart.

With hard strokes they hewed off the head and the neck,
Then swiftly from the sides they severed the chine,°   *backbone*
1355 And the corbie's bone they cast on a branch.⁸
Then they pierced the plump sides, impaled either one
With the hock° of the hind foot, and hung it aloft,   *joint next to hoof*
To each person his portion most proper and fit.
On a hide of a hind the hounds they fed
1360 With the liver and the lights, the leathery paunches,
And bread soaked in blood well blended therewith.
With sound of shrill horns they signal their prize,
Then merrily with their meat they make their way home,
Blowing on their bugles many a brave blast.
1365 Ere dark had descended, that doughty° band   *brave*
Was come within the walls where Gawain waits
                    at leisure.
            Bliss and hearth-fire bright
            Await the master's pleasure;

---

7. line 1347: **And this they named the numbles.** The modern expression "humble pie"
comes from *umble,* a variant from of *numble.*
8. line 1355: **The corbie's bone they cast on a branch.** *Corbie* is a name for the raven (cf.
French *corbeau*). Ravens, being carrion birds, would in all probability stay close at hand
during the butchering that followed a hunt. It was customary to throw a small piece of
gristle into the branches of a nearby tree for them.

1370   When the two men met that night,
              Joy surpassed all measure.

       Then the host in the hall his household assembles,
       With the dames of high degree and their damsels fair.
       In the presence of the people, a party he sends
1375   To convey him his venison in view of the knight.
       And in high good-humor he hails him then,
       Counts over the kill, the cuts° on the   *notches /*
                    tallies,°   *measuring sticks*
       Holds high the hewn ribs, heavy with fat.
       "What think you, sir, of this? Have I thriven° well?   *prospered*
1380   Have I won with my woodcraft a worthy prize?"
       "In good earnest," said Gawain, "this game is the finest
       I have seen in seven years in the season of winter."
       "And I give it to you, Gawain," said the good host,
       "For according to our covenant, you claim it as your own."
1385   "That is so," said Sir Gawain, "and the same say I:
       What I worthily have won within these fair walls,
       Herewith I as willingly award it to you."
       He embraces his broad neck with both his arms,
       And confers on him a kiss, the comeliest that he could.
1390   "Have here my profit, it proved no better;
       Ungrudging do I grant it, were it greater far."
       "Such a gift," said the good host, "I gladly accept—
       Yet it might be all the better, would you but say
       Where you won this same award, by your wits alone."
1395   "That was no part of the pact; press me no further,
       For you have had what behooves; all other claims
                         forbear."
                   With jest and compliment
                   They conversed, and cast off care;
1400   To the table soon they went;
                   Fresh dainties wait them there.

       And then by the chimney-side they chat at their ease;
       The best wine was brought them, and bounteously served;
       And after in their jesting they jointly accord
1405   To do on the second day the deeds of the first:
       That the two men should trade, betide as it may,
       What each had taken in, at eve when they met.
       They seal the pact solemnly in sight of the court;
       Their cups were filled afresh to confirm the jest;
1410   Then at last they took their leave, for late was the hour,
       Each to his own bed hastening away.
       Before the barnyard cock had crowed but thrice

The lord had leapt from his rest, his liegemen as well.
Both of mass and their meal they made short work:
1415   By the dim light of dawn they were deep in the woods
                     away.
                 With huntsmen and with horns
                 Over plains they pass that day;
                 They release, amid the thorns,
1420   Swift hounds that run and bay.

Soon some were on a scent by the side of a marsh;
When the hounds opened cry, the head of the hunt
Rallied them with rough words, raised a great noise.
The hounds that had heard it came hurrying straight
1425   And followed along with their fellows, forty together.
Then such a clamor and cry of coursing° hounds   *racing*
Arose, that the rocks resounded again.
Hunters exhorted them with horn and with voice;
Then all in a body bore off together
1430   Between a mere° in the marsh and a menacing crag,   *pool*
To a rise where the rock stood rugged and steep,
And boulders lay about, that blocked their approach.
Then the company in consort closed on their prey:
They surrounded the rise and the rocks both,
1435   For well they were aware that it waited within,
The beast that the bloodhounds boldly proclaimed.
Then they beat on the bushes and bade him appear,
And he made a murderous rush in the midst of them all;
The best of all boars broke from his cover,
1440   That had ranged long unrivaled, a renegade° old,   *loner*
For of tough-brawned boars he was biggest far,
Most grim when he grunted—then grieved were many,
For three at the first thrust he threw to the earth,
And dashed away at once without more damage.
1445   With "Hi!" "Hi!" and "Hey!" "Hey!" the others followed,
Had horns at their lips, blew high and clear.
Merry was the music of men and of hounds
That were bound after this boar, his bloodthirsty heart
                 to quell.°   *subdue*
1450   Often he stands at bay,
                 Then scatters the pack pell-mell;
                 He hurts the hounds, and they
                 Most dolefully yowl and yell.

Men then with mighty bows moved in to shoot,
1455   Aimed at him with their arrows and often hit,
But the points had no power to pierce through his hide,

And the barbs were brushed aside by his bristly brow;
Though the shank of the shaft shivered in pieces,
The head hopped away, wheresoever it struck.
1460 But when their stubborn strokes had stung him at last,
Then, foaming in his frenzy, fiercely he charges,
Hurtles at them headlong that hindered his flight,
And many feared for their lives, and fell back a little.
But the lord on a lively horse leads the chase;
1465 As a high-spirited huntsman his horn he blows;
He sounds the assembly and sweeps through the brush,
Pursuing this wild swine till the sunlight slanted.
All day with this deed they drive forth the time
While our lone knight so lovesome lies in his bed,
1470 Sir Gawain safe at home, in silken bower
                    so gay;
              The lady, with guile in heart,
              Came early where he lay;
              She was at him with all her art
1475   To turn his mind her way.

She comes to the curtain and coyly peeps in;
Gawain thought it good to greet her at once,
And she richly repays him with her ready words,
Settles softly at his side, and suddenly she laughs,
1480 And with a gracious glance, she begins on him thus:
"Sir, if you be Gawain, it seems a great wonder—
A man so well-meaning, and mannerly disposed,
And cannot act in company as courtesy bids,
And if one takes the trouble to teach him, 'tis all in vain.
1485 That lesson learned lately is lightly forgot,
Though I painted it as plain as my poor wit allowed."
"What lesson, dear lady?" he asked all alarmed;
"I have been much to blame, if your story be true."
"Yet my counsel was of kissing," came her answer then,
1490 "Where favor has been found, freely to claim
As accords with the conduct of courteous knights."
"My dear," said the doughty man, "dismiss that thought;
Such freedom, I fear, might offend you much;
It were rude to request if the right were denied."
1495 "But none can deny you," said the noble dame,
"You are stout enough to constrain with strength, if you choose,
Were any so ungracious as to grudge you aught."
"By heaven," said he, "you have answered well,
But threats never throve among those of my land,
1500 Nor any gift not freely given, good though it be.

I am yours to command, to kiss when you please;
You may lay on as you like, and leave off at will."
                          With this,
                    The lady lightly bends
1505   And graciously gives him a kiss;
                    The two converse as friends
                    Of true love's trials and bliss.

"I should like, by your leave," said the lovely lady,
"If it did not annoy you, to know for what cause
1510 So brisk and so bold a young blood as you,
      And acclaimed for all courtesies becoming a knight—
      And name what knight you will, they are noblest esteemed
      For loyal faith in love, in life as in story;
      For to tell the tribulations° of these true hearts,   *troubles*
1515 Why, 'tis the very title and text of their deeds,
      How bold knights for beauty have braved many a foe,
      Suffered heavy sorrows out of secret love,
      And then valorously° avenged them on villainous churls   *courageously*
      And made happy ever after the hearts of their ladies.
1520 And you are the noblest knight known in your time;
      No household under heaven but has heard of your fame,
      And here by your side I have sat for two days
      Yet never has a fair phrase fallen from your lips
      Of the language of love, not one little word!
1525 And you, that with sweet vows sway women's hearts,
      Should show your winsome ways, and woo a young thing,
      And teach by some tokens the craft of true love.
      How! are you artless, whom all men praise?
      Or do you deem me so dull, or deaf to such words?
1530   Fie!° Fie!   *For shame!*
                    In hope of pastimes new
                    I have come where none can spy;
                    Instruct me a little, do,
                    While my husband is not nearby."

1535 "God love you, gracious lady!" said Gawain then;
      "It is a pleasure surpassing, and a peerless joy,
      That one so worthy as you would willingly come
      And take the time and trouble to talk with your knight
      And content you with his company—it comforts my heart.
1540 But to take on myself the task of telling of love,
      And touch upon its texts, and treat of its themes
      To one that, I know well, wields more power
      In that art, by a half, than a hundred such
      As I am where I live, or am like to become,

1545 It were folly, fair dame, in the first degree!
     In all that I am able, my aim is to please,
     As in honor behooves me,° and am evermore   *I am obliged to*
     Your servant heart and soul, so save me our Lord!"
     Thus she tested his temper and tried many a time,
1550 Whatever her true intent, to entice him to sin,
     But so fair was his defense that no fault appeared,
     Nor evil on either hand, but only bliss
                    they knew.
               They linger and laugh awhile;
1555   She kisses the knight so true,
               Takes leave in comeliest style
               And departs without more ado.

     Then he rose from his rest and made ready for mass,
     And then a meal was set and served, in sumptuous style;
1560 He dallied at home all day with the dear ladies,
     But the lord lingered late at his lusty sport;
     Pursued his sorry swine, that swerved as he fled,
     And bit asunder the backs of the best of his hounds
     When they brought him to bay, till the bowmen appeared
1565 And soon forced him forth, though he fought for dear life,
     So sharp were the shafts they shot at him there.
     But yet the boldest drew back from his battering head,
     Till at last he was so tired he could travel no more,
     But in as much haste as he might, he makes his retreat
1570 To a rise on rocky ground, by a rushing stream.
     With the bank at his back he scrapes the bare earth,
     The froth foams at his jaws, frightful to see.
     He whets his white tusks—then weary were all
     Those hunters so hardy that hovered about
1575 Of aiming from afar, but ever they mistrust
                    his mood.
               He had hurt so many by then
               That none had hardihood
               To be torn by his tusks again,
1580   That was brainsick, and out for blood.

     Till the lord came at last on his lofty steed,
     Beheld him there at bay before all his folk;
     Lightly he leaps down, leaves his courser,
     Bares his bright sword, and boldly advances;
1585 Straight into the stream he strides towards his foe.
     The wild thing was wary of weapon and man;
     His hackles rose high; so hotly he snorts
     That many watched with alarm, lest the worst befall.

The boar makes for the man with a mighty bound
1590 So that he and his hunter came headlong together
Where the water ran wildest—the worse for the beast,
For the man, when they first met, marked him with care,
Sights well the slot, slips in the blade,
Shoves it home to the hilt, and the heart shattered,
1595 And he falls in his fury and floats down the water,
                    ill-sped.
              Hounds hasten by the score
              To maul him, hide and head;
              Men drag him in to shore
1600   And dogs pronounce him dead.

With many a brave blast they boast of their prize,
All hallooed in high glee, that had their wind;
The hounds bayed their best, as the bold men bade
That were charged with chief rank in that chase of renown.
1605 Then one wise in woodcraft, and worthily skilled,
Began to dress the boar in becoming style:
He severs the savage head and sets it aloft,
Then rends the body roughly right down the spine;
Takes the bowels from the belly, broils them on coals,
1610 Blends them well with bread to bestow on the hounds.
Then he breaks out the brawn° in fair broad flitches,°   *meat / slabs*
And the innards to be eaten in order he takes.
The two sides, attached to each other all whole,
He suspended from a spar that was springy and tough;
1615 And so with this swine they set out for home;
The boar's head was borne before the same man
That had stabbed him in the stream with his strong arm,
                    right through.
              He thought it long indeed.
1620   Till he had the knight in view;
              At his call, he comes with speed
              To claim his payment due.

The lord laughed aloud, with many a light word,
When he greeted Sir Gawain—with good cheer he speaks.
1625 They fetch the fair dames and the folk of the house;
He brings forth the brawn, and begins the tale
Of the great length and girth, the grim rage as well,
Of the battle of the boar they beset in the wood.
The other man meetly commended his deeds
1630 And praised well the prize of his princely sport,
For the brawn of that boar, the bold knight said,
And the sides of that swine surpassed all others.

Then they handled the huge head; he owns it a wonder,
And eyes it with abhorrence, to heighten his praise.
1635 "Now, Gawain," said the good man, "this game becomes yours
By those fair terms we fixed, as you know full well."
"That is true," returned the knight, "and trust me, fair friend,
All my gains, as agreed, I shall give you forthwith."
He clasps him and kisses him in courteous style,
1640 Then serves him with the same fare a second time.
"Now we are even," said he, "at this evening feast,
And clear is every claim incurred here to date,
                              and debt."
                    "By Saint Giles!" the host replies,
1645   "You're the best I ever met!
                    If your profits are all this size,
                    We'll see you wealthy yet!"

Then attendants set tables on trestles about,
And laid them with linen; light shone forth,
1650 Wakened along the walls in waxen torches.
The service was set and the supper brought;
Royal were the revels that rose then in hall
At that feast by the fire, with many fair sports:
Amid the meal and after, melody sweet,
1655 Carol-dances comely and Christmas songs,
With all the mannerly mirth my tongue may describe.
And ever our gallant knight beside the gay lady;
So uncommonly kind and complaisant° was she,   *intent on pleasing*
With sweet stolen glances, that stirred his stout heart,
1660 That he was at his wits' end, and wondrous vexed;
But he could not in all conscience her courtship repay,
Yet took pains to please her, though the plan might
                              go wrong.
                    When they to heart's delight
1665   Had reveled there in throng,
                    To his chamber he calls the knight,
                    And thither they go along.

And there they dallied and drank, and deemed it good sport
To enact their play anew on New Year's Eve,
1670 But Gawain asked again to go on the morrow,
For the time until his tryst was not two days.
The host hindered that, and urged him to stay,
And said, "On my honor, my oath here I take
That you shall get to the Green Chapel to begin your chores
1675 By dawn on New Year's Day, if you so desire.
Wherefore lie at your leisure in your lofty bed,

And I shall hunt hereabouts, and hold to our terms,
And we shall trade winnings when once more we meet,
For I have tested you twice, and true have I found you;
1680 Now think this tomorrow: the third pays for all;
Be we merry while we may, and mindful of joy,
For heaviness of heart can be had for the asking."
This is gravely agreed on and Gawain will stay.
They drink a last draught and with torches depart
1685   to rest.
                    To bed Sir Gawain went;
                    His sleep was of the best;
                    The lord, on his craft intent,
                    Was early up and dressed.

1690 After mass, with his men, a morsel he takes;
Clear and crisp the morning; he calls for his mount;
The folk that were to follow him afield that day
Were high astride their horses before the hall gates.
Wondrous fair were the fields, for the frost was light;
1695 The sun rises red amid radiant clouds,
Sails into the sky, and sends forth his beams.
They let loose the hounds by a leafy wood;
The rocks all around re-echo to their horns;
Soon some have set off in pursuit of the fox,
1700 Cast about with craft for a clearer scent;
A young dog yaps, and is yelled at in turn;
His fellows fall to sniffing, and follow his lead,
Running in a rabble on the right track,
And he scampers all before; they discover him soon,
1705 And when they see him with sight they pursue him the faster,
Railing at° him rudely with a wrathful din.   scolding
Often he reverses over rough terrain,
Or loops back to listen in the lee of a hedge;
At last, by a little ditch, he leaps over the brush,
1710 Comes into a clearing at a cautious pace,
Then he thought through his wiles to have thrown off the hounds
Till he was ware, as he went, of a waiting-station
Where three athwart his path threatened him at once,
                              all gray.
1715   Quick as a flash he wheels
                    And darts off in dismay;
                    With hard luck at his heels
                    He is off to the wood away.

Then it was heaven on earth to hark to the hounds
1720 When they had come on their quarry, coursing together!

Such harsh cries and howls they hurled at his head
As all the cliffs with a crash had come down at once.
Here he was hailed, when huntsmen met him;
Yonder they yelled at him, yapping and snarling;
1725 There they cried "Thief!" and threatened his life,
And ever the harriers° at his heels, that he had   *pursuing hounds*
      no rest.
Often he was menaced when he made for the open,
And often rushed in again, for Reynard was wily;
And so he leads them a merry chase, the lord and his men,
1730 In this manner on the mountains, till midday or near,
While our hero lies at home in wholesome sleep
Within the comely curtains on the cold morning.
But the lady, as love would allow her no rest,
And pursuing ever the purpose that pricked her heart,
1735 Was awake with the dawn, and went to his chamber
In a fair flowing mantle that fell to the earth,
All edged and embellished with ermines fine;
No hood on her head, but heavy with gems
Were her fillet° and the fret° that confined   *headband / net*
      her tresses;
1740 Her face and her fair throat freely displayed;
Her bosom all but bare, and her back as well.
She comes in at the chamber-door, and closes it with care,
Throws wide a window—then waits no longer,
But hails him thus airily with her artful words,
1745   with cheer:
      "Ah, man, how can you sleep?
      The morning is so clear!"
      Though dreams have drowned him deep,
      He cannot choose but hear.

1750 Deep in his dreams he darkly mutters
As a man may that mourns, with many grim thoughts
Of that day when destiny shall deal him his doom
When he greets his grim host at the Green Chapel
And must bow to his buffet, bating° all strife.   *giving up*
1755 But when he sees her at his side he summons his wits,
Breaks from the black dreams, and blithely answers.
That lovely lady comes laughing sweet,
Sinks down at his side, and salutes him with a kiss.
He accords her fair welcome in courtliest style;
1760 He sees her so glorious, so gaily attired,
So faultless her features, so fair and so bright,
His heart swelled swiftly with surging joys.

They melt into mirth with many a fond smile,
And there was bliss beyond telling between those two,
1765   at height.
                Good were their words of greeting;
                Each joyed in other's sight;
                Great peril attends that meeting
                Should Mary forget her knight.

1770 For that high-born beauty so hemmed him about,
Made so plain her meaning, the man must needs
Either take her tendered° love or distastefully refuse.   *offered*
His courtesy concerned him, lest crass he appear,
But more his soul's mischief, should he commit sin
1775 And belie his loyal oath to the lord of that house.
"God forbid!" said the bold knight, "That shall not befall!"
With a little fond laughter he lightly let pass
All the words of special weight that were sped his way;
"I find you much at fault," the fair one said,
1780 "Who can be cold toward a creature so close by your side,
Of all women in this world most wounded in heart,
Unless you have a sweetheart, one you hold dearer,
And allegiance to that lady so loyally knit
That you will never love another, as now I believe.
1785 And, sir, if it be so, then say it, I beg you;
By all your heart holds dear, hide it no longer
                    with guile."
                "Lady, by Saint John,"
                He answers with a smile,
1790   "Lover have I none,
                Nor will have, yet awhile."

"Those words," said the woman, "are the worst of all,
But I have had my answer, and hard do I find it!
Kiss me now kindly; I can but go hence
1795 To lament my life long like a maid lovelorn."
She inclines her head quickly and kisses the knight,
Then straightens with a sigh, and says as she stands,
"Now, dear, as I depart, do me this pleasure:
Give me some little gift, your glove or the like,
1800 That I may think on you, man, and mourn the less."
"Now by heaven," said he, "I wish I had here
My most precious possession, to put it in your hands,
For your deeds, beyond doubt, have often deserved
A repayment far passing my power to bestow.
1805 But a love-token, lady, were of little avail;

It is not to your honor to have at this time
A glove as a guerdon° from Gawain's hand,   *reward*
And I am here on an errand in unknown realms
And have no bearers with baggage with becoming gifts,
1810   Which distresses me, madame, for your dear sake.
A man must keep within his compass:° account it neither   *limits*
    grief
                    nor slight."
          "Nay, noblest knight alive,"
          Said that beauty of body white,
1815   "Though you be loath to give,
          Yet you shall take, by right."

She reached out a rich ring, wrought all of gold,
With a splendid stone displayed on the band
That flashed before his eyes like a fiery sun;
1820   It was worth a king's wealth, you may well believe.
But he waved it away with these ready words:
"Before God, good lady, I forego all gifts;
None have I to offer, nor any will I take."
And she urged it on him eagerly, and ever he refused,
1825   And vowed in very earnest, prevail she would not.
And she sad to find it so, and said to him then,
"If my ring is refused for its rich cost—
You would not be my debtor for so dear a thing—
I shall give you my girdle; you gain less thereby."
1830   She released a knot lightly, and loosened a belt
That was caught about her kirtle,° the bright cloak beneath,   *dress*
Of a gay green silk, with gold overwrought,
And the borders all bound with embroidery fine,
And this she presses upon him, and pleads with a smile,
1835   Unworthy though it were, that it would not be scorned.
But the man still maintains that he means to accept
Neither gold nor any gift, till by God's grace
The fate that lay before him was fully achieved.
"And be not offended, fair lady, I beg,
1840   And give over your offer, for ever I must
                decline.
          I am grateful for favor shown
          Past all deserts of mine,
          And ever shall be your own
1845   True servant, rain or shine."

"Now does my present displease you," she promptly inquired,
"Because it seems in your sight so simple a thing?

And belike, as it is little, it is less to praise,
But if the virtue that invests it were verily known,
1850   It would be held, I hope, in higher esteem.
For the man that possesses this piece of silk,
If he bore it on his body, belted about,
There is no hand under heaven that could hew him down,
For he could not be killed by any craft on earth."
1855   Then the man began to muse, and mainly he thought
It was a pearl for his plight, the peril to come
When he gains the Green Chapel to get his reward:
Could he escape unscathed,° the scheme were noble!   *unharmed*
Then he bore with her words and withstood them no more,
1860   And she repeated her petition and pleaded anew,
And he granted it, and gladly she gave him the belt,
And besought him for her sake to conceal it well,
Lest the noble lord should know—and the knight agrees
That not a soul save themselves shall see it thenceforth
1865   with sight.
            He thanked her with fervent heart,
            As often as ever he might;
            Three times, before they part,
            She has kissed the stalwart knight.

1870   Then the lady took her leave, and left him there,
For more mirth with that man she might not have.
When she was gone, Sir Gawain got from his bed,
Arose and arrayed him in his rich attire;
Tucked away the token the temptress had left,
1875   Laid it reliably where he looked for it after.
And then with good cheer to the chapel he goes,
Approached a priest in private, and prayed to be taught
To lead a better life and lift up his mind,
Lest he be among the lost when he must leave this world.
1880   And shamefaced at shrift° he showed his misdeeds   *confession*
From the largest to the least, and asked the Lord's mercy,[9]
And called on his confessor to cleanse his soul,
And he absolved him of his sins as safe and as clean

---

9. lines 1880–81: **And shamefaced at shrift he showed his misdeeds / From the largest to the least, and asked the Lord's mercy.** Gawain evidently does not confess his intention of withholding from the lord the girdle he has been given by the lady, thus failing to live up to the terms of their agreement. Because the intention to commit a sin (in this case primarily the sin of failing to be true to one's word) is itself sinful, his confession would seem to be invalid. Perhaps, as has been suggested, he feels that it is not sinful to break the rules of a mere "game" (line 1111). But he feels differently later, as is shown by his outburst in lines 2378–84. However Gawain's confession and absolution at Hautdesert are to be interpreted, it is fair to say that the absolution that strikes most readers of the poem as "real" is the secular one Sir Gawain receives later from the Green Knight (lines 2391–94).

As if the dread Day of Judgment should dawn on the morrow.
1885 And then he made merry amid the fine ladies
With deft-footed dances and dalliance light,
As never until now, while the afternoon wore
                           away.
              He delighted all around him,
1890   And all agreed, that day,
              They never before had found him
              So gracious and so gay.

Now peaceful be his pasture, and love play him fair!
The host is on horseback, hunting afield;
1895 He has finished off this fox that he followed so long:
As he leapt a low hedge to look for the villain
Where he heard all the hounds in hot pursuit,
Reynard comes racing out of a rough thicket,
And all the rabble in a rush, right at his heels.
1900 The man beholds the beast, and bides his time,
And bares his bright sword, and brings it down hard,
And he blenches from° the blade, and backward   *moves to avoid*
    he starts;
A hound hurries up and hinders that move,
And before the horse's feet they fell on him at once
1905 And ripped the rascal's throat with a wrathful din.
The lord soon alighted and lifted him free,
Swiftly snatched him up from the snapping jaws,
Holds him over his head, halloos with a will,
And the dogs bayed the dirge, that had done him to death.
1910 Hunters hastened thither with horns at their lips,
Sounding the assembly till they saw him at last.
When that comely company was come in together,
All that bore bugles blew them at once,
And the others all hallooed, that had no horns.
1915 It was the merriest medley° that ever a man heard,   *mixed chorus*
The racket that they raised for Sir Reynard's soul
                   that died.
              Their hounds they praised and fed,
              Fondling their heads with pride,
1920   And they took Reynard the Red
              And stripped away his hide.

And then they headed homeward, for evening had come,
Blowing many a blast on their bugles bright.
The lord at long last alights at his house,
1925 Finds fire on the hearth where the fair knight waits,
Sir Gawain the good, that was glad in heart.

With the ladies, that loved him, he lingered at ease;
He wore a rich robe of blue that reached to the earth
And a surcoat° lined softly with sumptuous furs;   *loose outer coat*
1930 A hood of the same hue hung on his shoulders;
With bands of bright ermine embellished were both.
He comes to meet the man amid all the folk,
And greets him good-humoredly, and gaily he says,
"I shall follow forthwith the form of our pledge
1935 That we framed to good effect amid fresh-filled cups."
He clasps him accordingly and kisses him thrice,
As amiably and as earnestly as ever he could.
"By heaven," said the host, "you have had some luck
Since you took up this trade, if the terms were good."
1940 "Never trouble about the terms," he returned at once,
"Since all that I owe here is openly paid."
"Marry!" said the other man, "mine is much less,
For I have hunted all day, and nought have I got
But this foul fox pelt, the fiend take the goods!
1945 Which but poorly repays those precious things
That you have cordially conferred, those kisses three
        so good."
        "Enough!" said Sir Gawain;
        "I thank you, by the rood!"°   *cross*
1950   And how the fox was slain
        He told him, as they stood.

With minstrelsy and mirth, with all manner of meats,
They made as much merriment as any men might
(Amid laughing of ladies and light-hearted girls,
1955 So gay grew Sir Gawain and the goodly host)
Unless they had been besotted,° or brainless fools.   *drunk*
The knight joined in jesting with that joyous folk,
Until at last it was late; before long they must part,
And be off to their beds, as behooved° them   *was proper for*
        each one.
1960 Then politely his leave of the lord of the house
Our noble knight takes, and renews his thanks:
"The courtesies countless accorded me here,
Your kindness at this Christmas, may heaven's
        King repay!
Henceforth, if you will have me, I hold you my liege,°   *feudal lord*
1965 And so, as I have said, I must set forth tomorrow,
If I may take some trusty man to teach, as you promised,
The way to the Green Chapel, that as God allows
I shall see my fate fulfilled on the first of the year."

"In good faith," said the good man, "with a good will
1970   Every promise on my part shall be fully performed."
He assigns him a servant to set him on the path,
To see him safe and sound over the snowy hills,
To follow the fastest way through forest green
                    and grove.
1975   Gawain thanks him again.
                    So kind his favors prove,
                    And of the ladies then
                    He takes his leave, with love.

Courteously he kissed them, with care in his heart,
1980   And often wished them well, with warmest thanks,
Which they for their part were prompt to repay.
They commend him to Christ with disconsolate sighs;
And then in that hall with the household he parts—
Each man that he met, he remembered to thank
1985   For his deeds of devotion and diligent pains,
And the trouble he had taken to tend to his needs;
And each one as woeful, that watched him depart,
As he had lived with him loyally all his life long.
By lads bearing lights he was led to his chamber
1990   And blithely brought to his bed, to be at his rest.
How soundly he slept, I presume not to say,
For there were matters of moment his thoughts might well
                    pursue.
                    Let him lie and wait;
1995   He has little more to do,
                    Then listen, while I relate
                    How they kept their rendezvous.

Part IV

Now the New Year draws near, and the night passes,
The day dispels the dark, by the Lord's decree;
2000   But wild weather awoke in the world without:
The clouds in the cold sky cast down their snow
With great gusts from the north, grievous to bear.
Sleet showered aslant upon shivering beasts;
The wind warbled wild as it whipped from aloft,
2005   And drove the drifts deep in the dales below.
Long and well he listens, that lies in his bed;
Though he lifts not his eyelids, little he sleeps;
Each crow of the cock he counts without fail.
Readily from his rest he rose before dawn,
2010   For a lamp had been left him, that lighted his chamber.

He called to his chamberlain,° who quickly   *personal attendant*
    appeared,
And bade him get him his gear, and gird° his good steed,   *equip*
And he sets about briskly to bring in his arms,
And makes ready his master in manner most fit.
2015 First he clad him in his clothes, to keep out the cold,
And then his other harness, made handsome anew,
His plate-armor of proof,° polished with pains,   *impenetrable*
The rings of his rich mail rid of their rust,
And all was fresh as at first, and for this he gave thanks
2020   indeed.
        With pride he wears each piece,
        New-furbished° for his need: *made bright*
        No gayer from here to Greece;
        He bids them bring his steed.

2025 In his richest raiment he robed himself then:
His crested coat-armor,° close-stitched with craft,   *cloth outer garment*
With stones of strange virtue on silk velvet set;
All bound with embroidery on borders and seams
And lined warmly and well with furs of the best.
2030 Yet he left not his love-gift, the lady's girdle;
Gawain, for his own good, forgot not that:
When the bright sword was belted and bound on his haunches,
Then twice with that token he twined him about.
Sweetly did he swathe him in that swatch of silk,
2035 That girdle of green so goodly to see,
That against the gay red showed gorgeous bright.
Yet he wore not for its wealth that wondrous girdle,
Nor pride in its pendants, though polished they were,
Though glittering gold gleamed at the ends,
2040 But to keep himself safe when consent he must
To endure a deadly blow, and all defense
             denied.
        And now the bold knight came
        Into the courtyard wide;
2045   That folk of worthy fame
       He thanks on every side.

Then was Gringolet girt, that was great and huge,
And had sojourned° safe and sound, and   *stayed there*
    savored his fare;
He pawed the earth in his pride, that princely steed.
2050 The good knight draws near him and notes well his look,
And says sagely to himself, and soberly swears,

"Here is a household in hall that upholds the right!
The man that maintains it, may happiness be his!
Likewise the dear lady, may love betide her!
2055   If thus they in charity cherish a guest
That are honored here on earth, may they have His reward
That reigns high in heaven—and also you all;
And were I to live in this land but a little while,
I should willingly reward you, and well, if I might."
2060   Then he steps into the stirrup and bestrides his mount;
His shield is shown forth; on his shoulder he casts it;
Strikes the side of his steed with his steel spurs,
And he starts across the stones, nor stands any longer
                  to prance.
2065   On horseback was the swain°   *fellow*
           That bore his spear and lance;
           "May Christ this house maintain
           And guard it from mischance!"

The bridge was brought down, and the broad gates
2070   Unbarred and carried back upon both sides;
He commended him to Christ, and crossed over the planks;
Praised the noble porter, who prayed on his knees
That God save Sir Gawain, and bade him good day,
And went on his way alone with the man
2075   That would lead him before long to that luckless place
To face the sad fate that must befall him there.
Under bare boughs they ride, where steep banks rise,
Over high cliffs they climb, where cold snow clings;
The heavens held aloof, but heavy thereunder
2080   Mist mantled the moors, moved on the slopes.
Each hill had a hat, a huge cape of cloud;
Brooks bubbled and broke as they ran between rocks,
Flashing in freshets° that waterfalls fed.   *streams*
Roundabout was the road that ran through the wood
2085   Till the sun at that season was soon to rise,
                  that day.
           They were on a hilltop high;
           The white snow round them lay;
           The man that rode nearby
2090   Now bade his master stay.

"For I have seen you here safe at the set time,
And now you are not far from that notable place
That you have sought for so long with such special pains.
But this I say for certain, since I know you, sir knight,

2095 And have your good at heart, and hold you dear—
Would you heed well my words, it were worth your while—
You are rushing into risks that you reck not° of: *are heedless*
There is a villain in yon valley, the veriest on earth,
For he is rugged and rude, and ready with his fists,
2100 And most immense in his mold of mortals alive,
And his body bigger than the best four
That are in Arthur's house, Hector or any.
He gets his grim way at the Green Chapel;
None passes by that place so proud in his arms
2105 That he does not dash him down with his deadly blows,
For he is heartless wholly, and heedless of right,
For be it chaplain or churl° that by the Chapel   *person of low class*
    rides,
Monk or mass-priest or any man else,
He would as soon strike him dead as stand on two feet.
2110 Wherefore I say, just as certain as you sit there astride,
You cannot but be killed, if his counsel holds,
For he would trounce° you in a trice,° had you   *thrash / an instant*
    twenty lives
               for sale.
          He has lived long in this land
2115   And dealt out deadly bale;°   *harm*
          Against his heavy hand
          Your power cannot prevail.

"And so, good Sir Gawain, let the grim man be;
Go off by some other road, in God's own name!
2120 Leave by some other land, for the love of Christ,
And I shall get me home again, and give you my word
That I shall swear by God's self and the saints above,
By heaven and by my halidom° and other oaths more,   *sacred relic*
To conceal this day's deed, nor say to a soul
2125 That ever you fled for fear from any that I knew."
"Many thanks!" said the other man—and
    demurring° he speaks—   *objecting*
"Fair fortune befall you for your friendly words!
And conceal this day's deed I doubt not you would,
But though you never told the tale, if I turned back now,
2130 Forsook this place for fear, and fled, as you say,
I were a caitiff° coward; I could not be excused.   *wretched*
But I must to the Chapel to chance my luck
And say to that same man such words as I please,
Befall what may befall through Fortune's will
2135   or whim.

Though he be a quarrelsome knave
With a cudgel° great and grim,   *club*
The Lord is strong to save:
His servants trust in Him."

2140 "Marry," said the man, "since you tell me so much,
And I see you are set to seek your own harm,
If you crave a quick death, let me keep you no longer!
Put your helm on your head, your hand on your lance,
And ride the narrow road down yon rocky slope
2145 Till it brings you to the bottom of the broad valley.
Then look a little ahead, on your left hand,
And you will soon see before you that self-same Chapel,
And the man of great might that is master there.
Now goodbye in God's name, Gawain the noble!
2150 For all the world's wealth I would not stay here,
Or go with you in this wood one footstep further!"
He tarried no more to talk, but turned his bridle,
Hit his horse with his heels as hard as he might,
Leaves the knight alone, and off like the wind
2155   goes leaping.
          "By God," said Gawain then,
          "I shall not give way to weeping;
          God's will be done, amen!
          I commend me to His keeping."

2160 He puts his heels to his horse, and picks up the path;
Goes in beside a grove where the ground is steep,
Rides down the rough slope right to the valley;
And then he looked a little about him—the landscape was wild,
And not a soul to be seen, nor sign of a dwelling,
2165 But high banks on either hand hemmed it about,
With many a ragged rock and rough-hewn crag;
The skies seemed scored° by the scowling peaks.   *scraped*
Then he halted his horse, and held the rein fast,
And sought on every side for a sight of the Chapel,
2170 But no such place appeared, which puzzled him sore,
Yet he saw some way off what seemed like a mound,
A hillock high and broad, hard by the water,
Where the stream fell in foam down the face of the steep
And bubbled as if it boiled on its bed below.
2175 The knight urges his horse, and heads for the knoll;
Leaps lightly to earth; loops well the rein
Of his steed to a stout branch, and stations him there.
He strides straight to the mound, and strolls all about,
Much wondering what it was, but no whit the wiser;

2180 It had a hole at one end, and on either side,
And was covered with coarse grass in clumps all without,
And hollow all within, like some old cave,
Or a crevice of an old crag—he could not discern
                          aright.
2185   "Can this be the Chapel Green?
               Alack!" said the man, "Here might
               The devil himself be seen
               Saying matins° at black midnight!"   *morning service*

"Now by heaven," said he, "it is bleak hereabouts;
2190 This prayer-house is hideous, half-covered with grass!
Well may the grim man mantled in green
Recite here his orisons,° in hell's own style!   *prayers*
Now I feel it is the Fiend, in my five wits,
That has tempted me to this tryst, to take my life;
2195 This is a Chapel of mischance, may the mischief take it!
As accursed a country church as I came upon ever!"
With his helm on his head, his lance in his hand,
He stalks toward the steep wall of that strange house.
Then he heard, on the hill, behind a hard rock,
2200 Beyond the brook, from the bank, a most barbarous din:
Lord! it clattered in the cliff fit to cleave it in two,
As if someone on a grindstone ground a great scythe!
Lord! it whirred like a mill-wheel whirling about!
Lord! it echoed loud and long, lamentable to hear!
2205 Then "By heaven," said the bold knight, "That business up there
Is arranged for my arrival, or else I am much
                          misled.
               Let God work! Ah me!
               All hope of help has fled!
2210   Forfeit my life may be
               But noise I do not dread."

Then he listened no longer, but loudly he called,
"Who has power in this place, high parley° to hold?   *conference*
For none greets Sir Gawain, or gives him good day;
2215 If any would a word with him, let him walk forth
And speak now or never, to speed his affairs."
"Abide," said one on the bank above over his head,
"And what I promised you once shall straightway be given."
Yet he stayed not his grindstone, nor stinted its noise,
2220 But worked awhile at his whetting before he would rest,
And then he comes around a crag, from a cave in the rocks,
Hurtling out of hiding with a hateful weapon,

A Danish ax devised for that day's deed,
With a broad blade and bright, bent in a curve,
2225 Filed to a fine edge—four feet it measured
By the length of the lace that was looped round the haft.
And in form as at first, the fellow all green,
His lordly face and his legs, his locks and his beard,
Save that firm upon two feet forward he strides,
2230 Sets a hand on the ax-head, the haft to the earth;
When he came to the cold stream, and cared not to wade,
He vaults over on his ax, and advances apace
On a broad bank of snow, overbearing and brisk
                            of mood.
2235   Little did the knight incline
                 When face to face they stood;
                 Said the other man, "Friend mine,
                 It seems your word holds good!"

"God love you, Sir Gawain!" said the Green Knight then,
2240 "And well met this morning, man, at my place!
And you have followed me faithfully and found me betimes,
And on the business between us we both are agreed:
Twelve months ago today you took what was yours,
And you at this New Year must yield me the same.
2245 And we have met in these mountains, remote from all eyes:
There is none here to halt us or hinder our sport;
Unhasp your high helm, and have here your wages;
Make no more demur than I did myself
When you hacked off my head with one hard blow."
2250 "No, by God," said Sir Gawain, "that granted me life,
I shall grudge not the guerdon,° grim though it prove;   *repayment*
Bestow but one stroke, and I shall stand still,
And you may lay on as you like till the last of my debt
                            is paid."
2255   He proffered, with good grace,
                 His bare neck to the blade,
                 And feigned a cheerful face:
                 He scorned to seem afraid.

Then the grim man in green gathers his strength,
2260 Heaves high the heavy ax to hit him the blow.
With all the force in his frame he fetches it aloft,
With a grimace as grim as he would grind him to bits;
Had the blow he bestowed been as big as he threatened,
A good knight and gallant had gone to his grave.
2265 But Gawain at the great ax glanced up aside

As down it descended with death-dealing force,
And his shoulders shrank a little from the sharp iron.
Abruptly the brawny man breaks off the stroke,
And then reproved with proud words that prince among knights.
2270 "You are not Gawain the glorious," the green man said,
"That never fell back on field in the face of the foe,
And now you flee for fear, and have felt no harm:
Such news of that knight I never heard yet!
I moved not a muscle when you made to strike,
2275 Nor caviled at° the cut in King Arthur's house;   *raised objections to*
My head fell to my feet, yet steadfast I stood,
And you, all unharmed, are wholly dismayed—
Wherefore the better man I, by all odds,
              must be."
2280   Said Gawain, "Strike once more;
              I shall neither flinch nor flee;
              But if my head falls to the floor
              There is no mending me!

"But go on, man, in God's name, and get to the point!
2285 Deliver me my destiny, and do it without delay,
For I shall stand to the stroke and stir not an inch
Till your ax has hit home—on my honor I swear it!"
"Have at you then!" said the other, and heaves it aloft,
And glares down as grimly as he had gone mad.
2290 He made a mighty feint, but marred not his hide;
Withdrew the ax adroitly before it did damage.
Gawain gave no ground, nor glanced up aside,
But stood still as a stone, or else a stout stump
That is held in hard earth by a hundred roots.
2295 Then merrily does he mock him, the man all in green:
"So now you have your nerve again, I needs must strike;
Uphold the high knighthood that Arthur bestowed,
And keep your collarbone clear, if this cut allows!"
Then was Gawain gripped with rage, and grimly he said,
2300 "Why, thrash away, tyrant, I tire of your threats;
You make such a scene, you must frighten yourself."
Said the green fellow, "In faith, so fiercely you speak
That I shall finish this affair, nor further grace
              allow."
2305   He stands prepared to strike
              And scowls with both lip and brow;
              No marvel if the man mislike
              Who can hope no rescue now.

He gathered up the grim ax and guided it well:
2310 Let the barb at the blade's end brush the bare throat;
He hammered down hard, yet harmed him no whit
Save a scratch on one side, that severed the skin;
The end of the hooked edge entered the flesh,
And a little blood lightly leapt to the earth.
2315 And when the man beheld his own blood bright on the snow,
He sprang a spear's length with feet spread wide,
Seized his high helmet, and set it on his head,
Shoved before his shoulders the shield at his back,
Bares his trusty blade, and boldly he speaks—
2320 Not since he was a babe born of his mother
Was he once in this world one-half so blithe—
"Have done with your hacking—harry me no more!
I have borne, as behooved,° one blow in this place;   *was proper*
If you make another move I shall meet it midway
2325 And promptly, I promise you, pay back each blow
                    with brand.°   *sword*
              One stroke acquits me here;
              So did our covenant stand
              In Arthur's court last year—
2330   Wherefore, sir, hold your hand!"

He lowers the long ax and leans on it there,
Sets his arms on the head, the haft on the earth,
And beholds the brave knight that bides there afoot,
How he faces him fearless, fierce in full arms,
2335 And plies him with proud words—it pleases him well.
Then once again gaily to Gawain he calls,
And in a loud voice and lusty, delivers these words:
"Bold fellow, on this field your anger forbear!
No man has made demands here in manner uncouth,
2340 Nor done, save as duly determined at court.
I owed you a hit and you have it; be happy therewith!
The rest of my rights here I freely resign.
Had I been a bit busier, a buffet, perhaps,
I could have dealt more directly, and done you some harm.
2345 First I flourished with a feint, in frolicsome mood,
And left your hide unhurt—and here I did well
By the fair terms we fixed on the first night;
And fully and faithfully you followed accord:
Gave over all your gains as a good man should.
2350 A second feint, sir, I assigned for the morning
You kissed my comely wife—each kiss you restored.

For both of these there behooved° but two   *were deserved*
    feigned blows
               by right.
             True men pay what they owe;
2355   No danger then in sight.
             You failed at the third throw,
             So take my tap, sir knight.

"For that is my belt about you, that same braided girdle,
My wife it was that wore it; I know well the tale,
2360 And the count of your kisses and your conduct too,
And the wooing of my wife—it was all my scheme!
She made trial of a man most faultless by far
Of all that ever walked over the wide earth;
As pearls to white peas, more precious and prized,
2365 So is Gawain, in good faith, to other gay knights.
Yet you lacked, sir, a little in loyalty there,
But the cause was not cunning, nor courtship either,
But that you loved your own life; the less, then, to blame."
The other stout knight in a study stood a long while,
2370 So gripped with grim rage that his great heart shook.
All the blood of his body burned in his face
As he shrank back in shame from the man's sharp speech.
The first words that fell from the fair knight's lips:
"Cursed be a cowardly and covetous heart!
2375 In you is villainy and vice, and virtue laid low!"
Then he grasps the green girdle and lets go the knot,
Hands it over in haste, and hotly he says:
"Behold there my falsehood, ill hap betide it!
Your cut taught me cowardice, care for my life,
2380 And coveting came after, contrary both
To largesse and loyalty belonging to knights.
Now am I faulty and false, that fearful was ever
Of disloyalty and lies—bad luck to them both!—
              and greed.
2385   I confess, knight, in this place,
            My faults are grave indeed;
            Let me gain back your good grace,
            And hereafter I shall take heed."

Then the other laughed aloud, and lightly he said,
2390 "Such harm as I have had, I hold it quite healed.
You are so fully confessed, your failings made known,
And bear the plain penance of the point of my blade,
I hold you polished as a pearl, as pure and as bright
As you had lived free of fault since first you were born.

2395 And I give you, sir, this girdle that is gold-hemmed
And green as my garments, that, Gawain, you may
Be mindful of this meeting when you mingle in throng
With nobles of renown—and known by this token
How it chanced at the Green Chapel, to chivalrous knights.
2400 And you shall in this New Year come yet again
And we shall finish out our feast in my fair hall,
                    with cheer."
                He urged the knight to stay,
                And said, "With my wife so dear
2405   We shall see you friends this day,
                Whose enmity touched you near."

"Indeed," said the doughty knight, and doffed his high helm,
And held it in his hands as he offered his thanks,
"I have lingered long enough—may good luck be yours,
2410 And He reward you well that all worship bestows!
And commend me to that comely one, your courteous wife,
Both herself and that other, my honoured ladies,
That have trapped their true knight in their
                    trammels° so quaint.   *nets*
But if a dullard should dote, deem it no wonder,
2415 And through the wiles of a woman be wooed into sorrow,
For so was Adam by one, when the world began,
And Solomon by many more, and Samson the mighty—
Delilah was his doom, and David thereafter
Was beguiled by Bathsheba, and bore much distress;
2420 Now these were vexed by their devices—'twere a very joy
Could one but learn to love, and believe them not.
For these were proud princes, most prosperous of old,
Past all lovers lucky, that languished under heaven,
                    bemused.°   *bewildered*
2425   And one and all fell prey
                To women that they had used;
                If I be led astray,
                Methinks I may be excused.

"But your girdle, God love you! I gladly shall take
2430 And be pleased to possess, not for the pure gold,
Nor the bright belt itself, nor the beauteous pendants,
Nor for wealth, nor worldly state, nor workmanship fine,
But a sign of excess it shall seem oftentimes
When I ride in renown, and remember with shame
2435 The faults and the frailty of the flesh perverse,
How its tenderness entices the foul taint of sin;
And so when praise and high prowess have pleased my heart,

A look at this love-lace will lower my pride.
But one thing would I learn, if you were not loath,
2440 Since you are lord of yonder land where I have long sojourned
With honor in your house—may you have His reward
That upholds all the heavens, highest on throne!
How runs your right name?—and let the rest go."
"That shall I give you gladly," said the Green Knight then;
2445 "Bertilak de Hautdesert, this barony I hold.[1]
Through the might of Morgan le Fay, that lodges at my house,[2]
By subtleties of science and sorcerers' arts,
The mistress of Merlin, she has caught many a man,
For sweet love in secret she shared sometime
2450 With that wizard, that knows well each one of your knights
                    and you.
                Morgan the Goddess, she,
                So styled by title true;
                None holds so high degree
2455   That her arts cannot subdue.

"She guided me in this guise to your glorious hall,
To assay,° if such it were, the surfeit° of pride   test / excess
That is rumored of the retinue of the Round Table.
She put this shape upon me to puzzle your wits,
2460 To afflict the fair queen, and frighten her to death
With awe of that elvish man that eerily spoke
With his head in his hand before the high table.[3]
She was with my wife at home, that old withered lady,
Your own aunt is she, Arthur's half-sister,
2465 The Duchess' daughter of Tintagel, that dear King Uther
Got Arthur on after, that honored is now.
And therefore, good friend, come feast with your aunt;
Make merry in my house; my men hold you dear,
And I wish you as well, sir, with all my heart,
2470 As any mortal man, for your matchless faith."

1. line 2445: **"Bertilak de Hautdesert, this barony I hold."** The first name appears, though it is of minor importance, in Arthurian tradition. A Bertolais and a Bertelak figure in two stories, one French and one English, but neither one has the slightest resemblance to the Green Knight. The name *Hautdesert* is not found elsewhere; it seems to be composed of two French words that would mean "high hermitage" and would thus imply the isolation of Lord Bertilak's castle from other human dwellings.
2. line 2446. **Through the might of Morgan le Fay, that lodges at my house.** Morgan le Fay, a famous "fairy" or enchantress, was, as we hear later (line 2464), the half-sister of King Arthur. (Why she should be a member of Lord Bertilak's household is not so clear.) Merlin, her lover, was a magician who plays an important role in a number of the Arthurian stories. See above, lines 2448–51.
3. lines 2456–62: **"She guided me in this guise to your glorious hall . . . / before the high table."** Few readers of the poem have been satisfied by this explanation of the opening episode. It is, however, in keeping with a tradition to the effect that Morgan le Fay was a bitter enemy of Queen Guenevere.

But the knight said him nay, that he might by no means.
They clasped then and kissed, and commended each other
To the Prince of Paradise, and parted with one
                          assent.
2475   Gawain sets out anew;
              Toward the court his course is bent;
              And the knight all green in hue,
              Wheresoever he wished, he went.

Wild ways in the world our worthy knight rides
2480 On Gringolet, that by grace had been granted his life.
He harbored often in houses, and often abroad,
And with many valiant adventures verily he met
That I shall not take time to tell in this story.
The hurt was whole that he had had in his neck,
2485 And the bright green belt on his body he bore,
Oblique, like a baldric,° bound at his side,   *band worn aslant*
Below his left shoulder, laced in a knot,
In betokening of the blame he had borne for his fault;
And so to court in due course he comes safe and sound.
2490 Bliss abounded in hall when the high-born heard
That good Gawain was come; glad tidings they thought it.
The king kisses the knight, and the queen as well,
And many a comrade came to clasp him in arms,
And eagerly they asked, and awesomely he told,
2495 Confessed all his cares and discomfitures many,
How it chanced at the Chapel, what cheer made the knight,
The love of the lady, the green lace at last.
The nick on his neck he naked displayed
That he got in his disgrace at the Green Knight's hands,
2500   alone.
              With rage in heart he speaks,
              And grieves with many a groan;
              The blood burns in his cheeks
              For shame at what must be shown.

2505 "Behold, sir," said he, and handles the belt,
"This is the blazon° of the blemish that I bear on   *heraldic symbol*
      my neck;
This is the sign of sore loss that I have suffered there
For the cowardice and coveting that I came to there;
This is the badge of false faith that I was found in there,
2510 And I must bear it on my body till I breathe my last.
For one may keep a deed dark, but undo it no whit,
For where a fault is made fast, it is fixed evermore."
The king comforts the knight, and the court all together

Agree with gay laughter and gracious intent
2515 That the lords and the ladies belonging to the Table,
Each brother of that band, a baldric should have,
A belt borne oblique, of a bright green,
To be worn with one accord for that worthy's sake.
So that was taken as a token by the Table Round,
2520 And he honored that had it, evermore after,
As the best book of knighthood bids it be known.
In the old days of Arthur this happening befell;
The books of Brutus' deeds bear witness thereto
Since Brutus, the bold knight, embarked for this land
2525 After the siege ceased at Troy and the city fared
amiss.
Many such, ere we were born,
Have befallen here, ere this.
May He that was crowned with thorn
2530 Bring all men to His bliss! Amen.

HONI SOIT QUI MAL PENCE[4]

4. line 2531: **HONI SOIT QUI MAL PENCE,** Evil be to him who evil thinks, is the motto of the Order of the Garter. The words have been added to the manuscript; apparently by some-one who thought there was, or wanted to suggest, a relationship between the adoption of the green girdle by Arthur's court and the founding of the Order in 1350. But there is general agreement that there is little basis for interpreting one in terms of the other (for one thing, the ceremonial Garter is not green but blue). By allowing the motto to stand after the con-cluding "Amen," as it does in the manuscript, I do not mean to indicate that I consider it part of the poem.

CONTEXTS

Sir Gawain in Middle English†

Note that the symbol Þ/þ [thorn], originally a runic letter, represents the *th* sound in modern English, and the symbol ȝ [yogh], also inherited from Old English, represents the velar, palatal spirant, as in modern English "young." After 1300, ȝ began to be replaced at the beginning of words by the letter "y" and by "gh" elsewhere, where it represents a guttural consonant sound, as in Scots *loch*. In modern English "gh" often signals a now-silenced yogh. Hence the Middle English word *þoȝt* (as in line 1867), is our modern word *thought*.

The Green Knight Enters

130 Now wyl I of hor seruise say yow no more,
For vch wyȝe may wel wit no wont þat þer were.
An oþer noyse ful newe neȝed biliue,
Þat þe lude myȝt haf leue liflode to cach;
For vneþe watz þe noyce not a whyle sesed,
135 And þe first cource in þe court kyndely serued,
Þer hales in at þe halle dor an aghlich mayster,
On þe most on þe molde on mesure hyghe;
Fro þe swyre to þe swange so sware and so þik,
And his lyndes and his lymes so longe and so grete,
140 Half etayn in erde I hope þat he were,
Bot mon most I algate mynn hym to bene,
And þat þe myriest in his muckel þat myȝt ride;
For of bak and of brest al were his bodi sturne,
Both his wombe and his wast were worthily smale,
145 And alle his fetures folȝande, in forme þat he hade,
   ful clene.
   For wonder of his hwe men hade,
   Set in his semblaunt sene;
   He ferde as freke were fade,
150   And oueral enker-grene.

Sir Gawain's Shield

Then þay schewed hym þe schelde, þat was of schyr goulez
620 Wyth þe pentangel depaynt of pure golde hwez.
He braydez hit by þe bauderyk, aboute þe hals kestes.

---

† For additional information about Middle English and its pronunciation, see J. A. Burrow and Thorlac Turville-Petre, *A Book of Middle English*, 3rd ed. (Oxford: Blackwell, 2005), pp. 9–13; and Fernand Mossé, *A Handbook of Middle English*, trans. James A. Walker (Baltimore: Johns Hopkins University Press, 1968), pp. 7–15. These excerpts are based on the text edited by Tolkien, Gordon, and Davis (Oxford: Clarendon Press, 1925). Reprinted by permission of Oxford University Press.

Þat bisemed þe segge semlyly fayre.
And quy þe pentangel apendez to þat prynce noble
I am in tent yow to telle, þof tary hyt me schulde:
625 Hit is a syngne þat Salamon set sumquyle
In bytoknyng of trawþe, bi tytle þat hit habbez,
For hit is a figure þat haldez fyue poyntez,
And vche lyne vmbelappez and loukez in oþer,
And ayquere hit is endelez; and Englych hit callen
630 Oueral, as I here, þe endeles knot.
Forþy hit acordez to þis knyȝt and to his cler armez,
For ay faythful in fyue and sere fyue syþez
Gawan watz for gode knawen, and as golde pured,
Voyded of vche vylany, wyth vertuez ennourned
635   in mote;
                   Forþy þe pentangel nwe
                   He ber in schelde and cote,
                   As tulk of tale most trwe
                   And gentylest knyȝt of lote.

The Gift of the Green Girdle

'Now forsake ȝe þis silke,' sayde þe burde þenne,
'For hit is symple in hitself? And so hit wel semez.
Lo! so hit is littel, and lasse hit is worþy;
Bot who-so knew þe costes þat knit ar þerinne,
1850 He wolde hit prayse at more prys, parauenture;
For quat gome so is gorde with þis grene lace,
While he hit hade hemely halched aboute,
Þer is no haþel vnder heuen tohewe hym þat myȝt,
For he myȝt not be slayn for slyȝt vpon erþe.'
1855 Þen kest þe knyȝt, and hit come to his hert
Hit were a juel for þe jopardé þat hym iugged were:
When he acheued to þe chapel his chek for to fech,
Myȝt he haf slypped to be vnslayn, þe sleȝt were noble.
Þenne he þulged with hir þrepe and þoled hir to speke,
1860 And ho bere on hym þe belt and bede hit hym swyþe—
And he granted and hym gafe with a goud wylle—
And bisoȝt hym, for hir sake, disceuer hit never,
Bot to lelly layne fro hir lorde; þe leude hym acordez
Þat neuer wyȝe schulde hit wyt, iwysse, bot þay twayne
1865   for noȝte;
                   He þonkked hir oft ful swyþe,
                   Ful þro with hert and þoȝt.
                   Bi þat on þrynne syþe
                   Ho hatz kyst þe knyȝt so toȝt.

Two Old French *Gauvain* Romances[†]

As early as the second verse-paragraph of the poem, the narrator of
Sir Gawain and the Green Knight indicates that the story he intends
to tell is not original with him: some men consider it quite a marvel,
he says, an exceedingly strange adventure among the wonders of
Arthurian tradition (lines 27–29). At a later point he seems to be saying that he learned his story from a book that was read aloud: Gawain,
in his quest for the Green Chapel, followed many bewildering routes,
"as I heard the book say" (line 690). At the end of the poem, we learn
that all who wore the green baldric after Sir Gawain had introduced it
to Arthur's court were honored, as it is told in "the best book of
knighthood" (line 2521), and that "the books of Brutus' deeds" bear
witness to the adventure (lines 2522–23). But no single source for the
poem's complicated narrative has ever been identified, nor is such a
story told in the historical account of King Arthur in Wace's earlier
poem *The Brut*, to which line 2523 may allude.

From what sources did the author of *Sir Gawain* derive the familiarity he displays in Part I with King Arthur's Round Table, the knights
of his court, and their customs and adventures? We know that his
readings in general included works in Old (that is, medieval) French,
because he alludes by name, in his poem called *Cleanness*, to the
author of the second installment of the famous thirteenth-century
allegorical poem *The Romance of the Rose*. In addition, some descriptive details in *Cleanness* apparently derive from Mandeville's *Travels,*
a popular quasi-factual, quasi-mythical report of wanderings among
exotic and fantastic places. This too the poet would have read in
French.

It is thus impossible to believe that, living as he did at a time when
the literary culture of France heavily influenced that of England, the
Gawain-poet did not know the Arthurian stories as retold by the most
famous poet of medieval France, Chretien de Troyes (ca. 1140–1200).
But the English poet's works contain no allusions to Chretien, and,
although Sir Gawain—called by his French name, Gauvain—is an
important member of the cast of characters in several of Chretien's
romances, he is not the hero of any of them, and no part of the narrative content of *Sir Gawain* is to be found in them.

There does exist, however, a pair of little-known poems in Old
French, evidently dating from the period when Chretien wrote, whose
central character is Sir Gauvain. The two are linked with each

---

† Translated by Marie Borroff, with the assistance of Brian J. Reilly from the text edited by
R. C. Johnston and D. D. R. Owens, *Two Old French Gauvain Romances* (Edinburgh:
Scottish Academic Press, 1972).

other, with Chretien, and with our late-fourteenth-century English romance. The unique extant copy is found in a manuscript copied in the late thirteenth or early fourteenth century in which they appear side by side. Modern editors have called them "The Knight of the Sword" and "The Mule without a Bridle." They are composed in the prosodic form that Chretien used in all his narrative poems: successive rhyming pairs of octosyllabic (eight-syllable) lines. What makes them of particular interest here is the fact that each contains one of the major narrative motifs brilliantly intertwined by the *Gawain*-poet in a single plot. In "The Knight of the Sword," Gauvain is sexually tempted when he must lie in bed next to a beautiful and receptive woman and is punished twice for making advances to her by a magic sword that gives him a superficial wound. In the end, it turns out that he is not killed by the sword, as the lady's would-be lovers usually are, because the sword will not kill the best knight in the world. In "The Mule without a Bridle," Gauvain stays in a castle in which his uncouth host, who wears a large ax or "gisarme" (*Gawain*, line 288) around his neck, offers him a "game" according to which he is to cut off the host's head in the evening and allow his own head to be cut off in return next morning. He accepts; later, the other man makes as if to perform the return blow but in the end withholds the stroke. It is also interesting that the last episode of "Sword," like that of *Sir Gawain*, includes an antifeminist theme. Sir Gauvain is impelled by the actions of the lady he has chosen as his love to break into an antifeminist diatribe similar to the speech made by Sir Gawain when he has learned the true meaning of Lord Bertilak's wife's earlier attempts to seduce him.

The opening passage of each poem alludes to Chretien. In "Sword," the narrator names him; defends him against the charge of having failed to include a romance about Sir Gauvain, the best of Arthur's knights, in his retellings of Arthurian legend; and proposes to remedy that lack in the story that follows. In "Mule," the narrator calls himself by the name "Paiens de Maisieres." This is a parody of Chretien's name in which *Pagan* is substituted for the given name *Christian* and the name of an unknown town for that of the illustrious Troyes, capital of the duchy of Champagne and seat of Chretien's patroness, the Countess Marie. A modern equivalent might be "Pagan of Podunk."

Some scholars have thought that these two poems should be added to the known works of Chretien. (The fact that the narrator refers to himself by name in the third person in the first poem is no argument against Chretien's authorship, as Chretien himself does this in the openings of several of his stories). But the use of another, parodic name in the second poem suggests both were written by someone other than the famous poet who was poking fun at him. What is more, they are far shorter than Chretien's Arthurian poems. The latter range from about 6650 to about 7050 lines, whereas "Sword" and "Mule" are 1206 and 1136 lines long, respectively.

Whether or not this pair of poems is to be ascribed to Chretien, it is hard, on reading them, to resist the supposition that the *Gawain*-poet knew them and might even have been stimulated by them to combine the themes of resistance to sexual temptation on the part of the hero with his acceptance of a "game" calling for reciprocal beheadings.

The translations here are summaries that include close renderings, in quotation marks, of the parts of the narratives that have parallels in *Sir Gawain*. I have put verbs in the past tense throughout, whereas in the originals, present and past tenses alternate in typical medieval fashion. In "The Knight of the Sword," Sir Gawain is the center of attention from the beginning; in "The Mule without a Bridle," the first section focuses on Sir Kay, the seneschal, or official master of ceremonies, of Arthur's court, who in early Arthurian tradition was viewed favorably but later came to be characterized in negative terms. Here he is used as a foil to the hero; he abandons, after some disconcerting experiences along the way, the quest that the more courageous Sir Gauvain then successfully completes.

The Knight of the Sword†

"Let all who love pleasure and joy come forth to hear about an adventure that befell the good knight who upheld loyalty, prowess, and honor, and never at any time loved a cowardly, perfidious, or uncourtly man. I tell of Sir Gauvain, who was so famed for elegant manners and great feats of arms that no one who wished to write a complete account of his virtues would ever come to the end of it. Yet though I cannot tell everything, that is no reason for me to remain silent. Chretien de Troyes must not be blamed—he who knew so well how to tell tales of the great and famed King Arthur, his court and his retinue—for never telling of Sir Gauvain. He was far too worthy to forget. Wherefore I am pleased to tell for the first time of an adventure that befell this good knight."

[Sir Gauvain, staying with King Arthur and his court at Carlisle, liked to ride out in the nearby forest during the day.]

"One day he had his horse made ready, and dressed himself in courtly fashion. He donned a pair of golden spurs over well-tailored hose of silk, fine white breeches, a shirt of pleated linen cut short and wide, and a mantle lined with miniver. He was indeed richly attired!"

---

† This is a summary of the poem, including excerpts closely translating the original. The latter are in quotation marks. *Gauvain* is the Old French version of the name *Gawain*.

[He rode on so far that he lost his way. Looking for the road back, he came upon a knight seated by a fire with his steed tethered to a tree. The knight told him that he lived close by and invited Sir Gauvain to be his guest, provided that he would stay with him in the forest that night. In the morning, the strange knight went on ahead to make preparations for the reception of a guest. Sir Gauvain, following him slowly, encountered a group of shepherds and heard one of them lamenting the fate that would surely befall him at the stranger's castle. They told Sir Gauvain that no one who stays there returns, and that the lord "kills any guest in his home who contradicts him on any point." Gauvain paid no heed to their story and went on to the castle. He was cordially received by the lord and his retainers.]

"There, running to meet him, was the lord of the castle, who made a great show of joy at his arrival. A valet took his arms, another took Gringolet, and a third relieved him of his spurs. His host took him by the hand and led him over the bridge. They found within, in the room in front of the tower, a splendid fire with luxurious seats all around it covered with purple silk. Outside, Sir Gauvain could see men leading his horse to a stable and bringing him grain and hay in abundance."

[The lord then introduced Sir Gauvain to his beautiful daughter. The lord said that he wished her to keep Gauvain company and that if he pleased her and he was pleased by her in return, it would be an honor to her. He left them together, and Sir Gauvain addressed her "courteously and without the least awkwardness" and "very graciously offered her his service." She, for her part, was reluctant to reveal the feelings he had aroused in her because she knew that he would never be able to possess her. She told him that no good could come of their friendship and cautioned him to refrain from contradicting her father on any point. A meal followed.]

"When they had washed, they sat down, and the servants set, on top of the beautiful white tablecloths, the saltcellars and the knives, followed by the bread, and the wine in cups of silver and fine gold. I have no wish to describe the courses in detail one by one; there was an abundance of meat and fish, roast pheasant and venison, and they fell to gladly. The host urged Gauvain and his daughter to drink. He told the damsel that she should encourage the knight, and said to Gauvain, 'You should be well pleased that I wish her to be your love.' When they had eaten their fill, the servants removed the cloths and brought them water and a towel with which to dry themselves."

[The lord left for a while, and Gauvain and the damsel had further conversation in which she repeated her words of caution and said she prayed that he might depart without having quarreled with her father. He returned, and they had a light supper of fruit and wine. The lord then told them that he wanted Gauvain to sleep in his bed, and that his daughter was to sleep with him. All three entered the bedchamber.]

"[It] was richly hung with tapestries, and twelve candles, set all around it, were burning there, casting a brilliant light. The bed was adorned with rich spreads and white sheets. But I have no wish to tarry in describing the luxurious sheets of foreign silks from Palermo and Romagna with which the bedroom was provided, or the fur coverlets of vair and miniver. I shall describe it all to you in a word: whatever is suitable for making the body of a knight or a lady comfortable in winter and in summer was there in great abundance. There were many costly furnishings in the room, so that Gauvain marveled greatly at the riches he saw. The host said to him 'This room is indeed beautiful. Both you and this young girl will lie there, and no one else will be present. Damsel, close the door, and do as he bids you, for I know well that people such as you and he have no need of a crowd of witnesses. But I solemnly warn you not to put out the candles—that would anger me greatly. I give you this command because I want him to see your great beauty when you lie in his arms, as that will increase his pleasure, and I want you to see his handsome body.' Then he left the bedroom and the damsel closed the door.

"Sir Gauvain lay down on the bed; the damsel returned and lay naked beside him; there was no need to entreat her to do so. All night, she lay in his arms. Sweetly he kissed and embraced her again and again, and things progressed so far that he was on the point of consummating his desire, when she said 'Sir, please! Things cannot continue thus. I do not lack protection here.' Gauvain looked around in every direction and saw no living thing. 'Belle,' he said, 'I pray you, who would stop me from having my way with you?' She answered, 'I shall willingly disclose to you all I know. Do you see the sword hanging there, the one with the decorative knot of silver below the pommel, and the hilt of fine gold? I am not inventing what you will hear me tell you, since I have seen it more than once in practice. My father prizes the sword highly, for it has killed for him many worthy knights of high repute. Be assured that he has caused more than twenty knights to be killed right here. I do not know what his reasons are, but I have never seen a knight escape who entered this door. My good father puts on a good show of hospitality, but as soon as any of them misbehaves, he seizes on him to kill him. It is imperative that his guests avoid the least hint of rude behavior; it is best to steer a wholly straight course. He immediately asserts his rights if he catches anyone in the smallest misdeed. If a guest behaves himself well and is not caught on any pretext, then he is told to sleep with me, and thus meets his death. Do you know why none escape from this room? If in any way a guest shows his intent to accomplish his desire for me, immediately the sword cuts into his body, and if he first goes toward it to seize and remove it, it straightway leaps out of the sheath and strikes him. Know that the sword is enchanted in such a way that it protects me without fail. I

might not have conveyed this knowledge to you, but you are so courteous and sage that it would be a great pity, and would weigh on my
mind forever after, if you were killed because of me.'

"Now Gauvain was at a loss. He had never in his life heard of such
a danger, wherefore he suspected that she had told him this to protect
herself from his desire to take his pleasure with her. On the other
hand, he thought to himself that the affair could never be kept secret:
that he had lain a whole night alone with a young girl in her bed,
naked body to naked body, and that, deterred solely by a word from
her, he had foregone his desire. Better it seemed to him to die honor-
ably than to live long in shame. 'Belle,' he said, 'I take no account of
what you have told me. Since I have come to this point, I wish here
and now to become your lover; you cannot escape it.' She replied,
'From this moment on you cannot blame me, whatever happens.' He
then drew so close to her that she uttered a cry. The sword leapt from
the sheath and flew through the air to his body, wounding his side in
such a way that it sliced off some of his skin but did not hurt him
severely. It also pierced the covers and all the sheets through to the
straw stuffing of the mattress. Then it shot back into its sheath. Gauvain lay there dumbfounded, his desire wholly extinguished. 'Sir,' she
said, 'Please hear me, in the name of God! You think that I spoke to
you as I did because I wanted to protect my body, but truly, I have
never done so for any knight except you. And believe me, it is a great
wonder that you were not immediately and without remedy killed by
this first blow. In God's name, lie here peacefully and from now on
refrain from touching me in any way. Even a wise man may undertake
something that turns out to his disadvantage.'

"Gauvain remained thoughtful and unhappy, not knowing how to
behave. Should God grant that he returned to his own country, the
affair could never be kept a secret. It would be known everywhere
that he had lain alone all night with a beautiful young girl and had
not touched her, with nothing to prevent him except a sword no
hand had wielded. He would be forever shamed if she escaped thus.
What vexed him all the more was the fact that the candles cast a
brilliant light by which he could see her beauty. Her hair was blond,
her forehead smooth, her eyebrows delicate, her eyes bright, her
nose well-positioned, her complexion fresh, her small mouth laughing, her neck long and graceful, her arms long, her hands white, her
sides soft and smooth, her skin white and tender beneath the sheets.
So lovely and well-made was her body that no fault could be found
with it.

"He moved gently toward her, being a man who was in no way
uncouth, and was about to make his conquest complete when the
sword leapt from its sheath and again assaulted him. The flat of the

blade struck his neck—he almost thought he had lost his wits. But it wobbled a bit, took three fingers'-breadth off his right shoulder, and cut a piece from the silken sheet, whereupon it flew back and thrust itself into the sheath once more.

"When Gauvain felt himself injured on his shoulder and his side, and saw that he could not succeed in his endeavors, he was vexed and grieved, not knowing what to do next and irked by this enforced abstinence. 'Sir,' said she, 'are you dead?' 'Damsel,' he replied, 'not I. But tonight I am giving you a gift: I hereby declare a truce with you.' 'Sir, by my faith,' she said, 'if it had been declared when it was asked for, you would now be in a more pleasant situation.' Gauvain was greatly discomfited, and the damsel as well. Neither the one nor the other slept; rather, their distress kept them awake through the night until it was day.

"Next morning, the lord came to the bedchamber and called out loudly. When he learned that no harm had befallen Gauvain, he was very much displeased. He saw some blood on the bed-linen, and said he was sure that Gauvain had wanted to possess his daughter, but had been prevented by the sword. Gauvain acknowledged that he had guessed the truth. The lord then demanded that he tell him his country and his name. When he learned who his guest was, he revealed that all the knights who had come there before him had been killed by the sword but that the sword would not kill the best of all knights. He then offered him his daughter and the lordship of his castle. Gauvain accepted the former with pleasure, but refused the latter.

"It soon became known throughout the countryside that a knight had visited the lord and had tried to possess the damsel, but that the sword had made two passes without harming him fatally. Many knights and ladies came there, and the lord served them sumptuously; entertainers amused them, and they listened to music and played games. At night, when all went to bed, the lord led Gauvain and his daughter to the room where they had lain before, and married them.

"He set them side by side without interference, then went out and closed the door. What more should I say? That night, Gauvain did as he wished; at no time did a sword fly at him through the air. It does not displease me to think that once again he assaulted the damsel, and she for her part was not distressed in the least."

[After many more days had passed, it came to Sir Gauvain that he had been away from the court for a long time and that his kinfolk and friends must think he had been killed. He sought permission from the host to leave and take the damsel with him and asked that she be dressed fittingly so that when he returned, her beauty and obvious nobility would be admired. The two departed, taking the road back to court through the woods. But they had hardly set forth when she took hold of the bridle of his horse and stopped them. She explained that she had forgotten the beautiful greyhounds she had raised herself and did not wish to leave without them. Gauvain returned and fetched them, and they traveled on together.

Suddenly a knight came riding toward them, fully armed and mounted on a fine steed. Without a word, he came up to them, took hold of the girl and drew her away without any objection from her. Gauvain challenged him for her, and, since he was lightly armed, asked him to wait while he went and obtained full armor so that they could fight for her on equal terms. Instead, the knight proposed that they withdraw from her on either side and let her choose which one she wished to accompany further.]

"But the damsel, who well knew how Gauvain was able to acquit himself, wanted next to assess the valor and prowess of the other knight.

"Know this, all of you, whether you be short or tall, whether you laugh or groan on hearing my tale: there is scarcely a woman in the world, were she the sweetheart of the best knight from here to India, whose love for him would be so great that, if he lacked prowess at home, she would prize him as much as a pinch of salt. You know well of what prowess I speak."

[Gawain was greatly vexed, but ceded the damsel to the knight without argument. He was so courtly that he did not address one word to her, but said to the knight, "May God never look on me with favor if I fight for something that doesn't care about me."

The knight and the damsel then departed, but at the edge of the woods, she halted, and told him that she could not be his sweetheart unless she had her greyhounds. The knight returned to Gauvain and accused him of taking them away even though they did not belong to him. Gauvain proposed that they play the same game they had played before: that they withdraw to either side, call the greyhounds, and let them choose which one to go to. The knight agreed, thinking that he would have them one way or the other. The dogs chose to go to Sir Gauvain, whom they knew, and this pleased him well.]

"But once again the damsel refused to accompany the knight unless she had her greyhounds. He ordered Sir Gauvain to stop and let the greyhounds alone, insisting that they did not belong to him. Gauvain replied:

'It is discourteous of you to oppose me thus. But I am in possession of the greyhounds, since they came to me. May God in His majesty disown me if I give them up. I gave the damsel to you because she attached herself to you, though she was mine and had come with me. Now it is reasonable that without threat you must leave the greyhounds to me, for they are mine and came to me, and of their own free will attached themselves to me. Know one thing for certain—and in me you can see the proof of it—that if you wish to take your pleasure with this girl, your joy will be short-lived. I fervently hope she hears me! I assure you that as long as she was with me, I did all that she wished. Now see how she has treated me! Know well that it is not with dogs as it is with women. Never will a dog leave for a stranger its master who has fed it. A woman will quickly abandon hers if he does not fulfill all her desires. Such inconstancy is hard to understand. The greyhounds have not abandoned me; thus I can prove, without contradiction from anyone, that the nature and love of a dog are worth more than the way a woman behaves.'"

[The knight then challenged him to combat, and they fought fiercely. Gawain finally knocked the knight and his horse down together, dismounted, pinned him against the ground, struck him a series of blows on the head, then dislodged a section of his body-armor and thrust his sword into his side. He left him lying there, retrieved his horse and the greyhounds and leapt into the saddle. The damsel begged him not to leave her, explaining that when she saw how poorly armed he was compared to the stranger, she was afraid to go to him.]

"'Belle,' said he, 'this amounts to nothing. Your excuses are worthless: apologies of this kind have no value. Such faith, such love, such a disposition one often finds in woman. He who wishes to harvest in his country a wheat other than he sows, and he who wishes to find in a woman a nature other than her own, are alike lacking in wisdom. Women have been thus since God made the first of them. The more a man takes pains to be of service to them, the more he repents himself in the end; the more a man honors and does as they wish, the more distressed he becomes, and the more he loses by it. Pity never moved your heart to uphold my honor and protect my life; rather, your feelings were quite the opposite. Country folk say 'It is at the end that one sees how each thing reveals itself.' May God never look graciously on him who finds a woman deceitful and false, yet cherishes and loves and protects her. Now keep the company you have chosen.' Thereupon he left her to herself, and never knew what became of her."

[He returned home; his friends rejoiced to see him, and they listened willingly as he told them all his adventures from first to last.]

The Mule without a Bridle[†]

"Country folks have a proverb saying that many old things which have been put aside are still useful. Therefore, each man should hold on to what he already possesses. The old ways are less esteemed today than the new ones, but often prove to be more valuable. For this reason, Paiens de Maisieres says people should follow the old ways rather than the new.

Here begins an adventure of a damsel on a mule who came to King Arthur's court.

[King Arthur was holding court at Carlisle, during Pentecost, with a great assembly of knights and ladies. A young girl came to the castle riding on a mule that had a halter but no bridle. She told the company that the bridle had been taken from her maliciously and that she would never be happy until she got it back. She promised anyone who would undertake the adventure that she would be his when he returned with the bridle and said that she would immediately give him her mule, which would take him to a castle. There he could obtain the bridle, but not peacefully.

Kay, the seneschal, offered to go in search of the bridle and departed, riding the mule. He wanted to kiss the girl before he left, but she refused, telling him that she would kiss him when he returned with the bridle. On his journey the mule took him through a forest full of lions, tigers, and leopards (who recognized the mule and did homage to her) and a deep and wide valley, bitter cold and full of a dreadful stench, in which were snakes, scorpions, and other creatures. Beyond it he entered a meadow with a fountain and then came to a black river crossed only by a very narrow footbridge made of iron. Here Kay, fearing even greater dangers than he had already encountered, turned back.

When, on his return, it was discovered that he did not have the bridle, he was disgraced and did not come again to court. Then Sir Gauvain said that he would undertake the errand. He was granted permission to do so by the king and queen.]

"[H]e wished to embrace the damsel before he left. It was right that she should kiss him, and she did so willingly. Now she felt at ease, since she was certain that she would get the bridle back without fail, however things might go."

[Gauvain rode through the forest and the valley, passed through the meadow, and found the footbridge over the black river, which looked as if it belonged to the devil. It was no wider than a hand, but he struck the mule and she jumped onto the bridge and crossed it.

He then came to a splendid castle surrounded by a deep river and enclosed by a circle of wooden stakes. On each was impaled the head of a

[†] Like the preceding text, this is a summary of the poem, including excerpts closely translating the original. The latter are in quotation marks.

knight. The castle itself was revolving rapidly; he succeeded in entering it by waiting until the gate came in front of him and immediately spurring the mule to jump. Within, the castle precincts were empty. Riding on, he came to a portico, where he was greeted by a dwarf who, after bidding him welcome, disappeared without saying more. Before him was a deep vault or cellar; soon, a shaggy, churlish fellow wearing a large ax around his neck ascended the stair from the vault and confronted him. He told Gauvain that he had wasted his journey, for the bridle was closely guarded and he would have to do battle for it. Gauvain assured him that he was ready to pay for the bridle in full.

The churl invited him to his lodging, stalled the mule, and served him dinner. He then made up a bed for him.]

"Now he approached him. 'Gauvain,' said he, 'you will lie alone all night in this very bed, without offering challenge or protest. Before you go to bed, I am making a request of you with peaceful intent. Since I have heard of the high esteem in which people hold you, and because the occasion has presented itself, I offer you a game, to accept if you will.' And Gauvain promised him that he would accept it, whatever it might be. 'Speak here and now,' he said, 'and I shall make my choice, so help me God, without deception, since I consider you my good host.' The other man said 'Tonight, cut off my head with this sharp gisarme, but on this condition, that I cut yours off when I return in the morning.' 'I would not know much,' said Gauvain, 'if I did not know what my decision would be. Tonight I'll cut off your head, and in the morning I will give you mine, if you want to take it.' 'Damned be he who asks for more,' said the churl, 'so come now!' Then he led him off. The churl rested his neck on a block. Now Gauvain took the ax, and without tarrying chopped off his head with one blow. The churl straight-way jumped to his feet and picked up his head. He returned to the cellar, and Gauvain went right to bed and slept soundly until morning.

"As soon as it was day, Gauvain got up and attired himself. Behold! the churl came back, entirely cheerful and in the best of health, with his gisarme around his neck. Gauvain might well think his wits had gone astray when he saw the head that he had cut off the night before. Nevertheless, he had no fear. Then the churl, who had lost nothing, spoke. 'Gauvain,' said he, 'I have come back, and I remind you of your agreement.' 'I have no objections at all, since I see what it behooves me to do, and I know there is no way of combatting it.' And indeed, he might well have done so, but he did not wish to commit a treacherous deed: since he had pledged himself, he wished to abide by the bargain. 'Come at once, then,' said the churl. Gauvain went to him and placed his neck on the block, whereupon the churl said 'Stretch your neck out all the way.' 'By God, there's no more of it, but strike it if you wish.' So help me God, there would have been great damage and grief if he had done so! The churl lifted the gisarme high to frighten him, but he had in fact no intention of touching him, since he had shown such great loyalty, and had so fully kept his promise."

[Now Gauvain asked him how he could obtain the bridle. The churl told him that he still had to fight two lions, kept shackled together there, who were so fierce that no one could fight them and survive. He assured him that he would give him as much help as he could. He brought him a suit of armor, gave him a steed to ride, and supplied him with seven shields. A fierce battle followed, in which Gauvain lost several of the shields but finally killed a lion with his sword. In his battle with the second lion, he lost all but one of the remaining shields but finally split the lion's head with his sword and killed him. He then asked again for the bridle, but the churl said that before he obtained it the whole sleeve of his armor would have to be covered with blood.

The churl then took him to a chamber where a wounded knight was lying. The knight welcomed Gauvain by name and said that it was necessary for them to fight each other. It was the custom in that land that every knight who came to the castle had to fight with the knight who was in residence there; if he lost, his head was cut off and impaled on one of the stakes outside. Gauvain and the knight fought fiercely for a long time, but finally Gauvain cleft the helmet of his opponent. He then begged for mercy and told him that it was he who had impaled on stakes the heads of all the knights who had come in search of the bridle. He had defeated each of them, but Gauvain was superior to them all.

Gauvain then asked yet again for the bridle. The churl told him that he would now have to fight two dreadful fire-breathing serpents and gave him a stronger suit of armor that he would need to wear in his encounter with them. He killed both serpents and cut them to pieces. The dwarf he had seen earlier reappeared and said that he must now eat with his mistress and that he might then take possession of the bridle. He took him to the lady, who, after they had eaten, expressed her gratitude for the help Gauvain had given her sister and offered to take him as her lord and give him the castle. Gauvain politely refused and said that he must leave, for he was overdue at King Arthur's court. She then gave him the bridle and ordered the churl to cause the castle to stop revolving so that he could depart unhindered. After he had crossed the bridge, he looked back and saw people dancing in the streets. The churl, who had led him out, told him that he had rescued the people by killing the beasts that persecuted them. God, through him, had delivered them, illuminating the people who were in darkness.[1]

Gauvain retraced his journey and arrived at King Arthur's castle. The damsel who owned the bridle kissed him a hundred times and more, and said that her person, by right, was wholly at his service and that she was sure no other knight could have obtained the bridle for her. Gauvain recounted

---

1. The language of the poem here clearly echoes a prophetic reference in Isaiah to Christ's deliverance of the Old Testament patriarchs in the so-called Harrowing of Hell: "The people who walked in darkness have seen a great light."

all his adventures to her. She then asked leave to depart. The king and
queen begged her to stay and take as her lover one of the knights of the
Round Table. She said she did not dare to and asked for her mule. Refusing any escort, she began her return journey, riding again into the forest.]

From The Alliterative Morte Arthure[†]

[*Feast at Christmas*]

Then he holds a Christmas feast at Carlisle Castle,
65   This acclaimed conqueror, in kingly state,
With dukes whose dominions lay in distant lands,
Earls and archbishops and other lords aplenty,
Bishops and bannerets° and bright-helmed knights   *knightly titles*
From all parts of his provinces: approach when they like!
70   But on Christmas Day, when the company assembled,
From that acclaimed conqueror there came a command
That no lord was to leave, but linger at court
Until a term of ten days had come to an end.
Thus in royal array he holds his Round Table
75   With princely pleasures and plenteous fare;
Never, to my knowledge, was a nobler feast
Made in midwinter in the West Marches.°   *borderlands*
But on New Year's Day, at noon, as it befell,
As the king was seated and served at the sumptuous feast,
80   There rushed in suddenly a Senator of Rome,
With a train of sixteen knights, trooping in together.
He saluted the sovereign and the assembly there;
To king after king he courteously bowed;
Guenevere, the gracious queen, he greeted as he liked,
85   And next, to the monarch he made known his errand.

[The senator tells King Arthur that he bears with him a notarized summons
ordering him to appear in Rome. There he must explain why, disregarding
his father's sworn fealty to the Roman Empire, he is occupying Roman
lands. If he ignores this summons, the emperor's forces will ravage his kingdom, and he himself will be captured and brought to Rome.]

The king gazed at him grimly; his great eyes shone
As bright as burning coals when the fire blazes high.

† Translated into modern English verse by Marie Borroff, from the text edited by Valerie
Krishna, *The Alliterative Morte Arthure: A Critical Edition* (New York: Bunt Franklin, 1976).
The *Alliterative Morte Arthure*, a poem composed in the late fourteenth-century in the
North Midlands area of England, offers a description of King Arthur's feast at Christmas-
time by a poet contemporary with the *Gawain*-poet.

His look was like a lion's; his lip he bites.
The envoys fell to the earth in abject fear;
120 Crouching before the king like curs° in a kennel;   *low-bred dogs*
As daunted by his demeanor° as if doom were at hand.   *manner*
Then a warrior, recovering, rose up among them,
And cried, "O crowned king, courteous and noble,
Let no envoy be hurt by so honorable a monarch,
125 Since we are wholly in your hands, and ask you for mercy.
We owe allegiance to Lucius, who is Lord of Rome,
The most marvelous man of all monarchs on earth.
We have come at his command—excuse us, we pray!"

[Arthur angrily calls the envoy a coward. The envoy replies that he and all
his company are utterly daunted by the fierce countenance of the king, who
is the lordliest personage he ever saw. Arthur says that out of respect for the
emperor, he will temporarily restrain himself, conferring with his lords and
doing as they advise. Meanwhile, he invites the Romans to stay with him
seven nights "to see what life we lead in these humble lands" (line 154). A
description of the feast follows.]

Then the first course came in, before the king himself:
Boar-heads borne high upon bright silver trays
By tall lads in livery elegantly attired;
Boys of royal blood, a band of three score.
180 There was flesh of fat deer, with frumenty° beside;   *wheat pudding*
Wild beasts and birds, brought fresh from the forests;
Peacocks and plovers on platters of gold;
Fillets of porcupine force-fed in pens;
Then herons under hot sauce; the slices heaped high;
185 Breasts of swan basted in bright silver chargers;
Tender tarts of guinea-fowl—taste when they like!—
Morsels most tempting, that melted on their palates;
Then shoulders of wild swine, the brawn sheared thick;
Bitterns° on embossed plates, and barnacle geese,   *heron-like bird*
190 Birds cooked under cover of crusts baked brown;
And great breasts of boar in bounteous display;
All in sumptuous sauces to solace their hearts,
With blue flames aflicker, to keep the fare hot . . .
195 Whose luster delighted all who looked on them there.
Then cranes and curlews°, cunningly roasted,   *long-legged bird*
Rich stews of rabbit, redolent with spices,
Pheasants fancifully served, with feathers in fans,
Panoplies° of pastries, puffed piping hot.   *splendid display*
200 Claret and Cretan wine copiously flowed
From conduits° crafted of silver, curiously wrought;   *pipes*

Wines from Alsace and eastern vineyards;
Rhine wine and Rochelle, none richer to savour;
Venetian vintages of various hues
205 That flowed from gold faucets—fill his cup who likes!—
The cabinet of the king was encased in silver,
With great gilded goblets, glorious to behold;
The chief butler, chosen among chevaliers of rank,
Was the courteous Sir Kay, who bore the cups round;
210 Sixty alike were set before the King himself,
Carven most cunningly by craftsmen renowned;
Embossed all about with brilliant gems,
That if poison were privily put in the wine,
The bright gold abruptly would break all to pieces,
215 Or else the venom be made void by virtue of the stones.
And the sovereign seated there in seemly splendor,
Clad in cloth of gold, with his company of knights
Adorned with the diadem duly on dais,°   *platform*
Who was deemed most doughty of all dwellers on earth.
221 Then the Conqueror cordially called to those lords,
Rallied° the Romans with ready speech: *mocked*
"Sirs, keep a cheerful countenance and comfort yourselves;
We know nothing here of nicely cooked fare;
Our barren lands bring forth no better than this.
225 Wherefore, without feigning, enforce yourselves all
To feed on such feeble food as you find before you."
"Sir," says the Senator, "as I hope for Christ's help,
Such royal fare ne'er reigned within Roman walls!
There is no prelate, nor pope, nor prince upon earth
230 Who would not be pleased to praise such peerless dishes."

CRITICISM

ALAIN RENOIR

Descriptive Technique in *Sir Gawain and the Green Knight*[†]

Literary scholars and critics are agreed that *Sir Gawain and the Green Knight* deserves a place of honor among the great works of mediaeval literature. Some seventy years ago, Gaston Paris labelled it "the jewel of English literature during the Middle Ages"; George Lyman Kittredge has called it "a very distinguished piece of work"; and Fernand Mossé has praised it as nothing less than "*the* masterpiece of alliterative poetry." The opinion of our age is perhaps best summed up by Albert C. Baugh when he simply refers to the poem as "the finest Arthurian romance in English." In general, modern critics agree with Bernhard ten Brink that its author "knows well how to hold our attention."

Those who have concerned themselves with the means whereby the reader's attention is aroused and maintained have generally turned to the extraordinary vividness which permeates the work from beginning to end. For instance, Emile Pons assures us that "*Sir Gawayne and the Green Knyght* is not only the most beautiful Arthurian poem in English but one of the most vivid works of Arthurian literature of all countries and of all times." He believes that this quality is due in large part to the poet's psychological insight: "In fact," he writes "there is no literary production, including that of Chaucer . . . which brings the fourteenth century nearer to us . . . by means of a richly equipped psychology . . ." On the other hand, Francis Berry, in a discussion of Gawain's quest for the Green Knight, accounts for that vividness with the observation that "the experience is actualized in the muscular images and rhythm, in the grasp of concrete particulars."

Every reader of the poem will agree with both of the views expressed above, for *Sir Gawain and the Green Knight* owes its compelling vividness equally to its author's psychological insight into the nature of the experiences he describes and to his flair for significant details. My purpose here is to argue that along with the qualities just noted, our poem is indebted for much of its vividness to the presence of a third element: the poet's use of a peculiar descriptive technique whereby the details selected for inclusion are set off in the most psychologically effective relation to the total picture presented to the reader. The nature of this technique may best be understood in reference to Erich Auerbach's account of the principal differences between the Homeric and Biblical styles. According to Auerbach, "it would be difficult . . . to imagine styles more contrasted than those of these

† From *Orbis Litterarum* 13 (1958): 126–32. Reprinted by permission.

two . . . texts. On the one hand, externalized, uniformly illuminated phenomena, at a definite time and in a definite place, connected together without lacunae in a perpetual foreground; thoughts and feeling completely expressed; events taking place in leisurely fashion and with very little of suspense. On the other hand, the externalization of only so much of the phenomena as is necessary for the purpose of the narrative, all else left in obscurity; the decisive points of the narrative alone are emphasized, what lies between is nonexistent; time and place are undefined and call for interpretation . . ." If, as Auerbach argues, the style of Homer be characterized by the uniform illumination of the scene, and that of the Bible by the selective illumination of a few immediately relevant details only, then the style of *Sir Gawain and the Green Knight* may be described as a composite of the two. The technique of our poet is to draw a single detail out of a uniformly illuminated scene which is then allowed to fade out in obscurity and of which we may be given an occasional dim glimpse at psychologically appropriate moments. The twentieth century is thoroughly familiar with this device. In effect, it is that most commonly associated with the cinematograph, where the camera may at will focus either upon the whole scene or upon a single detail, while illumination may be used so as to keep the audience aware of the background against which the action takes place. We must note that the device is primarily concerned with the utilization of space. Whether that space be a theatre's screen or a reader's mind, its size remains constant during the projection of the film or the reading of the poem, respectively. The importance assumed by a given detail depends largely upon the portion of that space it occupies; it may be diminished or increased by changing the proportion accordingly: the greater the magnitude of the picture before us, the less the importance of the individual detail.

The passage where Gawain beheads the Green Knight is clearly illustrative of the technique discussed here. We recall how the semi-gigantic green man has entered King Arthur's hall at Camelot and interrupted the New Year festivities to challenge any willing knight to beheading him on the spot in exchange for a return blow a year and a day later. Arthur has accepted the challenge, but Gawain claims the undertaking for himself on the ground that a king ought not to risk his life recklessly. Now the decision to grant Gawain his request rests with the barons, who immediately hold a brief consultation:

> Ryche togeder con roun,
> And syþen þay redden alle same
> To ryd þe kyng wyth croun,
> And gif Gawan þe game.
>
> (362–65)

Considered *in context*, this is a uniformly illuminated scene. Indeed, the greater part of the preceding 361 lines has been devoted to descriptions, both general and particular, which allow us to visualize with equal clarity every detail of the entire scene. We know that, with the exception of Arthur, Gawain, and the Green Knight, the company is sitting at table but has not yet begun the first course (133). We know the names of the most important knights there, as well as their places at the table (107–13). We even know the nature of the food and beverages served, the number of dishes available to each guest, and the very metal of which the plates and platters are made (116–29). Thus, the lines mentioning the barons' consultation create a picture as uniformly illuminated as any in the Homeric poems. Furthermore, they create a picture of immense magnitude, for the reader's imagination is made to sweep for an instant over the entirety of the festively crowded great hall at Camelot.

With the next line, however, this general picture suddenly vanishes into obscurity, and our field of vision is considerably narrowed when the poet focuses first upon Arthur and Gawain alone, and then upon Gawain and the Green Knight as they formulate the terms of their bargain. We now proceed to the description of the beheading proper, where the technique we have been discussing is pushed to its absolute extreme. For the sake of clarity, that description is printed here so as to indicate divisions relevant to the subsequent argument:

> The grene knyȝt vpon grounde grayþely hym dresses,
> A littel lut with þe hede, þe lere he discouereȝ,
> His longe louelych lokkeȝ he layd ouer his croun,
> Let the naked nec to þe note shewe.
>
> Gauan gripped to his ax, and gederes hit on hyȝt,
> Þe kay fot on þe fold he before sette,
> Let hit doun lyȝtly lyȝt on þe naked,
> Þat þe scharp of þe schalk schyndered þe bones,
> And schrank þurȝ þe schyire grece, and scade hit in twynne,
> Þat þe bit of þe broun stel bot on þe grounde.
>
> Þe fayre hede fro þe halce hit to þe erþe,
> Þat fele hit foyned wyth her fete, þere hit forth roled.
>
> (417–28)

We see at a glance that the passage quoted is divided into three clearly distinct but thematically related sections: the first of these (417–20) shows the Green Knight preparing himself for the blow; the second (421–26) shows the actual delivery of the blow; the third (427–28) shows the head tumbling down as a result of the blow. We also note that the first two sections follow similar patterns as they progressively narrow their respective fields of vision from a whole man down to a few inches; on the other hand, the third section precisely reverses the process.

These patterns deserve closer examination. The first section devotes four lines to what could be told in one, but the result is that each line brings the reader visually and emotionally closer to the climax. Exactly as if the action were taking place on a screen before us, the field of vision is progressively narrowed from the entire Green Knight, to his head, and eventually to his neck alone. It is significant that we are made to anticipate that last picture two lines before the word "neck" actually appears on the page. In mentioning the "lere" (418) and showing the Green Knight gathering his long hair upon his head (419), the poet accomplishes far more than he would with a straightforward description, for he forces us to visualize both the neck and the fate that awaits it. From the point of view of the reader, the actual mention of the neck, when it finally appears in the last line of the section (420), has all the emotional impact of a first-rate cinematographic close-up: everything else—the great hall, the barons, King Arthur, Gawain, even the Green Knight—has faded out of the picture; only the fated green neck stands out of the obscurity, in sharp focus and clearly illuminated.

As the first section began with a picture of the entire Green Knight, the second section begins with one of the entire Gawain. But note the intensity therein: we have just been concentrating on the very point where the ax will strike, and now we suddenly see that "Gauan gripped to his ax and gederes hit on hyȝt' (421). Nor is the superb picture a mere flash; the poet gives it time to gather emotional momentum as he allows Gawain a line to bring forward and steady "þe kay fot on þe folde" (422). Obviously, the most dramatically relevant object before us is the ax; and it is upon it that the field of vision is narrowed, in the next line, as we follow its swift downwards motion and see it touch the bared green flesh. At this point, the field of vision becomes even smaller, so that the only image before us is the very "scharp" of the blade as it irresistibly cuts its way through the back-bone and the flesh beneath (424–25). Students of the cinematograph will recall that Buñuel used precisely the same visual device in the *Andalusian Dog*, when he covered the screen with a razor blade cutting its way through an eyeball. The coincidence is significant, for the *Andalusian Dog* has often been regarded as an attempt to use the cinematographic medium for purely cinematographic ends. To return to our text, we should consider it a sign of the poet's narrative genius that he does not immediately show us the head rolling off the shoulders, as a less gifted writer would probably have done. Instead, he keeps the focus sharply on the edge of the blade, which he follows through the neck and down to the floor into which it sinks. In so doing, he contributes in three ways to the effectiveness of his narrative: (1) he not only impresses upon us the terrific force of the blow, but he makes it a part of our immediate visual experience; (2) he gains verisimilitude, for the law of inertia would prevent the head from falling instantaneously; (3) he avoids the stylistically awkward shift in point of view which would necessarily result from his abandoning in mid-course the object he has been closely following since the beginning of the section. To these three contributions, one may wish to add a fourth, less obvious one: the uninterrupted arc of a circle described by the swinging ax is aesthetically very felicitous and gives the decapitation a stylized quality which it might otherwise lack. Nor is this feature likely to prove accidental, for our poet reveals a constant concern with pictorial beauty. With the possible exception of Morgan the Fay, everyone and everything in the poem is beautiful. The Green Knight himself is beautiful (137–95), terrifying though he be.

As the opening line of the second section gained effectiveness from its proximity to the last line of the first, so the entire third section benefits from the last image in the second. The reader who has followed the beheading blow to its logical conclusion has had time to gather his wits so as to imagine the details that follow. As has already been suggested, the third section reverses the visual pattern discussed in regard to the first and second sections; it enlarges the field of vision instead of narrowing it. At first the poet centers upon the falling head (427), thus merely shifting from one small object—the ax—to another. With the next line, however, he enlarges the field of vision so as to include not only the severed head, but also the feet that kick it away as it rolls on the floor. This final image is particularly effective. On the one hand, the picture of the feet desperately kicking away the loathsome object renders the barons' horror far more realistic than any account of their feelings could ever hope to do. On the other hand, it brings the temporarily forgotten background back into our ken. To be sure, the illumination is dim, but it is sufficient to impress upon us the fact that the action we have just witnessed has taken place in a crowded hall where it has interrupted a New Year celebration. Furthermore, the reaction of the barons who have just returned into the picture is precisely the same as ours, so that we are no longer mere spectators; we are, in effect, emotionally drawn into the picture ourselves for a brief instant.

In short, the decapitation scene in *Sir Gawain and the Green Knight* consists of a series of pictures organized so as to emphasize the most strikingly suggestive details. Anyone at all familiar with the technical aspects of the cinematograph will realize that the organization of these pictures may be expressed in the terms of the cameraman's work without making a single alteration. In order, we have (1) a general, uniformly illuminated view of the entire cast and setting (the barons' consultation); (2) a series of individual pictures of the principal protagonists (Arthur, Gawain, the Green Knight); (3) a progressive close-up of the most significant detail on the object of the decapitation (the Green Knight's neck); (4) a progressive close-up of the most significant detail on the agent of the decapitation (the edge of the blade); and (5) an enlarging view of the result of the decapitation (the head rolling down) with inclusion of details reminiscent of the general view at the beginning of the scene (the feet kicking the head). It is significant that the reader's emotional reaction to the episode is the result of an entirely *visual* experience. From the line where the Green Knight prepares himself for the trial to the line where his head rolls on the floor, the poet neither glosses the action nor allows his protagonists to vent their feelings.

The technique discussed above is found elsewhere in the poem as well. In particular, the well-known episode of the hunting of the boar lends itself to the very same analysis as the beheading of the Green Knight. Here, the frame narrows swiftly from a general view of the boar at bay surrounded by dogs and men (1450) to a close-up of the very point of an arrow breaking itself upon his hide (1459). Throughout the poem, one detects a constant striving for what is in effect the primary concern of the cinematograph: the effective use of both space and motion. We find this concern clearly exemplified in Gawain's ride through a weirdly desolate forest of gigantic oaks (740) and in his first sight of Bercilak's castle, seen through the very same branches (765) which we have so often found on either side of the cinematographic screen under similar circumstances. The extent of that concern may be inferred from a passage in what is perhaps the most familiar episode of the poem: Gawain's third temptation by Bercilak's wife. Bent upon love-making, the lovely lady enters the room where the knight is asleep. But she does not immediately wake him up. Instead, she goes to the window, opens it, and stands there very lightly clad and perfectly framed in the sunlight, for Gawain—and the reader—to look at from the comparative darkness of the room (1740). It is significant that the comparison of relevant passages in the poem and in the analogues suggested by Sir Frederic Madden, Martha Carey Thomas, George Lyman Kittredge, and others likewise suggests a strong concern with the visual element on the part of the *Gawain* poet.

Obviously, one will find in other works isolated instances of the descriptive technique which I have termed "cinematographic," but one is unlikely to find it used anywhere with the same consistency. A remotely similar claim has been made by Joseph Frank for Flaubert's *Madame Bovary*, but a consideration of the two works merely emphasizes the extent to which the technique in question is used in *Sir Gawain*.

In conclusion, the analogy of the cinematograph allows us an insight into a hitherto neglected aspect of descriptive technique in *Sir Gawain and the Green Knight*. The very consistency with which that technique is used suggests in the *Gawain* poet an exceptionally fine sense of space distribution as well as an unmatched talent for transferring a visual experience into a poetic utterance. Indeed, the successful handling of a device which seems mere matter of course to an age familiar with the visual and animated medium of the cinematograph, represents a singular achievement when executed verbally by a poet whose only example was his mind's eye.[1]

MARIE BORROFF

[The Challenge Episode: A Stylistic Interpretation][†]

The entrance on the scene of the Green Knight is brilliantly handled. Lines 136–50, like the lines analyzed earlier, are composed in the traditional style of alliterative poetry, although they are somewhat less conventional in phraseology.[1] The words used in the two passages are similar; the proportion of traditional poetic words is small in both, and there is in both a small group of obscure words which turn out to be either distinctively poetic (*rekenly, fade*) or distinctively colloquial (*glaum, enker*), so far as the available evidence enables us to determine. But the two passages differ significantly in effect, and the tradition is utilized in the later passage in a different way.

---

1. Quotations from *Sir Gawain and the Green Knight* are from the edition by J. R. R. Tolkien and E. V. Gordon (Oxford: 1930). Other quotations and specific references are to the following texts, listed in the order in which they appear my text: Gaston Paris, *Histoire Littéraire de la France* (Paris: 1888), XXX, 73; George Lyman Kittredge, *A Study of Gawain and the Green Knight* (Cambridge, Mass: 1916), p. 3; Fernand Mossé, *Manuel de l'Anglais du Moyen Age: Moyen Anglais* (Paris: 1949), I, 268; Albert C. Baugh, *A Literary History of England* (New York: 1948), p. 236; Bernhard ten Brink, *History of English Literature*, trans. H. M. Kennedy (New York: 1899), I, 347; Emile Pons, *Sire Gauvain et le Chevalier Vert* (Paris: 1936), p. 15; Francis Berry, "Sir Gawayne and the Grene Knight", in *The Age of Chaucer*, ed. Boris Ford (London: 1954), p. 149; Eric Auerbach, *Mimesis*, trans. Willard Trask (New York: 1957), p. 9; Joseph Frank, "Spatial Forms in Modern Literature". *Sewanee Review,* Spring, Summer, and Autumn, 1945.

† From *Sir Gawain and the Green Knight: A Stylistic and Metrical Study*. Yale Studies in English, Vol. 152 (New Haven, Conn.: Yale University Press, 1962), pp. 110–29. Reprinted by permission.

1. A comparison between the number of parallels cited for lines 39–53 and those cited for lines 136–50 will show this clearly. Some of the key words of the latter passage, such as *sware, lyndes, etayn, muckel, smale,* and *folȝande,* are of infrequent occurrence in the extant alliterative poems; *womb* usually refers to women in childbirth or the belly to be filled with food, rather than to part of the human body as a visible form.

We may think of the poet, at the moment he is about to introduce the Green Knight, as faced with a problem of reference. The point of view in the narrative has so far been that of the company at Arthur's court, who are about to be confronted with a being of a sort completely unfamiliar and unpredictable. To refer to this being as a "Green Knight" at the outset would be to forego part of the suspense, part of the dramatic excitement which attends the gradual revelation of his identity and nature. What the poet does is to refer to him at first obliquely, as a *noise*. (He uses the same device in a more literal way at the moment of the Green Knight's second entrance: "Þene herde [Gawain] of þat hyȝe hil, in a harde roche, / Biȝonde þe broke, in a bonk, a wonder breme noyse," 2199–2200.) In doing this he takes advantage of the now rare meaning "an agreeable or melodious sound" (*OED* s.v. *noise* sb. sense 5). *Þe noyce* referred to in line 134 is the music of trumpets, pipes, and drums accompanying the serving of the first course, which, though loud, was delightful (cf. line 120). The *noyse* associated with the Green Knight, however, is of a different sort; it is indeed *ful newe,* so far as the life at court depicted in the earlier stanzas of the poem is concerned, and the implications of discord in the word will soon be fully realized.

In the first description of the Green Knight the poet creates a minor effect of climax by withholding the word naming the stranger's color until the end of the last line of the wheel. Thereafter, *grene* is used again and again. The word *kniȝt*, however, is not used with reference to him by the narrator until line 377, or about 140 lines later, and even here he is called "þe knyȝt in þe grene," the phrase "þe grene knyȝt" appearing first in line 390. Actually, there is justifiable doubt whether the visitor *is* a knight in the specific sense of that word. He is not dressed as one (cf. lines 203–204), nor is he carrying shield or spear (205). In 228 "To knyȝteȝ he kest his yȝe" he seems to be differentiated from the group of actual knights, and the synonyms used to refer to him (*freke* 149, 196, *gome* 151, *haþel* 221, 234, *wyȝe* 249, 252, etc.) thus mean "man, warrior" in a very general way, *freke* being of course especially ambiguous. The court's difficulty in identifying him is clearly brought out in the interchange between him and King Arthur. At first, Arthur addresses him simply as *wyȝe* (252) and invites him to dismount and stay, while obviously not knowing what sort of person he is or what he wants. The Green Knight in answering brings out the fact that he does own knightly weapons and could have brought them if he had wished to (268–70). Arthur, as if to remedy the error of identification, at once addresses him as "sir cortays knyȝt" (276). At the same time he attempts to place him within the world of the court by suggesting that he is seeking single combat in the traditional sense, this having been one of the possibilities suggested earlier in the poem (96–99).

In the first direct reference to the Green Knight (136) both the noun and the verb have implications of great interest. A priori, the logical choice for the noun might have seemed to be *wyȝt*. In Middle English this word had not only the meaning "a human being, man or woman" (*OED* s.v. *wight* sb. sense 2)—it is used by the poet to refer to the lady in line 1792—but "a living being in general" (s.v. sense I); and it was often applied to supernatural beings (sense Ib). But *mayster,* the poet's actual choice, is certainly much better.[2] As was pointed out above, *mayster* is used in alliterative poetry to refer to men, as a rule to men who are not warriors. But in addition to this general meaning, it has a host of more specific meanings which *wyȝt* does not have and which give it positive suggestions of great value. It differs, in fact, from all other words referring to persons in its associations with practical superiority, authority, and dominating or manipulating roles of various sorts in the real world. *Master* was used in the language of everyday communication to refer to persons having authority or competence not only in learning (*OED* s.v. *master* sb.[1] sense 12) but in such realms as government (sense 1), seamanship (sense 2), carpentry (cf. sense 14), and so on. (Cf. also sense 7: "One who has the power to control, use, or dispose of something at will.") The word thus leaves the Green Knight's identity open to doubt as *kniȝt* would not have done, while strongly implying the domineering role he is to play in the episode that follows.

The use of *hales* in this line, as in line 458, is comparatively rare in alliterative poetry. Of the meanings cited by the *OED* (s.v. *hale* v.[1]), the closest is "to move along as if drawn or pulled . . . hasten, rush; spec. of a ship, to proceed before the wind with sails set" (sense 4). *Gawain* 136 is cited; the other uses all refer to ships.[3] *Hale* also had the meaning "to flow, run down in a large stream," as in *Pearl* 125, and in this meaning survives in modern Scots and Northern dialects (s.v. sense 4b). Colloquial status for the nautical meaning is evidenced by the seventeenth- and eighteenth-century quotations in the *OED*. The metaphorical use of *hale* for the coming of the Green Knight on his horse thus suggests powerful and continuous motion.

2. To change *mayster* to *wyȝt* would presumably have involved recasting the line, since *wyȝt* seems always to occur within the line; cf. *Morte Arthure,* ed. Erik Björkman, Alt-und mittelenglische Texte 9 (Heidelberg, 1915), 959; *The Siege of Jerusalem,* ed. Eugen Kölbing and Mabel Day, Early English Text Society 188 (London, 1932), 348. In *Joseph of Arimathie,* ed. W. W. Skeat, Early English Text Society 44 (London, 1871), 196, 197, it occurs, with questionable meaning, within the line but does not alliterate.

3. *Hales* is cited 2x in the glossary of *The Wars of Alexander* (ed. W. W. Skeat, Early English Text Society Extra Series 47; London, Trübnen, 1886) in the meanings "to rush," "to draw quickly, come" (in both cases referring to a human being): lines 962 and 2817. The earliest meaning, according to *The Oxford English Dictionary* is "to draw or pull along . . . esp. with force or violence," which is cited from Lawman (s.v. *hale* v.[1] sense 1b). The intransitive senses developed later and the application to persons is apparently figurative and limited to poetry.

The third word in the line that describes the Green Knight, the
adjective *aghlich*, does not belong to the traditional diction of alliterative poetry; hence it does not have an established elevated meaning
like that of, for example, *kyd*. As with other words expressing fearfulness, its quality will depend directly on the context in which it is used
(cf. "a dreadful cold," "a dreadful catastrophe"; "an awful thought [of
Doomsday]," "an awful thought [of having left theatre tickets at
home]," etc.). Since the noun it modifies refers to real people rather
than to monsters or supernatural beings, and since the diction of the
line in general is colloquial, *aghlich* suggests the startling or even
frightening impact of a powerful presence suddenly appearing out of
nowhere; but it does not imply stark terror or solemn awe.

The statement of the Green Knight's entrance is thus made in
realistic rather than grandiose or exaggerated terms, and the poet's
method in describing the person of the Green Knight in the lines
that follow is a realistic and direct method. The passage contrasts in
this respect with that analyzed earlier, and the difference between
them is revealed with particular clarity if one examines the metrical
use of the descriptive adjectives in each. Compare, for instance, lines
50–54 of stanza 3:

> With all þe wele of þe worlde þay woned þer samen,
> Þe most kyd knyȝteȝ vnder Krystes seluen,
> & þe louelokkest ladies þat euer lif haden,
> & he þe comlokest kyng þat þe court haldes;
> For al watȝ þis fayre folk in her first age

with lines 137–41 of stanza 7:

> On þe most on þe molde on mesure hyghe;
> Fro þe swyre to þe swange so sware & so þik,
> & his lyndes & his lymes so longe & so grete,
> Half etayn in erde I hope þat he were;
> But mon most I algate mynn hym to bene

In the first group of lines only one adjective occurs in final position,
and this adds little to the content of the line. The assertions of ideal
quality are parallel and categorical; the essential meanings are carried by alliterating qualitative adjectives. In the second group of
lines three adjectives occur in final position; two of these, *hyghe* and
grete, although they do have abstract and idealizing meanings, are
here used concretely to refer to physical dimensions. The specific
details in lines 138–39 systematically bear out the general statement
in line 137. The size of the Green Knight's torso is measured from
throat to groin; then the size of "his lyndes & his lymes" is described.
In view of the carefully managed ordering of the details, *lymes*
should be interpreted as meaning "legs" (the word is cited by the

OED in this meaning from Mandeville's *Travels,* c1400, s.v. *limb* sb.[1] sense 2b), since the gigantic stature of the Knight would depend on the combined length of his torso and his legs.

But the narrator does not depend, as in the earlier passage, on the sheer intensity of his statements to impress the reader. The details he presents validate a clause of result, and the judgment is carefully qualified: "Half etayn in erde I hope þat he were; / Bot mon most I algate mynn hym to bene" (140–41). Again one is reminded by contrast of *Morte Arthure,* in which the description of the giant concludes with the statement

> Who þe lenghe of þe lede lelly accountes,
> Fro þe face to þe fote [he] was fyfe fadom lange.
>   [1102–03]

If the *Gawain*-poet does not wish to make the Green Knight monstrous in size, neither does he wish to make him repellent. He now praises his comeliness of form, but it should be noted that *myriest,* which here alliterates in an extended meaning, is substantiated by the details that follow as the superlatives in stanza 3 are not. The *OED* cites an entry from *Promptorium Parvulorum* (s.v. *stern* a. sense 4b) which seems almost designed as a gloss for *sturne* 143: "sterne, or dredful in syghte, terribilis, horribilis." Perhaps "formidable" would be a good modern equivalent. *Clene* 146 is not qualitative; it merely intensifies the meaning of *folȝande* 145 (see the *OED* s.v. *clean* adv. sense 5, "wholly"). The style of this passage is thus much more direct and down to earth than that of stanza 3. The meanings of most of the poetic and elevated words it contains are peripheral—*on þe molde, in erde.* The important meanings are expressed in colloquial and graphic language. The result is that the Green Knight materializes for us as the "kyd knyȝtes" and "louely ladies" did not. And his presence looms physically upon the scene with far more force as a result of a description tied to reality than it would have if the poet had presented him in grandiose and absolute terms.

The same technique is used again and again. As the Knight awaits the blow from Arthur's hand, he stands "herre þan ani in þe hous by þe hede & more" (333). His fearfulness as a potential opponent is expressed in relative terms: "Hit semed as no mon myȝt / Vnder his dyntteȝ dryȝe" (201–202). The phrasing is of course peculiarly appropriate to the ordeal Gawain must later undergo at his hand. The poet, in fact, seems to have inverted the traditional phrase "dele a dint" (Oakden, 2, 277) and created a formulaic linking of *dryȝe* and *dint* for the purposes of this poem. When Gawain is about to depart, the court grieves that one as worthy as he should "wende on þat ernde, / To dryȝe a delful dynt, & dele no more / wyth bronde" (559b–61). The most triumphant taunt the Green Knight utters takes the same

comparative form. After Gawain has flinched at the first feint of the
ax, the Green Knight exclaims that he had not flinched under the
same circumstances, "Wherfore þe better burne me burde be called /
þer-fore" (2278–79).

Assuming that style in narrative poetry manifests itself as the narrating "I"—the fictional being, implied by the language of the poem, by
whom the events are reported—let us assess the role of the narrator of
Gawain in the Challenge Episode, beginning with a summary of the
events themselves. The Green Knight rushes into the court during the
banquet and opens parley rudely, demanding to know which of those
present is the king. The court is frightened at his supernatural appearance, but Arthur speaks. The challenge is presented and at first the
court is silent. At this the Green Knight jeers; then Arthur accepts the
challenge, but Gawain requests that he be allowed to take his place.
The request is granted and he beheads the Knight, who picks up his
head and departs, after explaining how Gawain is to go about finding
him in a year's time.

   Given these events as the material of the story, the particular form
they will take—and this is true of all reporting, whether in life or in
fiction—will depend on who is narrating them, his attitudes, his interests, and his sympathies. In addition it will depend on the way his
mind and imagination work: any story can be told by one person
methodically, by another in random fashion, by one person in detail,
by another sketchily, and so on. The events, as mediated by the narrator, cease to be material; they are realized. Story becomes plot. The
story of the Challenge Episode could be made into a number of different plots. It could, for example, be treated as an adventure in which
the courage and courtesy of Arthur's court were demonstrated in an
encounter with the supernatural. This statement, however, would
constitute an inaccurate summary of the plot as we have it in *Gawain*.
Rather, the Challenge Episode appears to us as a series of humilia-
tions and discomfitures for the court which we feel as more comic
than tragic. Despite the fact that the challenge is successfully met,
the Green Knight departs from the scene as the victor in a kind of psychological warfare.

   His overwhelming presence throughout the episode results in part
from the simple fact that whereas he is described at length and in the
minutest detail, neither Arthur nor any of his knights is described at
all. The only detail of personal description prior to the entrance of the
Green Knight is the reference to Guenevere's *yȝen gray* (82). Five
lines plus the bob are devoted to the canopy and carpets surrounding
her, and a little later on, nine lines plus the bob to the dishes served at
the banquet. But the narrator goes into a lavish account of the Green
Knight's size, figure, dress, accouterments, horse, coiffure, beard, and

ax. It is much as if, in a group painting, one figure were drawn in the style of a Dürer engraving and the others sketched in a few lines. The Green Knight continues to receive the largest share of the narrator's attention throughout the events that follow. The fact that he has much more to say than anyone else aids in making his presence powerfully felt. This, of course, is not the narrator's responsibility (he reports all speeches verbatim); but the actions and gestures of the Green Knight are also given much more space than those of Arthur and the court.

After the challenge is delivered, for example, the narrator begins by telling of the reaction of the assembly:

> If he hem stowned vpon fyrst, stiller were þanne
> Alle þe hered-men in halle, þe hyȝ & þe loȝe
> [301–02]

There follow six lines of description, leading to the jeering speech which in a sense constitutes the climax of the episode: we are told how the Green Knight rolled his eyes, bent his brows, and wagged his beard and coughed as a preliminary to speaking. When Arthur accepts the challenge, two lines describe his handling of the ax (330–31), but these are followed by six lines plus the bob, describing the Green Knight's bold confrontation of the expected blow. When Gawain in his turn takes the ax and accomplishes the beheading, four lines are devoted to the Green Knight's gestures of preparation (417–20), six to Gawain's act of striking (421–26), but thirty-three (427–59) to the Green Knight's actions after the head falls. The picking up of the head, the final instructions, and the departure could have been dealt with in half as much space; instead, the narrator tells us of the rolling of the head among the beholders' feet, the glistening of the blood on the green clothing, the "ugly body that bled," and the head's lifting up its eyelids and "speaking with its mouth." The Green Knight continues to dominate the scene ("Moni on of hym had doute," 442) even though the blow he requested has been struck; and the loss of his head is, in fact, dealt with in the narration in such a way that through it he becomes more terrifying than ever. The king and Gawain begin to laugh (463–64) only after the sound of the green horse's hoofs has died away.

The material of the narrative, from the beginning of the poem on, is presented in such a way that certain relationships are tacitly emphasized, those which in another treatment of the same material might have been played down or suppressed altogether. One such relationship appears in what may be considered the first discomfiture of the court by the Green Knight, a discomfiture made possible by the fact that the king is not in his place at table. The narrator's account of the reasons for this behavior has been discussed in detail, and it has been shown that he takes pains to emphasize the part played in it by sheer youthful restlessness. Because Arthur is not in his place, the Green Knight can ask "Wher is þe gouernour of þis gyng?" (224–25) instead of greeting the head of the household as a preliminary to the delivery of the challenge. His question implies, moreover, that the king does not stand out from the rest in appearance or manner. And it is ambiguously, if not rudely, worded (*gyng* is cited by the OED from early Middle English on not only in the meaning "the retinue of a great personage" but "in depreciatory sense: a crew, rabble," s.v. *ging*, sb. senses 2, 3c). The minor humiliation undergone by Arthur in not being recognized is thus tacitly presented as deserved. It is the appropriate outcome of his youthful behavior, his *child-gered* mannerism. And this behavior in turn is a manifestation of the youthfulness of the court itself, which was earlier described as being in its "first age." The ironic reversal of this detail of the opening description is fully accomplished when the Green Knight, scoffing at the idea of meeting any one of them in single combat, says "Hit arn aboute on þis bench bot berdleȝ chylder" (280).

In a sense the coming of the Green Knight is the exact fulfillment of Arthur's desires as stated earlier. Here indeed is "sum mayn meru-ayle, þat he myȝt trawe" (94), and it is later "breued . . . ful bare / A meruayl among þo menne" (465–66). But what Arthur had been waiting for was not the marvel itself, but "of sum auenturus þyng an vncouþe tale . . . of alderes, of armes, of oþer auenturus" (93, 95). (*Alder* here surely is the traditional archaic-poetic word meaning "chief, prince or ruler" rather than the more colloquial word "elder."[4]) If someone actually came to the court, it was to be a warrior asking to "join in jousting" with one of his knights. With these expectations the Green Knight is utterly at variance, and his coming produces all the discord foretold by the initial reference to him as "anoþer noyse ful newe." His uncouth appearance and attire have already been discussed, and his manners are unconventional as well. The *gomen* he proposes is unheard of as a mode of knightly combat. It deprives Gawain of the use of sword and shield and involves a humiliating passivity, an inhibition of natural response and action. The Green Knight does in fact descend upon the court with all the irresistible force of a torrent or a ship in full sail, as the metaphorical verb *hales* implies. The implications of the reference to him as *an aghlich mayster* are fully realized. The physical paralysis and silence of the court, even the

---

4. *Alder* "chief, ruler," derives from old English *ealdor*, Anglian *aldor; alder* "elder" from old English *ieldra*, Anglian *œldra (eldra)*. J. R. R. Tolkien and E. V. Gordon (eds., *Sir Gawain and the Green Knight*; London: Oxford University Press, 1930) give the former derivation, Sir Israel Gollancz, Mabel Day, and Mary S. Serjeantson (eds., *Sir Gawain and the Green Knight*, Early English Text Society 210; London, 1940) the latter. See *The Oxford English Dictionary alder* sb.[2] and *elder* a. and sb.[3]

courteous behavior and quiet courage of the king and Gawain, are
overwhelmed by the blustering, rude speeches, the overbearing manner and vigorous gestures, the loud laughter, and the undaunted self-
possession, even when headless, of the Green Knight.

With all this, the narrator continues to play his time-honored role,
to express, in the words and phrases in which the details are presented, the traditional attitudes of respect and solemnity. Arthur's
knights are referred to as *siker knyȝtes* (96), as *aþel frekes* (241), as
burnes (337), as *renkkeȝ* (432), as the *fre meny* (101), as the *ryche*
(362); Arthur himself is "*þe stif kyng*" (107) and "*þe derrest on þe
dece*" (445). Whatever the relationship between these appellations
and descriptions and the facts being narrated, they keep their face
value, so to speak, in implying the narrator's manner. At one point,
indeed, he explicitly defends the court against the imputation of
cowardice. "I deme hit not al for doute" (246), he says, when the
court is too frightened to answer the question as to the whereabouts
of their king:

> Bot sum for cortaysye
> Let hym þat al schulde loute
> Cast vnto þat wyȝe.[5]   [247–49]

But their silence, prior to this statement, has been the subject of an
expanded and emphatic description (242–45), and the form of the
defensive statement makes the element of opinion intrusive. "I am
sure some of them refrained out of courtesy" is actually less
emphatic than "Some of them refrained out of courtesy."

It has already been seen that in the interaction between narrative
material and narrative style, the traditional alliterative phraseology is
sometimes significantly modified. "Bold on bent" becomes "hardy on
hille"; "stif in stour" becomes "stif in stalle." But the traditional phrases
themselves may take on an enhanced value as a result of the circumstances of the narration. Such a phrase, in the Challenge Episode, is
"burne on bench." This is listed by Oakden as traditional in alliterative poetry (2, 268, s.v. "baroun upon benche"). In origin it is a conventional mode of reference to the retainers at a banquet, and as such
doubtless antedates the Middle English period (cf. *Beowulf* 1013a
"Bugon þa to bence"—i.e. "went to the banquet-hall"). The phrase is
alluded to in the Green Knight's statement "Hit arn aboute on þis
bench bot berdleȝ chylder" (280). The knights are literally seated, as
is brought out in 242–43 "& al stouned at his steuen, & stonstil seten
/ In a swoghe-sylence þurȝ þe sale riche." It is Arthur, the only one

---

5. *Bot*, which begins line 248 in the MS, would seem to be an erroneous repetition, the eye
   of the scribe having presumably been caught by initial *bot* in the line preceding. The repetition of unstressed words (though usually within a single line) is one of the types of
   scribal error most prevalent in the *Gawain*-MS; cf., in *Gawain*, lines 95, 182, 1137, etc.

standing, who answers the challenge, and when he prepares to strike
the Green Knight with the ax, the latter awaits him as calmly as if
"any burne vpon bench hade broȝt hym to drynk / of wyne" (337–38).
Gawain then tacitly defends the posture of the court by asking permission to rise: "Wolde ȝe, worþilych lorde . . . Bid me boȝe fro þis
benche & stonde by yow þere . . . I wolde com to your counseyl"
(343–44, 347). And Gawain defends his fellow knights by alluding to
another phrase, phonetically similar but of contrasting significance. It
is not seemly, he continues, that the king should undertake the adventure "whil mony so bolde yow aboute vpon bench sytten" (351); there
are none stouter of purpose under heaven, "ne better bodyes on bent
þer baret is rered" (353). But Gawain's courtesy does not serve
entirely to dispel the passive implications of the former phrase.

The narrator of *Gawain,* we may safely say, is richly conscious of
the disparity between the reputation for valor and warlike prowess of
Arthur's knights and what actually takes place when the Green
Knight thrusts himself upon them. But this does not imply that his
attitude toward them involves either hostility or contempt. Because
he has avoided emphasis on material luxury and worldly power in
his depiction of the life of the court, the Challenge Episode is not
seen as a rebuke to arrogance or sensual self-indulgence. Arthur and
his knights are charmingly youthful and joyous; their pleasures are
innocent. And although it is overshadowed by the more conspicuous
presence of the Green Knight, Gawain's behavior is exquisitely courteous. His self-possession in requesting that the adventure be allotted to him and in actually dealing the blow indicates clearly that he,
at least, had refrained from speaking "for cortaysye" (247) rather
than out of fear. In such a passage as 366–71,

> Þen comaunded þe kyng þe knyȝt for to ryse;
> & he ful radly vp ros, & ruchched hym fayre,
> Kneled doun bifore þe kyng, & cacheȝ þat weppen;
> & he luflyly hit hym laft, & lyfte vp his honde,
> & gef hym Goddeȝ blessyng, & gladly hym biddes
> Þat his hert & his honde schulde hardi be boþe,

there is no ironic disparity between the implications of the traditional adverbs *radly* "with (courteous or befitting) promptness" and
luflyly "graciously, in a manner worthy of approval" and the circumstances of the action. Gawain's manner here fully validates the epi-
thet "þe hende," bestowed on him by the narrator when he is talking
to the Green Knight a moment later.

✳   ✳   ✳

The above-discussed features of style manifest themselves in the
poem as what might be called the characteristic mode of imagination

of the narrating "I," who is here also the narrating "eye." In general, the narrator of *Gawain* tends to imagine agents and objects as they assume particular relationships within a limited space (and in limited time). He tends also to adopt the point of view of the character central in a given narrative passage as that character responds to the circumstances of the action. The result is vividness, but it is vividness of a special kind. When it is visual, it depends as much on the exact appropriateness of what is seen, by whom, and from where, as on the color, texture, or other intrinsic sensory or aesthetic qualities of the object. It is the vividness of the frozen stream that "henged he3e ouer [Gawain's] hede in hard ysse-ikkles" (732), rather than of those streams that "thro' wavering lights and shadows broke, / Rolling a slumbrous sheet of foam below" in the landscape of "The Lotos-Eaters." In recognizing the dramatic implications of the successive details of the narrative, the reader is pulled in imagination into the world of the poem, and experiences it as a reality.

In the Challenge episode, as later in the poem, the narrator's attitude toward the hero is one of affection. And in this episode Gawain shows himself superior to the rest of the court (the king excepted) in his response to an unfamiliar, trying, and seemingly dangerous situation. As a result of this response, he is to be singled out for sore trials of chastity, of courtesy, and finally of courage. In the first there is no real question of failure. The second, conducted concomitantly by the lady in the bedchamber scenes, is the more subtle, the more suspenseful, and the more amusing of the two, though the hero's courtesy, like his chastity, is successfully maintained throughout. It is in the third that, showing himself less hero than human, he falls short, and as a result, abandons courtesy too for a few moments in an acrimonious outburst of antifeminism. In the account of these trials, as in that of the Challenge episode, the elements of discomfort, frustration, and annoyance inherent in each situation will be realized to the full, and the extent to which Gawain falls short of the ideal, by implication, clearly defined. But through it all, the narrator's time-honored attitudes of solemnity and deference—mixed with a genuinely felt affection—will be maintained.

This story and the way it is told—the "what" and the "how" of the narration—must, for the purposes of a study of style, be considered as two different things. The historical study of style reveals that in *Sir Gawain and the Green Knight,* the verbal expression of the story is thoroughly traditional, to an extent that is more and more fully apparent as one becomes more familiar with the other extant works belonging to the same tradition. But in *Gawain* the traditional features of style do not serve the traditional purposes. They become devices for the production of an effect in which the narrator—the presiding, interpreting "I," with his emotions and attitudes, his manner, and his particular mode of imaginative perception—is all-important. In the last analysis what this narrator has to tell and the way in which he chooses to tell it are one.

✳   ✳   ✳

J. A. BURROW

[Recognition and Confession at the Green Chapel]†

II

I come now to the central episode of the fourth fitt—Gawain's encounter with the Green Knight in the valley of the Green Chapel (II. 2160–2478). This is a long and obviously very important scene, and it will be convenient to consider it under three separate heads: first as a *recognition* scene, then as a *confession* scene and last as a *judgment* scene.

Aristotle says that the scene of recognition or 'discovery' is one of the most interesting and affecting parts of a tragedy; and the same can often be said of a romance. A familiar example is the Good Friday episode in Chrétien's *Perceval,* where the hero, after his mysterious visit to the Grail Castle, stays with the hermit and learns from him the identity of the Grail King and the nature of the Grail. The effect of such discoveries, coming after the mysteries and uncertainties of an Arthurian adventure, has been well described by one critic as a 'turning up of the houselights'.[1] This turning up of the lights is an interesting and, for the author, somewhat delicate business. Let us see how the *Gawain*-poet handles it in the present scene.

He opens dramatically, with what might be called a 'false discovery'. Gawain has been told by the guide to look for the Green Chapel on the left-hand side of the path when he gets down to the bottom of the valley; but when he gets there he cannot find it. Instead of whatever a Green Chapel might look like, there is merely a hollow mound or barrow with three holes in it:

> . . . nobot an olde caue,
> Or a creuisse of an olde cragge, he couþe hit noȝt deme
> with spelle.   (2182–84)

---

† From *A Reading of Sir Gawain and the Green Knight* (London: Routledge and Kegan Paul, 1965), pp. 122–133. Reprinted by permission.
1. D. C. Fowler, *Prowess and Charity* (Seattle, 1959), p. 5.

The depreciating colloquial use of 'old' twice in these lines helps to convey the shock of surprise and disappointment which this first discovery occasions.[2] The Green Chapel is not a real chapel at all—or not one of God's. So the 'Knight of the Green Chapel', Gawain at once concludes, cannot be a real knight either—he must be the Devil himself:

> Wel biseme3 þe wy3e wruxled in grene
> Dele here his deuocioun on þe deuele3 wyse.
> Now I fele hit is þe fende, in my fyue wytte3,
> Þat hat3 stoken me þis steuen to strye me here.   (2191–94)

The idea is a plausible one. The fiend does sometimes wear green; he does traditionally live in the 'strange countries' of the North; and he does make contracts and appointments with men in order to 'destroy' them.[3] On the other hand, *Sir Gawain* is a romance, not an 'exemplum'; and the experienced reader is likely to feel dissatisfied with Gawain's explanation. The true discovery, one should feel, is yet to come—as it does, in its proper place, after Gawain has received the Green Knight's return blow and so 'achieved' his adventure.

Even here, though, the poet does not turn up the lights all at once. The discovery is phased, divided into two stages. In the first stage (Bercilak's speech to Gawain immediately after delivering the return blow, ll. 2338–68) Gawain learns what the reader may be presumed to know already—that the Knight of the Green Chapel is identical with the nameless host:

> For hit is my wede þat þou were3, þat like wouen girdel,
> Myn owen wyf hit þe weued, I wot wel for soþe.
> Now know I wel þy cosses, and þy costes als,
> And þe wowyng of my wyf: I wro3t hit myseluen.   (2358–61)

This is for Gawain the crucial discovery, and we shall be concerned later with his reactions to it, which are immediate and violent. But there is nothing particularly new in it for the reader. *His* discovery comes later—in Bercilak's last speech, in fact (ll. 2444–70). By this time Gawain's first access of anger and remorse is spent, and he is

---

2. The colloquial shades of meaning in 'old' are rather elusive. The word is not recorded by the Oxford English Dictionary as an 'expression of familiarity' before Shakespeare. But the use presumably developed from sense 7c ('known or familiar from of old'); and 7c is recorded as early as Alfred. Like Chaucer, the *Gawain*-poet seems often to use 'old' in advanced colloquial senses. All three remaining occurrences of the word in *SGGK* present this possibility: 'þe olde auncian wyf', l. 1001 (a tautology? or *OED* 1c?); 'nobot an olde caue, / Or a creuisse of an olde cragge', ll. 2182–3 (*OED* 3? or 1c?).

3. All three points come out in Chaucer's *Friar's Tale The Works of Geoffrey Chaucer*, ed. F. N. Robinson, 2nd ed., (Boston, 1957): wearing green, III, 1382 (see D. W. Robertson, 'Why the Devil Wears Green', *Modern Language Notes* LXIX (1954), pp. 470–2); living in the north, III, 1413–16 (see Robinson's note—and compare *SGGK*, ll. 406–8 and 455); making a contract, III, 1404–5.

ready to leave for Camelot; but before he leaves he asks the Green
Knight one more question:

> Bot on I wolde yow pray, displeses yow neuer:
> Syn ȝe be lorde of þe ȝonde londe þer I haf lent inne
> Wyth yow wyth worschyp—þe wyȝe hit yow ȝelde
> Þat vphaldeȝ þe heuen and on hyȝ sitteȝ—
> How norne ȝe yowre ryȝt nome, and þenne no more?
>
> (2439–43)

It will be remembered that in the first fitt Gawain asked his challenger
to 'telle me howe þou hattes' (l. 401), and that the latter promised to
reveal 'myn owen nome' (l. 408) and later announced himself as 'þe
Knyȝt of þe Grene Chapel'. But this was a nickname or (in the old
sense) a 'surname'; and Gawain is now asking for more than that—for
the real or 'ryȝt' name. This distinction between nickname and 'right
name' can be illustrated from Malory: 'He was called in the courte of
kynge Arthure Bewmaynes, but his ryght name is sir Gareth of
Orkeney'; 'There was a knyght that was called the Knyght with the
Strange Beste, and at that tyme hys ryght name was called Pellynore';
'Sir La Cote Male Tayle was called otherwyse be ryght sir Brewne le
Noyre'.[4] In each of these cases, as in *Sir Gawain*, the nickname is
a descriptive tag referring to some characteristic feature or activity;
whereas the 'right name' is essentially the given name—though this
will itself usually have some descriptive appendage, as in 'Sir Gareth
of Orkeney' or 'Sir Brewne le Noyre'. The nickname is by its very
nature informative ('Par le *sornon* connoist on l'ome' was what Perceval's mother said); but it is the right name that counts in the end.
Nicknames come and go—and anyway they may, as in *Sir Gawain*, tell
you nothing which you do not know already. So Gawain is not content
to know his host and adversary simply as the Knight of the Green
Chapel. He wants to know his 'ryȝt nome'—who he *really* is.[5]

The Green Knight tells him. His given name is Bercilak; his real
'home' is in the castle where Gawain spent Christmas; and the castle's name is Hautdesert.[6] Hence, not 'the Knight of the Green
Chapel', but 'Bercilak de Hautdesert'. It is perhaps surprising how
much this simple discovery of a name contributes to the 'turning up

---

4. *The Works of Sir Thomas Malory*, ed. E. Vinaver (Oxford, 1947), pp. 350, 77, 476. Compare pp. 299 ('name of ryght'), 328, 329. ('Right name' is not always used in contrast to
   the chivalric nickname. It may mean little more than just 'name'.)
5. Compare the encounter between Lancelot and Perceval in Malory (Vinaver, p. 829).
   Lancelot at first gives his name as 'Le Shyvalere Mafete' (his current nickname); but a
   little later Perceval asks his 'trewe name' (a variant of 'right name'), and Lancelot, having
   in the meantime discovered Perceval's identity, reveals it.
6. 'Hautdesert' is commonly taken to be the name of the Green Chapel (e.g. by Tolkien and
   Gordon in their note to l. 2445), but this is almost certainly wrong. It would be very odd for
   both Bercilak's nickname *and* his right name to contain a reference to the Chapel. One
   would expect the latter to identify his real 'house and home' or ancestral dwelling-place

of the lights'. We feel that we are coming back rapidly to the world of everyday reality—the everyday reality of chivalry and romance, that is. The Green Knight, the nameless host, is known to his neighbours under a perfectly ordinary—if not actually familiar—knightly name:

> Bercilak de Hautdesert I hat in þis londe.   (2445)

But this answer raises other questions. How did this Bercilak come to play the part of the Green Knight? And why? Here again the answers given are conventional and even—so far as the case allows—'realistic'. Morgan le Fay's hatred of Guinevere, Arthur and the Round Table is one of the données of romance—something which, though explanations are to be found in various French sources, is generally taken to need no explanation.[7] Hence she provides the poet with a final and unquestionable answer to the reader's 'why?': 'Because Morgan wanted to humiliate the Knights of the Round Table and frighten Guinevere to death'. It is no more than one would expect from a woman who, in Malory's words, 'did never good but ill'. At the same time, economically, Morgan provides an answer to the other question, 'how?' It is true that we never discover how she could win Bercilak's consent to her schemes (though we would, I think, give Bercilak the benefit of the doubt on this); but we do discover how she managed the scheme itself. Here the poet shows an inclination to rationalize his wonders. He does not rest content, as he might have done, with the well-known fact of Morgan's magic powers. This time he does draw on the further explanations available to him in French tradition.[8] Morgan did not simply have her magic skills; she learnt them from Merlin, 'þat conable klerk'. They are a matter of 'koyntyse of clergye'—and this is, in the fourteenth century, at least a possible explanation of 'illusions' or 'appearances' such as the Green Knight and his returning head. A clerk *might* be able to produce such illusions—as we can see from Chaucer's *Franklin's Tale,* where a young clerk from the University of Orleans is able to do a similar trick: 'thurgh his magik, for a wyke or tweye, / It semed that alle the rokkes were aweye'. It is true that Chaucer treats such 'natural magic' with suspicion. He compares it with the

---

(cf. 'Gareth of Orkeney', etc.); and that is plainly not the Chapel but the Castle. There is no reason why 'Hautdesert' should *not* refer to the Castle. At least two medieval English castles, one in Warwickshire, the other in Staffordshire, were called 'Beaudesert' (i.e. 'beautiful waste (land)'); so there is no need to go to Celtic 'disert' ('hermitage') to explain the second element. See *Place-Names of Warwickshire*, English Place-Name Society, Vol. XIII (1936), p. 199, and *Introduction to the Survey of English Place-Names*, E.P.N.S., Vol. I, Part I (1924), p. 115.

7. On Morgan's hatred of Guinevere, etc., see L. A. Paton, *Studies in the Fairy Mythology of Arthurian Romance* (Boston, 1903), Chap. II.

8. L. A. Paton, *Studies in the Fairy Mythology of Arthurian Romance* (Boston, 1903), p. 226.

work of jugglers or illusionists at feasts, speaks of it as 'a supersti-
cious cursednesse' which 'hethen folk useden in thilke dayes', and
asserts that it is no longer possible in modern times:

> . . . swich folye
> As in oure dayes is nat worth a flye,—
> For hooly chirches feith in oure bileve
> Ne suffreth noon illusioun us to greve.[9]

At the same time he probably thought that (given a non-contemporary
setting) such learned magic provided the only reasonably plausible
explanation available to him—a clerk might be able to do it that way,
after all. It is in this spirit, I think, that one should take the *Gawain*-
poet's stress on Morgan's 'koyntyse of clergye'—as another contribu-
tion to the turning-up of the lights. It leads on, in fact, to the last and
most down-to-earth 'discovery' of all. This follows in the next stanza:

> Þat is ho þat is at home, þe auncian lady;
> Ho is euen þyn aunt, Arþureʒ half-suster,
> Þe duches doʒter of Tyntagelle, þat dere Vter after
> Hade Arþur vpon, þat aþel is nowþe.
> Þerfore I eþe þe, haþel, to com to þy naunt.   (2463–67)

Bercilak does not spare Gawain his last humiliating recognition: that
his real adversary has been, not the Knight of the Green Chapel, or
the Fiend, or even Bercilak de Hautdesert, but—most mundane of
relations—his own aunt. 'þerfore I eþe þe, haþel, to com to þy naunt':
it is not surprising that Gawain refuses the invitation and rides back
to Camelot.

I want now to consider Gawain's encounter under my second head,
as a *confession* scene. This means looking at that part of the episode,
so far not touched on, which lies between Bercilak's two speeches of
explanation; for this section (ll. 2369 ff.) is specially rich in penitential
matter—indeed it follows closely the actual order of the confessional.

It is Bercilak's first discovery speech which sets things in motion
here. He reveals that the exchange of winnings played a part in the
test—indeed, almost *was* the test—and Gawain consequently real-
izes for the first time the significance of his failure on the third day.
His reaction is strong:

> Þat oþer stif mon in study stod a gret whyle,
> So agreued for greme he gryed withinne;
> Alle þe blode of his brest blende in his face,
> Þat al he schrank for schome þat þe schalk talked.
>   (2369–72)

---

9. The *Works of Geoffrey Chaucer*, ed. F. N. Robinson, 2nd ed., (Boston, 1957), V, 1131–4.

Shame and mortification ('greme') may not be enough in itself to make up the contrition required by theologians in the sacrament of penance; but Gawain is clearly better 'disposed' here than he was during his formal confession to the priest at Hautdesert, where the poet failed to allow any expression of contrite feeling whatsoever. For what he evinces is at worst, one might say, the secular equivalent of contrition; and he may therefore claim to satisfy, in a sense, the first condition laid down by Bromyard for a proper 'disposition' ('quod doleat commissa'). In the same sense, he goes on to satisfy the second condition ('quod restituat ablata') when, in the following lines, he returns the girdle to its rightful owner:

> Þenne he kaȝt to þe knot, and þe kest lawseȝ,
> Brayde broþely þe belt to þe burne seluen.   (2376–77)

The style of the gesture is quite unsacramental; yet what Gawain is doing here is something which he should have done and, again, did not do as part of his confession at Hautdesert. It is, in its way, an act of restitution (though a tardy one), coming as a response to the moral drawn by Bercilak in the previous stanza:

> Trwe mon trwe restore,
> Þenne þar mon drede no waþe.   (2354–55)

'A true man must make faithful restitution—then he need fear no danger.'

The second 'act' of the confessional after 'contrition of heart' is 'confession of mouth'; and this stage too (or a secular equivalent of it) is easily recognized in the present case, when Gawain, after restoring the girdle, sets about analyzing his fault:

> For care of þy knokke cowardyse me taȝt
> To acorde me with couetyse, my kynde to forsake,
> Þat is larges and lewté þat longeȝ to knyȝteȝ.
> Now I am fawty and falce, and ferde haf ben euer
> Of trecherye and vntrawþe: boþe bityde sorȝe
>   and care!
>   I biknowe you, knyȝt, here stylle,
>   Al fawty is my fare.   (2379–86)

'Biknowe' is, with 'shrive', the established equivalent for the loan-word 'confess' in Middle English;[1] and Gawain's speech does in fact deserve to be taken as a formal, considered confession, despite what might at first seem a passionate and haphazard piling-up of moral

---

1. This comes out clearly in the Green Knight's reply, where 'be-knowen' is parallel to 'confessed' (l. 2391). See also *Piers Plowman* B. V. 200 and X. 416 (*The Vision of Piers Plowman II, Text B*, ed. W. W. Skeat, Early English Text Society 38, London, 1869), and *Middle English Dictionary* (University of Michigan Press, 1954) under 'biknouen', 4.

terms. The analysis turns quite specifically on three points and no more—both here and (the consistency is to be noted) in Gawain's two other brief confessional statements (l. 2374–75 and 2506–9). The first point is *cowardice* (ll. 2374, 2379, 2508); the second is *covetousness* (ll. 2374, 2380, 2508), with its traditional opposite 'larges' (l. 2381);[2] the third is *untruth* (ll. 2383, 2509), otherwise called 'trecherye' (l. 2383), with its opposite 'lewté' (l. 2381). In the present passage, furthermore, these three moral ideas are carefully related one to another, articulated into a coherent account of the case as Gawain sees it. The method is essentially allegorical—as indeed one might expect, seeing that the combination of confessional self-analysis and allegorical technique is such a persistent feature of medieval thought and writing. The moral ideas are brought together as if they were people. Consider how easily the passage might be converted into the scenario for an episode in a Morality Play. The hero (Everyman, Mankind, Humanum Genus . . .) has been summoned by Death; but Cowardice promises that he can save him. He is persuaded by Cowardice's arguments and, against his better judgment, goes with him to where his former enemies, Covetousness and Untruth, are waiting to welcome him. He 'accords him' with them and joins their party, leaving his former friends, the virtues Largess and Lewty, to lament his defection. It is a coherent and largely persuasive version of what happened when Gawain agreed to accept the lady's girdle—particularly in the role of 'teacher' assigned to Cowardice. The only difficulty arises from the presence of Covetousness. It is not easy to think of Gawain as covetous: indeed, as we have seen, the poet several times goes out of his way to stress that he was not interested in the gold of the girdle, its workmanship, etc. Yet the fact is that 'covetise' does appear, not only here but also in both the other two confessional statements. I shall return to this difficulty later.

Gawain's speech ends, in the wheel, with a general confession of guilt, a request for penance to be imposed, and a promise of future amendment:

> I biknowe yow, knyȝt, here stylle,
> Al fawty is my fare;
> Leteȝ me ouertake your wylle
> And efte I schal be ware.   (2385–88)

---

2. See *Cursor Mundi* (Fairfax Ms.), ed. R. Morris, Early English Text Society, O. S. 59–99 (London, 1874–92), l. 27404: 'Largesse gaine couaitise is sette'. In the *Castle of Perseverance* (*The Macro Plays: The Castle of Perseverance, Wisdom, Mankind*, ed. M. Eccles, Early English Text Society 262, London, 1969), Covetise fights against 'Lady Largyte'. This is a commonplace.

The line 'Lete3 me ouertake your wylle' could, as Tolkien and Gordon suggest, mean simply 'Let me win your goodwill'; but I would prefer, considering the context, to follow Gollancz here: " 'Let me understand your will", *i.e.* what do you want me to do now? Gawain, having confessed, asks for penance'.[3] Gawain's confession is over, and in the following line he fulfils, though again in a secular style, the third and last condition of a proper disposition ('quod promittat cessare'). The time has therefore come for the last of his 'acts' as a penitent—making satisfaction by penance. The Green Knight's reply, with its explicit use of technical language ('confessed', 'penaunce'), makes it clear that the author understood the situation in this way:

> I halde hit hardily hole, þe harme þat I hade.
> Þou art confessed so clene, beknowen of þy mysses,
> And hat3 þe penaunce apert of þe poynt of myn egge,
> I halde þe polysed of þat ply3t, and pured as clene
> As þou hade3 neuer forfeted syþen þou wat3 fyrst borne.
>   (2390–94)

Bercilak replies to Gawain's request for penance, then, by declaring that, so far as he is concerned, no penance is necessary, since Gawain has already made a clean confession and, what is more, received a wound in the neck. The idea that a contrite confession—besides being necessary in itself—counts towards a man's penance was generally accepted in the Middle Ages;[4] and so, of course, was the idea that bodily mortification might serve to pay off whatever debt of satisfaction remained when the confession was over. Naturally, wounds do not figure in the penance-books among the normal forms of such mortification (hair-shirts, uncomfortable beds, beating of the breast, etc.); but Gawain's cut does admirably all the same. Not only is it physically painful; it is also (unlike a well-concealed hair-shirt) visible to all, and hence a source of mental as well as physical mortification. It is in fact, as Bercilak himself points out, an open or public penance—'penaunce apert'.[5] We may recall, too, that wounds were well-established in Christian tradition as symbols of sin, in part through allegorical readings of the parable of the Good Samaritan. A sinful man is a wounded man. So the cut can, rather like the green

---

3. See the editors' notes to l. 2387. Doing penance is described as 'fulfilling the confessor's will and ordinance' in *Lancelot of the Laik*, ed. M. M. Gray, Scottish Text Society (Edinburgh, 1912), ll. 1420–I. See also *Cursor Mundi* (Fairfax Ms.), l. 26255, for a similar use of 'will'.

4. See Aquinas, *Summa Theologiae*, III, Supplementum, Quaestio VI, Art. I ('per confessionis erubescentiam . . . poena temporalis expiatur'); also *Dictionnaire de Théologie Catholique*, Vol. 13 (Paris, 1936), cols. 938, 954, 957. For a fourteenth-century English statement of the idea, see *The Book of Vices and Virtues* ed. W. N. Francis, Early English Text Society 217, London, 1942, p. 46.

5. Public penance was still practised in the poet's time. See H. C. Lea, *History of Auricular Confession and Indulgences* (London, 1896), Chap. XVI.

belt a little later, function as a 'syngne of surfet'—a symbol of, as well
as a satisfaction for, the hero's act of untruth. We shall see in due
course how the poet exploits this double symbolism of the wound and
the belt in the last part of the poem.

The confession ends, as it should, with Bercilak's 'absolution':

> I halde þe polysed of þat plyȝt, and pured as clene
> As þou hadeȝ neuer forfeted syþen þou watȝ fyrst borne.

The use of 'polysed' to mean 'absolved', or more generally 'cleansed
(of sin)', is paralleled in *Cleanness*:

> So if folk be defowled by unfre chaunce,
> Þat he be sulped in sawle, seche to schryfte,
> And he may polyce hym at þe prest, by penaunce taken,
> Wel bryȝter þen þe beryl oþer browden perles.[6]

The poet does not allow Bercilak to use the proper clerical term
'assoil'; but it is clear that the term which he does allow him is one
itself associated with the sacrament of penance—in the poet's mind,
at least. Notice, too, that Bercilak's next words, 'pured as clene /
As þou hadeȝ neuer forfeted syþen þou watȝ fyrst borne', are a variant
on those used of the priest's absolution, at the end of the Hautdesert
confession:

> And he asoyled hym surely, and sette hym so clene
> As domeȝday schulde haf ben diȝt on þe morn.[7]
>
> (1883–84)

What is the point of Gawain's second confession? How does it fit
in? Two things at least seem fairly obvious. First, it is not a 'real' confession, since Bercilak, being a layman, has no power of absolution.
Bercilak and Gawain are, as it were, playing at confession—though
in very different spirits, Gawain seriously, Bercilak with laughter.
They act it out between themselves, and God enters into the reckoning only insofar as Bercilak plays his part. For it is just Bercilak
who stands to be satisfied by Gawain's contrite confession and
penance: '*I halde* hit hardily hole, þe harme þat *I hade* . . . *I halde* þe
polysed of þat plyȝt'. This being so, we should not expect his 'absolution' to mark a final closing of the accounts—in fact, so far as

---

6. *Cleanness*, ed. R. J. Menner (New Haven, 1920), ll. 1129–32. Compare ll. 1068 and
1134.

7. Compare Bercilak's formula with the following passages: 'I yow assoille . . . as clene and eek
as cleer / As ye were born', *Pardoner's Tale*, *C.T.*, VI, 913–15; 'ȝee are als clene of syn, I
plyghte, / Als þat day borne were ȝee', *Sege of Melayne*, ed. S. J. Herrtage, Early English Text
Society, Extra Series 35 (1880), ll. 908–9; 'Now I haue power and dignyte / For to asoyle þe
as clene / As þou were houen off þe fount-ston', *Athelston*, ed. A. McI. Trounce, Early English Text Society, original series 224 (1951), ll. 676–8. It may well be that the *Gawain*-
poet's other, Doomsday, formula represents a pointed departure from this more common
birth/baptism type.

Gawain is concerned, we shall see that the account remains open, with a debit, to the very end of the poem. On the other hand, one should not neglect the fact that Bercilak *is* satisfied. Gawain's second confession is not 'real', but it is 'right'. He is contrite, he makes restitution, he resolves to sin no more. The play-acting is corrective: it makes good the imperfections of the confession at Hautdesert. For Gawain is only now at the point when he can appreciate both the full demands of 'trawþe' ('Trwe mon trwe restore') and his own failure to satisfy them. He can now see and feel what he could not before, and it is this which counts most for the reader in his scene with Bercilak. Of course, it is nonsense, theologically speaking, for a pretend, secular confession to 'make good' the inadequacies of a real, sacramental one; but here—as the reader will no doubt agree—it is necessary to remind oneself that even the confession at Hautdesert is not *really* real.

* * *

A. KENT HIEATT

Sir Gawain: Pentangle, *Luf-Lace*, Numerical Structure†

Whatever else *Sir Gawain and the Green Knight* may signify, it is certainly about keeping troth. Two novel pieces of evidence for this aspect of the poem are presented here. They possess general and methodological interest in addition to the light that they shed on *Sir Gawain*.

The distinction which J. A. Burrow, in his recent admirable study, draws between the symbolic qualities of the pentangle, or symbol of *trawþe* in this work, and of the *luf-lace*, the girdle of contrary signification, is germane here although the present article opposes it: 'Unlike the pentangle, the belt is not, so far as the poem is concerned, a "natural" symbol. It does not, that is, have any particular symbolic value on the strength simply of its intrinsic natural properties. So while the pentangle is necessarily a token of "trawþe" and could not possibly, in the poet's view, be otherwise, the belt is a token of untruth only because it happened to play the part it did in Gawain's adventure.'[1] Elsewhere, Burrow assigns these two symbols respectively to

---

† From *Silent Poetry: Essays in Numerological Analysis* ed., A. Fowler (New York: Barnes and Noble, 1970), pp. 116–40. Reprinted by permission.
1. *A Reading of Sir Gawain and the Green Knight* (1965), p. 158. Donald R. Howard takes an apparently opposite position (with which also I partly disagree) on the symbolic status of the pentangle. See his 'Structure and Symmetry in Sir Gawain', *Speculum*, xxxix (1964), 426:

the *impositio secundum naturam* and the *impositio ad placitum* or *impositio iuxta arbitrium humanae voluntatis* of fourteenth-century speculative grammarians.[2]

In fact, however, the *Gawain*-poet gives grounds for regarding the *lace* as a natural, not an arbitrary, symbol of imperfection. Its symbolic qualities oppose, but belong to the same class as, those singled out in the pentangle; and the relationship of these two objects is that of a balanced, two-part symbolic structure rather than that of an isolated construct (the pentangle) to a mere narrative motif (the *lace*) to which significance has been arbitrarily attached. That this two-part symbolic structure is likely to be the creation of an author writing a poem about troth is the implication of the first part of this article. The point of the second part is that the author almost surely built a numerical connection between the pentangle as a symbol of troth and important structural features of his poem. It may be that the same holds true for the *lace*. There is all the more reason, then, to think that the poem is mainly about keeping troth.

The explicit use made in *Gawain* of the intrinsic qualities of the pentangle is well known.[3] In the first place, this figure is a sign that 'Salamon set sumquyle / In bytoknyng of trawþe' (ll. 625–26) because each line in it immovably 'umbelappez and loukez in oþer' so that each angle braces all the others and so that the line defining the pentangle is 'endelez' (l. 629) in a sense well known to American school-children, who are taught to draw the five-pointed star of the national flag using only straight lines and never lifting the pencil from the paper. In fact it is called the 'endeles knot' (l. 630). In the same way, Gawain's excellences are said to fit together in an irrefragable and immutable pattern. This pattern had never failed. There had been no point in it to show a special juncture different from the rest ('ne samned neuer', l. 659). It had never broken. Like the pentangle, it had been without end at any angle or point ('noke') (ll. 657–61). In the second place, the pentangle has 5 points, and Gawain had 5 kinds of fivefold excellences, making a total of 25. For these two reasons, the pentangle appears on Gawain's shield in this romance, in red gold upon a red background (ll. 618–20, 662–63), and upon his coat-armour (ll. 637, 2026) against a background of red (l. 2036).

The *luf-lace* is similarly well known. It is a girdle worked in green and gold (l. 1832), with pendants (ll. 2038, 2431). It is a sign of *vntrawþe* (l. 2509)—disloyalty and inconstancy—and also, in Gawain's

---

'The pentangle has an *assigned* symbolic value; it is put into the poem to stand for an abstraction. . . . The shield and girdle, however, take their symbolic meaning from the situation.' As will appear, the disagreements here are mainly semantic.

2. P. 187.

3. All quotations from *Sir Gawain* follow *Sir Gawain and the Green Knight*, ed. J. R. R. Tolkien and E. V. Gordon, 2nd edn, rev., ed. Norman Davis (Oxford, 1968).

opinion, of an ensuing train of peccancy (ll. 2374–75, 2379–83, 2508). Going to his assignation with the Green Knight, he wears it bound twice about him, over the red of the coat-armour with its pentangle. When informed of its true significance, he undoes it and throws it from him, but subsequently wears it back to court, as a baldric, over his right shoulder and knotted under his left arm:

> Abelef as a bauderyk bounden bi his syde,
> Loken vnder his lyfte arme, þe lace, with a knot,
> In tokenyng he watz tane in tech of a faute.
>
> (ll. 2486–88)

Subsequently, the rest of the court adopt this device.

It has often been suggested, of course, that the color green in this *lace* has associations that make it naturally suitable for the principle associated with the Green Knight, or for Gawain's fault. In fact, Burrow himself very properly and subtly takes up the idea at several points.[4] Perhaps the most obvious secular association of green for the fourteenth century was disloyalty in love.[5] The liturgical connection with hope, however, and the other connections with the natural world, with vigor, with the Green Man, or with the recurrence of spring cannot be excluded. Yet none of these associations would justify classing the *lace* as a symbol arising from the *impositio secundum naturam* in the strong sense which holds for the pentangle. There is nevertheless another, more substantial association that makes the *lace* a natural symbol for Gawain's shortcoming.

One important meaning of *lace* (Chaucer's *las, laas*) is the OED's *Lace* 1: 'a net, noose, snare', corresponding to Old French *laz*, Italian *laccio*, and Spanish-American *lasso*, ultimately from Latin *laqueus*, of which the principal meaning is 'noose'.[6] The word is often used figuratively with the general meaning 'snare' or with one of the more specific meanings, in medieval and later verse. Typically, a personified principle or a divinity spreads a *lace* to catch the unsuspecting. Of Venus, for instance, 'Lo, alle thise folk so caught were in hire las, / Til they for wo ful often sayde "allas!"' ('Knight's Tale', *Canterbury Tales*, I, 1951–52); 'But Love had broght this man in swich a

---

4. E.g., pp. 14–17.
5. For the association of green with love, see, for instance, 'The Squire's Tale', *Canterbury Tales*, V. 646–7; the ballade 'Against Women Unconstant' ('Madame, for your newfangelnesse'), attributed to Chaucer in the *Works*, ed. F. N. Robinson, 2nd edn (1957), p. 540; and J. Huizinga, *De Herfsttij der Middeleeuwen*, 2nd edn (Haarlem, 1928), pp. 397–8. See also the English translation, *The Waning of the Middle Ages* (New York, 1954), p. 120, which, however, omits all footnote citations.
6. See *Oxford English Dictionary* and Walther von Wartburg, *Französisches etymologisches Wörterbuch* (Basel, 1950), 180 (*laqueus*, 'schlinge'). For purposes of this article, Wartburg's citation of Norman *mettre dans le là*, 'tromper', and Jersey *sous vos lâs*, 'sous votre puissance', are interesting. See also, in connection with 'love-lace', his Middle French, Modern French *lacs d'amour*, 'cordons repliés sur eux-mêmes de manière à former un 8 couché'. See also the OED's citations for *Lace* v. 1. 'to catch in, or as in, a noose or snare'.

rage, / And him so narwe bounden in his las' (Legend of Good Women, ll. 599–600); 'Women the haveth in hire las' (King Alisaundre, l. 7698); 'him þat bound is in loues lace';[7] the OED's quotation for 1491: 'the laces and temptacyons of the deuyll'. The laz laid by the Love God beside the Fountain Perilous in the Roman de la Rose may be nets (as used to entangle birds) rather than nooses: 'Cupido' sowed here 'd'Amors la graine' (ll. 1588–9) and

> fist ses laz environ tendre,
> E ses engins i mist, por prendre
> Damoiseles e damoisiaus,
> Qu'Amors ne viaut autres oisiaus.[8]
>
> (ll. 1588–94)

But specifically a noose (i.e., with some kind of knot, usually a running one) is often intended, as in the meaning of the original Latin word. In Italian, the primary meanings of laccio are 'noose', 'slip knot', 'thong', 'lace'.[9] The Gawain-poet's contemporary Petrarch, however, usually means 'noose' in using this word figuratively.[1] Remembering Laura, for instance, he says that Time now braids her hair in firmer knots so as to compress his heart with so powerful a noose that only Death can undo it:

> torsele il tempo poi in piú saldi nodi,
> e strinse 'l cor d'un laccio sí possente
> Che Morte sola fia ch' indi lo snodi.[2]

Conceivably he may sometimes mean a net, as in this use of the diminutive, 'Non volendomi Amor perdere ancóra / Ebbe un altro lacciuol fra l'erba teso' (cclxxi); but he more often means something like a lasso.

The Gawain-poet seems to have had two things in mind in using, or accepting, the concept and word lace for the device by which Gawain is successfully tempted. In the first place, he capitalizes on the habitual and general figurative meaning 'snare', 'trap', because snaring Gawain is what Bertilak's wife (in the first instance) is trying to do: the association is almost unavoidable when recognized. In the same connection, the association of lace with the catching of wild animals is supported by (and supports) the analogy between Berti-

---

7. Secular Lyrics of the XIVth and XVth Centuries, ed. R. H. Robbins (Oxford, 1955), No. clxxvii, l. 82.
8. Ed. E. Langlois, Publications de la Société des Anciens Textes Français, No. ccxii, Vol. ii (Paris, 1920).
9. Cambridge Italian Dictionary, ed. Barbara Reynolds (Cambridge, 1962).
1. See Kenneth McKenzie, Concordanza delle Rime di Francesco Petrarca (Oxford, 1912), laccio, lacciuolo.
2. Rime sparse, cxcvi, in Le Rime sparse e I Trionfi, ed. E Chiòrboli, Scrittori d'Italia, cxxvi (Bari, 1930).

lak's hunting and his wife's attempts to seduce Gawain on three successive days; and most readers seem to have accepted this analogy,
even when they cannot follow Dr H. L. Savage into all of the detailed
correspondences which he has enumerated between the hunting
scenes and the doings of Gawain and the wife of Bertilak.[3]

In the second place, however, the poet seems to wish to convey a signification directly contrary to that of the pentangle when he has
Gawain knot the *lace* around his body (it will be remembered that the
meaning 'noose' necessarily involves a knot). When Gawain attires himself to undergo his trial at the Green Chapel, he doubles the *lace* about
himself, over his red coat armour (ll. 2033–36). Apparently he knots it,
for when in his chagrin he takes it off to fling it to Bertilak, the operation is described thus: 'Þenne he kaȝt to þe knot, and þe kest lawsez' (l.
2376), although the meaning of *kest* ('fastening'?) is uncertain. Later
the physical situation is completely clear. As he returns to the court, the
lace is tied (*loken*) around him under his left arm 'with a knot' (l. 2487).

The 'endeles knot', or pentangle, is perfect because it is all of a
piece: each line 'umbellappez and loukez in oþer / And ayquere it is
endelez'. Like Gawain's former continuum of virtues, it 'ne samned
neuer in no syde, ne sundered nouþer, / Withouten ende at any noke
aiquere'. For this reason, mainly,

> Hit is a syngne þat Salamon set sumquyle
> In bytoknyng of trawþe.   [ll. 625–26]

In direct contrast (and with a partial verbal repetition) one reads on
the subject of the *lace*:

> þe blykkande belt he bere þeraboute
> Abelef as a bauderyk bounden bi his syde,
> Loken vnder his lyfte arme, þe lace, with a knot,
> In tokenyng he watz tane in tech of a faute.   [ll. 2485–88]

A now natural reading of these lines is that this 'token of vntrawþe' (l.
2509) opposes naturally the token of 'trawþe', not by authorial fiat, but
because the *lace* is not endless. Its ends must be tied together; and its
very visible knot shows where, in its imperfection, this frail and pliable
object must be 'samned' together in order to make an enclosure, unlike
the pentangle and, for instance, unlike the pearl which is 'endeleȝ
rounde' (*Pearl*,, ll. 738), being 'wemleȝ, clene, and clere' (l. 737).

In this connection, Gawain's statement about the knotted earnest
of his fault, 'Þer it onez is tachched twynne wil hit neuer' (l. 2512),
takes on more weight as emphasizing the snare-like qualities of the

---

3. *The Gawain Poet: Studies in His Personality and Background* (Chapel Hill, N.C., 1956).
See also introduction to *The Complete Works of the Gawain-Poet*, ed. John Gardner (Chi-
cago, 1965), pp. 76–8; F. L. Utley, 'Folklore, Myth and Ritual', in *Critical Approaches in
Medieval Literature*, ed. Dorothy Bethurum (New York, 1960), p. 90.

lace and perhaps the significance of the knot itself. Equally in accord with this interpretation is the lady's specifying that the *lace* should be fixed around the body (ll. 1851–52), not simply carried. It should be noted as well that the similar green, tasseled *lace* wrapped around the shaft of the axe with which Bertilak arrives at Arthur's court, 'louked' (l. 217) ('was attached', presumably 'was knotted') at the head of the shaft and was fastened ('halched ful ofte') at many points along the shaft—again, presumably, by knots.[4] The lengthy passage (ll. 187–95), in the same scene, on the horse's ornamentally knotted mane (green and gold, like the *luf-lace*) and the forelock and tail, both bound with a green band and the latter decorated with an intricate knot, may accord with this symbolism.

The *luf-lace*, then, like the pentangle, has traditional associations, which are most likely to have rendered its choice as a symbol in *Sir Gawain* an *impositio secundum naturam*. Its vividly scandalous character may be played down when it becomes the mark of an order of knighthood, but its geometrical imperfection in needing to be knotted and its character as a noose (as well as its no doubt startling *enker* green) are always there. Just as much as in the case of the pentangle, the *lace* seems to be the *Gawain*-poet's calculated symbolic device and not a chance narrative motif, whether inherited or not from other material. Further, the conceptually fixed, symmetrical, apparently calculated symbolic opposition (endlessness—incompleteness; knotlessness–knottedness; rigidity–pliability; protected area–trap) between these two most important symbols in the romance suggests that what they stand for—troth and untroth—are what *Sir Gawain* is about.

This discussion of pentangle and *luf-lace* in terms of their symbolic relationship now moves to certain structural considerations.

As J. P. Oakden points out, the *Gawain* stanza, in combining an indefinite number of unrhymed alliterative long lines with a bob and wheel, is a 'daring experiment'.[5] It is unprecedented in the extant verse from the Alliterative Revival. The experiment is, of course, hugely successful, partly because of the element of flexibility: the bob and wheel may be introduced *ad lib.*, within certain wide limits. But what I wish to show here is that the poet had an additional reason for desiring flexibility in stanza length.

As has often been noted, the number of stanzas in each of the poet's two *chefs-d'oeuvre* is 101. Presumably he was aiming at this total in both *Pearl* and *Sir Gawain*, for he would scarcely have hit it twice by

---

4. Larry D. Benson, *Art and Tradition in Sir Gawain and the Green Knight* (New Brunswick, N.J., 1965), p. 40, notes the parallelism between the *lace* on the axe and the *luf-lace*. Incidentally, the suggestions in Benson's passage here concerning the origin of the *luf-lace* in other magical tokens share one point with all other such suggestions with which I am acquainted: for this token, only the *Gawain*-poet uses the word *lace*.

5. *Alliterative Poetry in Middle English*, i (Manchester, 1935) 218.

chance.[6] Further, the echoing (and concluding) line in *Pearl*—the one which repeats elements of the first line—is No. 1212. The number 12, drawn from *Revelation*, is undoubtedly the most important one in the narrative of the poem: the Heavenly Jerusalem is built upon manifold units of 12s (length, breadth, foundations, trees, etc.) and the procession of virgins and innocents numbers 144,000. Duplication of a number in the fashion of '1212' is known elsewhere in medieval number symbolism.[7] It cannot, however, be automatically assumed that the total number 1212 was intended to have symbolic significance, for that total would inevitably follow, given a desire for 101 stanzas and a prior choice of an invariable stanza length of 12 lines (even though that choice in itself may have symbolic significance).

Nevertheless the echoing line in *Sir Gawain* also occurs at a point to which a parallel meaning may be attached: it is No. 2525. The number 25 is a highly significant number in the romance, for Gawain has 5 times 5 ('fyue and sere fyue syþes', l. 632) excellences. That is why he bears the pentangle. Moreover, since the length of the *Gawain* stanza is variable, the line number 2525 does not automatically arise from the stanza total of 101, as the number 1212 does in *Pearl*. Either one is faced with an extraordinary coincidence, or the poet wished to memorialize a significant number in the total number of lines up to and through the echoing one in both *Pearl* and *Sir Gawain*, at the same time that he wished to maintain a total of 101 stanzas in each.[8] If in fact he did this, then his way of doing it in *Sir Gawain* was curiously like that of Edmund Spenser in *Epithalamion* and may bear witness to a more general practice: in *Epithalamion*, according to my now widely accepted demonstration, Spenser's desire for a significant total of 365 lines in 24 stanzas led him to use stanzas of irregular length, as he does not do elsewhere.[9]

6. For 'significant' stanza totals or line totals in poems, see E. R. Curtius's appendix on arithmetical composition in his *Europäische Literatur und lateinisches Mittelalter* (Bern, 1963); an earlier edn was translated by Willard Trask as *European Literature and the Latin Middle Ages* (New York, 1953). 100 stanzas or lines make a more frequent total than 101. See 2 examples of the former in Samuel Singer (ed.), *Die Religiöse Lyrik des Mittelalters* (Bern, 1933), p. 43 and another in G. G. Perry (ed.), *Religious Pieces in Prose and Verse*, Early English Text Society, original series, 26 (1867 and 1914), No. ix (2 6-line stanzas plus 11 8-line stanzas). Others: Christine de Pisan's *Cent balades* and *Cent balades d'amant et de dame* (a continuous narrative), Jean Le Seneschal's *Livre des cent balades* (a continuous narrative), and Alain Chartier's *La belle dame sans merci* in 100 stanzas. But Christine de Pisan's *Proverbes mouraulx* contains 101 units. Chaucer's *Parliament of Fowls*, contains 99, 100, or 101 stanzas, depending on how the triolet near the end is counted, and may have been intended to contain 700 lines (by maximum allowable repetition of the refrain in the triolet).

7. See V. F. Hopper, *Medieval Number Symbolism* (New York, 1938), p. 9.

8. In the light of this poet's structural use of units of 5 in *Pearl* and his preoccupation with 5 in *Sir Gawain*, the structure of Jean de Castel's *Le Pin* is of some interest: 55 quatrains, each 5 being connected by rhyme.

9. *Short Time's Endless Monument* (New York, 1960), pp. 8–15.

It should perhaps be pointed out that a likely numerical structure has now been ascribed to the most famous alliterative poem in English. MLA Scholars' Conference 16, on the topic 'The Structure of *Beowulf*', 27 Dec. 1968, received from Thomas E. Hart a paper,

In versifying an action-filled, eventful narrative (unlike *Pearl*, for instance), a poet would find it much easier to reach a fixed number of lines in a fixed number of stanzas if he could vary the number of lines per stanza. But in the case of *Sir Gawain* a device would be needed to create a stanzaic impression, since the long, unrhymed, alliterative lines of this poem would in themselves seem no more stanzaic than, say, the alliterative *Morte Arthure*. A concluding, rhyming bob and wheel would provide the necessary punctuation, and in fact the 101 bobs and wheels of *Sir Gawain* are the only aural evidence for the 101 stanzas (a small, invariable marginal mark generally indicates to the eye the beginning of each stanza in the manuscript).

The echoing line 2525 in *Sir Gawain* is not the concluding one but is followed by the last, 5-line bob and wheel. But apparently the echo, not the concluding line, was the critical point for the author. In any case, within the stanzaic framework of *Sir Gawain* he could not have made his last line the echoing one even if he had wanted to. His choice of a stanza would have embarrassed him, since it is apparently impossible to repeat even the essentials (e.g., 'After segge sesed at Troye') of his long alliterative line 1 in the short line of any of his wheels.

In sum, the identity in number of stanzas, and the significant numbers 1212 and 2525 in the totals of lines through the echoing lines in *Pearl* and *Sir Gawain*, establish a very strong likelihood that their author intended the observed numerical patterns to have significance. They also provide a likely reason for the choice of an unprecedented stanzaic pattern in *Sir Gawain*. Possibly they provide the same for the choice of stanza in *Pearl*, in the sense that, arithmetically, 12-line stanzas form the most elegant means for arriving at the desired multiple of 12. All of these matters are of interest in the history of numerical composition in late medieval times. Above all, however, in the case of *Sir Gawain*, the apparent reference to the symbolism of the pentangle in the numerical structure of the poem is further evidence that the poet was composing a poem about troth, because that is what the pentangle represents.

I now come to a further set of structural patterns in *Sir Gawain* which are themselves of much interest but for which I am unable to offer a fully satisfactory explanation. They may be related to the motif of the imperfection of the *lace*. Before any discussion of them, the traditional division of the romance into 4 fitts, or parts, which has been called into question, must be rehabilitated. (This has, in fact, been recently and strongly done, but in somewhat different terms, as I shall point out.)

'*Ellen:* Some Tectonic Relationships in *Beowulf*', containing such a scheme. A description of the resemblances between the 'modular' units proposed in that paper and those proposed below for *Sir Gawain* awaits the publication of Professor Hart's results.

This division, corresponding to the 4 largest illuminated initial cap-itals in the part of the manuscript devoted to *Sir Gawain*, was intro-duced by Sir Frederic Madden in the first printed edition, for the Bannatyne Club in 1839. It has been continued in every other printed version since. Nevertheless Mrs L. L. Hill contended in 1946, 'It has become evident that there is no absolute fourfold division of *Gawain*. Such a division exists only in printed tradition and cannot be sup-ported by any attentive examination of *Cotton Nero A. x.* or of the poem itself.'[1] While admitting that Madden's divisions corresponded with the positions of some of the illuminated capitals, she pointed out that he failed to introduce such divisions at the no less than 5 other illuminated capitals in the manuscript text of *Gawain*. In her opinion, Madden had been led to make his divisions largely by another feature of the manuscript: 3 series of thin lines running across the page in each case at the same place in the text where the illuminated capital separates each of 'Madden's' fitts from the following one. But, she says, in the total manuscript (containing *Pearl, Purity,* and *Patience,* as well as *Gawain*) there are only 4 such 2-line elements. Of these, 3 occur in *Gawain,* as already stated, and the fourth occurs in *Purity* at line 1157, at the beginning of what Gollancz designated as Part iii. It follows that if the criterion of horizontal lines were applied in order to make divisions in the manuscript as a whole, then there should be only 'a twofold division of *Purity* despite the fact that the poet has said, "Þus vpon þrynne wyses I haf yow þro schewed," line 1805; and the same standard would leave *Patience* and *Pearl* with no divisions at all.'[2] The importance of Mrs Hill's thesis was enhanced when it was supported by Professor Morton W. Bloomfield in his review of *Gawain* studies: 'There is a good case for dividing the work into nine divisions. . . . It is surprising that this suggestion has not been taken up by literary critics.'[3]

There is reason, nevertheless, to believe that Mrs Hill somewhat overstated the case; in fact, the primacy of the 4 divisions has recently been reasserted by both Donald R. Howard and James W. Tuttleton.[4] The initials at the so-called fitt divisions are larger than the other 5 in *Sir Gawain*[5] and, unlike those 5, have at their heads, running across

1. 'Madden's Divisions of *Sir Gawain* and the "Large Initial Capitals" of *Cotton Nero A. X',* *Speculum,* xxi (1946), 67–71; quotation, p. 71.
2. *Ibid.,* p. 69.
3. '*Sir Gawain and the Green Knight:* An Appraisal', *PMLA,* lxxvi (1961), 7–19; quotation, p. 17.
4. See Howard, as cited above (n. 1), pp. 429–33. For Tuttleton, see 'The Manuscript Divi-sions of *Sir Gawain and the Green Knight',* *Speculum,* xli (1966), 304–10, esp. p. 305.
5. See *Pearl, Cleanness, Patience and Sir Gawain, Reproduced in Facsimile from the Unique MS. Cotton Nero A. X. in the British Museum, with Introduction by Sir I. Gollancz,* Early English Text Society, original series, clxii (1923). In 2 cases the initials at the fitt divisions are twice as large and in a third case even larger: the letter for Fitt i is 8 lines tall; for Fitt ii, 4 lines; for Fitts iii and iv, 6 lines. The other 5 are 3 lines high.

the page, horizontal blanks in the text.[6] More importantly, the inked lines running across the page at the fitt divisions are a more significant divisive feature than Mrs Hill recognized. She neglected to note 2 further cases of such lines. At the beginning of *Purity* (Folio 57a), and separating this poem from the preceding *Pearl* (the first poem in the manuscript), 3 such lines run from the top of the illuminated initial across the page. Similarly, at the beginning of *Patience* (Folio 83a) 3 lines running across the page from the initial separate that poem from the preceding *Purity*. (*Gawain*, the final poem, is in its turn separated from *Patience* by a large space at the top of its first page—about half the length of the text on that page.) As Mrs Hill says 2 horizontal lines (in appearance similar to the 3-line divisions which I have enumerated) separate each fitt from the other in *Gawain*. The only other horizontal division in the manuscript is the one in *Purity* (Folio 73a) that she mentions; but, as far as can be determined from the facsimile, it is a single line, not double like the ones in *Gawain*. It occurs at the beginning of the relation of the last episode in *Purity,* universally admitted to be one of the 2 main divisions of the poem. Each of these 6 units of horizontal lines in the manuscript occupies an otherwise blank horizontal strip, at least 1 line high, created by the initial's rising higher than the top line of text which it faces. There are places at the tops of pages in the manuscript text of *Pearl*—Folios 44a, 46b, 49a, 52b—where in each case there is room for such horizontal lines next to one of the initials which begin each of the 5-stanza units of *Pearl,* but the scribe has not added lines here, because (as I would claim) he or the scribe of the exemplar did not feel that this was a division important enough to merit that visual device for separating major portions of the poem. The case thus stands that there are 6 horizontal dividers in the manuscript—2 of 3 lines each, 3 of 2 lines each, and 1 of 1 line. The first 2 dividers separate poems from each other; the last, of only 1 line, is at a main division. Where the scribe had space for such lines next to an initial, but where there is not a prime logical division of the poem, he does not add lines. The 2-line divisions in *Gawain*, then, would seem to be of prime divisive importance in the scribe's or his exemplar's system, particularly as they are associated with the largest initials in the poem, exclusive of the opening one. It cannot be excluded, of course, that the smaller initials may correspond to subdivisions valuable for an interpretation of the poem (of which more later); but the case for 4 main divisions in *Gawain* seems secure.

If, then, the validity of the traditional fourfold division as it appears in all printed editions of *Gawain* is assumed, two series of numerical parallelisms are discernible in the poem. The first has to do with Fitt i (the first half of the Beheading Test) and Fitt iv (the

6. As Howard, p. 433, points out.

second half of the Beheading Test). (A) In Stanza 10 of Fitt i, the first axe and its *lace* make their appearance (ll. 208ff.). (B) In Stanza 20 of Fitt i, Bertilak as the Green Knight departs:

> Halled out at þe hal dor, his hed in his hande,
> Þat þe fyr of þe flynt flaȝe fro fole houes.
> To quat kyth he becom knwe non þere,
> Neuer more þen þay wyste from queþen he watz wonnen.
>
> (ll. 458–61)

(C) In Stanza 21, the axe, undoubtedly with its green *lace,* reaches its ultimate destination. It is hung against the wall-tapestry above the dais in Arthur's hall. That is the end of Fitt i. (A) In Stanza 10 of Fitt iv (the second half or the Beheading Test), an axe, with yet another gleaming *lace,* again appears (ll. 2222–6). (B) In Stanza 20 of this fitt, Bertilak again departs:

> Þe knyȝt in þe enker grene
> Whiderwarde-so-euer he wolde.
>
> (ll. 2477–78)

(C) In Stanza 21 of the same fitt, the *luf-lace* (knotted this time around a man, not an axe) reaches its ultimate destination in the poem. Wearing it over the pentangle and the red cloth of his coat-armor (ll. 2485ff.), Gawain reaches Arthur's court (l. 2489). This, however, is not the end of Fitt iv. An additional, 22nd stanza—the one-hundredth and first of the poem—goes beyond the natural arc of the parallelism with Fitt i, in order to relate the reaction to Gawain's shame, the founding of the order of the *lace.*

The second series of numerical parallelisms occurs in Fitt iii, the 3 days of the Temptation (see Table). In Stanza 11 (ll. 1402ff.) of this fitt, Gawain and Bertilak make an agreement—a *forward* or *couenaunt*—and the company of Bertilak's castle go to bed. In stanza 22 (ll. 1668ff.), after a succession of events corresponding precisely to the succession in the first sequence of 11 stanzas, another agreement in terms of *trawþe* is made, and the company go to bed. In Stanza 33 (ll. 1952ff.), after the same succession, a third promise 'in god fayþe' is made, and it is said to be time for the company to go to bed. As at the end of the other series, however, this is not the end of the fitt. A thirty-fourth stanza follows, in which Gawain makes his farewells to the inhabitants of the castle (ll. 1979–88). Except that Gawain goes to bed, the events of this stanza go beyond the natural arc of parallelism with the action of the other 2 series of 11 stanzas.

The promises which form the most important articulating points of the second numerical series are of paramount importance, although it is the cream of the jest that Gawain should not know this. Like the pentangle and the *luf-lace,* they concern *Sir Gawain's* great themes, *trawþe* and *vntrawþe*. In this second series at the end of the first sequence in Fitt iii, Bertilak and Gawain again agree to exchange what they gain on the following day, as they had done first at the end of Fitt ii, and they jocularly drink on the *couenauntez*:

Fitt III, The Three Sequences
(l., ll. = line or lines; s., ss. = stanza or stanzas.)

	FIRST DAY	SECOND DAY	THIRD DAY
I First stages of hunt	1126–78 (53 l.) 2 ss. + 1 l.	1421–68 (48 ll.) 2 ss. –7 ll.	1690–1730 (41 ll.) 1 s. + 12 ll.
II The happenings in Gawain's bed chamber to departure of lady	1179–1308 (130 ll.) 1 s. – 1 l. + 3 ss., + 1 s. – 10 ll. (4 ss. + 18 ll.)	1469–1557 (89 ll.) 7 ll. + 3 ss.	1731–1871 (141 ll.) 1 s. – 12 ll., + 5 ss., + 2 ll. (6 ss. – 10 ll.)
III Gawain's rising, religious observance, recreation with the two ladies of the castle	1309–18 (10 ll.)	1558–60 (3 ll.)	1872–93 (22 ll.) 1 s. – 2 ll., + 1 l.
IV Conclusion of hunt; dressing or skinning of deer, boar, fox; return to castle	1319–69 (51 ll.) 2 ss. – 2 ll.	1561–1620 (60 ll.) 1 s. – 3 ll., + 1 s., + 1 s. – 2 ll. (3 ss. – 5 ll.)	1894–1923 (30 ll.) 1 s. – 1 l. + 2 ll.
V Events of the evening: exchange of what has been gained during the day, entertainment; in 11th s. of each series: mention (1) of retirement of company for night; (2) of early activities of next morning; (3) of pledge(s)	1370–1420 (51 ll.) 2 ll. + 2 ss.	1621–89 (69 ll.) 3 ss. + 2 ll.	1924–78 (55 ll.) 1 s. – 2 ll. + 1 s.
TOTALS	11 ss. (295 ll.) Average stanza is 27–ll.	11 ss. (269 ll.) Average stanza is 24 + ll.	11 ss.(289 ll.) Average stanza is 26 + ll.) supernumerary 1979–97 (19 ll.) 1 s.

And efte in her bourdyng þay bayþen in þe morn
To fylle þe same forwardez þat þay byfore maden:
Wat chaunce so bytydez hor cheuysaunce to chaunge,
What nwez so þay nome, at naȝt quen þay metten.
Þay acorded of þe couenauntz byfore þe court alle;
Þe beuerage watz broȝt forth in bourde at þat tyme.

                                   (ll. 1404–9)

At the end of the second sequence of 11 stanzas, they make the same agreement:

Ande þer þay dronken, and dalten, and demed eft nwe
To norne on þe same note on Nwe ȝerez euen,

                                   (ll. 1668–69)

and at the same time Bertilak makes a second promise, in solemn form, although Gawain cannot know the gravity of Bertilak's involvement:

'as I am trwe segge, I siker my trawþe
Þou schal cheue to þe grene chapel þy charres to make
Leude, on Nw ȝerez lyȝt, longe bifore pryme.'

                                   (ll. 1673–75)

At the end of the third sequence of 11 stanzas, Bertilak repeats the promise in due form:

'In god fayþe,' quoþ þe godmon, 'wyth a goud wylle
Al þat euer I yow hyȝt halde schal I redé.'

                                   (ll. 1969–70)

The sting in its tail is sharpened by the parallel form of Bertilak's assurance when, metamorphosed into the Green Knight, he meets Gawain at the Green Chapel, apparently to cut off his head: 'And þou schal haf al in hast þat I þe hyȝt ones' (l. 2218).

One point worthy of note in the first series—the one having to do with the Beheading Test—is that the *lace* (the third in the narrative) which accompanies the second axe in the tenth stanza of the Fourth Fitt seems to have no function in the text unless it is there to fulfill the numerical parallelism with Stanza 10 of Fitt i, containing the first *lace*. The third *lace* is thus slipped in with its axe:

A denez ax nwe dyȝt, þe dynt with to ȝelde,
With a borelych bytte bende by þe halme,
Fyled in a fylor, fowre fote large—
Hit watz no lasse bi þat lace þat lemed ful bryȝt—.

                                   (ll. 2223–26)

If this means what it seems to mean, it is *ignotum per ignotius*—the length of an axe ratified by the unknown length of its *lace*. This *lace* then disappears from the story, its place in the arithmetical series taken (as I claim) by the *luf-lace*.

The 2 arithmetical series which I have posited—the 2 sequences of the Beheading Test and the 3 sequences of the Temptation—are unlikely to be coincidental, because their constituent parts differ greatly in length and in other respects. In the 2 halves of the Beheading Test there is, it is true, a rough episodic parallelism. The 2 antagonists go each to the other's abode and expose themselves to beheadings. But the 2 sequences of episodes differ so greatly in other respects as to suggest that the parallels of the tenth, twentieth, and twenty-first stanzas in the 2 fitts are the results of calculation. In the Temptation, the episodic parallelism is much closer among the 3 sequences, but the amounts of text devoted to parallel episodes differ quite enough to throw off the overall numerical parallelism if it were not the result of calculation. The exchange of gifts, for instance, arrives in the ninth stanza in the second sequence, in the tenth stanza in the first and third sequences. The reason for this is that the events of the bed chamber on the second day, being largely a repetition of those on the first, take up less space—3 stanzas plus 7 lines (ll. 1469–1557)—than the first day's 4 stanzas plus 18 lines (ll. 1179–1308). On the third day, on the other hand, the events in the bed chamber are quite involved, taking up more than 5½ stanzas, and the details of Gawain's confession and absolution take up almost 1 stanza (ll. 1876–84). Each of these discrepancies (as I call them) is compensated for so as to arrive at the assertion or reassertion of a promise in the eleventh stanza. On the second day, that is, the author allows himself a much fuller description of the evening's activities (ll. 1621–85) than on the other 2 days, which makes up for his brief bedroom scene; on the third day, however, the preliminary and concluding accounts of the hunt and the account of the evening's activities amount to less, stanzaically (about 4½ stanzas), than they do on the first day (6 stanzas) and the second day (7½ stanzas), and compensate for the other lengthy episodes. It is true that the more varied evening activities of the third day down through the eleventh stanza of this sequence actually occupy more lines than those of the first day (55 against 51), but the author has allowed considerably more lines in his eleventh stanza on the third day than on the first (27 against 19) so that the scheme still works, stanzaically. This is apparently an instance of his capitalization on his initial choice of an unprecedentedly flexible stanza.

What the poet may have intended by this ordering is very much in question. It may have been simply his way of going to work: so many stanzas arbitrarily allotted for this part of the story, so many for that, particularly if he intended to arrive at a fixed total of 101 stanzas. At the same time, one notes that the number of stanzas in each of the series here considered is a multiple of 5, plus 1: 101 stanzas, 21 stanzas and 11 stanzas.[7] I see no way of proving that the author's intention here was to build a numerical conception of the *lace* into the work as I believe he built into it the concept of the pentangle. Still, the idea is worth pursuing for a moment.

What such an arithmetical conceit would signify is that, as the *luf-lace*, with its knot, adds an element which ruins the perfection signified by the knotless pentangle, so 5 plus 1, or a multiple of 5 to which 1 unit is added, signifies imperfection.[8] A way of carrying out this system in the remaining fitt, the second, is to divide the fitt into 4 units of 6 stanzas each (5 + 1). At 2 points, this division corresponds in a sense to smaller illuminated capitals in the manuscript. In stanza 6 (ll. 619ff.) of this fitt—a stanza beginning with an illuminated capital—there appears for the first time the pentangle, highly significant as a symbol but destined to be overcome. In stanza 12, which also begins with an illuminated capital, there appears the castle, apparently by a miracle in answer to Gawain's prayer but also to be the stage for his undoing. In stanza 18, Gawain celebrates, for the first time after his prayer, what he had prayed for so urgently—'þe servyse of that syre'—in the chapel at evensong, but he also meets there his ultimate undoers, Bertilak's wife and Morgan la Fay (ll. 928–69). In the twenty-fourth stanza of this fitt, Bertilak induces Gawain to undertake the first of the apparently jocular but in fact solemn promises of the Temptation:

7. Of course 5 is the number of the pentangle, and all but 1 of the stanza groups in *Pearl* contain 5 stanzas each. Perhaps the initial choice of the number 5 for *Sir Gawain* depended upon its well-known medieval association with the Virgin. There are 5 letters each in *Maria, virgo, mater*. Mary is often said to know 5 joys. In the Christmas service, the two antiphons *Ad Laudes*, namely 'Quem vidistis' and 'Genuit puerpera', have each 5 X 5 X 5 = 125 letters, as is pointed out in an important book which I have drawn on elsewhere in this article: J. A. Huisman, *Neue Wege zur dichterischen und musikalischen Technik Walthers von der Vogelweide, mit einem Exkurs über die symmetrische Zahlenkomposition im Mittelalter*, Studia Litteraria Rheno-Traiectina, i (Utrecht, 1950), 95–6, n. For the antiphons, *see Liber usualis Missae et officii pro dominicis festis et festis I, vel II, classis, cum cantu gregoriano, ex editione vaticana adamussim excerpto* (Paris, Turin, Rome, 1932), pp. 361–2. See also the 'Song of the Five Joys', *Religious Lyrics of the XIVth Century*, ed. Carleton Brown (Oxford, 1967), pp. 44–6, in 5-line stanzas; the 'Orison of the Five Joys', *ibid.*, pp. 29–31, in 5-line stanzas if the refrain is included; 'A Prayer to the Five Joys', *English Lyrics of the XIIIth Century*, ed. Carleton Brown (Oxford, 1932), pp. 27–8, in 5 stanzas; and a fifteenth-century carol of the 5 joys, in 5 stanzas, *Ancient Christmas Carols*, ed. Edith Rickert (London, 1928), p. 205.

  Gawain's chief fealty seems to be to the Virgin. Her image appears on one side of his shield; the pentangle, the symbol of 5 in the poem, appears on the other. One of his 5 classes of excellences has to do with the 5 joys of Mary (646–7). She apparently helps him in his most need when Bertilak's wife is closest to seducing him (ll. 1768–9). In the matter of the connection of 5 with *Pearl*, the daughter in that poem, a queen in heaven as Mary is Heaven's Queen, honors the Virgin highly (*Pearl*, ll. 433–44).

8. The notion that perfection is ruined by adding 1 unit is known to medieval number symbolism in the number 11, going 1 beyond the 10 commandments, and in 13, going 1 beyond the 12 apostles. See Hopper, pp. 87 (St Augustine), 101, 152 (Dante), 131.

'Swete, swap we so, sware with trawþe' (l. 1108). Further such promises, jocular according to Gawain's estimate but grave in formula and
fact, define the divisions which I have posited in Fitt iii.

As I have just shown, of the 5 smaller illuminated initials, which
do not introduce fitts, 2 correspond to sequences which I propose
in Fitt ii. The significance of the other 3 smaller ones may be
touched on now.[9] One, at line 1421, corresponds to the beginning
of the second of the sequences I propose for the Temptation, in Fitt
iii. The other 2 do not correspond to any of the units here proposed,
but are of some independent interest. One (l. 1893) introduces the
stanza in which Bertilak strikes at the fox, who draws aside from the
blow but is immediately caught by one of Bertilak's dogs. The other
(l. 2259) introduces the stanza in which Bertilak, as the Green
Knight, strikes his first blow at Gawain, and Gawain winces aside.
Possibly the author wished to introduce these 2 remaining capitals
in order to call attention to the parallel, which goes into some
detail. Bertilak

> watz war of þe wylde, and warly abides,
> And braydez out þe bryȝt bronde, and at þe best castez.
> And he schunt for þe scharp, and schulde haf arered;
> A rach rapes hym to, ryȝt er he myȝt,
> And ryȝt bifore þe hors fete þay fel on hym alle,
> And woried me þis wyly with a wroth noyse.
>
> (ll. 1900–5)

On the other hand, as the Danish axe descends toward his neck
Gawain

> schranke a lytel with þe schulderes for þe scharp yrne.
> Þat oþer schalk wyth a schunt þe schene wythhaldez,
> And þenne repreued he þe prynce with mony prowde wordez.
>
> (ll. 2267–69)

Gawain's answer begins, 'I schunt onez, / And so wyl I no more' (ll.
2280–1). It goes without saying that there is the possibility of a parallelism between the fox's and Gawain's wincing aside, and, lightly
touched, between the fox's and Gawain's alternative escape-routes,
foredoomed because of the efficiency of Bertilak's creatures (his
dog, his wife, his *lace*). There is also the verbal agreement of
'schunt' (ll. 1903, 2268, 2280) and 'scharp' (ll. 1902, 2267), and the
canine and churlish surquidry (ll. 1905, 2269).

---

9. Howard suggests that the smaller capitals are probably significant, but less so than the 4
   large ones (pp. 429–31). The former 'were probably placed in accord with the author's—
   or scribe's—sense of dramatic rhythm' (p. 433). It should be noted that Professor
   Howard's analysis of the structure of *Sir Gawain* is a very interesting one, too complex to
   be summarized here.

In the matter, then, of the 9 initials in the manuscript text of *Gawain*, 7 (4 beginning the fitts, and 3 others) correspond to either the initial or final stanzas of sequences which I have suggested, and the remaining 2 initials point to a parallelism of a kind well known in the romance, mainly through the work of H. L. Savage. But 3 of the sequences that I suggest (the last 2 in Fitt ii, the last 1 in Fitt iii) have no illuminated capital initially or finally.

It must be said finally and regretfully that the overall numerical scheme proposed here for the fitts is so complicated as to be unsatisfactory, not because the *Gawain*-poet may not have followed it (I believe that he did, at least in Fitts i, iii, and iv), but because I see no way of demonstrating it fully. The sequences of stanzas, as noted, run like this: Fitt i, 21; Fitt ii, 6 + 6 + 6 + 6; Fitt iii, 11 + 11 + 11 + 1; Fitt iv, 21 + 1. I have included this scheme here only in the hope that someone else may see further than I do.

One other feature of the poem strongly suggests numerical calculation. In the later Middle Ages, the traditional life-span of Christ is 33 years, or 33 and a fraction years, or (perhaps more commonly) 32 and a fraction years.[1] One of these numbers is often a part of the numerological structure of medieval poems.[2] In *Sir Gawain*, the most extensive references to Christ—both to his birth and to his cross—appear in stanza 32. Gawain rides on Christmas Eve,

> Carande for his costes, lest he ne keuer schulde
> To se þe seruyse of þat syre, þat on þat self ny3t
> Of a burde watz borne oure baret to quelle;
> And þefore sykyng he sayde, 'I beseche þe, lorde,
> And Mary, þat is myldest moder so dere,
> Of sum herber þer he3ly I my3t here masse,
> Ande þy matynez to-morne, mekely I ask,
> And þerto prestly I pray my pater and aue
>   and crede.'
> He rode in hys prayere,
> And cryed for his mysdede,
> He sayned hym in sypes sere,
> And sayde 'Cros Kryst me spede!'

(ll. 750–62)

---

1. Cf. *The Pricke of Conscience*, ed. R. Morris (Berlin, 1863), v, 4987–8: 'þan was he of threty yhere elde, and twa, / And of thre monethes ar-with alswa.' Lucifer in *Piers Plowman* gives Christ 32 winters; see the three-text edition, ed. W. W. Skeat (Oxford, 1886), I, Passus xviii, 296 (B-Text); Passus xxi, 334 (C-Text).
2. Aside from the obvious example in the *Commedia*, see E. W. Bulatkin, 'The Arithmetic Structure of the Old French *Vie de Saint Alexis*', *PMLA*, lxxiv (1959), 495–502, where the tradition of 33 and a fraction is followed. A number of similar examples are cited in Fritz Tschirch, 'Schüsselzahlen', in *Beiträge zur deutschen und nordischen Literatur, Festgabe fur Leopold Magon* (Berlin, 1958), pp. 32–5.

Stanza 33 begins immediately thereafter, with an illuminated capital: 'Nade he sayned hymself segge, bot þrye' (l. 762). Apparently as Gawain crosses himself for the third time, he sees the castle within which he can accomplish his desire. The occurrence of the threefold action in Stanza 33 seems to be another example of duplication, as with lines 1212 and 2525. And the appearance of these references to Christ in Stanzas 32–3 is likely to be, as in other poems making use of the number 33, a gesture in the direction of a numerological concept.[3]

Speaking generally, the extent to which numerical structure and numerology are to become factors in the study of Old and Middle English literature remains a matter of guesswork. Important as instances of these practices may be in establishing some idea of a possible tradition, each instance must as yet be judged in comparative isolation. At a minimum, given the likelihood of the numerical ordering outlined here, it is obvious that an important new shaping factor in the amounts of material devoted to the several parts of the *Gawain* narrative has to be taken into account. Even if considerable adjustment were initially available to the author (conceivably other multiples or powers of 5 than 2525 for the total of lines), the limitations as the plan progressed would increase, until for the articulation of succesive episodes of the 3 days of the Temptation it is not a great exaggeration to find an analogy in the simultaneous articulation of space in fourteenth-century vaulting, where the complicated pattern of rib and boss in one bay is given by that in all of the others.

Such methodological considerations are of less significance here, however, than the production of strong evidence for the theme of *Sir Gawain* itself, and two such pieces of evidence have been brought forward. It is true that, like other classics, this poem can be usefully looked at in an extraordinary number of ways. Urbanity and courtesy, for instance, and their opposites, are certainly preoccupations of the fourteenth-century author and his hero. It is entirely within the realm of possibility, also, that the author sees certain historical figures behind his characters. He seems to be concerned with the historical destiny of Britain. Certainly a seasonal myth is somewhere in the folkloristic origins of the plot. The alternations of nature and civilization in the work are as plain as the difference between the hunters' quarry-strewn landscape and the life of the castle. The faultiness of many women and the perfection of the Virgin obviously strike him as notable truisms. But it seems wilful to say that the principal theme of *Sir Gawain* is anything but the consistent maintenance of explicitly and implicitly undertaken covenants with others. This remains true

3. A close parallel to the practice in *Sir Gawain* is cited in Tschirch, p. 37: in Stanza 33 of the South-German *Annolied* (c. 1080–1110) Cologne is said to have been converted by 3 missionaries, and then to have had 33 bishops up to Anno himself.

whether it is maintained that the author's particular set is towards glorifying a remarkable approximation of this theme taken as an ideal, or examining the baneful or beneficial consequences of falling short of it, or describing the common limitation upon the common human potential for it. The architectonic balance between the rigid, endless, and seamless pentangle of troth and the apparently yielding, incomplete noose of untroth with its ends knotted together is one of the pieces of evidence produced here for this theme; the other is the set of numerical structural considerations of which the most obvious is the signification of the pentangular excellences in the echoing line 2525. Just as strong evidence for this theme exists, in the present writer's opinion, in the tissue of expressed and implied promises which lie on the surface of the poem at first reading. This latter evidence, however, has not proved sufficient to convince a number of critics.[4]

W. A. DAVENPORT

[The Hero and His Adventure]†

It was possibly in pursuit of his interest in the 'difficult case' that the poet turned, in *Sir Gawain*, to secular material. God is a tricky subject and the poet has to contend with greater resistance in both material and audience when he deals with scriptural and doctrinal matter. If instead of codes of universal justice and belief, one starts from the earthly code of chivalry, then the values are more ambivalent. It is possible for the poet to set up oppositions between a hero and his challenger without a clear identification of the moral agency which that challenger represents. And so, around the central concept of a traditional hero undertaking a romance quest, the poet creates a shifting, hazardous world, where the ideas which in many other romances are taken for granted are explicitly or implicitly questioned.

The poet's choice of a literary form with a well-defined tradition could be assumed to arouse certain expectations in his audience; it is the poet's ingenious pleasure to attempt to satisfy his reader's interest in adventure while partly frustrating such expectations by eschewing the easy romance path and attempting a more penetrating treatment of the knight, showing him as an individual struggling to accomplish

4. Professor Rudolf Willard resigned to me his interests in numerical structure in *Gawain* long ago, and Professor Helaine Newstead helped me to present a paper on the subject at an early stage before the Arthurian Section of MLA. Professor Talbot Donaldson kindly helped me with final additions. I am grateful to all three but wish to implicate none.

† From *The Art of the Gawain Poet* (London: Athlone Press, 1978), pp. 180–94. Reprinted by permission.

an impossible task. The poet also avoids the hero's easy triumph and colours his 'happy ending' with a sense of partial failure and anticlimax, placing idealism in the light of unheroic reality and deflating comedy. Again, he chose a hero who would already be known to his hearers, and the existence of conflicting traditions of Gawain's nature may well have been something which the poet wished to exploit.[1] The resistance to sexual temptation of a hero who elsewhere in Arthurian tales acts as an impulsive libertine seems a particularly teasing example of moral conduct, intended to surprise the audience as much as the failure of this exemplar of courage completely to pass his more traditional test. The 'dangerous edge of things' is offered for our interest as much as with Jonah [in *Patience*], though more lightly, and, like Jonah, Gawain eventually appears as something of an heroic fool who thought wrongly that life played fair and according to the rules, even while he fails to conduct his own life according to them.

Unlike Jonah, however, Gawain is indisputably a hero, though the result of the poet's complex and equivocal treatment of his adventure is that the nature of the heroic role is continually in doubt, and the ending of the poem is designed to make us wonder whether Gawain has fulfilled such a role or not. We are certain, at least, that Gawain is hero in the sense of the central figure of the narrative; once he enters the action in the fifteenth stanza, he is present in every stanza except six scattered verses describing the hunts. Further, once he has left Camelot, the poet shows more and more of his thoughts and feelings, and often, though not always, focuses scenes from Gawain's point of view. He is identified as 'our luflych lede' and the idea of 'our' hero implicitly calls for the reader's sympathetic involvement. It is also clear that he is considered within the world of the poem as a model of noble behaviour, who performs actions fitting to the traditions of chivalry. He is presented in traditional heroic situations such as being equipped in armour and riding alone into danger. He is given words which ring with echoes of epic stoicism, and he is even accompanied by epic epithets: *Gawayn the gode, Gawayn the hende, gode Gawan*. He is associated throughout with high ideals and standards of behaviour, even if at times ironically; he is praised by the poet and by his opponent. But, of course, the model proves to have a flaw, and the outcome of the story displays the idea of the hero as a model of behaviour in conflict with the idea of the individual who is our emotional concern. This is the poet's major change in the traditional beheading tale. Whereas in the analogues the keeping of the promise alone

---

1. See B. J. Whiting, 'Gawain: His Reputation, His Courtesy and His Appearance in Chaucer's *Squire's Tale*', *Medieval Studies* 9, 1947, 189–234, Gordon M. Shedd, 'Knight in Tarnished Armour: The Meaning of *Sir Gawain and the Green Knight*', *Modern Language Review* 62, 1967, 3–13 and comments in *Two Old French Gawain Romances* ed. R.C. Johnston and D. D. R. Owen (Edinburgh: Scottish Academic Press, 1972).

proved the hero's courage and saved his life, the author of *Sir Gawain* portrays a hero who shows courage, keeps his promise, saves his life, and yet does not end with the conventional hero's triumph. Gawain possesses the necessary qualities for the fictional automaton which the hero of romance often seems, but these are played off against ordinary human, even unchivalrous, qualities, particularly fear, to create a figure who eventually seems to possess character and not just characteristics. The change of ending is a turning towards both realism and comedy, for Gawain's failure is no tragic fall, but an anticlimax. Hence from the start the tone of the poem is intermittently and insidiously comic, and indicates to us that the outcome, though it may be unexpected, is not to be serious. This is of a piece with the poet's other uses of levelling realism and marks *Sir Gawain*, from one point of view, as a romance moving in the direction of *Don Quijote*.[2] But the poet's basic choices, the choice of a testing story and the choice of treatment, indicate not so much a desire to deflate romance as that same interest in the antithesis of opposites, and in the interplay of ideal behaviour and actual experience, that one can observe, in various ways, in the other three poems. The Beheading Game measures Gawain against the heroic figures of legend, and in following their path, Gawain partakes of their heroic stature. The poet wants us to respond to the elevated, romantic aspects of his tale. At the same time the poet's treatment brings Gawain, like Jonah, to the reader's level of experience.

So, although Gawain fulfils a hero's role, the hero himself is continually being diminished. He is shown repeatedly as subordinate, and therefore being obliged to be deferential, and as passive. At Camelot he appears as liege, nephew and inferior; he is subject to the approval of Arthur and the court, advised and, at the close of the scene, patronised by the King, lectured on his obligations by the Green Knight, and even warned by the narrator, who, by the end of Part I, has left his pretended role of the minstrel repeating a tale, and has turned into the all-seeing, ironic commentator on the action. In Part II Gawain is shown setting out on an adventure in which he is doomed to be the passive recipient of a death-blow, and in which, in the court's eyes, he is the victim of kingly pride and folly. In the arming scene he is presented as a lay-figure being accoutred in equipment whose heroic associations have to contend with a sense of its irrelevance and uselessness in the particular quest he is undertaking. The elaborate explication of Gawain's device accompanies praise of the hero with emphasis on his reliance on forces outside himself and on his possesssion of virtues which are gentle and mild and show deference to the

2. See D. D. R. Owen, 'Burlesque Tradition and *Sir Gawain and the Green Knight*', *Forum for Modern Language Studies* 4, 1968, 125–45.

feelings of others, and this is followed by an account of Gawain's journey which gives a brief summary of his acts of valour but enters in
detail into his experience of loneliness, cold and anxious uncertainty.
The poet thus begins to establish a distinction between the hero's
humanity and the heroic pattern of behaviour expected from him; this
distinction forms the basis of the complex treatment of the hero,
whereby the poet repeatedly reduces Gawain's heroic quality in a variety of related ways, while maintaining in the reader's mind elevated
senses of his nature and behaviour.

Much of the time we are asked not to look at him but to perceive
through him; as he is faced by unknown places, an unfamiliar society
and startling and unnerving experience, so we live through it with him
as impressions are presented in the order in which he receives them.
This is strikingly so in the last part of the poem, where the poet builds
up the suspense preceding the Green Knight's reappearance and the
delivery of the blow. The careful focusing through Gawain's perception of the scene in which he first hears and then sees the Green
Knight again is characteristic of the way in which the poet creates a
bond of sympathy between reader and hero, which is implicitly identifying the hero as an ordinary man, who reacts to the unfamiliar with
embarrassment and fear, and whose limitations are inevitably exposed.
His 'inadequate' reactions are among the effects in the poem of which
the reader can be most sure, because the poet tells us of Gawain's
inner thoughts, reminding us from time to time of his fear of the
encounter with the Green Knight, and identifying his embarrassment
by the Lady of Hautdesert and his sense of the dilemma in which he
is placed. On the last day at the Castle, the poet enters into his hero
with particular point and emphasis, first identifying his preoccupation
during sleep and ominously reminding us of the passive, doomed role
which Gawain has yet to fulfil:

> In drey droupyng of dreme draveled that noble,
> As mon that watz in mornyng of mony thro thoghtes,
> How that destiné schulde that day dele hym his wyrde
> At the grene chapel, when he the gome metes,
> And bihoves his buffet abide withoute debate more.
>
> (1750–54)

The hero is shown, that is, at his most vulnerable. Then, as he
hastily recovers his wits to deal with the laughing and alluring Lady,
bending over him with her fair face, throat and breast enhanced in
beauty by jewels and fur, Gawain's instinctive sexual response is
indicated both directly and by innuendo:[3]

---

3. I have argued the point more fully and commented on this passage as a whole in 'The
Word *norne* and the Temptation of Sir Gawain', *Neuphilologische Mitteilungen* 78, 1977,
pp. 256–63.

He sey hir so glorious and gayly atyred,
So fautles of hir fetures and of so fyne hewes,
Wight wallande joye warmed his hert.
With smothe smyling and smolt thay smeten into merthe,
That al watz blis and bonchef that breke hem bitwene,
  and wynne.
 Thay lanced wordes gode,
 Much wele then watz therinne.

       (1760–67)

Beneath the decorous surface description of conversation runs the current of sexual, physical nuance, identified clearly in 'Wight wallande joye' and obliquely suggested in the physical verbs, *smeten*, *breke* and *lanced*. The threat that the warm courtesies of speech may burst into the hotter pleasures of physical contact is then made explicit by the voice of the all-seeing poet, who states Gawain's moral dilemma, shows his hero suppressing his sexual arousal and at last recognising that he can no longer go on temporising with the Lady without being false to her husband:

 Thay lanced wordes gode,
 Much wele then watz therinne.
 Gret perile bitwene hem stod,
 Nif mare of hir knyght [hym] mynne.

For that prynce of pris depresed hym so thikke,
Nurned hym so neghe the thred, that nede hym bihoved
Other lach ther hir luf, other lodly refuse.
He cared for his cortaysye, lest crathayn he were,
And more for his meschef, yif he schulde make synne
And be traytor to that tolke that that telde aght.
'God schylde,' quoth the schalk, 'that schal not befalle!'

       (1766–76)

This is, of course, a disputed and much discussed passage and one which several critics have seen as central to one's understanding of the moral sense of the tale.[4] It seems to me that the poet is ingeniously combining his reducing and his enhancing of the hero. Gawain's thoughts are on a level of plausible feeling; he wants to maintain a reputation for courtesy to women, but he comes to a moment of self-knowledge in recognising that he cannot, in his situation, both do that and maintain faith to his host. He is a normal

---

4. See J. A. Burrow, *A Reading of Sir Gawain and the Green Knight*. (London: Routledge, 1965), pp. 99–101 and A. C. Spearing's detailed discussion of the question of Gawain's chastity (*The Gawain-Poet: A Critical Study*. Cambridge: Cambridge University Press, 1970. p. 194ff.), with specific comments on Burrow's view of the passage at pp. 204–6. Also Ian Robinson, *Chaucer and the English Tradition* (Cambridge, 1972), p. 231.

male and his physical reactions to the Lady declare (*Nurned*) that
he is shamefully near crossing the boundary of another man's territory (*thred*), and so, because faith is more important than courtesy,
he forces down, subdues and checks (*depresed*) his urgent sexual
desire. The physical undertones of the passage make one view the
hero in ordinary terms and enjoy his comic struggle between being a
gentleman and avoiding adultery. The morality by which Gawain
acts also seems to emphasise common-sense ideas at the expense of
romantic notions of knightly conduct; Gawain is no dashing blade,
but a cautious man who realises that being polite to a woman stops
short of going to bed with her, if one is a guest in her husband's
house. The diminishing of the chivalrous hero to bourgeois standards of social behaviour is, however, counter-acted by the sense of
a real struggle against temptation and of a decisive act which is ideal
in social terms rather than those of either *amour courtois* or Christian celibacy. The decision of a *prynce of pris* to respect the rights of
a social inferior, even at the expense of his own reputation for courtliness, is a piece of ideal behaviour which displays Gawain as one of
those who have that true 'gentillesse' of which another bourgeois
character, the Wife of Bath, so eloquently speaks, through the lady
in another intimate bedroom scene, in Chaucer's version of the tale
of the Loathly Lady. Again we have a moment in the poem where
beneath the surface is a debating point about knighthood, as to
which of the two, courtesy to a woman or loyalty to one's host, is the
more important. The emphasis on the hero's own overcoming of
temptation in lines 1770–91 seems to make the idea of the intervention of the Virgin Mary, which most editors curiously prefer to
emendation in line 1769,[5] quite out of keeping with the rest of the
section; the poet is thinking more in social than in religious terms.

Gawain's resistance to temptation and his loyalty to his host occur,
with an irony which comes to seem typical of the poet, just before the
crucial scene in which he yields to the Lady's persuasion and commits
himself to an act of disloyalty. The alternation of building-up and
letting-down is present throughout the poem and is a second way in
which the heroic aspect of Gawain and his enterprise is diminished.
The Castle itself, which at first sight seemed full of rich potentiality,
is, in romance terms, an anti-climax. There are no besieged maidens,
no predatory giant; its inhabitants turn out to be, apparently, normal,
concerned with sensible matters such as food, warmth and Christmas
entertainment. Gawain is, on his arrival, rapidly disarmed, domesti-
cated, led to the lulling comfort of fine fresh clothes, fire, food and
drink. What have pentangles and high courage to do in such a setting?

5. See the note on lines 1768–9 in *Sir Gawain and the Green Knight* ed. J. R. R. Tolkien and
   E. V. Gordon, second edition, revised by N. Davis (Oxford: Oxford University Press,
   1967), p. 121.

It is no surprise that the Green Chapel turns out to be just around the
corner. The whole business of Gawain's quest is deflated and made to
sound ridiculously easy:

> 'The grene chapayle upon grounde greve yow no more;
> Bot ye schal be in youre bed, burne, at thyn ese,
> Quyle forth dayez, and ferk on the fyrst of the yere,
> And cum to that merk at mydmorn, to make quat yow likez
>   in spenne.
>   Dowellez whyle New Yerez daye,
>   And rys, and raykez thenne.
>   Mon schal yow sette in waye;
>   Hit is not two myle henne.'

> (1070–78)

Gawain will not even need to get up early! When he comes to depict
the actual fulfilment of the quest, the poet again builds up a sense
of climax in the account of Gawain's setting forth, his rejection of
the Guide's advice, and the description of the desolate valley. The
Chapel itself is a let-down, but Gawain's imaginings invest it with
eerie force and lead to a further build-up of suspense with the Green
Knight's re-appearance and the preliminaries to the blow. After the
cut all is, for Gawain, bathos. The revelation of the Lady's deceit, of
the meaning of the challenge and of the identity of the agent leads
to the ultimate insulting cosiness of Bertilak's invitation to Gawain
to come back and stay with his elderly aunt.

The poet thus seems to take pleasure in putting his hero in false
positions and it is in the scenes at the Castle that he most ingeniously devised ways of doing it. In this part of the poem Gawain is
imagined as a kind of Wimbledon champion of chivalry, who has to
find again those qualities that made him champion. Since there is
no question that Gawain will, if challenged to direct knightly contest, display superlative powers, his humbling has to be achieved by
guile. Hence the methods at the Castle are devised to subject him to
what is in essence a psychological trial. He is first encouraged by
comfort and relief to relax and to consider himself off duty, but, at
the same time, is placed beneath a weight of obligation by the overwhelming hospitality which puts him into the role of grateful and
deferential guest; the weight grows heavier as he finds himself
expected to put on a performance worthy of the reputation accorded
to him. Then the Lord deprives Gawain of the opportunity to show
his masculine, active qualities of courage and strength in the field.
This is typically justified in naturalistic terms: Gawain needs rest
and food after his long winter journey. But it reduces him to a passive role and this is highlighted by the constrast of the vigorous,
active Lord, fulfilling the role of a leader of men, the 'lowande leder
of ledez' which Gawain might have been, in a realistic picture of the

activities of the rural nobility. So Gawain is held within a pleasant prison, reduced to inactivity. Then he is further placed in a false position and further imprisoned by the Lady, who takes on the lover's role, captures him naked and flat on his back, disarmed in every sense of the word.

This double reversal of roles is made ingeniously comic and subtle by the Lady's use of Gawain's own reputation as a weapon against him. The juxtaposition of the romantic and the real is expressed in their conversations almost in terms of a distinction between literature and life: Gawain appears to have read fewer romances than the Lady and to be ill-versed in the role which is persuasively thrust upon him. This twist of the situation works both to convince the reader of Gawain's reality, since we sympathise with the one who appears the imperfect actor on the stage, struggling to keep up with a plot he is unaware of and to improvise appropriate lines, and further to draw a distinction between the limited, actual man and romantic conceptions of a knight as an idealised being. Measured against the example of the hunting Lord and against the Lady's picture of a prototype lover-hero, the real Gawain is continually disconcerted and his standards are questioned by being deliberately confused. On the one hand he is presented with an exaggerated model of fine breeding and courtly expertise by the flattery of the Lady and the courtiers, against which he is forced to demur and to counter over-praise with modest disclaimers; on the other hand, he is forced to defend himself against undervaluation when the Lady accuses him of failing to do what a gentleman ought. The disconcerting of Gawain takes place in a situation where he is constantly under obligation to express courtly sentiments of service to the Lady, and to defer to his host. He is forced to receive repeated generosity in the form of the Lord's winnings and to give little in return—a situation repeated in the symbolic moment when Gawain confesses himself bankrupt of courtly gifts and the Lady in reply presses him to accept a valuable ring. He is further put out of countenance by the Lord's teasing and by the Lady's embarrassing hints in her husband's presence. Another element in the concerted attack on him is the attempt to catch him off guard by the exertion of pressure just when the situation might allow him to relax: so the Lord proposes the exchange-bargain just when Gawain has been relieved of anxiety about finding the Green Chapel; the Lady first persuades him to accept a kiss just as she seemed on the point of leaving; the Lady starts the crucial discussion about giving love-tokens only when she appears to have given up her attempt to make Gawain act as lover. Such strategy contributes to an over-all sense of deliberate displacement in the poem, whereby not only is the hero continually caught off-guard, but also the reader is cleverly confused and challenged to read the situation truly.

Trapped at the centre of a web of invidious comparison and subtle teasing attack, Gawain is shown to us from within and without. We are given an intimate, identifying knowledge of him, a knowledge both comic, since we share his experience of embarrassment and uncertainty, and also serious, since we are given private access to his fear, his resistance to temptation and his single-mindedness and determination. But this view of the hero is not consistently maintained and we are shown Gawain's acts at times as they appear to others, the courtiers at Hautdesert, the Lord, the Lady, the Green Knight in the valley, and the Round Table. The outer view of him also has a comic and a serious aspect. His improvised displays of elegant words for the Lady's benefit and his returning of the kisses to her husband are conceived as dramatic scenes offered for the reader's detached, amused enjoyment; the serious aspect is his performance as a keeper of promises, shown mainly in dramatic externalised terms. The effect of the combination of points of view is to create a division between Gawain's thoughts and his acts, so that the hero's actual conduct is presented as a performance of what is fitting to the moment, whether, in other terms, it is genuine or false. The poet most significantly chooses to withdraw knowledge of Gawain's inner mind in the scenes immediately after his acceptance of the green belt, so that we are shown his going to confession, his mirth, and the last exchange of winnings, from outside. These acts exist in the poem as a performance of virtue, a completely convincing appearance of truth. As we know later, Gawain is here at his most wrong and that he should show at this moment the greatest self-confidence that he displays anywhere in the poem is another of the poet's ironies. The fact that the author makes so little of the matter of Gawain's confession is a sure indication that he is more interested in creating an effect of dramatic irony than in making the moral point which so many commentators have tried to elicit from the scene.[6] Gawain is later blamed for lack of loyalty to a fellow man, not for false religious observance, and the sensible conclusion is that the poet wears his religion, as so many other things, lightly and comfortably, recognising that this tale is not the place for making points about whether an unconfessed intention to commit sin is to be added to the list of Gawain's failings. The poet remains, interestingly and effectively, vague, leaving us either to assume that 'the more and the mynne' did really include everything and that the priest belongs to the 'good face' of Hautdesert uninvolved in the plot, or that Gawain with sensible practicality went to confession before he had actually done anything wrong and even, if we care to press it that far, before he had finally made up his mind. But the reader is not actually invited to consider such questions: his attention

6. Especially Burrow, *Reading*, pp. 104–10. See also G. J. Engelhardt, 'The Predicament of Gawain', *Modern Language Quarterly* 16, 1955, 218–25.

is directed to enjoyment of the performance and the ironic confrontation between a confident, joyful, truthful, open-handed hero and a
crest–fallen Lord apologising for his measly fox-pelt.

That Gawain's deeds and words should, in part, be presented to us in
terms of putting on an act is the inevitable product of the antitheses
basic to the whole poem, between ideal and actual, between the reputation and the real man, between mystery and explanation, between
anonymity and identification. Gawain is repeatedly measured against
models of behaviour. He is measured against an archetypal sense of
the hero's role in a setting with the authority of historical tradition.
He is measured in Christian and partly allegorical terms as an Everyman existing in a world of mutability and human weakness. He is
measured in terms of a social, courtly, romance ideal of knighthood.
Most subtly he is compared to the idea of himself, since the poet
offers us definitions of what a Gawain should be, or might be considered to be. Teasingly he is accused of being an impostor, of not really
being Gawain at all, first by the Lady:

> 'Bot that ye be Gawan, hit gotz in mynde.'
> 'Querfore?' quoth the freke, and freschly he askez,
> Ferde lest he hade fayled in fourme of his castes.
> (1293–95)

The phrase 'in fourme of his castes' places emphasis on the idea of
the performance of Gawain which Gawain is managing to put on,
and this performance is again questioned by the Lady on the next
day (1481–3). It is left to the Green Knight to make the strongest
accusation of imposture:

> And thenne repreved he the prynce with mony prowde
>   wordez:
> 'Thou art not Gawayn,' quoth the gome, 'that is so goud
>   halden,
> That never arwed for no here by hylle ne be vale,
> And now thou fles for ferde er thou fele harmez!
> Such cowardise of that knyght cowthe I never here.'
> (2269–73)

In the face of these challenges that he is failing to deserve a famous
name, Gawain is required to define his own nature, to reply in
effect: 'I am Gawain, but Gawain is other than you think.' No other
hero of medieval romance is so frequently shown as talking about
himself, first with modest, conventional self-depreciation:

> 'I am the wakkest, I wot, and of wyt feblest,
> And lest lur of my lyf, quo laytes the sothe:
> Bot for as much as ye ar myn em I am only to prayse;
> No bounté bot your blod I in my bodé knowe.'   (354–57)

This courtly modesty gradually becomes more than conventional as self-depreciation becomes necessary in the face of too great generosity and praise:

> 'In god fayth,' quoth Gawayn, 'gayn hit me thynkkez,
> Thagh I be not now he that ye of speken;
> To reche to such reverence as ye reherce here
> I am wyye unworthy, I wot wel myselven.'   (1241–44)

From this the poet is able to move his hero to a real recognition of limitation, first in response to the Green Knight's scornful words:

> Quoth Gawayn, 'I schunt onez,
> And so wyl I no more;
> Bot thagh my hede falle on the stonez,
> I con not hit restore.'   (2280–83)

This ruefully humorous and true declaration that the comparison between the Green Knight and Gawain is unfair and unreal, rescues Gawain in the reader's eyes from any accusation of cowardice and prepares for the fuller acknowledgement of human frailty which Gawain is later obliged to make:

> 'For care of thy knokke cowardyse me taght
> To acorde me with covetyse, my kynde to forsake,
> That is larges and lewté that longez to knyghtez.
> Now am I fawty and falce, and ferde haf ben ever
> Of trecherye and untrawthe . . .'   (2379–83)

The contest remains an unfair one, and one inducing cynical disillusion with women, if nothing else, but all men must accept the heritage of sons of Eve.

The hero's answer to the question 'What is Gawain?', which the poem implicitly poses, is humble, and his verdict on the quality of the performance of Gawain which he managed to produce, uncharitable, but the poet's combination of inner and outer senses of his hero forces the reader to take a larger view. We have been shown by the end a hero subordinate, deferential, nervous, who is tested, tempted and tricked, and whose difficult path is overhung by reminders of idealistic and romantic conceptions of knighthood. Treading between quicksands, Gawain shows his positive qualities by his *ad hoc* behaviour in the peculiar situations in which he is unexpectedly placed. The poet gives us dramatised instances of his resistance to sexual temptation, his refusal of rich gifts and his rejection of the opportunity to run away. Throughout, the reader is made conscious of the difficulty of fulfilling a heroic role and is asked to respond to a hero who has sufficient imagination to feel fear and to be sensitively aware that at the end of the road waits death. In a difficult place Gawain acts with

modesty, courtesy, quick-wittedness and discretion, even to the extent
of knowing when to pretend; he has a sympathetic lack of aggressive
self-confidence, a capacity for civilised pleasure, a stern sense of duty,
and sensible, conventional moral standards. His morality fails him
only when basic self-protection is at issue, when he acts, in a way
with which the reader is encouraged to sympathise, with sudden irra-
tionality and gullibility.

The picture created by the poet amounts to a characterisation of
Gawain, a portrait complex enough to have a kind of realness uncom-
mon in romance literature. The journey in *Sir Gawain* is a journey
inward, into the nature of the hero, a journey in which a young, over-
serious, inexperienced Gawain, armed with ideal standards of heroic
conduct, is gradually transformed through struggling against fear, by
resistance to psychological trial, and by discovered weakness into
the experienced and self-condemning figure at the close. The comic
conception of the poem is based on the idea that such a voyage of discovery is inevitable for all men, leaving us with the sense that Gawain
fulfils the role of hero essentially in surviving, particularly since he
has survived an unfair trial with honour dented no more than can be
accepted as the inevitable price of experience.

The world which the poet has created to embody this experience is
a maze through which the bewildered hero has to pick a path. The
only way we can account for the figures whose ambiguous faces make
up the labyrinth, and can relate to the literal story the nebulous suggestions of allegorical figures, of a masque of testing and temptation,
of the fable as a schematised abstraction and so on, is to see the poet's
intention as that of creating images and figures who are, in various
ways, manifestations of the shifting powers which operate in the sub-
lunary world, the powers of fortune, mutability, hazard, time and
mortality. The images of youth and age, of good and bad fortune, of
the passing seasons, of the new and old year, fuse together to form
a broad, shadowy backcloth to the action. Against this backcloth
Gawain's test may be seen as a test not only of knighthood but of
humanity, but the poet, having made use of shadows and suggestions
as part of the suspense and mystery of his tale, seems to dismiss them
as illusions at the end, when the adventure is seen simply. As we
read there is no danger of the poet's ingenuity over-reaching itself,
because, first, we go through the maze with the hero, and have the
shadows and complexities focused for us through his eyes or by having
our attention continually directed to him, and, secondly, we are given
an over-all, distanced sense of the poem as something belonging to
the legendary past, something completed and, therefore, following a
course whose conclusion we, in a sense, know in advance; the details
may be surprising but, whatever the particular outcome for Gawain,

we know that it will be something which we can absorb into our existing knowledge of Arthurian history.

Though I have referred to the ending of the poem as ambiguous, it is not really so; rather it is humanely ironic. Gawain at the end is powerfully abashed and overcome by his failure, as he sees it. What Gawain feels ashamed of is the *result* of his weakness, that because of fear he was led to act in a way unworthy of his code, and be false to his nature as a knight. His fault is not that of feeling fear but allowing fear to pervert his judgement, allowing human instinct to overcome the acquired ideals of perfect behaviour. But the poet makes it clear that for this result Gawain has been punished, and therefore left subsequently free of guilt; the green band is a reminder of the punished fault. The actual weakness, instinctive love of life, Gawain is not blamed for and Gawain himself, though naturally enough with some rueful bitterness, accepts it. His anti-feminist cynicism is implicitly as much an acceptance of his share in the Fall as the explicit statement a few lines later of human frailty, and the poet's choice of this way of recognising one's limitations clearly identifies wry and worldly humour as his conception of a mature attitude to life. Gawain's sorrow and shame convey the bitter sadness of recognising limitation and uphold the value of the romantic ideals with which literary knighthood is identified. What else can men do but build civilisations, establish standards of fair dealing, affront destiny, and attempt to surpass the boundaries of man by creating ideals, orders and structures? The beauty of an ideal life, such as it can be in the world, remains. But the poet persuades us that the joyous assembly at the end is right, even if in all human dealings there is an element of folly, to laugh and to honour Gawain and the belt. By the standards of common sense what matters is that Gawain 'the grace hade geten of his lyve'. The cause of Gawain's failure is itself the reason for going on, absorbing experience and joyfully continuing to pursue ideals which will inevitably have to combat the mutations of time and human nature. The view the poem represents is an essentially generous and comic sense of life, a sympathetic, mature view, containing a dash of cynicism as to whether honour can set to a leg, which accepts the weakness of men but shows the pain of living with intelligence and sympathy. Gawain's progress through the courtly maze of experience to a kind of bitter-sweet maturity seems, eventually, to be a fair enough fictional image of one part of life.

RALPH HANNA III

Unlocking What's Locked:
Gawain's Green Girdle†

Modern understanding of *Sir Gawain and the Green Knight* has been advanced substantially by a distinguished series of articles on the poem's symmetry. Central to this view of the poem stand those two objects most closely associated with the protagonist—the pentangle he bears on his red blazon and the green girdle which replaces it as his device late in the poem.[1] The device on the shield, a sequence of lines carefully "locked" both geometrically and spatially (see 628),[2] is poised against a strip of cloth which Gawain first sees "locked" about the lady's waist and then "unlocked" from it (see 1830–1834). The critical articles which have drawn out the connections between these objects have insisted carefully upon the relationship between the two implements as a sign of Gawain's fault or fall: the promise of the shield is replaced by the guilt of the pentangle.

But in so describing the poem, these readings have attended more carefully to the less dynamic member of this duo, the pentangle. The shield description in the poem brims with everything readers take to be literary significance—it not only demands a careful reading but also delimits the nature of that reading. The poet elaborates a variety of relationships which the outlined star adumbrates, and these relationships have an explicit, a fixed and "locked" form which the star bodes. Moreover, identification of meaning here is public—the shield, after all, is a sign for those Gawain meets to read; and the poet insists on its status as an openly legible device:

> Hit is a syngne þat Salamon set sumquyle
> In bytoknyng of trawþe, bi tytle þat hit habbez . . .
> And ayquere hit is endelez; and Englych hit callen
> Oueral, as I here, þe endeles knot . . .

† From *Viator* 14 (1983): 289–301. Reprinted by permission. © 1983 by The Regents of the University of California.

1. See especially Donald R. Howard, "Structure and Symmetry in *Sir Gawain*," *Speculum* 39 (1964) 425–433; and also Robert W. Ackerman, "Gawain's Shield: Penitential Doctrine in *Sir Gawain and the Green Knight*," *Anglia* 76 (1958) 254–265; Richard Hamilton Green, "Gawain's Shield and the Quest for Perfection," *ELH* 29 (1962) 121–139; Roger Lass, "'Man's Heaven': The Symbolism of Gawain's Shield," *Mediaeval Studies* 28 (1966) 354–360; A. Kent Hieatt, "*Sir Gawain*: Pentangle, *Luf-Lace*, and Numerical Structure," *Studies in Language and Literature* 4 (1968) 339–359; Theodore Silverstein, "Sir Gawain in a Dilemma, or Keeping Faith with Marcus Tullius Cicero," *Modern Philology* (MP) 75 (1977) 1–17; and Robert E. Kaske, "Sir Gawain and the Green Knight," forthcoming in *Proceedings of the Southeastern Institute of Medieval and Renaissance Studies* 10 (for 1979).

2. I cite from the standard text, Norman Davis's revision of J. R. R. Tolkien and E. V. Gordon (Oxford 1967).

Þat is þe pure pentaungel wyth þe peple called
With lore.   (625–626, 629–630, 664–665)[3]

These qualities of publicness and legibility control the kind of
meaning the poet assigns Gawain's blazon. The pentangle links and
locks three discrete areas of experience, two of which the poet asserts
as well known—the eternal value of truth and the pentangle as its
fixed sign (according to the testimony of a famous biblical authority).
Because Gawain's personal habits and attainments correspond to the
form of the device, and because, to pursue geometry a little further,
things equal to the same thing are also equal to each other, Gawain's
unknown and untested personal qualities manifest the qualities of
truth. Understandably, as a summary of Gawain's claims for himself,
the passage has attracted a rich and merited attention.

But in this process of reading, the other half of this central symmetry has been too often ignored. If the pentangle is a fixed emblem, the
girdle is anything but delimited in its potential significance. Although
it stands to the pentangle as failure to perfection, its significance
remains slippery and equivocal. And that, presumably, is just the
point of the poem: Gawain in his failure (however measured) finds
himself inhabiting a world where the promise of perfection is distant
indeed. The pentangle, the emblem of a world where meaning is clear
and exemplary (if not locked to the point of rigidity), becomes
replaced by an object, the girdle, to which meaning must be assigned.
And after that point when Gawain accepts the belt from the lady, at
least one major interest of the poet becomes the proliferation of possible meanings which might be assigned this strip of cloth. Characters
and poet delight in conferring, qualifying, and denying significances.
Gawain's failure in the poem becomes his introduction to (or initiation into) a world where meaning is not an obvious reading-out of geometrical relationships but a slippery and chancy business. And this
world is, of course, that inherent in the entire narrative—the world of
magic where things may not be as they seem, where signs may not (as
the pentangle does) represent transcendent signifieds.

To illustrate and elaborate this process, to explore the significance
of the green girdle, I want to examine part of the process of according
meanings to this object as it occurs in the last quarter of *Gawain*.
Although I will look at what I call "four versions of the girdle," I make
no claim for this nomenclature as implying an exhaustive list and
indeed remain conscious of a good many other obvious "versions" I

3. This public and legible status exists, of course, only within the poem. For no assiduous
   reader of the *Clavis Salamonis* has yet found a pentangle signifying truth; nor do the terms
   "pentangle" and "endless knot" seem to occur elsewhere in Middle English, much less
   "oueral"; nor is Gawain's blazon elsewhere in Middle English a pentangle at all, but rather
   griffins of gold (see alliterative *Morte Arthure* 3869, *Awntyrs off Arthure* 509).

might have suggested. I thus ignore such potential significances as: the girdle as simply a piece of green cloth with no inherent value; the girdle as a token of sexual conquest;[4] and the girdle as illgotten goods taken wrongfully and responsible for a false confession.[5] Although these senses are relevant and involve some very interesting problems unlike those I shall discuss, their analysis would form a supererogatory critical gesture: limiting myself to four versions of the girdle explicitly suggested by the characters will be sufficient for my purposes.

These four "versions" are adequate because they illustrate three major features of the endeavor of finding meaning in the girdle. First, the very existence of a variety of projected readings of the girdle indicates a world where significance is moot and debatable, unlike that world implied by the pentangle. Moreover, since I believe that logically no two of these interpretations can be simultaneously correct as stated, this world is one which demands judgment, the poising and evaluation of conflicting claims to "truth." Second, in this situation all interpretations begin to appear fragile and tentative; they are personalized, a reflection of dramatic situation and point of view. Meaning in some measure ceases to be an identification or intuition of some idealized and exemplary sense of the "real"; it becomes the effort of a limited perceiver to draw conclusions from experience.[6] Third, in multiplying possible significances of the girdle, the poet directly involves the reader in that process of adjudicating meanings which the poem describes. Like our contact with all poems, we as readers respond to *Gawain* serially: from the moment we begin to read, we intuit meaning and attempt to perceive the author's intended sense. We come, as we proceed, to certain hypotheses about what is important in the poem and to hypotheses interrelating these

4. Such a reading is inherent in the context in which Gawain accepts the girdle (see 1774–1775, or the reference to the object as a *drurye* 2003); see Albert B. Friedman and Richard H. Osberg, "Gawain's Girdle as Traditional Symbol," *Journal of American Folklore* 90 (1977) 301–315. Such an identification produces an implausible reading but one relevant to the kinds of problems I shall discuss below. For if one seriously entertains this identification, the girdle represents an event which never occurred. There is at least one analogue for such an extraordinary dissolving of the narrative—the adultery in *The Manciple's Tale*, which does occur but which the conclusion of the poem virtually denies.

5. See especially John Burrow, "The Two Confession Scenes in *Sir Gawain and the Green Knight*," MP 57 (1959) 73–79 and the later expansion in *A Reading of "Sir Gawain and the Green Knight"* (London 1965); the corrective to Burrow's earlier views, P. J. C. Field, "A Rereading of *Sir Gawain and the Green Knight*," *Studies in Philology* 68 (1971) 255–269; and some provocative comments by Donald R. Howard, *The Three Temptations* (Princeton 1966) 240. The tendency of all these treatments to engage in the language of traditional penitential casuistry I take as germane to my thesis, for arguments *de casibus conscientiae* presuppose the difficulties of interpreting and assessing experience.

6. As a thing of this world, a literal object, the girdle inevitably functions as a sign, but what it signifies depends on the context in which it appears, and most importantly, on the acuity of the eye that perceives it"; R. A. Halpern, "The Last Temptation of Gawain: 'Hony Soyt Qui Mal Pence,'" *American Benedictine Review* 23 (1972) 379. Halpern argues (353–384) that Gawain's interpretation of his experience is valid.

various leading ideas. Near the end of *Gawain*, when we first see the green girdle, we think we have a clear sense of what is at issue in the poem. But this meaning that we have intuited the poet quite deliberately seeks to obscure. Issues we had thought settled become unclear; that fragility and tentativeness which I have associated with various readings of the girdle by the characters become part of our reading experience as well. Rather than clarifying the poem's issues, the climax of Gawain's adventure makes that very problem of evaluation and interpretation with which the characters are involved the center of our reading experience.

Version 1 of the girdle, the lady's claim that it has magical properties, epitomizes certain attributes of all the potential meanings assigned the girdle. All these "definitions" share two features: they are not susceptible to any validation, and any reading against the narrative events of the poem confuses issues that have seemed clearly explained elsewhere. These qualities measure the extent of Gawain's failure, his descent from the emblematic world of the pentangle into one of opinion and uncertainty.

Similar properties become inherent in the language of the poem at just the moment when Gawain considers accepting the girdle:

> Þen kest þe knyȝt, and hit come to his hert
> Hit were a juel for þe jopardé þat hym iugged were:
> When he acheued to þe chapel his chek for to fech,
> Myȝt he haf slypped to be vnslayn, þe sleȝt were noble.
> (1855–1858)

Although explicitly not a jeweled ring (and not even especially rich in ornament—see 1832–1833), the belt, to Gawain's thinking, becomes momentarily a thing of gemlike value. And far from visualizing his activity as that of the disciplined and codebound pentangle knight, Gawain now sees his hope as "slipping," as escaping from the locked organization of his blazon into some other realm of action. Further, nobility becomes no longer the attribute of a warrior knight (see 623) but of *sleȝt*, "trickery." The degree to which the protagonist has already entered a world of slipperiness is measured both by the embarrassing rhyme *knyght: sleight* and by the fact that Gawain, for once in bedroom duel, has surrendered his own language for the lady's terminology, if not her perspective (see *slyȝt*, 1854). And even before he has accepted her offer, Gawain has fallen prey to the lady's suggestiveness: his acceptance of her terms indicates both a willingness to take as somehow true what is not experiential and in excess of available fact (the girdle is no jewel), and, insofar as experience is at issue, to treat it from an evaluative but potentially nonidealistic perspective (in which such oxymora as "noble sleȝtes" are possible verbal constructions).

The nature of the girdle's magic is defined by the lady when she produces the object:

> . . . quat gome so is gorde with þis grene lace,
> While he hit hade hemely halched aboute,
> Þer is no haþel vnder heuen tohewe hym þat my3t,
> For he my3t not be slayn for sly3t vpon erþe.   (1851–1854)

The girdle is a device of power, one that renders its bearer invulnerable, but most especially (and appropriately) invulnerable to dismemberment, *tohewynge*. This claim of magical potency is apparently validated in the poem by Gawain's survival: although not unscathed, he is not *tohewen*.

As every reader knows, however, things in *Gawain* are not quite so simple. Making the girdle into the token of salvation accords to it a unique causal role in the narrative: it, and it alone, is the proximate cause of the hero's living through the experience. But, as all readers know, causality (even literary causality) is potentially far more complicated than this reading suggests. Moreover, if the girdle ensures Gawain's safety in danger, the reader must reject the force of important pieces of the narrative: if the girdle is causally coercive on the acts at the Green Chapel, neither the symmetry of the Green Knight's feints, nor the skill of his axwielding, nor his explanations of having stagemanaged the entire scene (a claim that he controls the girdle rather than it him) can be allowed any real effect. From this point of view, the girdle as causal factor competes with other, perhaps more proximate, causal possibilities, and choosing to identify it as the magic object responsible for the action, thus validating the meaning assigned by the lady, begins to appear capricious at best.

An additional issue should prove yet more unsettling: adopting with any seriousness that magical significance the lady assigns the girdle forces the reader to challenge ideas which he takes as givens of the poem. If one accepts that the girdle represents some magic power which allows Gawain to elude that physical harm for which he has contracted, one must hold in abeyance what seems one of the poem's most basic and explicit *données*. In the poem the girdle must then function in at best an oxymoronic fashion (cf. *noble sle3t*). Rather than a thing which magically dissolves a situation of expected death, the girdle is that thing in the poem which brings Gawain into gravest danger, which provokes the possibility of death. Accepting the girdle does not allow Gawain to elude physical correction; indeed, it is the single act which makes it most apparent that he must be corrected. If one accepts the lady's identification and uses it to read the poem, the girdle becomes both the magical thing by which Gawain is sustained in life and what most thoroughly threatens his life. It is possible to resolve this dilemma quickly by saying that the lady either lies or is mistaken. But it seems to me wrong to do so, or to do so without pause: the persistence of this kind of dilemma as the poem nears its conclusion indicates that the poet emphasizes such problems deliberately. Thus the reader must, at a minimum, recognize that he has faced and tried to adjudicate contradictory views.

Version 2 of the girdle holds a particularly central place in the literature about *Gawain*, and, indeed, is often taken as if it were the only effort in the poem to assign a significance to the green belt.[7]

> Corsed worth cowarddyse and couetyse boþe!
> In yow is vylany and vyse þat vertue disstryez . . .
> For care of þy knokke cowardyse me taʒt
> To acorde me with couetyse, my kynde to forsake,
> Þat is larges and lewté þat longez to knyʒtez.
>
> (2374–2375, 2379–2381)

Gawain, angrily discomfited at being caught in his trick, here names what he takes to be his sins. Later (see 2429–2438, 2506–2510) he imposes these identifications upon the girdle: it becomes the sign of the failure of his quest, explicitly in terms of these sins. Like the lady, who asserts a magic power which gives the girdle value, Gawain also attempts to name that value resident in the object, to render it significant within his experience. Unlike the lady's identification, and much more in the spirit of Versions 3 and 4, Gawain's claim represents a variety of symbolic reading. But one has to understand such symbolmaking as not at all susceptible to standards of validity. There is no inevitable connection between a symbol and its referent (signs are generally arbitrary), and the only measure of validity is public acceptance, whereby the symbol enters usage and passes current. But it should not surprise the reader that the poet has gone out of his way to suggest the peculiarly arbitrary quality of Gawain's reading.

If the reader accepts Gawain's identification of the girdle as a sign of covetousness and cowardice, some very serious difficulties in interpretation result. If Gawain is cowardly or covetous, then these words cannot mean in the poem what they normally mean in Middle English, and the literary portrayal cannot be analyzed in any straightforward way.[8] The poet is explicit in his view that Gawain does not take the girdle for reasons at all associated with avarice (see 1832–1837

---

7. See Burrow, *Reading* (n. 5 above) 129ff.; David Farley Hills, "Gawain's Fault in *Sir Gawain and the Green Knight*," *Review of English Studies* 14 (1963) 124–131; and G. V. Smithers, "What *Sir Gawain and the Green Knight* Is About," *Medium Aevum* 32 (1963) 171–189.

8. A notable effort in this regard is Hills (n. 7 above), who associates *couetyse* with Latin theological uses of *cupiditas*; Hills is ably answered by John Burrow, *Review of English Studies* 15 (1964) 56. Similarly, Silverstein (n. 1 above) 11–13 offers Ciceronian glosses for Gawain's language; these I find forced, in part because Silverstein uses considerable sleight of hand in revealing the Ciceronian tradition.

and 1846–1848, mentioned above, and particularly 2037–2042): accepting Gawain's view that the girdle represents such an avaricious proclivity flatly conflicts with direct narrative statement.

The case against branding Gawain a coward is similar, though more difficult. Although Gawain clearly takes the girdle "for to sauen hym-self" (2040) and although he flinches once at a proffered blow (2267), his pusillanimousness is of a minor and muted sort. Both bearing the girdle and flinching become less than adequate demonstrations of cowardice in the context of Part IV where Gawain performs, if any-thing, with a valor far beyond the ordinary. He could, after all, accept the guide's offer and flee; he could, even later, be overcome by the the-atrical eeriness of the Green Chapel and Green Knight's appearance; he could flinch a second time, rather than upbraid the Green Knight for toying with him; he could be considerably less plucky and sensitive to the possibility of divine protection (however dramatically ironic the statements at 2132–2139 and 2156–2159, Gawain plainly believes them, and they bolster his resolve).[9] To assert bluntly, as Gawain does, that he is a cowardly failure misses much of the narrative dedicated to defining a figure not cowardly at all. The reader must find Gawain's creation of symbolic readings for the girdle just as problematic as the lady's claim for its magical powers.

More interesting than the possible perversity of Gawain's symbol-making should be its familiarity as a human activity in the poem. That is, Gawain's identification of the girdle with his sin forms an act of symbol-making of precisely the same type as that represented in the pentangle. The blazon embodies a universal and abstract nexus of meaning and joins it with the properties of the person who bears it. Here matters are very similar: Gawain has in some way failed, been found faulty; the girdle becomes a sign linking personal faultiness with a universal sense of fault. But the very act of identifi-cation suggests the limitations of the procedure itself: having, as he thinks, forfeited any claim to the purity of the pentangle, Gawain finds a new blazon and tries to assert the same parameters of mean-ing for it. However, losing the pentangle and the world of perfection which it signifies may render this form of symbolic relationship for-ever impossible for Gawain. The pentangle forms an appropriate sign because it bodes a world of Trawþe—a relation of identity and unity. But having forfeited the pentangle as proper emblem, Gawain now inhabits a world where such relations of identity are not neces-sarily true, where, like the quality of his knighthood, the very "kynde" or nature (2380) of things may have changed. Rather than truth

---

9. Two studies offer useful comments on the narrative qualities of Part IV: Paul Delany, "The Role of the Guide in *Sir Gawain and the Green Knight*," *Neophilologus* 49 (1965) 250–255; and Stoddard Malarkey and J. Barre Toelken, "Gawain and the Green Girdle," *Journal of English and Germanic Philology* 63 (1964) 14–20.

being available, emblematic, and unified, it may now need to be discovered. The competing versions of what the girdle is (or might be) are testimony to such a world of experiential truthseeking: Gawain, at the moment he labels the girdle "sin," may merely demonstrate a naivete in believing he inhabits a simpler and less problematic world.

Further, Gawain may quite literally overlook and thereby misread an emblem more relevant to his state:

> Þe scharp schrank to þe flesche þurȝ þe schyre grece,
> Þat þe schene blod ouer his schulderes schot to þe erþe;
> And quen þe burne seȝ þe blode blenk on þe snawe,
> He sprit forth spenne-fote . . .
> Neuer syn þat he watz burne borne of his moder
> Watz he neuer in þis worlde wyȝe half so blyþe.
> (2313–2316, 2320–2321)

The knight's blood, sign both of his guilty mortality and (because he is unaccountably alive to see it) his vital force regained, stains the blank field about him. The powerful evocation of rebirth, a newfound possibility, is balanced against the wilderness snowfield—a *tabula rasa* on which Gawain must learn to write what he (not the world) now is. This scene may come as close to an adequate reading of the girdle as any: an unexamined vitality, apparently valued for itself, yet undefined and not clearly reflecting whatever values produced its pursuit.

Version 3 of the girdle is promulgated by the Green Knight:

> And I gif þe, sir, þe gurdel þat is golde-hemmed;
> For hit is grene as my goune, Sir Gawayn, ȝe maye
> Þenk vpon þis ilke þrepe, þer þou forth þryngez
> Among prynces of prys, and þis a pure token
> Of þe chaunce of þe grene chapel at cheualrous knyȝtez.
> (2395–99)[1]

Just as Gawain has done, the Green Knight attempts a symbolic reading, in which the girdle should be construed (with the Green Knight showing greater awareness than Gawain that symbolic readings achieve validity only as they achieve public acceptance) as a sign of the chivalric adventure in which Gawain has been involved. Just as Gawain's reading, this effort is not validated within the poem; just as Gawain's identification, it affects and is affected by the reading of the poem. The two symbolic efforts differ, however, in manner: Gawain's reading, in a justifiably self-centered effort at finding significance in failure, overelaborates the girdle; the Green Knight, dialectically, minimizes its significance. The girdle becomes, in his rendering, merely

---

1. I have altered Davis's punctuation slightly to remove the full stop after "goune" (2396).

another trophy for a Camelot display case, and this typically Green Knightish matter-of-factness creates difficulties for the reader.

Identifying the girdle as simply the "token" of a chivalric adventure reduces and qualifies one basic assumption of any reading, that girdle and pentangle are significant objects in some poised relationship. The Green Knight's reading creates different and unsettling balances in the literary relations of the poem. In his telling, the girdle becomes less like the pentangle and more like the ax of Part I (see 478–480), both implements associated with the quest, the one a sign of its acceptance, the other of its achievement. In these terms, the Green Knight's reading gains further support as demonstrating a link between the two halves of the poem's double plot. As the ax reflects the beheading game, the girdle becomes a sign of the private testing Gawain has undergone in his bedchamber. This reading renders the second plot a symmetrical and balanced portion of Gawain's experience.

But reading *Gawain* this way will surely not appeal to most, for such an interpretation flattens the poem's significance. What readers take to be the supreme testing of the superlative Round Table knight becomes in the Green Knight's handling merely one of innumerable Arthurian adventures. Just as Gawain senses himself the center of his world, the most important person he knows, and tries to construct a significant version of his experience, readers of the poem desire a peculiar and special significance, in the poem conveyed by the shield and its coat of arms.

From such a perspective, the Green Knight's sense of significance exhibits the same personalized quality as Gawain's treatment of the girdle. For the Knight, however appreciative of Gawain's virtues he may be (see 2362–2365, 2469–2470), all Arthur's men are "bot berdlez chylder" (280): significance for them is established merely by contact with him. Moreover, for him, Gawain's shield has none of those resonances of Gawain's personal history which the poet explains to the reader; in their contact, where Gawain performs only as houseguest and passive recipient of his blow, the shield lacks function. For a reader determined to see the poem as exhibiting Gawain's unique significance, this symbolic reading will seem easy to reject. But the Green Knight's view of the girdle is part of a larger pattern and shares with other versions that power to force the reader to examine significance, to assess potential meanings.

The fourth reading of the girdle is introduced in the closing lines, yet remains the only one which achieves any general currency in the poem:

> Þe kyng comfortez þe knyȝt, and alle þe court als
> Laȝen loude þerat, and luflyly acorden
> Þat lordes and ladis þat longed to þe Table,

Vche burne of þe broþerhede, a bauderyk schulde haue,
A bende abelef hym aboute of a bryȝt grene,
And þat, for sake of þat segge, in swete to were.   (2513–18)

The members of the Round Table define (and aggressively assert their definition of) the green girdle as a sign of their human complicity and sympathy, their fellowship with the discomfited Gawain. The badge, especially in the mood of hilarity with which it is created, the laughter which greets Gawain's overly dire confession of failure, becomes the inverse of the sign Gawain intended. Rather than a badge of grief and shame, the girdle now betokens courtly civility, that mirth and courtesy which binds the Round Table. This signification is explicitly designed to reject the moralistic obduracy and naive despair of Version 2.

Yet although it passes current at the end of the poem, even gaining an ironic historical validity by notice in "þe best boke of romaunce" (2521), this interpretation seems as qualified as the poem's other assays at assigning meaning to the girdle. First, the reading is created in a clear dramatic context which underscores the capriciousness and self-indulgence of its making. As an act, assigning to the girdle the implications of good fellowship is designed to have an effect—the reintegration of Gawain into chivalric society, the cessation of his moralistic moping over his failure. Meaning here is centered entirely in context and situation and carries with it that fortuitousness which seems inevitably to hover about jests.

Moreover, this reading resembles the Green Knight's in its denial of significance to an experience the reader has felt to be significant. As a positive gesture, of course, the fellowship of the Round Table means to indicate to Gawain that he is no worse than they, that he is overly morbid about the discovery of his faulted humanity. But in making this claim the members of the Round Table create dissonances similar to those I have analyzed earlier. The generalization of the girdle as heraldic badge indicates a community of experience, but Gawain's experience the Round Table has not shared. Indeed earlier its members suggested that to undertake the quest was folly (see 539ff., 672–86). Further, in defining the girdle as they choose, the courtiers deny that most unique, and for the reader most significant, aspect of Gawain's adventure—his effort at self-discovery. Whatever else it may indicate, Gawain's shame, which the Round Table finds so unsettlingly risible that it must attempt to dissipate it, reflects the protagonist's sense that his experience is something to be learned from, a reminder of past misperception of his human nature. This possibility, which most readers take to be of considerable import, the Round Table interpretation of the girdle severely truncates.

All four efforts at according significance to the girdle, then, seem problematic insofar as they create potential disruptions in the meaning of the poem. In the characters' persistent effort to assert meaning, they manage only to draw the reader's attention to the difficulty of defining both what the girdle is and what Gawain's acceptance of it signifies. And that is, of course, the major point. The pentangle promises a world where Trawþe is a primary value, where identity is secure, and where unity defines a real relationship. Once Gawain fails by accepting a girdle he does not intend to exchange, he has denied his identity as previously constituted, has ceased to be the knight of Trawþe. His world becomes filled with the possibility of mistake, illusion, or magic, a place where values lack that clarity they had before. This world is not one where truths may be identified but one where they must be read out, intuited and interpreted, or read in, imposed. The poet's insistent creation of interpretive situations for both characters and reader forms a designed emphasis, a requirement that the reader apprehend the difficulty of such a world, one more significantly like the reader's own than like Camelot.

Another way of saying the same thing is to draw attention to the poem's repeated description of acts involving exchange. Generally, up to the point when Gawain accepts the girdle, exchange always appears to be even in practice; although the objects swapped (a kiss and venison steaks, for example) may differ in terms of market value, the covenanted rules of exchange games seem to imply that getting a bad deal is undone by the fun of playing the game (see 69: "Ladies laȝed ful loude, þoȝ þay lost haden"). Because of the leveling activity of mirth, this system can be visualized as one in which objects all become roughly equivalent through the courtliness with which they are offered and accepted. But Gawain's retention of the girdle breaks the equivalence structure and introduces a more deceptive, yet potentially more hardminded, standard, that of valuation. Keeping the girdle is the act of determining that one priority (saving one's neck) should deserve more attention than another (playing an exchange game); thus the girdle becomes too valuable to be returned. To say this is to indicate that Gawain's consciousness of fault is merely a belated discovery of what has always been present but unclear to him. Gawain's quest-centeredness has obscured for him the extent to which he has depended upon conventional signification (the pentangle, for example) rather than perceiving its potential limits as a purely human construction.[2]

In pursuing this theme, the *Gawain*-poet is, of course, at one with his great contemporaries. Similar examinations of the power of the transcendent and of its distance from the awkward muddle of human

2. Such issues have not been much discussed in the literature; there are provocative comments in P. B. Taylor, "Commerce and Comedy in *Sir Gawain*," *Philological Quarterly* 50 (1971) 1–15; and Martin Stevens, "Laughter and Game in *Sir Gawain and the Green Knight*," *Speculum* 47 (1972) 65–78.

affairs so typify the works of other Ricardian writers that those themes I have been discussing in *Gawain* may define one major interest of a literary period. In works such as *The Canterbury Tales*, *Piers Plowman*, and *Mandeville's Travels*, other leading authors of the late fourteenth century show an abiding interest in such difficulties.

As the most thorough exemplar of this theme, one might consider *The Canterbury Tales*.[3] Partial and limited human perspective inheres in the gross form and manner of the poem, for Chaucer as poet can only say what he wants to say in the *Tales* by an act of imaginative fragmentation. To write the work he wishes, he must divide himself into a series of twenty-odd voices, each of which speaks separately and uniquely. Moreover, each voice in its primary mode offers only an interpretation, a tale. Personalized interpretation, a leading theme near the end of *Gawain*, is the central concern of Chaucer's *Tales*.

The tales interpret because, even while they differ, they show a common and constant interest in mimesis, an effort at describing external reality. (Compare the Host's injunction to tell "aventures that whilom han bifalle," A 795.)[4] Given the paucity of instructions for what would constitute an adequate tale (only "best sentence and moost solaas," A 798), each of Chaucer's voices, in theory, begins with the same range of human experience to draw upon. That the tales vary in setting, in manner, and in genre testifies to human unpredictability in responding to experience: what each voice tells (and how it tells it) reflects Chaucer's definition of a limited fragment of his total poetic personality. In its partiality, each voice is created in order to view the world in a particular manner, to emphasize certain aspects of

3. Since I choose to concentrate upon only one of these works, some suggestion of how I would support my contentions from the others may be in order. *Piers*, of course, reverses the pattern held in common by *The Canterbury Tales* and *Gawain*. Langland fervently seeks for a way in which the transcendent can become an animating force in human experience while demonstrating the utter impossibility of such a conjunction. The poem's persistent fits and starts are created by the readiness of the characters to substitute short-term human goals, mere interpretations of felicity, for the uncompromising, forbidding, and unattainable eternal word of the gospels. For two outstanding discussions, see Anne Middleton, "Two Infinites: Grammatical Metaphor in *Piers Plowman*," *ELH* 39 (1972) 169–188; and Charles Muscatine, "Locus of Action in Medieval Narrative," *Romance Philology* 17 (1963) 115–122. *Travels*, a French work which enjoyed an enormous English vogue in the period 1390–1425, creates one set of guidelines for interpretation in its relatively sober and conventional guide to Palestinian pilgrimage spots; in the more extensive description of the wonders of the East, the reader is then forced to come to terms with a variety of experiences calculated to shock and rebuff that very piety to which the Jerusalem itinerary appeals. "Mandeville" shows, for example, no moral qualms while describing the Hindu juggernaut; the reader, primed by description of the scenes of Christ's sacrifice, has to reevaluate and expand his sense of appropriate religious action to accommodate an event which looks suspiciously like a paradoxical holy suicide. In this process, "Mandeville" coerces the reader into redefining his notions of barbarity and religious behavior, into forsaking a narrow and unific system of judgment for some broader sense of the "natural." But the work gives no hint of how to do this save through the imperturbable voice of its narrator. For the best of the very few literary discussions, see Donald R. Howard, "The World of *Mandeville's Travels*," *Yearbook of English Studies* 1 (1971) 1–17.

4. I cite the standard text, F. N. Robinson, *The Works of Geoffrey Chaucer*, ed., 2 (Boston 1957).

experience and to exclude others. The resulting work, with its variety of nontangential and often antithetical views of the same subject (marriage, for instance), provides a wealth of possible interpretations of the world and its problems. And since in fragmenting his voice Chaucer has denied himself the possibility of invoking any transcendent standard through authorial commentary (the voice identified as "I" is one of the poem's most clearly limited), the collision of various interpretations, of possible ways of viewing the experiential world, is never resolved within the *Tales*.

But Chaucer's involvement with interpretation does not stop with the governing conception of the *Tales*. For besides their primary role as separate vehicles for the interpretation of experience, the created voices collide in a secondary role. Commentary upon the tales, a superadded patina of interpretation, fills the frame which carries the larger pilgrimage narrative. And here also diversity is a keynote, since opinions range from the Host's constant efforts at tying interpretive tales to specific human situations to the Parson's denunciation of fiction as a useful device to the Man of Law's attempt at analyzing the Chaucer canon. In addition to a diverse interpretation of experience, the *Tales* go far beyond *Gawain* in providing a wideranging discussion of literary interpretation.

Moreover, the theme of interpretation is perhaps one of the most constant features of the tales themselves. Since Chaucer's voices tend to describe the world through fabliaux (itself a surprising interpretation in the context of Chaucer's career as courtly poet), the treatment is most frequently comic. The tales emphasize those misperceptions and misreadings of experience to which man is ceaselessly prone. Life, for characters in the tales, frequently involves an assessment of the world we inhabit—most often in terms which experience shows to have been sadly short-sighted. Even within the narrow focus of the individual tale, reality proves more various than the characters can conceive. This interest in the faulted assessment of experience produces an evaluative vocabulary which insists on human perception and its difficulties. Chaucer's voices constantly discuss the characters' *entente, illusion, fantasye*, or *affeccioun*. All these terms direct attention to the human predilection for creating mental images of the world; in the action of the tales, these interpretive visions are measured against other interpretations, the worlds created by Chaucer's voices.

And given the fiction of an evaluative contest into which Chaucer places his fragmented voices, the interplay between tale and a critical audience invokes interpretation as well. Many of Chaucer's voices seem aware that the act of interpreting the world by a tale invites an evaluation, a new interpretation, of that interpretation offered. *The Canterbury Tales* is crammed with voices so oppressively aware of

this fact that they offer within their tales a constant stream of interpretation designed to forestall evaluation. Ironically, such self-
consciousness proves almost invariably faulted: in the cases of the
Physician or the Manciple, to take only two examples, the tale testifies to truths of which the interpreter-voice seems unaware. Such nar-
rators may, within their very different modality, remind readers of
Gawain's insistence that his experience is meaningful—and in only
the way he says it is.

The great Canterbury tales offer more sophisticated examples of
this interplay. Although the tours de force of the Clerk and Pardoner
and the subdued conscientiousness of the Knight surely rival it, the
Franklin provides perhaps the most notable example of such behavior.
At the end of his tale, a thoroughgoing demonstration of the capacity
of human *fantasye* or *illusioun* to pervert the glories of God's creation
and bring disorder into existence, the Franklin eschews explicit interpretation. Having already evoked tolerance as a standard by which to
measure human relations (see F 761–86), he invites the audience's
indulgence of and participation in his narrative interpretation: "Which
was the mooste fre, as thynketh yow?" (F 1622). The question, like
many of those definitions of the girdle introduced near the end of
Gawain, neutralizes audience response (none of the characters has
seemed a paragon of *frenesse* or nobility at most points in the tale).
And by inviting an audience evaluation which is potentially quite
diverse, this Chaucerian voice posits a colloquy in which no definitive
answer may be forthcoming.[5]

Similarly, at the end of *Gawain*, the point is not that the girdle
means any single finite thing but that it has become a "token" to be
interpreted by both characters and reader. In this procedure, *Gawain*
forces one into a direct perception of that world of "blysse and blun-
der" (18)[6] which the poet has affirmed as his subject from the opening lines:

> Þe tulk þat þe trammes of tresoun þer wroȝt
> Watz tried for his tricherie, þe trewest on erthe:
> Hit watz Ennias þe athel. . . .   (3–5)

5. In Chaucer's creation, where the poet has dissolved into a variety of constituent voices, the
Franklin's question represents, I think, one of two ideal endings. The other, the actual ending of the *Tales*, reasserts an unquestionable transcendent standard but places it so far from
the human world of interpretation as to show the total limitation of all human voices. Thus
the poet who is the sum of all the poem's interpreters, tellers and characters, retracts his
creation. For two powerful recent statements of similar views of the *Tales*, see H. Marshall
Leicester, Jr., "The Art of Impersonation: A General Prologue to the *Canterbury Tales*,"
PMLA 95 (1980) 213–224; and David Aers, *Chaucer, Langland, and the Creative Imagination* (London 1980), esp. 81ff. Although ironic readings of the Franklin's Tale seem currently in vogue, I find compelling in its scope Harry Berger, Jr.'s "The F-Fragment of the
Canterbury Tales: Part II," *Chaucer Review* 1 (1967) 135–156.
6. See John M. Ganim, "Disorientation, Style, and Consciousness in *Sir Gawain and the
Green Knight*," *PMLA* 91 (1976) 376–384.

The poem unfolds in such a world of ambiguity, where treachery and nobility may coexist, where events are not necessarily what they seem.[7] In this world, the emblematic and exemplary represents only a willed assumption, a simplifying condition which defines the noble life of leisure and courtesy. But the fundamental tone of *Gawain*, especially as it nears its conclusion, has little to do with the exemplaristic or the gravity of departing from it, of falling as Gawain does. Rather the poem approximates a process of discovery or exploration, the process of recognizing the persistent intractibility of experience, its potential variousness, and the often self-willed limitation of human efforts to comprehend that variousness. The multitude of interpretations to which characters subject a green silk belt adorned with gold thread suggests both the difficulty of knowing a simple physical object and the potential caprice involved in all human claims to knowledge. This is the world which Gawain, to his sorrow, inhabits, perhaps a uniquely fourteenth-century world,[8] one suggested in the poem most forcefully by the green girdle.

LYNN STALEY JOHNSON

[Regenerative Time in *Sir Gawain and the Green Knight*][†]

*   *   *

Both a vision of history as a series of cycles and a vision of history as a process of dissolution underline the effects of time and thus the theme of mutability. In both cases, man is a prisoner of time, and human history may perhaps teach only certain lessons about the art of living in time. In his efforts to cope with time, man is alone. The universe and the earth undergo a similar process of change, but only man knows he changes and knows his time is limited. In *The Cosmo-*

---

7. These lines are taken as proleptic of the whole by Alfred David, "Gawain and Aeneas," *English Studies* 49 (1968) 402–409. See also Derek W. Hughes, "The Problem of Reality in *Sir Gawain and the Green Knight*," *University of Toronto Quarterly* 40 (1971) 217–235; and Morton Donner, "Tact as a Criterion of Reality in *Sir Gawain and the Green Knight*," *Papers in English Language and Literature* 1 (1965) 306–315.

8. There seem at least interesting analogues to be drawn between the difficulties of significcation the *Gawain*-poet and Chaucer propose and the presumptions of fourteenth-century philosophy, most especially Ockhamist skepticism. But one should note that there are analogies to *Gawain* in early romance tradition; see Robert W. Hanning, *The Individual in Twelfth-Century Romance* (New Haven 1977), esp. 171–193 on multiple perspective within romance. (See also the references to *Gawain*, 163 and 275 n. 29.).

† From *The Voice of the Gawain Poet* (Madison: University of Wisconsin Press, 1984), pp. 52–69. Reprinted by permission.

graphia, Bernard Silvestris distinguishes between man and nature in their relations to time:

> The nature of the universe outlives itself, for it flows back into itself, and so survives and is nourished by its very flowing away. For whatever is lost only merges again with the sum of things, and that it may die perpetually, never dies wholly. But man, ever liable to affliction by forces far less harmonious, passes wholly out of existence with the failure of his body. Unable to sustain himself, and wanting nourishment from without, he exhausts his life, and a day reduces him to nothing.[1]

Man, unlike nature, perceives time's limits and is therefore forced to use time or to escape it. An awareness of change need not, however, end with a simple recognition of mutability. For the Middle Ages, the Bible described the end of time itself in apocalypse. Decay could therefore become a providential process, ushering in a new golden age without the strictures of time, as Gower affirms:

> And seide how that is goddes myht,
> Which whan men wene most upryht
> To stonde, schal hem overcaste.
> And that is of this world the laste,
> And thanne a newe schal beginne,
> Fro which a man schal nevere twinne;
> Or al to peine or al to pes
> That world schal lasten endeles.[2]

For Gower, as for other medieval writers, change is a natural process, and man's insecurity in a universe of change should align him with infinite and changeless principles. This process of reorientation is, of course, the lesson Lady Philosophy teaches Boethius and the lesson deduced by numerous medieval and Renaissance personae who contemplate the process of time. Change exists, but it need not threaten man.

The liturgical calendar thus offered another way of ordering time. Like the natural cycle, the liturgical cycle describes a circular motion, but it revolves from spring (March 25) to spring, not from winter to winter.[3] This year begins and ends in new life and has as

---

1. Bernard Silvestris, *The Cosmographia,* trans. Winthrop Wetherbee (New York, 1973), p. 126.
2. Gower, *Confessio Amantis,* in *The complete works of John Gower,* ed. G. C. Macaulay (Oxford, 1901), Prologue, lines 655–622. For a survey of late medieval ways of considering history, see M.W. Bloomfield, *Piers Plowman as a Fourteenth-Century Apocalypse* (New Brunswick, 1962) pp. 98–103. See also J. A. Burrow, *A Reading of Sir Gawain and the Green Knight* (London: Routledge, 1965), p. 34.
3. See Sherman Hawkins's discussion of time in "Mutabilitie and the Cycle of the Months," in *Form and Convention in the Poetry of Edmund Spenser,* Selected Papers from the English Institute, ed. William Nelson (New York, 1967), pp. 76–102.

Sir Gawain's Year

Date	Liturgical Date	Liturgical Significance of the Day	Event in Poem
January 1	Feast of the Circumcision		Green Knight's appearance
November 1	Feast of All Saints		Gawain celebrates at Camelot
November 2	Feast of All Souls		Gawain leaves Camelot
	Advent	"Christi est duplex in Scriptura, scilicet Adventus in carnem, & Adventus ad judicium. Primus fuit amorosus, sed secundus rigorosus; primus fuit clementiae, sed secundus justitiae; primus fuit pietatis, sed secundus severitatis."	Gawain journeys north
December 24	Eve of the Nativity		Gawain prays to Mary; he arrives at Hautdesert
December 25	Feast of the Nativity	"Primus fuit nativitatis ex matre Virgine, in quo notatur constantiae stabilitas . . .	Feasting at Hautdesert
December 26	Feast of St. Stephen, Protomartyr	"in quo notatur constantiae stabilitas . . .	Feasting at Hautdesert

December 27	Feast of St. John the Evangelist	"… qui comparatur Aquilae, in quo notatur contemplationis sublimitas …"	Feasting at Hautdesert
December 28	Feast of the Holy Innocents	"… in quo notatur innocentiae synceritas. …"	Unaccounted for
December 29	Feast of St. Thomas à Beckett	"… qui fuit audacissimus martyr; in quo notatur spiritualis audaciae virilitas. …"	Hind-hunt; temptation of lust
December 30		"… a nullo denominatur, quo notatur ipsius mirabilis humilitas …"	Boar-hunt; temptation of pride
December 31	Feast of St. Sylvester (receiver of the Donation of Constantine)	"qui fuit sanctissimus Episcopus, in quo notatur suae praelationis auctoritas. (Et iste assimulatur veneri seu lucifero, qui sc. Episcopi lucem scientiae & honestatis prae caeteris debent habere.)"	Fox-hunt; temptation of avarice: Gawain's failure in truth
January 1	Feast of the Circumcision	Octave of Christmas, denoting resurrection, or the New Man	Beheading scene

Note: Latin quotations from Petrus Berchorius, *Dictionarium morale,* in *Opera* (Colona, 1730), s.v. "Adventus," "Circumciso."

seasons central events in the life of the Church. The liturgical calendar allows an individual to transcend time by participating in
moments that transcend time. He can thus celebrate the eternal
truths figured by Church festivals and escape time's limits by figuratively aligning himself with those truths.

Although *Sir Gawain* addresses itself to the ethical lessons of time
and history, the poet also provides us with a cycle of regenerative
time. The poet's careful references to certain significant dates in the
life of the Church serve to remind his audience of the lessons of
another way of reckoning time. While we recognize the lessons of
history implicit in *Sir Gawain*, and the reality of decay, we also see
Sir Gawain and Camelot against the framework of another sort of
year whose lessons concern spiritual renewal, eternal life, and the
duties of the Christian warrior in the battle of life.

Every event in the poem occurs on a meaningful date in the liturgical calendar. *Sir Gawain* begins on New Year's Day, the Feast of
the Circumcision, and moves quickly through the seasonal cycle to
begin again on the Feast of All Saints, November 1, the day Gawain
prepares to leave Camelot. Gawain's adventure occurs between
November 2, All Souls' Day, and the Feast of the Circumcision, the
next New Year's Day. The poet's references to the liturgical calendar
are particularly important because the lessons of the Church year
are reflected in the action of the poem. As the chart illustrates, the
poet uses the framework of the liturgical calendar to suggest Gawain's
spiritual progression from ignorance to knowledge and thus the possibilities of man's regeneration in time.[4]

The Feast of All Saints, the last full day Gawain spends at Camelot,
is an especially auspicious day for his preparation for what will be a
test of inner chivalry. The poet notes that the day is a feast day (536–
537) and is celebrated at Camelot by "reuel and ryche of þe Rounde
Table" (538). The Beatitudes are the assigned Gospel reading for All
Saints' Day.[5] As we have seen in relation to *Patience*, the Beatitudes
outline the steps from fear to wisdom that culminate in recreation of
spirit. All Saints' Day celebrates this process of perfection by com-
memorating the physical and spiritual struggles of those who have
achieved this standard. In his translation of *The Golden Legend* Caxton stresses the importance of this festival, which should be celebrated as a recognition of "the debt of interchanging neighborhood":
"For the angels of God and the holy souls have joy and make feast
in heaven of a sinner that doth penance, and therefore it is right

---

4. The Feast of the Holy Innocents (December 28) is not mentioned in the poem, but see J.
   R. R. Tolkien and E. V. Gordon eds., *Sir Gawain and the Green Knight* (Oxford: Clarendon Press, 1967), n. 1022.
5. See *Missale ad Usum Insignis et Praeclarae Ecclesiae Sarum*, ed. F. H. Dickinson (Hants,
   England, 1969), cols. 953–956.

when they make of us feast in heaven, that we make feast of them in earth."[6] Furthermore, on this day, death becomes a sign of triumphant change: "What thing is more precious than death, by which sins be pardoned and merits increased?"[7]

The despair of the Round Table over Gawain's proposed journey sharply contrasts to the Church's affirmation of death and change:

> Þere watz much derue doel driuen in þe sale
> Þat so worthé as Wawan schulde wende on þat ernde,
> To dryʒe a delful dynt, and dele no more
>   wyth bronde.
>
> (558–61)

Whereas the Church celebrates the everlasting life of the saints of God, Camelot mourns Gawain's death in a way that underlines Arthur's court's dependence upon the world, or mortal life. The fact that, after he keeps his bargain with the Green Knight, Gawain shall no longer fight with a sword seems to be Camelot's only way of confronting Gawain's departure.

In both *Sir Gawain* and *The Golden Legend*, we may find an emphasis upon the theme of chivalry in relation to the Feast of All Saints. The *Golden Legend* exhorts those now living to emulate the spiritual discipline of the saints by evoking the ideals of military discipline in the figure of the Christian warrior:

> . . . whereof S. John Chrysostom saith to us: Thou, christian man, art a knight delicate if thou ween to have victory without fighting and triumph without battle. Exercise thy strength mightily, and fight thou cruelly in this battle. Consider the covenant, understand the condition, know the noble chivalry, know the covenant that thou hast made and promised, the condition that thou hast taken, the chivalry to whom thou hast given the name. For by that covenant all men fight, and by that condition have all vanquished, and by that chivalry.[8]

The scene in Camelot at this point in the poem includes a knight who has made an agreement, or a covenant, with the Green Knight and who is pledged to battle. But the *Golden Legend* refers to the battle of life, while Camelot and Gawain appear to recognize only a test of

---

6. *The Golden Legend; or, Lives of the Saints of England,* trans. William Caxton, ed. F. S. Ellis (London, 1935), vol. 6, pp. 97, 102. For "the debt of interchanging neighborhood," the Latin reads "debitum mutuae vicissitudinis." See Jacobus de Voragine, *Legenda Aurea,* ed. Th. Graesse (Leipzig, 1850), p. 720. Caxton's translations are accurate for those passages I have cited.

7. *The Golden Legend,* trans. Caxton, vol. 6, p. 102.

8. Ibid., pp. 102–103. For "covenant," the Latin reads "pactum." According to Lewis and Short (*A Latin Dictionary* [Oxford, 1879]), "pactum" was used to refer to a Biblical covenant, such as "pactum Domini." See Deut. 29:25; 3 Kings 11:11; 2 Par. 6:14. For "chivalry," the Latin reads "militiam."

physical endurance. Camelot's limited perception is especially striking because the Green Knight challenges not strength but fame, and,
from the beginning, the test is clearly spiritual rather than physical.

Gawain arms, attends Mass, and leaves Camelot on November 2,
the Feast of All Souls. The prayers and responses for All Souls' Day
celebrate the deaths of the faithful, affirming that their souls live eter-
nally and sleep only to rise at the Second Coming. The Epistle is 1
Thessalonians 4:13–18, part of which reads: "For if we believe that
Jesus died, and rose again; even so them who have slept through Jesus,
will God bring with him."[9] The Gospel reading is the story of the raising of Lazarus. In spite of the penitential awareness that permeates
the day, the Feast of All Souls teaches the lesson of rebirth through
grace.[1]

The court's response to Gawain's departure leaves no room for hope,
and, in fact, marks Gawain's departure with extraordinary sorrow:

> . . . "Bi Kryst, hit is scaþe
> Þat þou, leude, schal be lost, þat art of lyf noble!
> To fynde hys fere vpon folde, in fayth, is not eþe.
> Warloker to haf wroʒt had more wyt bene,
> And haf dyʒt ʒonder dere a duk to haue worþed;
> A lowande leder of ledez in londe hym wel semez,
> And so had better haf ben þen britned to noʒt,
> Hadet wyth an aluisch mon, for angardez pryde."
>
> (674–81)

These lines are, in part, a eulogy for Gawain, whose nobility will be
ignobly destroyed by an "elvish" man. Not only does the court expect
Gawain to die, but it laments his death in a way that suggests the
finality of death. Once more, the attitude of the court contrasts to
that of the Church, for the Church similarly recognizes death but
relieves death of its power by calling it sleep and by reaffirming eternal life. Camelot mourns death as the end of all fair things, as a mysterious process of destruction. However, the poet has noted the reality
of death, or winter, in his description of the seasonal cycle with
which he opens the second section. There, death is neither mysterious nor ignoble; it simply exists. In fact, winter most threatens things
without fruit for harvest. In relation to the year's cycle of growth and
decay, Camelot, in its spring, appears dangerously inadequate to the
demands of fall and winter. Winter and death exist in nature, and

---

9. *Missale . . . Ecclesiae Sarum*, col. 957.
1. The penitential tone of the day is underlined by the use of the Dies Irae sequence for the
feast. F. J. E. Raby (*A History of Christian-Latin Poetry* [Oxford, 1953], pp. 443, 449) notes
that the sequence was used liturgically for this feast during the lifetime of Bartholomew of
Pisa (d. 1401). The Sarum Missal does not contain the Dies Irae, but the responses and
prayers for the day reflect a similar awareness of judgment and, consequently, an emphasis
upon penance.

Camelot only mourns their existence without seeming to prepare for their coming.

Gawain journeys north during Advent, a season devoted to penance and preparation. Because Advent precedes Christmas, it was, in the Middle Ages, a time of fasting and of self-examination when men were exhorted to prepare themselves for the message of mercy figured in the Feast of the Nativity. For example, in a sermon on Advent, Hugh of St. Victor discusses what should be men's attitude toward the season:

> In hoc itaque tam sacro tempore debemus in bone propensius exerceri, ut per ejus gratiam mereamur abundantius visitari. Certe si rex dignaretur ad nos venire, et nobiscum facere mansionem, diligenter et nos, et nostra in ejus susceptionem praepararemus. [Therefore, in this so sacred time, we should more willingly be employed in the good, in order that through his grace we may deserve to be visited more abundantly. Certainly, if the king deems it worthy to come to us, and to make us a mansion, diligently likewise we should prepare ourselves in advance for his undertaking.][2]

The emphasis upon preparation and worthiness is likewise apparent in the figure of Saint John the Baptist who presides over this season. Saint John was considered the last prophet of Israel, and his cry, "Prepare the way of the Lord," was thought to be directed to the human heart during Advent. As Saint John's strict life in the desert and spiritual preparation led him to recognize Christ, so each man should emulate John and move toward the message of human redemption through penance.

Gawain's journey through a wilderness mirrors the theological concerns of the season in which he travels. Both the land and the battles he fights are reminders of hardship and of the constant battle against temptation characteristic of the season.[3] The landscape itself is bare and inhospitable to man and beast: "With mony bryddez vnblyþe vpon bare twyges, / Þat pitosly þer piped for pyne of þe colde" (746–747). Gawain himself suffers from the cold and the loneliness:

> Ner slayn wyth þe slete he sleped in his yrnes
> Mo ny3tez þen innoghe in naked rokkez,

---

2. Hugh of St. Victor, Sermo V—"In Adventu Domini," in *Sermones Centum, Patrilogia Latina* 177, col. 911. See also P. Berchorius, "Adventus," in *Dictionarium Morale* (Coloniae Agrippinae: Joannis Wilhemi Huisch, 1730) p. 84.

3. For an allegorical reading of these preliminary battles, see H. Schnyder, *Sir Gawain and the Green Knight: An Essay in Interpretation* (Bern, 1961), chap. 4. The *Glossa Ordinaria* (PL 114, col. 179) says of the wilderness, "Ubi vicit diabolus. . . ." The fourteenth-century Holkam picture Bible, on one page, juxtaposes three pictures—of John the Baptist preaching, of his recognition and baptism of Christ, and of the temptation of Christ. The series underlines the relationship between Advent, the wilderness, and temptation (London: Mus., British Add. 47682 fol. 19ro.).

> Per as claterande fro þe crest þe colde borne rennez,
> And henged heȝe ouer his hede in hard iisse-ikkles.
>
> (729–32)

The poet's description of privation, harsh weather, and struggle is similar to the descriptions in the mystery plays of the shepherds' hard life
at the moment just before the angels announce the Incarnation. The
world is dark and cold and unsympathetic to man. Whereas the shepherds of the mystery plays move directly from darkness and privation
to the light stable and God's bounty, Gawain moves to a castle that
only appears bright and safe. His worst trials occur after the hardships
of his physical journey end on December 24, in Hautdesert.

The fact that Gawain's worst trials occur after the more obvious
struggles of Advent is less surprising when we consider the warnings
many writers expressed about the dangers inherent in the Christmas
season. Whereas Advent is a time of vigilance and spiritual preparation, Christmas is a season given over to rejoicing. The sudden shift
from privation to plenitude has its own dangers; for it was thought
all too easy to relax during the Christmas season, to forget the reality of human sin that inspired the Incarnation. Writers focused on
the temptations of luxury: abundant meat and drink and too much
thoughtless merrymaking can provide an ideal occasion for certain
types of sin.[4] Gawain's own situation at Hautdesert during Christmas
captures in many ways what were considered the temptations of the
Christmas season. Gawain moves abruptly from harsh weather and
loneliness to luxury and hospitality, and, once in Hautdesert, he lets
down his guard and relaxes the vigilance that sustained him in the
wilderness.

The poet heightens our sense of Gawain's spiritual lassitude by
emphasizing the secular tone of Hautdesert's Christmas celebrations. Though the court observes the literal requirement that Christmas Eve continue the fast of Advent, Hautdesert's fast involves little
hardship:

> Seggez hym serued semly innoȝe
> Wyth sere sewes and sete, sesounde of þe best,
> Double-felde, as hit fallez, and fele kyn fischez,
> Summe baken in bred, summe brad on þe gledez,
> Summe soþen, summe in sewe sauered with spyces,
> And ay sawes so sleȝe þat þe segge lyked.
>
> (888–93)

---

4. See Hugh of St. Victor, Sermo XXIV—"In Nativitate Domini," in *Sermones Centum*, col.
948; Sermo XLVIII—"In Nativitate," col. 1031. In Sermon 48, Hugh of St. Victor employs
the metaphor of the spiritual warrior, or knight. See also Raymond Oliver, *Poems without
Names* (Berkeley, 1970), pp. 56–57; Berchorius, *Super Apocalypsim* in *Opera*, cap. XXIII,
p. 248.

The poet follows up this description of fish cooked in a variety of ways with Bercilak's remarking to Gawain, "' Þis penaunce now ȝe take, / And eft hit schal amende" (897–898). The words "penance" and "amend" serve several purposes here. First, they alert us to the nature of the meal the court is about to eat: the "fast" should remind men of man's spiritual want that is satisfied by the central event of Christ's nativity. The penance man observes during Advent prepares him for Christ's coming and, hence, for his own amendment. Second, the words alert us to Bercilak's irony, an irony Gawain appears not to fathom. Bercilak has neither penance nor amendment to offer Gawain, or any member of Arthur's court, but Gawain accepts the merely literal nature of the fast and prepares to enjoy his meal. Bercilak's remark may also have been intended to awaken a more literary awareness of the nature of Hautdesert. For example, G. R. Owst cites John Bromyard's detailed account of the Devil's Castle, where "Gluttony holds the office of Master of the Kitchen." Conversely, in the *Abbey of the Holy Ghost,* the cook is Penance.[5]

Gawain's inability to perceive the dangers of prosperity is his major weakness in the poem, and his misapprehension reflects the inherent spiritual weaknesses of Camelot. Gawain comes from a court that celebrates the Christmas season in much the same way, as illustrated by the poet's description of Camelot's own festivities earlier in the poem. Thus Gawain's ignorance, though not excusable, is understandable. Faced with a court that mirrors Camelot, Gawain ignores the fact that temptations may be concealed in the pleasures of noble living. It is worth remarking, at this point, that the two courts are similar in many ways: both contain a charismatic leader, a lovely lady, a magician, and all the trappings of wealth in clean linen, silver spoons, fine apparel, and elaborate preparations for the dinner table. Gawain finds himself tempted in terms of Camelot's values, which are its weaknesses.

The period from Advent to the Feast of the Circumcision was thought to describe a progression from ignorance and darkness to knowledge and light. The week between Christmas and Circumcision, which Gawain spends at Hautdesert, contains important feasts that celebrate the saints, or spiritual warriors, of the Church.[6] Gawain, a temporal warrior, fails his own struggle on December 31, the Feast of St. Sylvester.[7] On the Feast of the Circumcision, Gawain

---

5. G. R. Owst, *Literature and Pulpit in Medieval England* (Cambridge, 1933; rev. ed., Oxford, 1966), pp. 81–82. The Devil's Castle also contains Sloth as a chamberlain, "who draws the curtains and makes men lie for long in wantonness, and makes priests to celebrate after midday, fearing more to give offence to their lords than to God."

6. *The Golden Legend* verifies these dates and offers a compilation of popular legends and sermons associated with each one. See also C. R. Cheney, *Handbook of Dates for Students of English History,* Offices of the Royal Historical Society (London, 1961); *Missale . . . Ecclesiae Sarum.*

7. In Scotland and in some parts of northern England, December 31 was called Hogmanay, a day on which children received oatmeal cakes or on which gifts were given.

is punished for his failure, receiving a nick in the neck as payment. The lessons of the Feast of the Circumcision centered upon the virtue of humility which signified the resurrection of the *novus homo,* born again in knowledge and grace. Curiously, Berchorius's remedy for what he considers the proud sins of January is a more humble inclination of the head, ". . . contra Januarium, humilitatem in capitis inclinatione, quia inclinato capite emiset spiritum, id est, superbiam."[8] For Berchorius and others, the Feast of the Circumcision should teach us the humility that releases us from the justice otherwise rendered human pride.

The medieval celebration of the Feast of the Circumcision was a celebration of Christ's circumcision, for by his act Christ fulfilled the requirements of the Law, offering man a new covenant of mercy. The actual circumcision recorded in the Old Testament was considered a sign of the old covenant made between God and Israel by which Israel pledged faithful worship and obedience and God pledged his care for Israel's safety. As a sign of this covenant, circumcision was seen as ineffectual, for the bargain was inevitably and frequently broken by Israel. Israel's act of circumcision may have signified its good intentions, but, given human nature, it was also a reminder of human failure. In terms of Old Testament history, failure was met with punishment, and thus, for medieval Christians, circumcision became a sign of justice.[9]

By his obedience to the Law, Christ was thought to have released man from the necessity of circumcision; instead, he offered man a sacrament of mercy. Baptism was usually discussed as the sacrament signifying man's acceptance of this new covenant. Rather than the punishment afforded disobedience, Christ offered man the opportunity for renewal through baptism and for continuous renewal through humility and penance. Circumcision was discussed as a figure for spiritual circumcision, an operation that cut away the old man and that released the new man to life. In a sermon on this feast, Hugh of St. Victor captures the emphasis upon renewal: "Renovemur in novo homine per novam circumcisionem, in hoc novo ano in hoc mundo, ut in ipso renovari mereamur in coelo."[1] The word *novo* provides him with the basis for his argument and with the basis for his vocabulary. He speaks of renewal, the new man, the new circumcision, the new year, all fitting considerations for a feast celebrated on New Year's Day.

---

8. Berchorius, *Super Apocalypsim,* cap. XXIII, p. 248.
9. See Peter Lombard, *Sententiae* (Florence, 1916), IV, I, cap. vii, pp. 748–749. In IV, III, cap. viii, p. 761, Peter Lombard discusses the original significance of circumcision in relation to its New Law significance. See also Bruno Astensis, *Sententiae, PL* 165, IV, v, col. 987.
1. Hugh of St. Victor, Sermo XLIX—"In Circumcisione Domini," in *Sermones Centum,* col. 1039.

Warnings against temptations were often a part of sermons on the Circumcision. If the feast concerns, as Saint Bernard says, the cutting away of nonessentials, the nonessentials are those things that tempt man away from his own renewal, such as the lures of worldly adulation ("alii adulationibus in vanam gloriam").[2] In juxtaposition with the false light of worldly glitter and glory, Saint Bernard places the true light of discretion.[3] Man, then, must determine what parts of himself need cutting away; he can do this through the act of penance. Taken figuratively, circumcision offered man an escape from his own inadequacy; for, by recognizing temptation for what it is and by turning from lesser goods, he might move toward God in humility and penance. Taken literally, circumcision remained a bargain between man and God that could be made only once although it could be broken many times. As such, circumcision was a sign of the justice man receives for broken bargains. However, as a spiritual operation, man could, each New Year's Day, remind himself of those things he might cut away that kept him from true faith and obedience.

In *Sir Gawain,* the poet describes the events of two New Year's Days in a way that evokes the lessons of the Feast of the Circumcision. On the first New Year's Day, Gawain makes a bargain; on the second, he appears to fulfill his promise but receives a wound for a bargain he has broken with the same man. Significantly, Gawain is wounded in the name of justice—because he has broken faith with his host. The themes of true and false renewal are also central to the poet's description of the two days: the Green Knight's physical renewal after his beheading in Arthur's court anticipates Gawain's true spiritual renewal at the Green Chapel. The Green Knight comes to Camelot to test it. He first tests the court's bravery by calling for a Christmas game; later, in Hautdesert, he tests the nature of its fame and chivalry by testing Gawain's good faith. Gawain, like man, fails in perfect truth but redeems his loss through penance. Finally, Gawain returns to Camelot having "cut away" those aspects of himself that are superfluous and that hinder his spiritual growth. Thematically, then, the poet evokes both the ineffectual bargain of good faith and the truly valuable bargain man can make and remake with God through penance. The cut Gawain receives, while a sign of his inadequacy, is the mark of his rebirth into humility. The events of the second New Year's Day supersede those of the first; for, on the first day, we are reminded of the realities of justice as they apply to human weaknesses.

2. St. Bernard, "In Circumcisione Domini," Sermo III, *PL* 183, col. 139. See also Bernard S. Levy, "Gawain's Spiritual Journey: *Imitatio Christi* in *Sir Gawain and the Green Knight,*" *Annuale Medievale,* 6 (1965), 65–106.
3. St. Bernard, "In Circumcisione Domini," col. 142. In *Il Convivio,* IV, viii, Dante says that *discrezione* is the most beautiful branch that springs from the root of reason.

The poet's description of the first New Year's Day suggests the ideas of justice associated with circumcision under the aegis of the Law. First, the Green Knight enters the hall carrying an ax in one hand and a holly branch in the other. As a Christmas decoration, holly was a symbol for renewal because it remains green all year. The ax, used by headsmen and by warriors, appears to be an instrument of justice.[4] The poet emphasizes the ax, rather than the holly bough, devoting nine lines to a description of its size, sharpness, color, and design. The ax directly threatens Camelot, for it is the instrument the Green Knight has chosen for his test of the court's fame. The Green Knight states that Camelot's reputation for prowess and courtesy have brought him ("wayned me hider," 264), and that he now wishes to play a Christmas game: he will exchange one stroke for another. The game itself recalls the idea of justice; for a stroke is given for a stroke just as, for the Middle Ages, the old covenant was frequently compressed into "an eye for an eye." When we consider the picture the poet has just painted of Camelot's youth, ignorance, and self-absorption, the ax appears doubly ominous, "For now the axe is laid to the root of the trees. Every tree therefore that doth not yield good fruit, shall be cut down, and cast into the fire" (Matt. 3:10). These are Saint John the Baptist's words to a Jerusalem he considered corrupt and unprepared for the coming of the Messiah; they are words frequently used as warnings in medieval discussions of national weakness. The Green Knight's ax is certainly laid at the roots of Camelot, for he comes to judge the nature of its "fruit"—its fame.

The language the Green Knight uses to describe his proposal even more strongly recalls the idea of justice. First, he states the terms of the game he wishes to play to the court in general. His language is legalistic, for "quit-clayme" (293), "barlay" (296), "respite" (297), and "a twelmonyth and a day" (298) were commonly used in situations involving legal agreements.[5] He restates the terms once Sir Gawain accepts the challenge. Once more, the Green Knight's tone is legalistic, for he begins by saying to Sir Gawain, "'Refourme we oure forwardes, er we fyrre passe'" (Let us restate our agreements before we proceed, 378). A few lines later, the Green Knight refers to their agreement as a "couenaunt" (393). Finally, upon leaving the court

---

4. One of the meanings the Oxford English Dictionary assigns to "axe" is that instrument used by the headsman on condemned traitors; in addition, it is a weapon. The ax acquires further significance as an instrument of justice because Saint John the Baptist used it as a metaphor for Jerusalem's destruction. This association is evoked by John of Salisbury in the *Policraticus (The Statesman's Book*, ed. J. Dickinson, New York, 1927), for he frequently refers to the ax of the Day of Judgment and the punishment it will render upon impenitent societies. See, for example, *Policraticus*, IV, 12. See also St. Gregory, Hom. XX, in *XL Homiliarum in Evangelia, PL* 76, col. 1164; Rabanus Maurus, *Commentaria in Matthaeum, PL* 107, col. 771; Filippo Picinelli, *Mundus Symbolicus* (Colona, 1687), XVII, xxvi, p. 215.

5. See Tolkien and Gordon, *Sir Gawain and the Green Knight*, n. 298.

with his head under his arm, the Green Knight reiterates the terms of
his bargain with Sir Gawain:

> "Loke, Gawan, þou be grayþe to go as þou hettez,
> And layte as lelly til þou me, lude, fynde,
> As þou hatz hette in þis halle, herande þise kny3tes;
> To þe grene chapel þou chose, I charge þe, to fotte
> Such a dunt as þou hatz dalt—disserued þou habbez
> To be 3ederly 3olden on New 3eres morn."
>
> (448–53)

The Green Knight's tone here is imperative; he commands Sir Gawain
to appear at the Green Chapel to receive the blow he deserves. Furthermore, the Green Knight stresses the legal nature of the agreement between them by alluding to the fact that Gawain promised
before witnesses to meet him on the next New Year's morning.

The events of this first New Year's Day also suggest the theme of
renewal. After Gawain has taken the challenge and chopped off the
Green Knight's head, the Green Knight leaps up with an unearthly
vitality:

> And nawþer faltered ne fel þe freke neuer þe helder,
> Bot styþly he start forth vpon styf schonkes,
> And runyschly he ra3t out, þere as renkkez stoden,
> La3t to his lufly hed, and lyft hit vp sone . . .
>
> (430–33)

In a sense, the Green Knight's physical renewal parodies the spiritual
renewal celebrated in the feast. More important, the Green Knight's
renewal has no effect on Camelot's perception of itself. After the
knight has left the hall, the court returns to the feast: "Wyth alle maner
of mete and mynstralcie boþe, / Wyth wele walt þay þat day, til worþed
an ende / in londe" (484–86). The Green Knight threatens the court
when he first appears; he should doubly threaten them now. They,
however, keep their manners and their feast. Camelot's sophistication
is made to seem foolish in the line following—"Now þenk wel, Sir
Gawan"—for the poet interposes the voice of the narrator as a means
of underlining the necessity for thought, given what has just happened.

The second New Year's Day is the day of Gawain's renewal, but his
renewal is neither as simple nor as quick as that of the Green Knight.
First, at the hands of the Green Knight, he receives two mock blows,
before receiving a third, which only nicks him. After the third blow,
Gawain experiences a physical renewal: "Neuer syn þat he watz burne
borne of his moder / Watz he neuer in þis worlde wy3e half so blyþe"
(2320–21). These lines echo Christ's words to Nicodemus on being
born again (John 3:3), and the poet heightens their effect in line 2328
when Gawain announces that the "couenaunt" has been fulfilled.

However, only the literal covenant has been fulfilled, for Gawain then learns that the ax has rendered spiritual judgment: "'At þe þrid þou fayled þore, / And þerfor þat tappe ta þe'" (2356–57). Had Gawain not deceived his host, the ax would not have touched him: it punishes broken bargains. Only at this point does Gawain begin to experience true renewal, a model for the process of spiritual rebirth.

He begins the process with contrition and confession, finally moving to satisfaction.[6] The first New Year's Day, Gawain accepts the Green Knight's challenge, using the empty language of social politeness: "'I am þe wakkest, I wot, and of wyt feblest, / And lest lur of my lyf, quo laytes þe soþe'" (354–55). A year later, he confesses to spiritual inadequacy: "Now am I fawty and falce, and ferde haf ben euer / Of trecherye and vntrawþe: boþe bityde sorȝe / and care!'" (2382–84). There is a real difference between a polite murmur about physical weakness and intelligence and an anguished cry acknowledging treachery and untruth. The first defines humility in terms of the court and is relevant only to the social microcosm of Camelot. The second defines humility in human, mythic terms. Like Adam in the York Cycle, who cries "'Allas! for sorowe and care! oure handis may we wryng,'"[7] Gawain mourns the result of his own broken oath. Gawain then goes on to compare himself to Adam and Solomon who also gave in to the weaknesses of the flesh.

Gawain ignores the Green Knight's levity about the seriousness of his sin and moves beyond confession to satisfaction: he wishes to keep the girdle as a symbol of his weakness:

> Bot in syngne of my surfet I schal se hit ofte,
> When I ride in renoun, remorde to myseluen
> Þe faut and þe fayntyse of þe flesche crabbed,
> How tender hit is to entyse teches of fylþe;
> And þus, quen pryde schal me pryk for prowes of armes,
> Þe loke to þis luf-lace schal leþe my hert.
>
> (2433–38)

He wears the girdle in humility, and with his humility he is a different man who can return to court and admit his failure. Gawain's spiritual progression in this sequence is a paradigm of what should be everyman's movement away from self. Gawain has cut away those nonessentials, such as the pride he takes in his reputation and worldly glory. At the end of the poem, he can humbly confess to being a man.

6. For a discussion of this scene, see Burrow, *A Reading of Sir Gawain and the Green Knight*, pp. 127–133.
7. "Man's Disobedience and Fall from Eden," in *York Plays*, ed. L. T. Smith (New York, 1885; rpt. 1963), lines 175–176, p. 28. Trevisa (in Ranulph Higden, *Polychronicon Together with the English Translations of John Trevisa and of an Unknown Writer of the Fifteenth Century*, Rolls Series (London, 1865), II, p. 215) uses much the same wording to describe the human condition: ". . . profit of berþe is sorwe and care in lyuynge. . . ." Cf. Burrow, *A Reading of Sir Gawain and the Green Knight*, p. 140.

The poem's liturgical framework suggests a cycle of renewal. The poem begins with reminders of justice and mercy, hints of the choices man must make in time. The poet then focuses on the period from November 1 to January 1, a time that contains central feasts in the life of the Church. The lessons of All Saints' Day concern issues central to Sir Gawain's coming adventure—the movement from humility to wisdom suggested by the Beatitudes, a reminder that man should consider himself a Christian warrior, sworn to a spiritual covenant. On the Feast of All Souls, Gawain leaves Camelot. While the court mourns his death, a sign of its superficial spiritual understanding, the Church celebrates the resurrection of the faithful in Christ. Gawain's journey north embodies the privation of Advent. The week from Christmas to New Year's, the week Gawain relaxes at Hautdesert, is a sequence that celebrates spiritual heroes who have triumphed over temptation. Gawain's activities at Hautdesert—eating, sleeping late, talking to his hostess—provide a sharp contrast to those of the saints celebrated for their discipline and devotion. The final day of this sequence brings us back to the Feast of the Circumcision, a day of justice for Gawain; for he receives his reward for a broken covenant. However, on this day, he gains both humility through failure and renewal through penance and thus evades spiritual death.

The poem, like its liturgical frame, describes the movement from worldliness, pride, and thoughtlessness to spiritual knighthood, humility, and self-awareness. The concept of time the poet adumbrates in his references to the liturgical calendar, unlike natural and cyclic time, offers transcendence because it lifts man above the limits of winter, death, and justice. Thus the poet suggests that time can offer man more than worldly fame and more than dissolution; used properly, it can offer him regeneration.

JONATHAN NICHOLLS

[The Testing of Courtesy at Camelot and Hautdesert]†

Despite having a consistent Christian framework, *SGGK* explores more fully the social meaning of courtesy than its companion poems. There are only three occasions in the poem when 'courtesy' or 'hende' is used in an explicitly religious context: twice when Gawain offers thanks to Jesus and St Julian for finding him a lodging at Christmas, and once in connection with Mary, 'þe hende heuen-quene', (647)

† From *The Matter of Courtesy: Medieval Courtesy Books and the Gawain-Poet* (Woodbridge, Suffolk, UK: D. S. Brewer, 1985), pp. 112–31. Reprinted by permission.

Other verbal contexts for the words suggest a less explicit religious reference, although the poet's normal sensitivity to the complexity of the idea never allows us to view its use as simplistic.

The most prominent use of 'courtaysye' occurs in the pentangle-passage where it is enumerated along with 'clannes', 'fraunchyse', 'fela3schyp', and 'pité', as the fourth quality of the 'fyft fyue'. (651) Here the word must pick up resonances of Christian virtue from its proximity to the other emblematic explanations of the pentangle, but it is equally true that the other qualities in its immediate group are applicable as much to chivalry as to Christianity. Their prominence in the analysis of the pentangle is emphasized by the poet, not only by their final position, but also by the poet's statement that 'þyse pure fyue/Were harder happed on þat haþel þen on any oþer'. (654–55) Thus it should be no surprise that the subsequent events of the romance seem designed to test the virtues that are most operable in the social sphere of knighthood. We are aware that Gawain is Mary's knight (646–50), but it is as well to remember that on the 'vrysoun' of his helmet, Gawain wears embroidery of 'papiayez', 'tortors', and 'trulofez'. (608–12) As Gawain sets out, he journeys not as a knight ascetic, but as one who carries with him the symbols of courtly life in all its richness.[1]

This does not preclude, as John Burrow points out, that the final sections of the poem have a penitential movement to them.[2] The poet encourages us to compare the confession that Gawain makes in the castle to the confession and absolution that the Green Knight hears and grants in the wilds of Cheshire.[3] But the very fact that the final scene with the Green Knight is a secular confession, almost a distortion of religious practice by its location at a 'Green Chapel', which Gawain thinks of as an 'vgly' 'oritore' where the devil might hear Matins (2188, 2190), may make us re-assess the nature of his trial. In the Green Knight's opinion, the Exchange of Winnings and the Sexual Temptation are inextricably linked. In his explanation of the three strokes of the axe, he emphasises the surrender of all the gains which Gawain made: 'Trwe mon trwe restore'. (2354) Gawain suffers a 'nirt in þe nek' (2498) because he withheld the girdle, and lacked 'lewte'. (2366) The retention of the girdle is part of the 'wowyng of my wyf' (2361) because the lady manoeuvres Gawain

1. Cf. John A. Burrow, *A Reading of* Sir Gawain and the Green Knight (London, 1965), p. 41: 'This should put us on our guard against taking too narrowly ascetic a view of the ideal which he represents.'

2. *ibid.* esp. pp. 127–33, a view repeated in the same author's *Ricardian Poetry* (London, 1971), pp. 106–11. Since Burrow pointed this out, the idea has become something of a critical commonplace.

3. There has been much debate on the efficacy of Gawain's first confession to the castle-priest. Rather than agreeing with Burrow, *A Reading*, pp. 104–09 that his first confession is invalid, I follow Spearing, *The Gawain-poet* (Cambridge, 1970), p. 225 who says that Gawain does not mention the girdle in confession because he fails to see its withholding as a sin.

into a position where he can no longer keep faith both to her and to Bertilak. Presented with a chance to save his life, Gawain forgets the bonds of hospitality which tie him to Bertilak, supposing an obligation to the lady that runs counter to his over-riding agreement with his host. More than a matter of chastity, it is, as Burrow stressed, a question of 'trouthe' that is involved[4] a test that is appropriate to the pentangle, 'a syngne þat Salamon set sumquyle/In bytoknyng of trawþe', (625–26) and at which the poet probably hints in his comment (on the third day of temptation) that:

> He cared for his cortaysye, lest craþayn he were,
> And more for his meschef ȝif he schulde make synne,
> And be traytor to þat tolke þat þat telde aȝt.   (1773–75)

It seems to me, following Burrow, that 1775 qualifies 'synne' in 1774, and if this is so, then our attention is being drawn to the treacherous consequences of adultery in destroying the fabric of society, as much as to its consequences for the individual soul.[5] Adultery, as Lancelot and Guinevere discovered, can easily create intolerable tensions in a society that exists on the mutual trust and obligation of lord and retainer.[6] Gawain's eventual breach of loyalty does not portend the end of his society, and in not succumbing to the lady's full sexual temptation, he proves himself to be 'on þe fautlest freke þat euer on fote ȝede'. (2363)

However, as well as accusing himself of 'trecherye and vntrawþe', (2383) Gawain also stresses other facets of his weakness, enumerating

---

4. Burrow, *A Reading*, esp. pp. 23–25, 42–45. For an assessment of earlier views of the poem, see Morton W. Bloomfield, 'Sir *Gawain and the Green Knight*: An Appraisal', *PMLA* 76 (1961), 7–19. The most outspoken critic of Burrow's commentary on the poem's meaning is by Spearing, *Gawain-poet*, pp. 206–09, although his comments seem to misrepresent the wider implications of Burrow's reading, especially in connection with the nature of contracts in the poem: 'In the narrow sense of fidelity to contracts, it does not appear that the poem is centrally concerned with *trawthe*'. (p. 207) William R.J. Barron, '*Trawthe and Treason: The Sin of Gawain Reconsidered*, Publications of the Faculty of Arts, University of Manchester 25 (Manchester, 1980) has the most recent discussion of 'trawthe' in *SGGK*, although he tends to emphasise the religious rather than the social aspect of the quality.

5. Burrow's view of these lines can be found in *A Reading*, p. 100. Spearing, *Gawain-poet*, pp. 204–206 takes the opposite view. Davenport, *The Art of the Gawain-poet* (London, 1978), pp. 184–85 sees the lines as encapsulating a 'debating point about knighthood', (p. 185) holding essentially the same view as Burrow, but strengthening it by his proposed emendation of 1769 which he revises to, 'Nif mare of hir knyght (hym) mynne', a point elaborated in his article 'The word "norne" and the Temptation of Gawain', *Neuphilologisches Mitteilungen* 78 (1977), 256–63. Most other commentators follow Burrow or Spearing, although Joseph E. Gallagher, '"Trawþe" and "Luf-Talkyng" in *Sir Gawain and the Green Knight*', *Neuphilologisches Mitteilungen* 78 (1977), p. 373 sees the poet joining the two sins into 'a single possible act'.

6. Larry D. Benson, *Art and Tradition in* Sir Gawain and the Green Knight (New Brunswick, 1965), pp. 44 (with extended discussion of *Le Chastelaine de Vergi*, pp. 47–48) makes the point that in many medieval examples of the 'Potiphar's Wife' story, to which *SGGK* is surely related, the tempted knights repulse the ladies because of loyalty to the ladies' husbands rather than out of personal concern for chastity. That it would be Bertilak's honour that Gawain preserves by not committing adultery is indicated by Derek S. Brewer, 'Honour in Chaucer', *Essays and Studies* n.s. 26 (1973), 1–19, esp. p. 9.

a number of possible vices. This extreme reaction, natural perhaps to a perfectionist, may not be the view of the poet, and should be balanced by the moderating voice of the Green Knight. It is worth noting that for him, the fact that Gawain 'lufed' his 'lyf' (2368) extenuates further what he sees as Gawain's minor failing. Undoubtedly it is possible to take a stern moral view of this last scene and support such a view with examples from penitential literature and homilies.[7] But in spite of the Christian perspective which Gawain adds to his trial, it seems to be the social tests that have been the Green Knight's concern, and which the poem best illustrates. During his stay at Hautdesert, trial is made of Gawain's social virtues by associating them with a code that ultimately contradicts Gawain's beliefs.[8] The most central of these values is courtesy, and in the action of the poem, the poet explores the meanings and consequences of following a courteous mode of behaviour, linking it both with the integrity of society and of the individual.

Arrival and Reception

The two main elements of plot in *SGGK*, a Beheading Challenge and a Sexual Temptation, each have as a prelude the arrival of a knight at court. The Green Knight's entry into Camelot begins the 'outtrage awenture', (29) and Gawain's reception at Hautdesert begins the sequence of sexual temptations and agreement about the Exchange of Winnings which is the crucial phase of the story. Of the two arrivals, the Green Knight's is characterised by a deliberate flouting of normal convention, whereas Gawain's reception at Hautdesert is described as the consummation of courteous conduct and good manners. The 'principle of good manners' is something that Kittredge sees as being a common element in a number of analogues to this poem.[9] In both *Le Chevalier à l'Épee* and the *Carl of Carlisle*, it is the hero's strict adherence to the host's commands that saves him from a beating or death, and Kittredge cites a number of other similar *exempla* or tales that illustrate the same point.[1] In all,

---

7. A recent example of this kind of reading has been made by Vincent J. Scattergood, 'Sir Gawain and the Green Knight and the Sins of the Flesh', *Traditio* 37 (1981), 347–71. But both Spearing, *Gawain-poet*, p. 227–31 and Davenport, *Art*, pp. 180–94 are suspicious of taking too seriously Gawain's judgement on his failings, or of reading the poem as an essay on gross moral failure.

8. This view of the test is also supported by Burrow, *A Reading*, p. 80, D.S. Brewer, 'Courtesy and the Gawain-poet', in *Patterns of Love and Courtesy*, ed. John Lawlor (London, 1966), p. 84, and Benson, *Art and Tradition*, pp. 44–55; 218–26. Spearing, *The Gawain-poet*, pp. 200–01 sees the ambiguity residing in the term 'cortaysye' itself, and the different sorts of 'courtesy' have also been emphasised by John F. Kiteley, 'The *De Arte Honeste Amandi* of Andreas Capellanus and the Concept of Courtesy in *Sir Gawain and the Green Knight*', *Anglia* 79 (1961), 7–16.

9. George L. Kittredge, *A Study of* Sir Gawain and the Green Knight (Harvard, 1916), pp. 101–03.

1. *ibid.*, pp. 90–101, including Italian *Canzoni*, Latin *exempla*, as well as romances such as *Hunbaut* and *Rauf Coilȝear*. Other folktale versions are discussed by Hamilton M. Smyser, The Taill of Rauf Coilyear *and its Sources, Harvard Studies and Notes in Philology and Literature* 14 (Cambridge, Mass., 1932), pp. 135–38.

it is the point of the story that the guest does not contradict the host in his own house, a dictum which, as Kittredge also realised, lies at the heart of a guest's behaviour to his entertainer as depicted in non-fictional works. Kittredge cites two examples from courtesy books to substantiate his case, but there are many others, both in the general and the particular, that make it quite clear that to do what the host wanted was a fundamental point of courtesy.[2]

Because Gawain is treated with such good manners at Haut-desert, and responds in kind, there are limitations as to what he may do. Being a conscientious guest involves a loss of self-determination. As will be shown, this explains in part why he appears to act with passivity at Hautdesert; he does not go hunting because his sense of obligation to Bertilak requires him to carry out his host's wishes, even though this means that he is placed in dangerous proximity to the lady. But because the Green Knight breaks all rules of courteous behaviour when he 'hales' (136) into Camelot, he is not hampered by the restrictions of ritualised politeness. His lack of concern for the principles governing that society gives him the licence to harass and intimidate the court, and to insist upon his strange request. In order that this disruptive presence has the greatest possible impact, the poet describes the interruption from the viewpoint of the court, and establishes the joy and harmony at Camelot before their disruption.

The poet is at pains to stress the excellence and courtesy of Camelot at Christmas time. Of all Britain's kings, Arthur was the 'hendest', (26) the 'luflych lorde' are 'ledez of the best', (38) 'þe most kyd knyȝtez vnder Krystes seluen', (51) and their ladies are 'þe louelokkest . . . þat euer lif haden'. (52) Their festivities are described in the same glowing terms and with the same kind of superlatives. Recognisable social decorum is observed when everyone washes before the meal (72), and twice the poet particularises the seating arrangements at the high table, which enables us to reconstruct the order of the guests

2. Kittredge quotes from *Le Castoiement d'un Père à son Fils* (a translation of *Disciplina Clericalis*) and *Enfant qui veult estre courtoys*. Other examples are not difficult to find. Cf. Heinz-Willi Klein, "Anonymi Doctrina Mense" (*Mittellateinisches Jahrbuch* 13 [1978]: 184–200), line 56; *Carmen Iuvenile de Moribus*, ed. and trans. H. Thomas (Oxford, 1949), line 69; *De Ingenuis*, in Sister M. T. Brentan, *Relationship of the Latin Facetus Literature to the Medieval English Courtesy Poems* (Lawrence, Kansas, 1935), lines 145–46; *Le Petit Traitise*, in H. R. Parsons, "Anglo-Norman Books of Courtesy and Nurture," *PMLA* 44 (1929): 383–455, lines 116–18; and *Urbanus Magnus Danielis Becclesiensis*, ed. J. G. Smyly (Dublin, 1939), lines 1064–70. Some of these are in the context of drinking and therefore bear a close relationship to the anonymous *Canzone* retold by Kittredge, *A Study*, p. 93, in which the host singles out as a particular discourtesy he has suffered, a guest telling him to drink first. The general connection between loyalty and courtesy can be found by the inclusion of a number of precepts praising truth, loyalty, and honour in the courtesy poems. Cf. *Urbain*: 'later version', in Parsons, "Anglo-Norman Books," pp. 408–19, line 28 (Harley MS); *Stans Puer Ad Mensam*: Ashmole MS, in *Queene Elizabethes Achademy etc.*, ed. F. J. Furnivall, Early English Text Society, Extra Series 8 (London, 1868), line 213; William Caxton, *Book of Courtesy* (ed F. J. Furnivall, Early English Text Society, Extra Series 3, London, 1868), line 492; and *Young Children*, in *Babees Book*, Part I, ed. F. J. Furnivall, Early English Text Society 32 (London, 1868), pp. 17–25, line 146.

confronted by the Green Knight.[3] The impression that we obtain
from the description of the Christmas feast is of conventional courtesy and luxury being taken to their highest level. As an image of society it is one of an elite in perfect accord.

This is the over-riding impression, although some commentators
have wished to see in certain phrases an implied criticism of the
court and of Arthur in particular.[4] But any note of disapprobation
that may be imagined in the phrase 'rechles merþes' (40) should be
dissipated by the same line when the poet talks of 'rych reuel oryȝt',
a qualifying statement that seems to approve of the fun and games
as being appropriate to a celebration of Christmas. In the same way,
the description of Arthur's easy dissatisfaction with a settled existence, particularly the much discussed phrase 'sumquat childgered',
(86) may be just as appropriate to a young king at the head of a
group of knights all in their 'first age'. (54) 'Childgered' would only
have a distinctly critical connotation if used of a much older man,
and in the only other known use of the compound (as a noun rather
than an adjective), it describes Alexander at the age of fourteen going
on his first expedition, where it serves to emphasise the responsibility undertaken by one so young.[5] Even if the poet leads us to expect
that the court may be unequal to the Green Knight's challenge
because of its immaturity, the expectations are confounded by the
response of Arthur to the challenge (apart from a momentary lapse
of control quickly restored by Gawain's intervention) despite these
earlier suggestions of brittle resolve.

One of the manifestations of Arthur's restless spirit is that he
'wolde not ete til al were serued', (85) a new aspect of the well-known
custom that Arthur would not dine at certain feasts (often Pentecost
rather than Christmas) until he had heard or seen a marvel. A presiding Lord at a banquet would normally expect to be served first;[6] Arthur
inverts these normal rules of precedence, but does not act discourte-
ously. Everything is still effected with the utmost attention to the
requirements of good manners and the deliberate reversal of ranks
(here only in the order of serving, not in the position of the guests)

3. 73–74, and 109–15. The latter passage is explained by Oliver F. Emerson, 'Shakespearean
   and Other Feasts', *Studies in Philology* 22 (1925), p. 181. Also see J. R. R. Tolkien and E.V.
   Gordon, eds. *Sir Gawain and the Green Knight*, 2nd ed. N. Davis (Oxford, 1967), n. to 107.
4. For a good summary of the various critical responses to phrases such as 'childgered' and
   'rechles merþes', see Patricia A. Moody, 'The *Childgered* Arthur of *Sir Gawain and the
   Green Knight*', SMC 8–9 (1976), 173–80.
5. Walter W. Skeat, ed., *The Wars of Alexander*, Early English Text Society, Extra Series 47
   (London, 1866), *826–24 (Dublin MS).
6. Cf. Johannes de Garlandia, *Morale Scholiarum*, ed. L. J. Paetow (Memoirs of the University of California 4, 2 [Berkeley, 1927]), line 400; and *Urbanitatis*, eds. D. Knoop, G. P.
   Jones, and D. Hamer (in *The Two Earliest Masonic MSS*, Publications of the University of
   Manchester 259 [Manchester, 1938], pp. 146–51), lines 45–48. It is also tacitly assumed
   in serving manuals, such as *Ffor To Serve a Lord* (ed. F.J. Furnivall, *Babees Book*, pt. I,
   EETS Extra Series 3, London, 1868), p. 369.

has been a feature of Christmas celebrations since at least the Roman
Saturnalia when slaves ate with masters and all marks of rank were
discarded. It found a counterpart in the Middle Ages with the celebrations such as the Feast of the Boy Bishop, and even today, in some
units of the British Army, officers act as serving men on Christmas
Day in the privates' mess.[7] To follow such customs is a kind of game,
the taking of delight in a brief reversal of the normal course of events.
In *SGGK* it is another aspect of the gaiety and joy which pervades this
young court at its feast. There have been carols, interludes, a game of
forfeits, and a traditional disregard of everyday rules within the wider
terms of courtesy. The general impression of this feast-day is one of
concord, social well-being, and fine manners.

But the first course has hardly been served when, without warning,
the Green Knight bursts in. It is not learnt that the knight is green
until the last line of the wheel (150), and although this adds to the
shock of revelation, it also means that the first thing that is known
about the newcomer is his enormous height. A stranger rushes into
the hall, and the poet says that he was the largest man alive (137).
The Green Knight's colour, his height and size, and his precipitous
entrance obviously contravene what is reasonable. Not only his physical appearance, but his behaviour too, lack 'mesure'.[8] As in *Cleanness*,
we have a further example of the interrupted feast, and the poet's
most elaborate example of the unwanted-guest motif. Following a
similar pattern in *Cleanness*, the poet has described in detail the state
of the society (represented by the order and cohesive good-will of the
feast) before its disruption by a potentially dangerous intruder. Much
of the interest in this opening scene now rests on seeing how the dis-
rupted society copes with the stranger, who, unlike the ragged beggar
at the wedding feast, can not be thrown into chains and hauled out of
the door.

Although the Green Knight is like no other human being, the poet
takes care not to dismiss him as a monster or another 'wild man'.
(Benson, *Art and Tradition*, pp. 83–90) The admission that 'Bot mon
most I algate mynne hym to bene', (141) and the care taken to
describe his clothing and other physical features as being in accord
with the ideals of beauty and fashion, means that the reader reacts to
this visitor as a knight as well. Courtesy is due to and from a knight,
and although the Green Knight's appearance is shocking, and subsequent events prove that he is supernatural, much of the dramatic tension in this scene is generated by expectations of courteous behaviour
being disregarded, reflecting the fact that though he is a 'mayster', he

7. Henry L. Savage, 'The Feast of Fools in *SGGK*', *Journal of English and Germanic Philology*
   51 (1951), 537–44 elaborates further on this point.
8. Benson, *Art and Tradition*, pp. 86–89 describes well the energy of the Green Knight/
   Bertilak.

is also 'aghlich', though (in a sense) a courtier, he is also a monster. This ambiguity is the most fundamental aspect in the presentation of the Green Knight, and it is essential to respond to it in order to respond adequately to the subtlety of the poem.[9]

In his analysis of this scene, Burrow argues that the Green Knight's entrance is an example of what he terms the topos of the 'hostile challenger'.[1] He picks out two distinguishing actions in the knight's behaviour (refusing to greet the king and addressing him with the singular pronoun), and quotes examples from Chrétien de Troyes and the Vulgate Romances to further his argument. Such instances and comments are helpful in an assessment of the tradition behind the Green Knight's challenge, but Burrow underestimates the role which deliberate discourtesy plays in the convention that he describes. Politeness is a veneer over the violence latent in human affairs, and courtesy, however frigid or strained, acts as a restraining force between a violent thought and a violent act. If courtesy is ignored and disregarded, then the rules of mediation and 'mesure' cease to apply, with potentially dangerous results.

The importance of the Green Knight's discourtesy in SGGK can be seen by comparing his actions with those of the knights in some of the analogues to this part of the story. The three versions of the Carados story do not contain the same details of disrespect for the court.[2] In none does the knight omit to greet Arthur. In all, he states his mission reasonably, using the polite form of the second person pronoun. This neutralises some of the menace in the approach, and the gaiety and courtesy of the knight's entry contrasts with his strange request. The later Middle English ballad, *The Grene Knight*, does not describe Sir Bredbeddle bursting into the court, but pictures him waiting at the gate for the porter to request an audience with Arthur.[3] It will be seen, when Gawain's arrival at Hautdesert is discussed, that this was one of the accepted courtesies when seeking a lodging. Like Carados's father, Sir Bredbeddle greets Arthur with becoming courtesy when he does enter the hall. These analogues all contain essentially the same story in which the intention of the visitor is, at least in part, hostile. In none, however, does the intruder cause the same degree of alarm as results from the Green Knight's interruption. The Green Knight undoubtedly acts with more hostility than either Carados's father or Sir Bredbeddle, but without his

9. Burrow, *A Reading*, pp. 13–17 also explores the 'suggestiveness' of the Green Knight.
1. *ibid.*, pp. 17–20. Burrow challenges John Speirs, *The Non-Chaucerian Tradition* (London, 1957), p. 226 who notices the 'outrageously discourteous' behaviour of the knight.
2. Most easily read in L. Elisabeth Brewer, *From Cuchulainn to Gawain* (Cambridge, 1973).
3. John W. Hales & Frederick J. Furnivall, eds., *Bishop Percy's Folio Manuscript*, II (London, 1868), pp. 56–77. Also in L. E. Brewer, *From Cuchulainn*, pp. 83–91.

deliberate neglect of polite forms of behaviour, his hostility would also be less threatening, especially since he claims to come in peace without the trappings of war (265–71).

Without announcement, therefore, the Green Knight rides into the hall on horseback. This refusal to dismount is another indication of his disruptive purpose. When Guy of Warwick goes as a messenger to the Sowdan's tent without peaceful intentions, one manuscript records that, 'Into that pauylon Guy is went/On horsbak, y telle you, verament', and repeats the information a little later to emphasise his point: 'And Guy on horsbak sate there'.[4] In another English romance, *Sir Degrevant*, the squire sent by Degravant to the Earl's to challenge him about his crimes, 'nolde nat down lyght' from his horse, and gives his message while mounted.[5] To remain on horseback indicates mobility and the capability of attack. It also gives the mounted person a height advantage which emphasises his challenge for superiority. When Gawain arrives at Hautdesert, dismounting is one of the first signs of his peaceful intention.

It was shown, when the first feast passage in *Cleanness* was discussed, that some form of greeting was expected from anyone entering another's dwelling. Thus the poet's comment that, 'haylsed he neuer one', (223) is a further example of the Green Knight's calculated surliness. In this case, the insult is compounded by the splendid haughtiness of, '"Where is," he sayd,/"þe gouernour of þis gyng?"' (224–25) justified, perhaps, because Arthur is not at that moment sitting at the head of the high table, but still scornful of the other insignia of rank which Arthur is presumably wearing.

As Arthur is of a higher rank than the Green Knight, the latter's consistent use of the less polite form of the pronoun also increases our sense of the lack of regard that has been manifest in his disruption of the feast.[6] The challenge to identity or reputation ('What, is þis Arþures hous', 309) is a recurrent motif of the poem, and becomes of crucial importance later, as will be seen, when the Lady questions the identity of the Gawain she has before her with the phrases,

4. Julius Zupitza, ed., *The Romance of Sir Guy of Warwick: The First or 14th century version*, Early English Text Society, Extra Series 42, 49, 59 (London, 1883–91), Caius MS 3883–84; 3889. Burrow, *A Reading*, p. 18, n. 16, claims that such behaviour is not necessarily hostile, and refers to examples of suppliants and donors riding into hall. However, in the right context, such an action can only denote hostility and discourtesy.

5. Leslie F. Casson, ed., *The Romance of Sir Degrevant*, Early English Text Society 221 (London, 1949), Cambridge MS 117.

6. My comments on the use of the second person pronoun in *SGGK* owe much, once again, to W. W. Evans, "Dramatic Use of the Second-Person Singular Pronoun in *Sir Gawain and the Green Knight*," *Studia Neophilologica* 39 (1967): 38–45; and A. A. Metcalf, "*Sir Gawain* and 'You'," *Chaucer Review* 5 (1970–71): 165–78. The use of the pronoun in *SGGK* is also specifically treated by Basil Cottle, *The Triumph of English 1350–1400* (London, 1969), pp. 280–84. Also see Israel Gollancz, ed., *Sir Gawain and the Green Knight*, Early English Text Society 210 (London, 1940), n. to 1071.

'"Bot þat ȝe be Gawan, hit gotz in mynde,"' (1293) and '"Sir, ȝif ȝe be Wawan."' (1481)[7]

Arthur's initial reaction to the Green Knight's disruptive presence is to remain courteous and attempt to restore the status quo.[8] We are told that 'rekenly hym reuerenced', (251) and he welcomes the stranger to court, reasserting his own authority as head of the court ('þe hede of þis ostel Arthour I hat', 253) while readily telling the stranger his name. Arthur wants the Green Knight to dismount and stay (254), and he seems to try to neutralise the possible effects of the Green Knight's challenge by treating him as if he were a normal guest of the court. At this point, no one knows whether the Green Knight is going to follow his threatening behaviour with direct action, and Arthur, through the use of courtesy, does not precipitate immediate violence. The Green Knight abruptly refuses any offers of friendship (nor does he reveal his name) with claims that he has come in peace. Despite having just been treated with some degree of polite tolerance, he insinuates that the 'courtesy' of the Round Table is hearsay ('as I haf herd carp', 263) and seems to suggest that their courtesy, as well as their courage, will be solely determined by whether they will play his 'gomen'. (273) Arthur, now perhaps responding more to the axe than the holly-bob, offers the Green Knight 'batayl bare', (277) calling him with ill-concealed irony 'Sir cortays knyȝt'. (275) Throughout these exchanges, Arthur has addressed the Green Knight with the second-person singular pronoun, (as he does Gawain), which, like his offers of hospitality, is an assertion of normal social codes. A king would naturally address an inferior with the less polite form of address. Having had his kingship questioned by the stranger, Arthur behaves as a person of authority and maintains his tone of command.

But the Green Knight is not satisfied with individual combat, and as his purpose becomes known, his impatience is as threatening as it is insulting:

> Þe renk on his rouncé hym ruched in his sadel,
> And runischly his rede yȝen he reled aboute,
> Bende his bresed broȝez, blycande grene,
> Wayued his berde for to wayte quo-so wolde ryse.
>
> (303–06)

7. A final detail in this picture of the rude stranger is the way in which the Green Knight rolls his eyes (228–29). Apart from connotations of madness and aggression, Hugh Rhodes in his *Book of Nurture* (ed. Furnivall, *Babees Book*, pp. 63–114), condemns rolling the eyes when speaking to another man (p. 76, II.173–74), and *Facetus: 'cum nihil utilius'*, ed. J. Morawski, *Le Facet en Françoys*. (Société Scientifique de Poznan: Travaux de la Commission Philologique II.1 [Poznan, 1923], pp. 3–19), lines 169–70 advises that a visitor should always show a happy face to his host. On the redness of the eyes, see Robert B. White, jr., 'A Note on the Green Knight's Red Eyes (*SGGK*, 304)', *English Language Notes* 2 (1962), 250–52.

8. Several commentators have noted Arthur's courtesy, including Benson, *Art and Tradition*, p. 97, Burrow, *A Reading*, p. 29, and Spearing, *Gawain-poet*, pp. 175–77, 182–83.

His imputation of cowardice on the part of the Round Table stings Arthur into an angry and shamed response, and he prepares to carry out the beheading. Arthur's anger, however natural as the reaction of a man whose manhood has been doubted, is impotent in the face of the Green Knight's impassivity ('No more mate ne dismayd for hys mayn dintez/Þen any burne vpon bench hade broȝt hym to drynk/Of wyne', 336–38), and Camelot loses its focal point of order when the king steps off the dais.[9] It is at this point that Gawain intervenes, and the respite this gives Arthur, enables him to regain his self-control. He behaves with regal grace towards Gawain (366), and even finds the presence of mind to offer him some witty advice (372–74).

Just as it was Arthur who attempted to act normally when the court was initially confronted by the Green Knight, so it is Arthur again, who, after the headless and no more polite Green Knight has rushed out of the door, restores calm to the uneasy court. He remains 'þe hende kyng' and speaks to Guinevere 'wyth cortays speche', (467, 469) and he controls any natural apprehensiveness ('He let no semblaunt be sene', 468) for the sake of his companions. The incident is brushed off as 'Laykyng of enterludez', (472) and he redirects attention back to the feast by admitting that his condition of a marvel has been fulfilled (474–75). This display of courtly wit and politeness is rounded off by a punning reference to the whole business ('Now sir, heng vp þyn ax, þat hatz innogh hewen', 477) with which he signals an end to the disruption of the feast. Although it may seem, from subsequent events, that Arthur treats the whole matter too lightly, we know of his true feelings, that he 'hade wonder', (467) and his public comments are appropriate for the restoration of the court's well-being. Arthur acts as a king acutely conscious of his social duties, and despite the Green Knight's suggestions to the contrary, he also shows a becoming regal authority.

But at the critical moment when it seems that Arthur loses some of his composure and makes ready to use the axe, it is Gawain who re-establishes the order and courtesy of the Round Table by re-affirming faith in Arthur as the head of the court. His speech, with its careful flattery of the king and its courteous subordination of self, relaxes the tension in the hall.[1] Authority is restored to Arthur because Gawain, although assuming control of the situation, leaves the matter of whether he should proceed with the Green Knight's request solely to his king and his fellow-knights.

Like his sovereign, Gawain also treats the Green Knight with some degree of courtesy. It is true that he consistently uses the singular

9. Benson, *Art and Tradition,* p. 216 sees Arthur becoming churlish, but I do not see Arthur's reaction as a complete breakdown of his courtesy, only as a momentary relinquishment of his regal authority.

1. Gawain's speech has been well analysed by Anthony C. Spearing, *Criticism and Medieval Poetry,* 2nd ed. (London, 1972), pp. 43–47.

form of the second-person pronoun to him, in marked contrast to his use of the plural form to Bertilak. But in the latter case, Gawain is a guest and Bertilak is the lord of a castle. By using the singular form to the Green Knight, Gawain makes the assumption that the intruder is an equal, and refuses to cede any authority to him by being over-polite, a politeness that could be misconstrued as an inferior's deference. Besides, having used the plural form to Arthur, and having heard Arthur call the Green Knight by the singular form, it would be insulting to treat them as of equal rank.

One of the main indications that Gawain acts politely towards the Green Knight is the ready way in which he reveals his name: '"In god fayth," quoþ þe goode knyȝt, "Gawan I hatte."' (381) Burrow points out that Gawain was particularly noted for revealing his name when asked, and substantiates the remark by reference to Le Haut Livre du Graal.[2] There does seem to be a connection between refusing to conceal identity and Gawain's traditional character, although it should not be thought that this is a peculiarity of Gawain, as the practice was a universally recognised point of good manners. Arthur, at an earlier moment in this scene, willingly reveals who he is (253), and the custom can be illustrated from many other romances as well. When Guy of Warwick is asked for his name by Amis, the lord of the castle in which Guy is hospitably received during his search for Oisel and Tirri, he readily answers (6021–23), to be repaid with similar information by the host a few lines further on (6039). In the same romance, Tirri also comes to lodge at this castle after having been set free by Guy, and he too is asked for his name (6367), although this time there is no need for an exchange, as Tirri has already called the host by his proper name (6359). The same kind of thing happens during an episode in the Continuation de Perceval, when Perceval, with several companions, takes lodging at a castle:

> Aprés souper molt belement
> Li sires de cele maison
> A mis Percheval a raison,
> Son non li demande et enquist.
> Et Perchevaus son non li dist
> Et puis li demande le sien.[3]

As often with the examples of courteous behaviour from romances, the custom has a non-fictional basis too, and the right to ask a name

2. A Reading, p. 58, referring to Wiliam A. Nitze, and collaborators, ed., Le Haut Livre du Graal, Perlesvaus, II: Commentary and Notes (Chicago, 1937), pp. 241–42, n. to 1492, and B. J. Whiting, "Gawain: His Reputation, His Courtesy, and His Appearance in Chaucer's Squire's Tale," Mediaeval Studies 9 (1947), p. 196, n. 25.
3. Gerbert de Montreuil, Continuation de Perceval, ed. Mary Williams, (III, ed. Marguerite Oswald), 3 vols. Classiques Français du Moyen Age 28, 50, 101 (Paris, 1922–25–75), 1132–37.

is an established precept in courtesy books, especially in the context of travel. *Facetus: 'cum nihil utilius'* advises that, 'Cum quocumque tibi prope vel procul accidit ire/Nomen et esse suum, quo, qua, quis, et unde require',[4] which was repeated by the *Sloane Courtesy Book* as:

> With woso men, boþe fer and negh,
> The falle to go, loke þou be slegh
> To aske his nome, and qweche he be,
> Whidur he wille kepe welle þes thre.   (299–303)

It would not be worth dwelling on this point were it not for the fact that names and identities play an important part in *SGGK*, a poem in which the ambiguity of reputation is fully explored.

Gawain's reply to the Green Knight's question fulfils certain obligations when two strangers meet. The Green Knight, for the moment, keeps his identity secret, and even when Gawain asks some understandable questions:

> 'Where schulde I wale þe,' quoþ Gauan, 'where is þy place?
> I wot neuer where þou wonyes, bi hym þat me wroȝt,
> Ne I know not þe, knyȝt, þy cort ne þi name.'   (398–400)

the stranger avoids the request. When he does tell Gawain who he is, he uses a riddling reference, almost a nickname, 'þe knyȝt of þe grene chapel', (454) which does not satisfactorily solve the problem of his identity. The description does not give Gawain any clearer idea of the stranger's motives or reputation than does his appearance, and even during these final exchanges with the Green Knight, the values of the court are largely powerless in defining this mysterious figure. But despite the Green Knight's intransigence and his consistent refusal to conform to the courteous values of Camelot, Gawain comes through the encounter with great presence of mind, and without compromising his own code of social ethics.

Having examined Arthur and Gawain's reaction to these events, it is illuminating to observe the way in which the court behaves. At no point does any other member of the court rise to the same mastery and control as does Gawain, which serves further to pick him out from his companions as the knight who best embodies the ideal qualities of Camelot. After the Green Knight's first challenging speech, the court stare rudely at him (232), and without respect for his trappings as a knight, show only an awed interest in him as a freak: 'Al studied þat þer stod, and stalked hym nerre'. (237) In the face of this supernatural visitant, an uneasy hush settles over the hall, which the poet says is 'not al for doute/Bot sum for cortaysye'. (246–47) Contemporary

---

4. Passages such as this lie behind the 'curious piece of advice' (Burrow, *A Reading*, p. 60) given to Perceval by his mother in Chrétien's romance (557–62) when she advises him to ask a stranger for his name at meeting.

etiquette demanded quiet attention when a superior was talking, which may explain the poet's claim that the silence was courteous in origin.[5] It may also refer to the fact that it was not their duty to welcome the stranger, so they 'courteously' defer the obligation to Arthur, as the next lines ('Bot let hym þat al schulde loute,/Cast vnto þat wyȝe', 248–49) imply.

However, in reminding the reader that the silence can partly be explained by the polite habits of the knights, the poet only further underscores the bewildered awe which the Green Knight provokes. It is almost as if the majority of the court takes refuge in a corporate reputation for courtesy to hide its real feelings.

When the court does talk, it is to whisper together before deciding whether Arthur or Gawain should meet the challenge. Gawain's clear and eloquent courtesy contrasts sharply with this mode of discussion, and further marks him off as an individual. Throughout the poem the opinions of courtiers are generalised, their opinions often being misleading or ambiguous. At Hautdesert, and at Camelot, broad statements are offered by members of the court which need modification in the light of the other information that we can gather from both the events and the poet's interpretation of his story. The knights of Camelot, for example, imply that Arthur is to blame for not preventing Gawain's quest (677–83), although they are only too delighted to share in Gawain's success on his return: 'for þat watz acorded þe renoun of þe Rounde Table'. (2519)

The reader's attitude to the courtiers is conditioned by the obvious superiority of Gawain and Arthur over their companions. Not only do they behave with more poise than the court, but the poet is also not afraid to question the qualities of the other knights so that Gawain's conduct is seen to be more exemplary. The last reference to the court in this opening scene does not give much credit to it either, and illustrates the possible dissolution of courteous values in the face of the Green Knight's threat, were it not for the ethical resilience of Arthur and Gawain. After Gawain decapitates the Green Knight, 'þe fayre hede fro þe halce hit to þe erþe/Þat fele hit foyned with her fete, þere hit forth roled'. (427–28) Even if this is not a reference to medieval football, a sport which was generally frowned upon by the authorities as being disorderly and ignoble, it shows an unbecoming attitude to a 'defeated' opponent, and in its contrast to the standards of behaviour displayed before the Green Knight's arrival, it indicates how thin the veneer of courtesy can be.[6]

5. Cf. *Facetus: 'cum nihil utilius'*, 197–98, *L'Apprise de Nurture*, in Parsons, 'Anglo-Norman', 115, *Urbanitatis*, 87, *Stans Puer Ad Mensam* in John Lydgate, *Minor Poems*, ed. H. N. Mac-Cracken, Early English Text Society 192 (London, 1934), pp. 739–44, lines, 69–70, and *Babees Book*, 75–77.
6. See the articles by Francis P. Magoun, jr., '*Sir Gawain* and Medieval Football', *English Studies* 19 (1937), 208–09, and 'Football in Medieval England and in Middle English Literature', *American Historical Review* 35 (1929–30), 33–45.

Even when under duress, the retention of courteous modes of behaviour by Gawain and Arthur hold the society together, its potential disintegration being represented by the reaction of the courtiers to the events. Gawain and Arthur are shown to be the leaders of their society: Arthur because of his rank and the acceptance of responsibilities that go with leadership, and Gawain because of his possession of qualities that will come under closer scrutiny at Hautdesert. Thus the poet underlines the importance of courtesy and etiquette, associating such concepts not only with 'sleȝtez of þewez', (916) and the 'teccheles terms of talkyng noble', (917) but with the whole meaning of society and the forces that bind it together. At both Camelot and Hautdesert, the potency of courtesy is in evidence, whether this potency is shown in the deliberate breaking of accepted codes and patterns of behaviour, or whether in the acceptance and fulfilment of them.

In contrast to the Green Knight's arrival at Camelot, Gawain's reception and entrance into Hautdesert is seen through his eyes. The Green Knight appears from nowhere (rather like his departure from the poem, 'Whiderwarde-so-euer he wolde', 1478) whereas we are made acutely aware of the spiritual and physical discomfort that Gawain encounters before the sudden discovery of the castle. For an Arthurian knight to come fortuitously to a dwelling where he will be offered hospitality, is a common episode in romances.[7] The poet of *SGGK* makes full use of this traditional element, emphasising and expanding upon details of hospitality (to be found in other such incidents) in order to stress the courteous reception that the knight receives.

After gazing at the impressive architecture of the castle, Gawain decides to ask for lodging. He calls out (807) to indicate his presence, and a porter soon appears who greets him pleasantly (810). Courtesy books do not often deal with admission into another's dwelling, but there is a brief reminder in *Facetus: 'cum nihil utilius'* of the need to wait at the gate after making a noise to draw attention to the inhabitants, and in the much later *Sloane Courtesy Book*, fuller treatment is given to the same procedure.[8] In accordance with the ideas advocated there, Gawain asks the porter to act as an emissary to the lord, a task which the porter gladly undertakes, adding that he is certain that Gawain will be able to stay for as long as he likes (814). It is not

---

7. *Cf. the examples cited by* Roy J. Pearcy, 'Chaucer's Franklin and the Literary Vavasour', *Chaucer Review* 8 (1973), 32–59; some of these are also cited by Scattergood, 'Sir Gawain', pp. 350–51. Hakan Ringbom, *Studies in the Narrative Technique of* Beowulf *and Lawman's* Brut, Acta Academiae Åboensis, Ser. A. Humaniora 36, 2 (Åbo, 1968) shows how typical arrivals are in heroic poetry. He counts (p. 99) sixty-two arrivals with spoken salutation in the *Brut*.

8. *Facetus: 'cum nihil utilius'*, 255–56, and cf. Robert de Blois, *Chastoiement des Dames*, ed. J. H. Fox (Paris, 1950), 487–90. *Sloane Courtesy Book* (5–14), in Furnivall, *Babees Book*, pp. 299–327.

difficult to find parallel examples in other romances of castle porters showing similar respect to travelling knights, and such a detail would have been viewed as typical of courteous reception.[9] Rude porters can be found in medieval literature (as, for example, in *Sir Cleges*, when one tries to bar Cleges's entrance into the hall, in order to prevent him from showing the king the miraculous cherries), but they are deliberate elements of discord that indicate an atypical reception for the knight.[1]

Other elements in Gawain's arrival and reception can also be paralleled in the romances, showing them to be connected with a traditionally polite mode of conduct that both guest and host were expected to follow.[2] Although they do not share many similarities with the customs to be found in religious houses, the adherence to a ritualised procedure is common to both the secular and the religious forms. In the passage that has already been partially quoted from Gerbert de Montreuil's *Continuation de Perceval* (1094–1116), for example, a similar order of events takes place to those in *SGGK*.

Perceval, Agravain, Saigremour, and two maidens arrive at a lodging. The *preudom* who owns the *Manoir* comes out to greet them, the travellers dismount, and the ladies are helped from their horses. The horses are then stabled, the guests are led by hand into the hall, where the men are disarmed and given robes suitable for indoor wear. In *Ywain and Gawain*, Colgrevaunce's reception at the castle where he is impressed by the excellence of the hospitality, matches that shown to Perceval. He mentions particularly that 'Mi sterap toke þat hende knight/And kindly cumanded my to lyght'. (173–74) His horse is taken to the stables, and he is also taken by the hand and undressed in a chamber (193–204). In the episode in *Guy of Warwick* that has already been discussed, Guy too is led by the hand into Amis' castle and dressed in a mantle. (6009–12) References such as these could be duplicated at length from other romances, and the details of greeting, asking permission, alighting and being helped from a horse, the taking by the hand, dressing in a robe, and the stabling of the horse, establish a strong pattern of courtesy that necessitates a similar response.

Some of these customs are also recorded by the courtesy books as well. Giving a welcome or greeting to the assembled company when

9. Cf. Albert B. Friedman & Norman T. Harrington, eds., *Ywain and Gawain*, EETS 254 (London, 1964), in which Ywain, on coming to a 'fayre castell', (2712) calls out (2713) whereupon a porter soon appears who welcomes him; and *Sir Degrevant*, Lincoln MS, ed. L. F. Casson, Early English Text Society 221 (London, 1949), 389–400 when Degrevant going to the Earl's castle, dismounts and asks the porter to be his messenger to the Earl.

1. Alexander Treichel, '*Sir Cleges*, eine mittelenglische Romanze', *Englische Studien* 22 (1896), 345–89, II. 259–70.

2. For further examples, apart from those adduced below, see Henri Dupin, *La Courtoisie au Moyen Age* (Geneva, 1973), pp. 18–35.

arriving in hall, was, as we have seen in the discussion of *Cleanness*, recommended by several poems. *Facetus: 'cum nihil utilius'* also contains the advice that help should be given to any one who has trouble dismounting, 'Si quis descendat ab equo vel equum grave scandat/te praesente, strepae manus obsequium cito pandat', and no doubt the precept about removing the spurs after dismounting, also in the same poem (213–14), bears a close relationship to the disarming passages, which symbolise the peaceful intentions of the visitor.

In *SGGK*, a very similar sequence of events can be observed. Gawain is greeted and greets all the attendants who meet him, he is helped from the saddle (822), and his horse is taken to the stables. Courtiers help to disarm him, and he is led to the hall where Bertilak meets him with great reverence. Also in accordance with other passages, Gawain is stripped of his war-like gear and given an indoor robe when he is taken to his chamber.

For a medieval audience, Gawain's arrival and reception at Hautdesert would have contained many recognisable and conventional gestures of courtesy. But even though it is useful to compare Bertilak and Hautdesert with a *vavasor* and his castle, Scattergood is correct in qualifying his parallel between the two by stating that Hautdesert 'is a much more splendid place'. ('Sir Gawain', p. 350) The Gawain-poet takes some pains to emphasise the meticulous attention paid to his hero, and the sumptuous richness of his new surroundings. It is a large crowd of people who come to greet Gawain, not just a few attendants but 'sere seggez', (822) 'kny3tez and swyerez', (824) and 'mony proud mon'. (830) Apart from greeting him, they treat him to especial reverence, even though it is the middle of winter, 'And kneled doun on her knes vpon þe colde erþe'. (818) When he takes off his helmet, 'þer hi3ed innoghe/For to hent hit at his honde, þe hende to seruen'. (826–27) In the chamber, the trappings and furnishings are of the best, and prominence is given to the luxurious garments that Gawain wears. After the privations of the journey, the comfort seems even greater, and Gawain responds to this treatment, his servants thinking that Christ never made a more comely knight (869–70).

The meal or feast in this part of the poem figures prominently as an image of relaxed and harmonious good-will, as it does in *Cleanness*. To be offered a meal as a stranger is a sign that participation in the household has been effected to an intimate degree. Even today, to serve a visitor with a meal is to acknowledge to the recipient that they have been treated with a familiarity that distinguishes them from other people. The meal that honours Gawain on this first night consists of a grandeur commensurate to his surroundings, and is made more of an honour by being brought to him in his chamber. Some writers in the Middle Ages condemned this particular custom, but it was generally seen as a privilege reserved for special guests or dignitaries. *Ffor to serve a Lord*, p. 373, gives instructions on how 'grand Guests' are to be served in chambers after the main course in the hall, and several accounts of feasts, such as the *Nevill Feast*, pp. 95–97, and the testimony of the Czechs who visited England in 1465, (Rozmital, *Travels*, p. 47) support the notion that the private meal was a respected honour.[3]

The details of the meal served to Gawain in his chamber, given prominence by selectivity and intensifying adjectives, also illustrate the excellent courtesy on display at Hautdesert. That the meal is generally attended to with due regard to the forms of polite society can be determined by the poet's choosing to draw attention to Gawain washing before the meal (887). This particular courtesy, that occurs at Camelot, and is notable in *Cleanness*, can also be found in many other romances where meals are described.[4] As in these other cases, the particularisation of it at Hautdesert seems to be a traditional signal that the meal was passed with full attention to courteous behaviour.

The meal itself, as Davis's note says (edn., n. to 897) is recognisable from contemporary descriptions of such fast day feasts. From John Russell's *Book of Nurture,* we can see the possible elaboration and skill in preparing a meal from fish, skills which were developed to counter the Church's restrictions on diet on certain dates in the calendar. There is no suggestion from the poet that a various and sumptuous fish meal is to be viewed as either immoral or casuistical. Some church reformers would have been unhappy with this shadow of abstinence, but there are no such strictures here, just as in *Cleanness* it is not the luxury of Belshazzar's feast that is being criticised, but the misuse of the expense for an egotistical and perverted end.[5]

Since Gawain's arrival at Hautdesert, the words 'hende' or 'cortaysye' in their various forms have appeared with remarkable frequency (nine times between 773 and 946) and particularly in this scene describing the meal, during which the compliments between guests and hosts are rapidly swapped. Gawain has completely

---

3. In William Langland's *Piers Plowman*, Dame Study criticises the custom, X, 98–101 (ed. A. V. C. Schmidt [London, 1978]), and the ninth of Robert Grosseteste's *Household Statutes* (ME version) advises the reader to make his/her household sit together in the hall at mealtimes. For other references critical of the habit of eating alone, see Jill Mann, *Chaucer and Medieval Estates Satire* (Cambridge, 1973), p. 157, n. 38. Criticism of the custom may have had its origins in the association, in some romances, of private meals and scenes of love. See *Sir Degrevant*, for example, 1393–1440 and the editor's note on this passage.

4. Cf. the episode from the *Continuation de Perceval,* by Gerbert de Montreuil (ed. M. Williams, Classiques Français du Moyen Age 28, 50, 101. Paris 1922, 1925, 1975), 1125, *Guy de Warwick* (ed. J. Zupitza, Early English Text Society, Extra Series 42, 49, 59. London 1883–1891), 6850, and *Sir Degrevant*, 1408.

5. This is the view too of Burrow, *A Reading*, p. 57, although Scattergood 'Sir Gawain', p. 355 sees the episode as one in which 'overindulgence would be easy', and E. Wilson, *The Gawain-poet*, Medieval and Renaissance Poets (Leiden, 1976), p. 124 finds the meal 'disturbing'.

accepted the standards of Hautdesert, and even becomes a little tipsy (899–900), recalling to the reader the poet's comment on the effects of 'mayn drynk'. (497) It would be wrong to seize upon this and elaborate a scheme of moral censure by which the poet is condemning Gawain.[6] But it does seem to suggest that Gawain's unsuspicious enjoyment of his courteous treatment ensures that he will be drawn into the darker designs of Bertilak. During Gawain's first night at the castle, the poet explores the conditions under which Gawain feels obliged to enter into another agreement with Bertilak/ The Green Knight, and to remain in the castle while the lord goes hunting. As the courtesy becomes more extravagant, so it becomes more difficult for Gawain to avoid doing what is demanded of him.

After the meal, Gawain again finds himself being asked for his identity in a significant passage that in some ways parallels the Pentangle description because it too defines the qualities of Gawain's character. This time, however, the emphasis is solely on the secular virtues as seen by other courtiers, and their expectations of Gawain are ambiguous enough to prepare the reader for the difficulties of definition that characterise the temptation scenes. For a stranger to be questioned after a meal as to his identity was another established courteous practice in the Middle Ages. To entertain a visitor first and only then to enquire who, or what, he was, placed strong faith in him, and has echoes in the ideal code of hospitality practised in monasteries. *Urbanus Magnus* is quite clear about the propriety of waiting until after the meal:

> Advena dum comedit, verbis non sit stimulatus,
> Quelibet interea rumorum questio cesset
> Querere si placeat, post cenam questio fiat. (2389–91)

In the episode from the *Continuation de Perceval* that has been quoted from before, it is 'aprés souper' that host and guest exchange names (1132), and Rauf Coilȝear also waits until after supper before asking the anonymous Charlemagne for his dwelling-place, his occupation, and his name.[7] As at Camelot, Gawain readily responds to the attendants' enquiries, but it is noticeable, as Burrow points out (*A Reading*, p. 59), that Bertilak never reveals his name throughout Gawain's stay, a fact which has all the significances of ignorance and mystery that Burrow describes so well.

As soon as the court and Bertilak know they are entertaining Gawain, 'þat fyne fader of nurture', (919) his name conjures up a

---

6. Scattergood, 'Sir Gawain', p. 350 also sees this as a sign of Gawain's eventual moral failure, but Burrow, *A Reading*, pp. 57–58 is not too critical of Gawain here.

7. Ed. Sidney J.H. Herrtage, *The English Charlemagne Romances* VI, Early English Text Society, Extra Series 29 (London, 1882), II. 227–42. Unlike Burrow, *A Reading*, p. 58, I cannot detect 'a sinister touch of cunning in the attendant's behaviour' here.

reputation which incorporates a wider interpretation of courtesy than that of which Gawain has hitherto shown himself master. We are reminded of his 'pured þewes', (912) and the court not only think that they will see 'manerez mere', (924) 'sleʒtez of þewez', (916) and the 'teccheles termes of talkyng noble', (917) but also that they will hear the skills of 'luf talkyng'. (927) This last quality need not necessarily imply the specious blandishments of the seducer, and there may be little difference between the art of talking about love and the art of 'talkyng noble'. During his stay at Hautdesert, Gawain is not inept at talking to women, either alone or in company, and such conversational ease (which comes under extreme pressure) is all part of the courteous man. There is ample evidence to suggest that talking about love was a courtly pursuit, and one at which Gawain would no doubt be proficient. It seems to be fairly clear that, apart from anything else they do, the Lady and Gawain discuss the subject of love because this was a topic that becomes a courtly pastime: 'Much speche þay þer expoun/Of druryes greme and grace'. (1506–07) In the *Knight's Tale*, Chaucer says he will not discuss the finer points of Theseus's feast: who sat highest on the dais, who danced and sang best, 'Ne who most felyngly speketh of love', (*CT, The Knight's Tale*, I, 2203) an aspect of the feast which is bracketed quite innocently amongst other points of interest in its organisation.[8] What Gawain has to repudiate is the idea that such conversation necessarily means that there is a sexual interest too.[9] The Lady assumes that courtesy shown towards women must have an ulterior motive, and will not be offered as a polite refinement. Gawain shows that courtesy is a worthy virtue in and of itself, even though he is handicapped by being a guest, a social role that allows him little room for manoeuvre when subjected to the testing motives of Hautdesert.

The remainder of Fitt 2, which describes the events leading up to the three days before New Year, explores further the ambiguity of courtesy and courtly love, as well as the limitations placed on Gawain by a solicitous host. There can be little doubt of the excellence of the court-life at Hautdesert. The Christmas feast, with its particularisation of the seating arrangements (1001–05, paralleling the feast at Camelot), the Christmas games of the lord and the conversation of Gawain and the Lady, 'Wyth clene cortays carp closed fro fylþe,/þat hor play watz passande vche prynce gomen,/in vayres', (1013–15) which is probably another reference to the 'game of love', all suggest

---

8. For further discussion of the 'game of love' and its place in courtly discussion, see John E. Stevens, *Music and Poetry in the Early Tudor Court* (London, 1961), pp. 159–64, and R. F. Green, *Poets and Princepleasers* (Toronto, 1980), pp. 101–34.

9. Pandarus's smirk when Criseyde asks him whether Troilus 'kan wel speke of love' (*Troilus and Criseyde* in Robinson, ed., II, 503) indicates the thin line that separated speaking about love, and love-making. Like the lady, Pandarus hopes to exploit the subtle distinction.

another society in which the pursuits of the noble life are followed to the highest degree. However, there are several indications of the passive role that Gawain plays in the Christmas celebration, and the poet takes pains to emphasise that he rarely does anything of his own volition. There are overtones of control for instance, in the way the lord 'laches' Gawain by 'þe lappe and ledez hym to sytte' (936) when they go to the chapel, although Bertilak shows a generous warmth to his guest.[1] The words are repeated when 'þe godman hym lachchez,/Ledes hym to his awen chambre' (1029–30) before they have their crucial conversation about the length of Gawain's stay, and even the manner in which the ladies 'tan hym bytwene hem, wyth talkyng hym leden/To chambre' (977–78) after the meeting in the chapel, suggests the powerlessness of Gawain's will when he has accepted the courtesies of Hautdesert.

Gawain's subservience to the desires of his host and hostess is encapsulated by his request to be the ladies' servant, an innocent gesture of chivalric politeness, but which is used to great effect by the lady in the temptation scenes when she also pretends serviture to Gawain's desires (1239–40) so that Gawain, in order to neutralise any possible sexual implication, has to reiterate his own willingness to serve her in word or deed (1245–47). His obligation to the lady is of a slightly different nature to his obligation to Bertilak, founded as it is upon medieval notions of respect for noble women by a single knight, but we are still aware of the lady's role of hostess, and how this further complicates Gawain's predicament.

If there is any doubt, at this point, of the restrictions that Gawain must feel as a guest at Hautdesert, the poet gives explicit attention to clearing these up in the conversation between Bertilak and Gawain just prior to the end of the fitt. While Bertilak (supposedly) does not know of Gawain's quest, Gawain is perfectly correct in refusing any further hospitality at the holiday season, although his words first bring to mind the debt he feels to his host: 'And I am wyʒe at your wylle to worche youre hest,/As I am halden þerto, in hyʒe and in loʒe,/bi riʒt'. (1039–41) But when Bertilak informs him of the Green Chapel's proximity, any further thought of rudely departing is banished. It is at this point that Bertilak's speech takes on an authoritative tone, with words and phrases that imply necessity or command: 'Now leng þe byhoues', (1068) 'Dowellez', (1095), and 'ʒe schal lenge in your lofte'. (1096) In the face of this, Gawain can only express his

---

1. To lead someone by the 'lappe' can imply both intimacy and control. Two uses by Chaucer illustrate this, the first from the *Second Nun's Prologue*, when the nun says that until a man be seized 'by the lappe' he is not aware that the devil 'hathe hym in honde' (*CT*, VIII, 12–13), and the second from *Troilus and Criseyde* when Pandarus leads Criseyde to Troilus's bed: 'And Pandarus, that ledde hire by the lappe,/Com ner, and gan in at the curtyn pyke'. (III, 59–60)

willingness to stay, repeating the debt of gratitude he feels by stating the other side of the guest-host bargain, 'I schal at your wylle/Dowelle, and ellez do quat ʒe demen', (1081–82) and, 'Whyl I byde in yowre borʒe, by bayn to ʒowre hest'. (1092) Having said this, Gawain can hardly refuse, what seems in retrospect, the ambiguous suggestion that he stay in bed, 'Tomorn quyle þe messequyle, and to mete wende/When ʒe wyl, wyth my wif', (1097–98) particularly as it seems sensible in view of his long journey and the tiredness he must feel.[2] When he agrees to this, Bertilak then proposes the Exchange of Winnings agreement, and with elaborate courtesy ('Frenkysch fare', 1116) they part and go to bed.

*   *   *

GERALDINE HENG

Feminine Knots and the Other *Sir Gawain and the Green Knight*

Analysis means, etymologically, the undoing of a knot.
—Shoshana Felman, "Postal Survival"

When Derek Brewer, writing in 1976, declared that *Sir Gawain and the Green Knight* "is self-evidently the story of Gawain: Morgan and Guinevere are marginal, whatever their significance to Gawain. . . . [T]he protagonist is central, and all must be interpreted in relation to his interests" ("Interpretation" 570, 574), he was arguing from textual assumptions that we now recognize, with the unfair judgment of hindsight, as implicated in a fantasy of textual closure and command.[1] His homogenizing of the text—underwriting, as such acts

---

2. Some critics, notably Scattergood, 'Sir Gawain', wish to argue that Gawain is guilty of sloth in staying in bed and not hunting with Bertilak. Although the point is well-argued, it takes no account of the obligations Gawain must feel to Bertilak. Benson, too, *Art and Tradition*, p. 108 thinks that it is dangerous to stay in bed, even if he finds it not entirely inappropriate for Gawain.

† From *PMLA* 106 (1991): 500–514. Reprinted by permission.

1. Another instance where feminine agency is bypassed or minimized by an influential critic is represented in an otherwise unexceptionably fine reading by Spearing: it is, he says, "the poet" and "the plot of the poem," not Morgan or the Lady, that act against Gawain (Gawain-Poet 190). Shoshana Felman seems to speak to just such attitudes as these when she suggests that we learn "how to read femininity; how to *stop reading* through the exclusive blind reference to a masculine signified, to phallocentric meaning" ("Rereading" 27). Unfortunately—but perhaps unsurprisingly—Brewer extends his confident pronouncements on female marginality to the readers of poems as well. Writing some ten years before Valerie Krishna's production of a critical edition of the alliterative *Morte Arthure* (and eighteen years before Mary Hamel's), he finds this text "a fascinating poem for any middle-aged soldiers and politicians who may be able to read a slightly difficult Middle English dialect: not much likely to attract women and undergraduates" ("Courtesy" 82).

often do, a gender hierarchy—is observable today as a routine deployment and affirmation of the protocols naturalized by a critical-scholarly establishment. That meaning is produced rather than unproblematically "there" for discovery, and that hidden ideologies stalk each instance of seeming interpretive obviousness, has become axiomatic. We are careful to announce the politics of our reading, to admit at the outset the inevitability of a dialogic and transferential relationship between readers and texts.[2]

Underpinning present stories of reading and textuality is a view of the text as a ground simultaneously occupied by presence and absence, a site divided ever and always against itself by conscious and unconscious reflexes. A text is a "weave of knowing and not-knowing" (Spivak 120), a heterogenous signifying field that, because it is constituted only in and through language, is infected with all the investments of desire, resistances, unrepresentables, and repressions of language itself. "A" text is thus a heuristic fiction, since a text is really many texts in the same body and to select among them for significance is to draw attention to the programmatics of choice. Because analysis is invariably partial (that is, both incomplete and discursively inflected), traversed like the textwork it questions (and through which it is questioned) by its own unthought and unsaid (*impensé, non-dit*), the impossibility of mastery must be acknowledged. What remains is the explicit acknowledgment of the specificities of one's particular reading pact.

Under present conditions of reading it is possible to distinguish a feminine text in *Sir Gawain* in those regions where the logic of the poem as the stage of the masculine actors founders and fails. There, at the limit of the masculine narrative—in the repeating moments where masculine command slips and misses—appear the sedimentations of feminine desire: a desire always plural in nature, accommodated to a tracery of spaces in the poem coded as feminine, and signaling its presence through a medley of practices, figures, and signs.

It has disturbed many, for instance, that the founding fiction of the poem turns on the inexplicable design of a woman, the infamous Morgan la Fée, and on the game she sets in motion for reasons so apparently tenuous that they require continual scholarly rehearsal. At once dismissed and elaborately justified by readers, reviled for its improbability and defended as crucial, Morgan's responsibility for the plot mechanism has been resurrected, debated, minimized, multiplied,

---

2. Dramatically changing interests perceptible in the reception of the poem over the last several decades might in themselves force a recognition of this relationship. See Bloomfield for a brief survey of general trends in criticism and scholarship from the nineteenth to the mid-twentieth century; see also the annotated bibliography by Blanch (*Reference Guide*). For succinct theorizations of the reader-text relationship from the viewpoint of French psychoanalysis, see Felman, "To Open," and Brooks.

classified, and reimagined—only to be reappropriated once again
(albeit with difficulty) to serve the masculine narrative, whose priority
customarily goes unchallenged.[3] Yet the unsettling of the poise and
presumed knowledge of that narrative's logic should hinge attention
on precisely what escapes and vexes its command, thus serving to
gravitate attention toward the vectors of another, intersecting text—
a drama of feminine presences in dynamic relationship, whose field of
play is referenced, not to the masculine text and its signifieds, but to
the figures and turns of a different desire. Repeatedly crisscrossing
the narrative plane established by such characters as Gawain, Arthur,
and Bertilak and by the worlds of the two courts are, after all, the
reticulated angles and interstices of a feminine nexus, a spacing of
women; and this other script, read for itself, recuperates the move-
ments of another desire, in a feminine narrative folding into and
between the masculine.

To receive the poem from this other direction is to acquire the
familiar outlines unfamiliarly, to reconceive their foreignness and
difference. Morgan, named "þe goddes," directs an emissary to the
Arthurian court to trigger a drama whose intended destination is
Guenevere, the secular queen who is the desired audience or reader
of its effects. A player, Gawain, is drawn into Morgan's game, under
the apparent patronage of the "heuenquene," the Blessed Virgin. In
the course of his journey, Gawain's supplication to this Christian
goddess for a safe residence in which to perform Christian religious
rites, a plaint invoking the personal name of this sacred mistress,
Mary (736–39, 754),[4] seems to occasion the appearance of the cas-

3. The practice is so habitual that it escapes particular notice. Examples include Benson; Burrow; Eadie, "Morgain" 303 and "Sir Gawain" 60–61; Eagan 83; Hulbert 454; Kittredge
   132–36; L. H. Loomis; Spearing, Gawain-*Poet*; Williams; and the lively Baughan-Friedman
   dispute—with Mertens-Fonck representing a curious exception. More recently, feminist
   essays, while continuing to read the poem as the narrative of its masculine characters—thus
   unintentionally colluding with the masculine text once again to confirm the marginality of
   the women—have nonetheless argued the putative marginality in politically useful ways.
   (See, e.g., Fisher's "Leaving Morgan Aside." Her more nuanced "Taken Men and Token
   Women," which unfortunately appeared after the completion of my paper, could not be
   taken into account here.) My own retroping of the narrative pretext in the register of an
   unfamiliar-familiar story of elusive, enigmatic women aims at evoking, not (inherently) mar-
   ginalized figures, but the resonances of a countertext that erodes the assumption of an all
   powerful masculine narrative.
4. All line references to *Sir Gawain*, henceforth designated by numbers alone, are to the
   Tolkien, Gordon, and Davis edition. Like the editors, I follow Israel Gollancz's lead in
   spelling the Green Knight's name Bertilak. A reader's report leads me to believe I should
   clarify my use of citations from the poem's critical tradition in support of my arguments. It
   might appear to some that by selectively abstracting material from the poem's critical history that happens to coincide with my views (much of this material often being buried in, or
   incidental to, the writing of the authors I cite), I am generating an impression of critical
   continuity for my reading strategy: I should therefore perhaps state the obvious—that the
   authors I quote in my support would not, in fact, necessarily support or approve the ways in
   which I deploy their work, and that the points of convergence that seem to emerge effort-
   lessly between parts of my arguments and theirs are sometimes the result of a highly
   inflected, polemical, and admittedly interested retroping of the criticism and scholarship on
   the poem.

tle where an aggressively secular courtly mistress (the nameless Lady) resides—the scene for the performance of amatory rites. There a feminine game of seduction is enacted, a seduction of language and identity that forms the principal *aventure* of this romance, but its precise outcome and consequences are veiled from the knightly participant's understanding, being hidden within the screen game of a masculine economy of exchanges. The Lady marks Gawain with her personal sign—a "luf-lace," or sexualized signifier, which is later disseminated throughout the Arthurian court—as well as with a small neck wound, a token cut that leaves a scar. The end limit of her play is signaled by the Virgin's rescue of "hir knyȝt" from "[g]ret perile." Finally, when the feminine subscript is read to him, Gawain in self-defensive fury attributes all responsibility and power to women, in what is commonly cited as his "antifeminist diatribe," a tirade witnessing the belief that women dominate and shape the destinies of men. Morgan's signature in the drama is deciphered by the Green Knight, who unravels it backward to the beginning of the poem's action.[5]

This familiar-unfamiliar story transmits the registers of the feminine text, whose key players are curiously elusive, enigmatic women. Plans initiated by one woman are directed at another, performed by a third, and modulated by the actions of a fourth: read in this fashion, the romance is the theater of its feminine figures, a field in which forces of tension and filiation circulate within a feminine relay. Each woman, moreover, even the most shadowy (the Blessed Virgin and Guenevere, who exist principally as names and attenuated presences), is intricately elaborated in multiple identifications with every other woman, so that a sense of the limits of individual identity is never accomplished, troubled always by the repeated crossing over of division among the women. The result is the emergence of a feminine example in the text of identity as plural, heterogenous, and provisional, elusively reforming elsewhere just as it might seem most fixedly locatable.

The Shadow of a Knot: Multiplying Identity and Desire

Where they first appear, for instance, Guenevere and the Virgin share the status of fetishized objects: Guenevere, evoking the puissance and grandeur of the Arthurian court, by being set in state on her dais a

---

5. Because limitations of space require me to focus my discussion narrowly, I concentrate on two important structural cruxes in the poem—the pentangle and the girdle—though they make up only one skein of the feminine narrative summarized here. I am, however, currently revising a paper that teases out another strand of the feminine text, examining sexuality, erotic speech, theatricality, courtly relations, and gender identity in the seduction scenes.

royal jewel amid other gorgeous treasures;[6] the Virgin, signaling Christian adventitiousness and advocacy, by being blazoned on the inner surface of Gawain's shield like a talisman (74–84, 649). In the framework of the poem, however, Guenevere is also inextricably bound to Morgan by the push and direction of the desire in Morgan's game, which claims Guenevere for its subject; as the desired recipient of the game's meaning or affect, she is to be drawn, willingly or not, into an intersubjective relationship with Morgan.[7] The significance of this uneasy alliance, whose ambiguities bear silent witness to the existence of a prior relationship of undecidable tension between the two women, finally escapes the text, and perhaps Arthurian tradition altogether. Critics who wish to stabilize the meaning of the women's relationship in the context of the poem, however, have sometimes sought to normalize the uncanniness of Morgan's game by characterizing the game itself as a convoluted "chastity test" for Guenevere (e.g., Carson 14; Hulbert 454; Kittredge 132; and Moon 48).

Partnered thus with the Virgin and Morgan, Guenevere is also deliberately linked by spatial and verbal continuities with the Lady, for the Lady's first appearance is peculiarly designed to trigger our memory of Guenevere, whom she simultaneously reproduces and supplants. Like Guenevere in an earlier setting (109), the Lady is seated near Gawain at a magnificent court (1003). Indeed, that tableau of knight and great lady together seems lifted out of one context and transplanted into another—different, yet spatially familiar—with little alteration in format. The (ap)proximity of the women is skillfully highlighted, moreover, by a remarkable play upon Guenevere's name to describe the Lady's physical person: by being *"wener* þen *Wen*ore"—the orthography here is arguably unique (Silverstein 141n945)—the Lady's bodily beauty is caught and communicated through the body of Guenevere's

6. "Guinevere . . . seems transformed from a person into an elegant courtly artifact" (Hanning 11). We may wish to remember, in the context of her talismanic place in the Arthurian court—on display, framed by other precious objects, each announcing the court's magnificence and plenitude—that Freud's essay "Fetishism" apportioned to the fetish the work of both marking an absence and simultaneously warding off any recognition of absence.

7. One purpose of the game, according to Bertilak, is "to haf greued Gaynour and gart hir to dyȝe" (2460). Guenevere is also strategically conjoined with Morgan in being a silent presence at court, like Morgan accessible only through the response of others to her. Fisher observes, with wit and acuity, that the women are positioned at opposite ends of the poem—Guenevere at the beginning, Morgan at the close—with the Lady occupying the middle ("Leaving" 135).

   Among the critics invoking the tradition of hostility or competition between Guenevere and Morgan are Carson 14; Clark and Wasserman 64; Friedman 268; R. S. Loomis 88, 115; Mertens-Fonck 1075; Moon 56–57; Novak 122; and, most notably, Paton, esp. 60. The Middle English *Sir Launfal* and Marie de France's *Lanval* dramatize tension between Guenevere and a fairy mistress—and many believe (following Paton or Loomis, French or Celtic schools of source scholarship) that Morgan is a celebrated representative of this type. Myra Olstead's persuasive hypothesis that the "larger than life" figure of the courtly mistress has its origin in supernatural women, including the fay, would further reduce the distance between Guenevere and Morgan—perhaps finally conflating them (128–29).

name, itself the embodiment of beauty in the Arthurian universe (Tolkien, Gordon, and Davis 102n945). Such impressive coincidence inspired one critic to go so far as to advance the hypothesis that the Lady is in fact a second Guenevere, albeit in the guise of the "false Guenevere" of the Old French prose *Lancelot* (Griffith 261).[8]

Other interconnections are hinted at or suggestively relayed. Morgan and the Virgin are like each other in being, unlike others, powerful supernatural figures. Both the Lady and the Virgin, however, perform variations of the courtly mistress[9]—the Virgin materializing in this capacity during a fractional hiatus in the last seduction scene, where she and the Lady are momentarily shown to contend explicitly for Gawain as their desired prize (1768–72). The Lady's desire functions in this instance to create a breach wherein an otherwise unsuspected vein of desire, the Virgin's, may appear, when the Lady's blandishments to Gawain provoke an urgent response from the Virgin—not as "moder," but simply as "Maré," a jealous mistress calling back "*hir kny3t*" from the brink of erotic surrender to another woman (1769; italics mine). At this brief intervention, the only explicit textual recognition of the Virgin as a player in Morgan's theater, one more nucleus of desire is suddenly made visible. In that instant, another scene breaks through, displacing the male-female contest between Gawain and the Lady and at the same time reversing the earlier relationship between that knight and the sacred patron whose image is caught on his shield, for it is now not the Virgin but Gawain who stands revealed as the captive, prized object; he is contended over by two female players in a drama that is suddenly elsewhere—no longer between the sexes but within the psychomachia of a feminine narrative.[1]

---

8. Eagan hints at another connection between Guenevere and the Lady (72), through the nearly identical descriptions of the tapestries that form part of the backdrop against which each of the women appears, the "tapites" from "tars" around Guenevere and the "[t]apitez . . . of tuly and tars" in Gawain's bedchamber, the Lady's setting (77, 858).

9. Many have argued or assumed that the Virgin, though a divine figure, functions for Gawain as a courtly mistress. Novak remarks that, viewed as Gawain's lady, she conjoins the themes of chastity and troth (127–28); Spearing describes Gawain as the Virgin's "man" (*Gawain-Poet* 196); McAlindon calls him "Mary's knight" (126); Taylor mentions his "allegiance to Mary" (11); and Hieatt points out that Gawain's "chief fealty" belongs "to the Virgin" (354n25). Gawain thrice invokes the personal form of her name, Mary—when he is cold and lonely on Christmas Eve (737, 754) and again on the first morning with the Lady (1263). Significantly, it is as "Maré" that she intervenes between him and the Lady at the critical moment on the third morning (1769). Thus deployed, a commonplace medieval topos—the eroticized (but necessarily sublimated) relationship between a knight and the Blessed Virgin—assumes a strategic discursive shape and significance in this text.

1. The images of the Lady and the Virgin telescope complex psychic discourses of the feminine that extend far beyond the poem to operate an infinitely suggestive tension between secular and sacred forms of literature in the Middle Ages. Since C. S. Lewis's *Allegory of Love* in 1958, much has been written on the courtly mistress's vexed relationship to the Virgin Mary. Kristeva's distinguished formulation in the brilliant and provocative "Stabat Mater" falls somewhere between strictly historicist and broadly universalizing models:

The example par excellence of conjunction and identification among the women in the poem remains, nonetheless, the extraordinary relationship between Morgan and the Lady. Critics whose arguments may dramatically diverge in other respects often concur in identifying each of them as the other's double (Carson 6, 15; Clark and Wasserman 69n22; L. H. Loomis 535; R. S. Loomis 89; Moon 44–46; Williams 49, 52)—that is, as a split in the subject that has been projected outward. While every woman in the poem may be said to refigure another—to function as a point of reference and construction, an other for the others—the twinned descriptions of Morgan and the Lady adopted by the text particularly insist on the characters' simultaneous differentiation and nondifferentiation.[2] As nonidentical doubles, they are awarded diametrically contrasting, virtually symmetrical qualities at their first appearance, each establishing a specular surface for the other as its near opposite, and being thoroughly constituted therefore as the other's reference. The specular relationship between the two women situates both in an exchange, a filiation of identities, that finally works to obscure the horizon of their division:

"Initially, the cult of the Virgin, which assimilated Mary to Jesus and pushed asceticism to an extreme, seems to have contrasted sharply with courtly love for the noble lady. . . . Yet even in its carnal beginnings courtly love had this in common with Mariolatry, that both Mary and the Lady were focal points of men's aspirations and desires. Furthermore . . . both were embodiments of an absolute authority that was all the more attractive because it seemed not to be subject to the severity of the father. This feminine power must have been experienced as power denied, all the more pleasant to seize because it was both archaic and secondary, an ersatz yet not less authoritarian form of the real power in the family and the city, a cunning double of explicit phallic power" (106–07). For a representative Anglo-American feminist account, see Penny Schine Gold's *Lady and the Virgin*.

Interestingly, the Lady and the Virgin also appear in a line Spearing identifies as the "sovereign mid point" in *Sir Gawain*: "'Madame,' quoþ þe myry mon, 'Mary yow ȝelde . . .'" (1263). Applying to medieval texts Alastair Fowler's suggestion that a symbolic, iconological, or organizational center can be located, where kingship or "sovereignty" is apt to manifest itself, or be figured, in a poem, Spearing identifies this line as the point at which a "sovereign" (Arthur) should appear, but fails to. It must be Gawain himself, then, Spearing reasons, who displaces the king in this romance, to occupy the poem's most significant location; fittingly, since the knight is "Arthur's surrogate," "the hero," a possessor of royal blood, and so forth ("Central and Displaced Sovereignty" [260]). A feminist reading accepting his notion of an all-important textual fulcrum might wish to emphasize instead the two feminine presences that are unarguably inscribed, along with Gawain, in this august position, a double inscription Spearing himself glances at in recommending Gawain's claims: "At the centre of the poem's central line, we find . . . Gawain himself. Appropriately enough, he is accompanied by his seductive hostess . . . but l. 1263 does not merely pair together Gawain and the lady; *it places him between two ladies*, with both of whom he is linked by alliteration—'Madame,' the hostess, and 'Mary,' the Blessed Virgin. This arrangement is powerfully symbolic" (261; italics mine). If two feminine figures materialize where a masculine figure of sovereign power might be expected, hedging between them a principal player of the masculine text, their appearance might well indeed make a "powerfully symbolic" statement—on behalf of the feminine text.

2. Morgan and the Lady's most extensive and elaborate linking occurs, of course, at their introduction. The text nonetheless continues to refer to the presence of "þe ladyes" together on each occasion of communal merrymaking, and at least twice takes special pains to ensure their unmistakable identification ("Þe alder and þe ȝonge" [1316–17], "Boþe þe ladyes" [1373]).

> Bot vnlyke on to loke þo ladyes were,
> For if þe ȝonge watz ȝep, ȝolȝe watz þat oþer;
> Riche red on þat on rayled ayquere,
> Rugh ronkled chekez þat oþer on rolled;
> Kerchofes of þat on, wyth mony cler perlez,
> Hir brest and hir bryȝt þrote bare displayed,
> Schon schyrer þen snawe þat schedez on hillez;
> Pat oþer wyth a gorger watz gered ouer þe swyre,
> Chymbled ouer hir blake chyn with chalkquyte vayles,
> Hir frount folden in sylk, enfoubled ayquere,
> Toreted and treleted with tryflez aboute,
> Pat noȝt watz bare of þat burde bot þe blake broȝes,
> Pe tweyne yȝen and þe nase, þe naked lyppez,
> And þose were soure to se and sellyly blered;
> A mensk lady on molde mon may hir calle,
> > for Gode!
> Hir body watz schort and þik,
> Hir buttokez balȝ and brode,
> More lykkerwys on to lyk
> Watz þat scho hade on lode.   (950–69)

That is to say, Morgan and the Lady form a hyphenated term in the narrative of desire—their representation a conspicuous instance of doubling, which at the same time doubles up as the representation of, or figure for, a conspicuous slippage of meaning and decidability in the text.[3] By being alike and unlike, by appearing now as subordinate, now as superior, to each other, Morgan and the Lady figure the ease of misrecognition and the concomitant difficulty of anchoring textual significance or responsibility. For the Lady, who appears the dynamic (and sole) female speaking subject, that individual whose desire seems to activate and dispose the drama of seduction, is discovered in her articulation with Morgan to be herself spoken, a term in the lexicon of Morgan, who is silent, the subject without speech, but the accents of whose desire nonetheless apparently play upon, and at least in part produce, the Lady's own desire, which then assumes the character of a ventriloquized double.

Having thus argued that the construction of each woman entails a point of anchoring in another—and, through the dissemination of traces, in the others of that other—one might go on to suggest that a simple, schematic graph of feminine relationships in the poem would plot an interlinked, overlapping tracery, culminating in a pattern not unlike the familiar one invoked in the pentangle description. Like each constituent of the pentangle, the path of every woman in the

---

3. Both Kane and Hanning discuss the notorious difficulty of anchoring meaning, value, and emphasis in this poem.

poem is articulated with that of every other, so that each approximately "vmbelappez and loukez in oþer," "vchone . . . in oþer, þat non ende hade" (628, 657), a knitting together that reproduces the shadow of a different "endeles knot" in the poem—a knot of the feminine and the figure of another desire and its text.[4]

A Tale of Two Knots: Or, Desire in the Sign

Unsurprisingly, a knot of some kind in *Sir Gawain* is always a place where the pressure of an investment speaks itself—a moment of becoming visible. It offers up that revealing "detail" which Naomi Schor theorizes in her now historic feminist readings, *Breaking the Chain* and *Reading in Detail*, that peculiar hitch or halting point in a text on which attention catches, and which announces the working of a certain demand. The pentangle and love lace, notorious examples of the knot, are also knots of this kind. In the narrative ambit, the pentangle marks the site of a second model of identity, one contextualized as masculine by association with Gawain. Although the example of the women in the poem would seem to set forth a view that identity (and desire) remains always multiple and unfinished, there persists nevertheless a competing suggestion—expressed more explicitly through the intertwined descriptions of pentangle and Gawain—that knightly identity can still in some circumstances be somehow singular and undivided, static and finished. As the sign for Gawain and his perfect knighthood, the "perfect" knot is glossed as that which is permanently in place, whole. Never requiring to be tied, untied, or retied, the pentangle is the ultimate guarantee, on the symbolic level, for the existence of fixed and stable identity: the basis of that identity, its completeness and closure, being here predicated on a reassuringly exact equivalence between the announcement of Gawain's attributes and his actual possession of them—or, expressed in linguistic values, on the absolute adequacy of referent to sign. Just as the pentangle is the sign for which Gawain is the perfectly corresponding referent, we are to understand, so must the declaration of Gawain's virtues—the sign—find its own perfect referent also in his possession of them. This wishful vision undergoes an important correction when the pentangle as a personal emblem for Gawain is subsequently overtaken by an "imperfect" knot (Eadie, "Sir Gawain"; Englehardt 225; Kiteley 48; Malarkey and Toelken 20; Taylor 10), that which fastens and unfastens the love lace and, therefore, stands as its synecdoche (Hieatt 342–43). With the substitution of an imperfect knot, the Lady's lace, for the pentangle, a signifier is produced that situates

---

4. This metaphorical "knot of the feminine" is of course—like the "luf-lace"—an "endeles knot" different in kind from the pentangle.

identity as more tenuous and incomplete—a fragile, uncertain prospect that is always on the verge of unraveling and reconstitution in infinitely varied sequences of possibility.

Significantly, pentangle and love lace can organize the question of identity and its representation only through an intimate association with the Virgin and the Lady, the two female figures for whom they exist as markers. For the pentangle is no more than the outside of what is inside Gawain's shield: the image of the Virgin (as, in a parallel example, the host's exchange-of-winnings game is the outside of, and camouflage for, the hostess's seduction game). When the five sets of virtues that trace the outline of the pentangle are being described, the image of the Virgin suddenly appears, interrupting and displacing the series that supposedly produces her (the fourth set of virtues being the apparent trigger of her emergence), as she later displaces and substitutes for the pentangle in her protection of Gawain during his severest testing. Hieatt astutely notices that the pentangle, mentioned once and never again, is something of a decoy, a tactical diversion:[5]

> Gawain's chief fealty seems to be to the Virgin. Her image appears on one side of his shield; the pentangle, the symbol of 5 in the poem, appears on the other. One of his 5 classes of excellences has to do with the 5 joys of Mary (646–47). She apparently helps him in his most need when Bertilak's wife is closest to seducing him (1768–69).   (354n25)

Pentangle and Virgin's picture together collocate (co-locate) what Jacqueline Rose has called in a different context "the twin axes of identification and fantasy" (141), the continuousness of the pentangle allegorizing the linking up of all points of Gawain's imaginary subjectivity, in order that a particular fantasy of identity might be authorized and sustained. The pentangle hypothesis is thus a metaphysical statement of presence, the presence of a fully confirmed and locatable identity in a ground of ultimate reference. It stands, moreover, for an aspiration, a psychic yearning that takes up and reenacts an archaic, preoedipal moment of fantasmatic plenitude—the moment of presubjectal infancy, where loss and uncertainty, division, are still absent—since it leads back inexorably, umbilically, via the route of an uncut knot, the pentangle, to the (divine) mother whose image appears on the other side, "[i]n þe inore half."[6]

---

5. The "conysaunce of þe clere werkez / Ennurned vpon veluet" (2026–27) might or might not refer to the pentangle, since there is no earlier mention that the pentangle is displayed anywhere except on Gawain's shield.

6. The curious positioning of the pentangle and the Virgin's image, each on one side of Gawain's shield, has occasionally spurred attempts to read a relationship between them. To Novak, for instance, the pentangle is a metaphor for Mary's "virgin knot" (185), itself a metaphor, while Kiteley seems to assume that the images function as interchangeable figures (48–49). Marina Warner, in contrast, finds a metonymic relation between the Virgin's girdle and the state of incipient or actual motherhood in late medieval art (278–79).

But however compelling this fantasy of an uncut knot leading
back to a mother might be, the force of its authority has already
begun to slip away with the attempt to make of the pentangle an
absolutely intact knot, always and everywhere present to itself. For it
must be remembered that the comforting illusion of unity and continuity that the pentangle design supports is also a condition that renders impossible a sufficient separation, or a proper spacing, of the
five points and their constituent sets of virtues in such a way as to
discriminate their meaning(s): since the possibility of establishing
such meaning, such differentiation, is contingent on the activity of
that punctuated series of breaks which, paradoxically, enables individual units of signification to combine for the making of overall
intelligibility. If the points and virtues of the pentangle can never be
"sundred" or "samned" (659), neither can they be held apart and distinguished: lacking lack, or imperfection, their meanings run one
into another endlessly without the punctuation of a gap. The apparently different (and meaning[s]-full) qualities gathered by the pentangle are then finally *in*different: faultlessness in actions ("fyngres"),
senses ("wyttez"), and trust (in "þe fyue woundez") would absorb, or
seamlessly vanish into, "fraunchyse," "felaȝschyp," "clannes," "cortaysye," and "pité"; and even as a group, though claimed in the
poem's critical history for specifically Christian virtues, these properties are equally indifferent, collectively, from courtly ones (Spearing, Gawain-*Poet* 197).[7]

The inference is useful in a cautionary way for the rest of the
poem, since it positions a reminder that the determined pursuit of
determination invariably misses its object, issuing instead in an
indetermination that signals the failure of every attempt at containing and regulating, policing, a sign. Such an attempt would require
abbreviating the sign—which, qua sign, is characteristically unstable
and traversed by excess—into a cipher, with the incidental but concomitant effect here of also rewriting Gawain into a simplified
palimpsest, the subject of (and subjected to) the provenient univo-
cality of the pentangle logos: very simply, only a pentangle('s) knight.

One might also suspect that the Virgin's image on Gawain's shield is a residue from an
earlier period of Arthurian legendary history, since in the *Historia Britonum* Nennius also
describes Arthur as carrying an image of the Virgin on his shield: "Arthur portavit imag-
inem sanctae Mariae perpetuae virginis super humeros suos" is usually treated by editors
and translators as an error, to be rendered more accurately as "Arthur carried the image of
the holy Mary, the everlasting Virgin, on his [shield]," not "on his shoulders" 'super
humeros suos' (Morris 76, 35).

7. Long before the advent of deconstructive readings, Englehardt made the casual but shrewd
remark that "the 5 virtues assigned to Gawain in that *dilatatio* are not determinative or even
quite discriminable" (219). Finlayson, moreover, reads the "papiayez," "peruyng," "tortors,"
and "trulofez" in lines 611–13 as the devices of the courtly lover: "the author is quite clearly
signalling to his audience that the Gawain of *this* romance is the Gawain of courtly reputation . . . the knight known for his 'daliaunce and fair langage'" (9).

But the patient investment of the pentangle's abstract geometry, itemized over forty-three lines in the poem (an effort sometimes thought to be wholly improvised, its signification here being arbitrary rather than traditional),[8] only produces an overinvested sign and an overdetermination of meaning, that is the very symptom of excess; so that it quickly becomes difficult even to tell whether the pentangle "acordez" to Gawain because it functions as a description of, a prescription for, an aspiration by, an inspiration to, or a flattering idealization of that knight.[9] In the end, to the questions, What exactly—and, as important, how exactly—does the pentangle, in its sum and parts, signify? and, What is the precise relation of that signification, if any, to Gawain? there remains only the suspension of the possibility of answer.

Inasmuch as the pentangle is an abstract, bodiless sign, the girdle is a sign that is also a fully material object, one that carries, in its function and appearance, the impress and memory of the body itself. It is a detail of encirclement bearing the mark of the body and becomes metonymically, in the course of the Lady's theater of seduction, a sexualized, desiring, feminine term. It is an object, moreover, that mirrors the concentricity of other encirclements mapping out the poem: the circle of the Lady's arms pinioning Gawain (1224); the circumambient, overlapping spheres of influence (the Green Knight's, the Virgin's, Bertilak's, the Lady's) in which the knight is caught; Gawain in the circle of Bertilak's household; the brief, enframing histories, or "chronicle" accounts that trace the circumference of this romance; the beheading game that surrounds and holds within it the other two games, the exchange of winnings and the seduction; and Gawain's innumerable physical adventures with "wormez," "wolues," "wodwos," "bullez and berez, and borez," "etaynez" that are constructed as a circling outer edge, the before and after of his feminine adventure with language. A narrative within narratives, a game inside games, an adventure enclosed by adventures: reading anatomically, concentrically, from this term of the body, the Lady's, we arrive at "the odd truths revealed in the

8. Tolkien, Gordon, and Davis state flatly that "[n]othing like the symbolism attributed to [the pentangle] here is known anywhere else" (93n620), an opinion shared by others: "The symbolism of the pentangle is artificial, fabricated *ad hoc* for this poem, and has to be explained explicitly and meticulously because the hearer's [sic] have little in their culture that goes out to meet it" (Friedman and Osberg 315). The ostensible necessity of yoking that signification to Gawain in an ostentatious fashion also prompts speculation: "It has recently been suggested that the reference in *Sir Gawain* to the 'pentangel nwe' (1. 636) means not only that the device was newly painted but also that it was newly imposed as a sign, and that the author had just granted new arms to his hero" (Arthur, "Signs" 77, *Medieval Sign* 53).

9. Lines 632–35 and 655–56 seem to be description, but lines 642–50 might indicate inspiration, aspiration, or prescription, while Gawain's apparent failure as a pentangle knight suggests to some that his virtues, as encapsulated here, are somewhat exaggerated.

accidental [but never innocent] material of language . . . a different kind of reading, no longer a sublimated relation to the spirit of the text, but an intercourse with its body" (Gallop 29)—a reading enabled, invited, by the imprint of a female body on a sign and its macrostructural reverberations throughout the text.[1] By contrast, the cut that Gawain receives, extending causatively from the Lady's successful imposition of her girdle, is the imprint of a sign on a body (the Lady's on Gawain's). Transferred from the pentangle, where it does not appear, to the girdle (a circle with a break in it, a cut), where it does, and thereafter to Gawain's body, this cut may be read there as the vestige of a displacement, the trace of a symbolic beheading that is itself displaced from, and vestigially symbolic of, castration: the organizing dynamic in a psychic economy marked as masculine. That this gash vanishes, leaving only the residue of a scar to suggest its former place, even as the girdle travels successfully across several signifying systems, passing from the Lady's, to the Green Knight's, to Gawain's, and finally into the signifying system of the entire Arthurian court and its history, might be read, therefore, as a fantasied, fabulous parable of the subtextual narrative—a "speculative turbulence" that imagines another, feminine, organization of greater mobility imbricated with and overtaking the masculine (of which something nonetheless remains, in the scar that is the *entre-deux*).[2]

Feminine Terms: Signifying Mobility and Transformation

If the pentangle is the "too much," an overspecification that must fail, the girdle is the "too little," or underspecification that facilitates the girdle's retroping at an exigent moment in the Lady's third engagement with Gawain[3]—in order that her desire, momentarily blocked and at an impasse, can negotiate a passage by being mapped onto and disseminated through the object. Before the transfer can be accomplished, however, Gawain's objections and extreme suspiciousness,

1. Practices of this kind might constitute "a hermeneutics focused on the detail, which is to say, on those details of the female anatomy generally ignored by male critics and which significantly influence our readings of the texts in which they appear" (Schor, *Breaking* 160). On "concentricity" and the organization of female sexuality and the feminine unconscious, see Montrelay's "Inquiry into Femininity."
2. Although I have coded the neck wound as masculine, reading from a conventional Freudian model of castration, it might also be argued that by virtue of its suggestive shape, the wound (and the consequent scar) can be retroped as feminine; as a cross-sectional representation of the circle, it is after all powerfully reminiscent of the vulvaic or vaginal "gash." The wonderful expression "speculative turbulence" is Leo Bersani's.
3. There is "a peculiar imbalance in the symmetrical opposition of pentangle and girdle. For though the poet spends forty-three verses [sic] (623–65) carefully, almost pedantically, expounding the symbolism of the pentangle, he says nothing explicitly about the symbolism of the girdle" (Friedman and Osberg 301–02).

roused to keenness by the Lady's theater of seduction, have to be overcome. In the intimate circumstances of this final appointment (a
man's private bedchamber, a beautiful seductress, provocative "luf-
talkying," the exchange of kisses—all in an aura of intimacy and
secrecy, "we bot oure one") any gift from the Lady, especially one
worn on her body (whether a personal token of jewelry, such as her
ring, or an item of clothing, like her girdle), would carry a strongly
sexual coloring, be inflected by an unmistakably erotic charge.
Gawain's polite but determined refusal of the Lady's ring aptly com-
municates his recognition of the field of suggestion the offer invokes.[4]
The prospect of the girdle as a gift is complicated, moreover, by a further difficulty, in that the girdle's meaning as a sign, even outside
the context of seduction and lacking commentary of any kind in the
poem, is perhaps already overfamiliarly cathected. Friedman and
Osberg brilliantly argue, for instance, that the history of the girdle in
tradition and literature conveys so heavy a burden of intimate contact
with the feminine—with female sexuality and fertility, genitalia, "cos-
mic sovereignty," heroism and magic (304)—and so forcefully com-
municates the idea of binding, to exact the "psychic adherence" and
"mystical incorporation" of whoever accepts and wears the girdle, that
these intimations must be carefully veiled or dissembled when the
object is presented (303, 309).

The Lady, in an inspired retroping, accordingly codes her proffered
gift as a magical rather than a sexual object (perhaps "magical
because sexual," say Friedman and Osberg [307]), a move assisted by
conspicuous textual silence on the meaning of this sign. Already
caught in an appearance of churlishness, having repeatedly denied
the Lady's requests, Gawain responds with relief to this other form of
seduction and hence arrives at a serious misrecognition: he mis-takes
the detour and occlusion of the Lady's desire for its renunciation. For,
undetected by him, her desire has already turned aside, and by covering over its apparition, the Lady manages to trick Gawain into receiving the instrument of its conveyance, as she makes her gift appear
entirely innocent, a mere aid to Gawain's earnest wish to escape
imminent death in the beheading game. With the acceptance of her
girdle for its putative magic, however, the desire Gawain believes to be
his own becomes annexed to that of the Lady, the Other—and functions, thereupon, as the deflected-reflected form of the other's desire.
The apparent integrity of Gawain's will, carefully maintained through
all his encounters with the Lady, also proves to be an illusion, since his
will exists here only as a mirrored sliver of the will of the other to

4. Both "a ring [and] a girdle . . . are, under one aspect, universal vaginal symbols, under
another, instruments of binding magic" (Friedman and Osberg 308–09).

which he has become accomplice. The girdle is then the join at which two registers of desire meet, the junction of a triumphal capture:[5]

> 'Now forsake ȝe þis silke,' sayde þe burde þenne,
> 'For hit is symple in hitself? And so hit wel semez.
> Lo! so hit is littel, and lasse hit is worþy;
> Bot who-so knew þe costes þat knit ar þerinne,
> He wolde hit prayse at more prys, parauenture;
> For quat gome so is gorde with þis grene lace,
> While he hit hade hemely halched aboute,
> Þer is no haþel vnder heuen tohewe hym þat myȝt,
> For he myȝt not be slayn for slyȝt vpon erþe.'
> Þen kest þe knyȝt, and hit come to his hert
> Hit were a juel for þe jopardé þat hym iugged were:
> When he acheued to þe chapel his chek for to fech,
> Myȝt he haf slypped to be vnslayn, þe sleȝt were noble.
> Þenne he þulged with hir þrepe and þoled hir to speke,
> And ho bere on hym þe belt and bede hit hym swyþe—
> And he granted and hym gafe with a goud wylle—
>   (1846–61)

With the Lady's subsequent plea to Gawain to "lelly layne" her gift "fro hir lorde," however, the temporary attribution she has improvised for the girdle falls away, and the girdle is returned to its role as a guilty prop in a presumed love scene—

> And bisoȝt hym, for hir sake, disceuer hit neuer,
> Bot to lelly layne fro hir lorde; þe leude hym acordez
> Þat neuer wyȝe schulde hit wyt, iwysse, bot þay twayne
>   for noȝt;
> He þonkked hir oft ful swyþe,
> Ful þro with hert and þoȝt.   (1862–67)

—the very scene that has been acted out, though never to its completion and always with great care on Gawain's side to prevent self-incrimination, in all their private encounters together, including this final occasion. As something to be concealed from a rightful husband, the girdle is by inference a love gift; and the necessity of its concealment entails a guilty conspiracy of silence that instates two persons, "þay twayne," in an apparent transgression against a third,

---

5. In an excellent structural reading of the poem, Hieatt mentions the Oxford English Dictionary's gloss of the word *lace* as "a net, noose, snare" (341). Like Benson (40), he discovers a second lace besides the Lady's—wrapped around the shaft of the Green Knight's ax when that character appears at the Arthurian court (line 217). He reads line 2226, furthermore, as referring to a third lace, distinguishable from the Lady's lace on Gawain's body. All three nooses wind up, by a suggestive coincidence, around either the trunk of a man or the protruding shaft of a weapon (Hieatt 344, 350)—a coincidence in positioning that seems curious, to say the least.

in effect producing a version, albeit here in a form empty of content, of the common courtly theme of triangulated, adulterous love. The text goes on to hint of the return of the girdle's other cathexis: "Twice (ll. 1874, 2438) the girdle is called a 'luf-lace,' once (2033) a 'drurye,' glossed by the editors as a 'love-token,' the same word later applied by the poet to the illicit dalliance of Merlin and Morgan" (Friedman and Osberg 307).

Thereafter, each occasion of unknotting and reknotting witnesses the girdle's passage into and out of other, subsidiary vocabularies and lexical frames. It is a magical prophylactic to Gawain when it leaves the Lady (doubly prophylactic, in that it is thought to ward off both death and further sexual demands from the Lady). Immediately after the Green Knight's revelations, however, Gawain seeks to make of the girdle the conveniently extrovertible carrier of his moral unease—that part of him he attempts to excoriate from his "kynde," or true authentic nature, in an orgy of symbolic excision: flinging away the offending (part-)object and transferentially attributing to all womankind, woman's "kynde" (including, by tacit accusation, the Lady), the worst, false, and now presumably extruded portion of that nature.[6] The expurgation apparently complete, Gawain can then take up the girdle again, but explicitly as "syngne"—that is, as a thing that he sees as a-part from him, separate, and with which he exists only in a proximate confabulation. Gawain's rendering of the girdle as "syngne" thus slyly testifies to the tactical apprehension of a distinction between an inside characterized as Gawain and an outside characterized as an overlay, his "faut," "surfet," "fayntyse." That division is interposed through the subtle deployment of two tropes during his public self-accounting to Arthur's court: first, a trope of capture, where an unsuspecting Gawain is supposedly "tan" by "vntrawþe" imaged like a waiting trap; and second, a trope of infection, where the same "untrawþe" is visualized as a kind of extrinsic disease, which fastens ("is tachched") upon Gawain, creating an ailment that is then "caȝt" by the hapless victim (2508–12). Even as Gawain is passionately averring that his "harme" can never be removed from him, therefore ("twynne wil hit neuer"), his mechanism of strategic distancing, of inserting a space between what is

6. One critic notices that "the girdle is presented almost as an active agent of deceit—*þe falssyng*" (Mills 637). Gawain's flaw, by his own reasoning, did not exist in him in any form whatever, neither as a trace nor as the possibility of a trace, before the seduction game. Rather, he imagines it as produced by the Lady's game, as an unjust effect that is subsequently laid to his charge and interfaced with him ("Now am I fawty and falce," "cowardyse *me* taȝt," "*my kynde* to forsake" [2382, 2379, 2380; italics mine]). Dove contributes the important reminder that in both Middle English and Old French literature an antifeminist and misogynist Gawain is as fully a part of the Gawain tradition as is a courteous one.

self and what is not-self (but an unfortunate supplement or addition devised by a woman), has already enacted a scenario of self-removal, an escape through the disjunctions afforded by metaphor.[7]

Where the girdle as a sign is intended by Gawain to deliver an alibi of sorts, it appears to promise his erstwhile adversary, the Green Knight, the possibility of mastery and command over the Lady's text and all its strategies. By claiming the girdle as his possession ("my wede") in his disclosures to Gawain, the Green Knight is able also to lay claim to rightful ownership of the seduction game after the fact ("I wroȝt hit myseluen") and thereby assert his dominion over its supervisor, the Lady ("my wyf"). To legitimate his access to the girdle, he artfully alludes to its colors, green and gold, which are pointedly his own colors as well ("For hit is grene as my goune," "þat is golde-hemmed"),[8] and stealthily reintroduces the motif of the hunt, a motif we are habituated to think of as belonging to him, by casually offering Gawain the girdle for a souvenir: "And I gif þe, sir, þe gurdel . . ." (2358–96). That single gesture at once recalls all the earlier instances when, in his role as Bertilak the hunter, he had offered other prizes to Gawain, and it surreptitiously reconstructs the girdle as merely another of his trophies to give away, a prize, this time from a manhunt. It is a move that seeks to eclipse the primacy of the Lady's part and her responsibility for the stalking of Gawain, since it works to dissolve the specificity of her particular subtle hunt and all its scenes into a panoramic generality of hunts dominated by Bertilak-the Green Knight: the Lady's project is to appear as only one act in a grander, vaster design overseen by a male supervisor, with its crucial preeminence accordingly withheld.

The potential violence of the move is immediately disengaged, however, by the slipperiness of the girdle as a sign. Once Gawain's brief, furious outburst has served its intended task of suggesting his innate innocence, he lapses quite unselfconsciously into calling the girdle a "luf-lace," a reference that meaningly signals the quiet surfacing, once again, of the Lady's discourse (2438). With this recurrence, the layers of signification wrought by the Lady return to haunt the text, and her

7. By resorting to the *blasme des femmes* tradition, Gawain deftly codes his own "faut" and masculine weakness in general as feminine, naming as "woman" all that is demonstrably wrong with man and invoking in shorthand form ("Adam," "Salamon," "Samson," "Dauyth") certain misogynist strains in biblical history to support his weighting of the figure. In his hasty conversion of what Barbara Johnson calls "a difference *within* . . . into a difference *between*" (105), Gawain naively fails to notice, however, that his assignment of blame inadvertently registers an implicit assumption that ultimate power over men's actions and destinies *rests with women*—an assumption useful to feminist readings (see, e.g., Heng).

8. Much has been said about the traditional, innovative, or ambiguous use of color in *Sir Gawain* (see, e.g., Blanch, "Games"; Eagan; Kittredge; Robertson; and Zimmer), particularly by critics taking anthropological, folkloric, or religious approaches to the poem. An entire branch of the poem's scholarship is in fact devoted to the interpretation of color. As indicated in this paper, my interest in the use of color is strictly local and limited.

desire overshadows the momentum of refiguration, fleetingly halting it. That is to say, feminine desire breaks in to dispel (dis-*spell, unspell*) the masculine assertion of mastery at the very juncture where that control and mastery would seem most secure; riding the protean elusiveness of the sign, feminine desire doubles back on, and ironizes, in a countermovement, the process of the girdle's refiguration.[9] In that moment when masculine discursive command falters—at the point where the sign slips away from the narrative in which it has been ambitiously embedded—the feminine text ineluctably emerges once again. To expand and consolidate its moment, this incursion by the feminine dilates into a celebratory testament to Morgan la Fée: in a dizzying turnaround, the Green Knight not only admits Morgan's overarching authority and powers in an astonishing, prolonged excursus—an admission that represents him no longer as master-manipulator but only as a servant, and Morgan's obedient creature—but also hints at the extent of her reach and possible status, when he respectfully describes her as "Morgne þe goddes" (2446–67).

The slippery reversals of hierarchy and priority asserted in the quick substitution of one construction after another (the Lady's, Gawain's, the Green Knight's, the Lady's again, then Morgan's) echo once more when the girdle, in its final appearance toward the end of the poem, metamorphoses into a "bauderyk" and multiplies in number at the Arthurian court. There, Gawain's gloomy projection of the girdle as a penitential sign—his lodging it, in other words, within a closed signifying system that would stabilize its meaning along a moral-ethical axis, with himself at the center—is given short shrift by Arthur and the knights. The court refuses Gawain's melancholy prognosis, with its joy and laughter,[1] and Arthur overturns the girdle's signification once again by quite literally turning the sign over on its side, an act that records its entrance into yet another order of reference by mutating it into another object altogether, a girdle-become-baldric. But even here in its celebrated afterlife the referent(s) of the once-girdle cannot be grasped with any finality. So much may be hazarded by that sign—perhaps joy,

9. More traditional views on how a trope of disenchantment functions in the poem (represented by scholars ranging from Kittredge to the Indologist Ananda Coomaraswamy) center primarily on the interaction between the Green Knight and Gawain.

1. Gawain's insistence that the girdle is "þe token of vntrawþe þat I am tan inne," a claim as subtle as it is exaggerated, represents a last, late attempt at fixing an identity for himself—even if it is that of the shamefaced wrongdoer and sincere penitent. This final stab at securing a known and knowable, clearly defined identity is little different from the earlier, more conspicuous attempt with the pentangle. As a ploy, however, it is no more successful: the court, by turning back Gawain's moralizing, defers not only the girdle's meaning but also the temptation and opportunity to stabilize an identity. A poignant misunderstanding is also registered in Gawain's use of "trawþe" and "vntrawþe" here—apparently terms of considerable meaning for him. Critics rightly point out that "trawþe" to one idea, value, or character in the poem is instantly "vntrawþe" to another; the concepts, as they are exercised in the poem, are treacherously shifty and elusive, impossible to anchor.

affection, honor, esteem, renown, a lesson, a romance, a coun-
ternarrative, a postscript, and, not least of all, the allegorized fable
of an endless desire—that its signifying horizon vanishes at the very
point where its multiplication and dispersal take effect. With the
girdle-baldric firmly ensconced as an institution, the chronic uncertainty and dilation of desire staged through it are dramatically
enshrined also as permanent conditions.

It is because the girdle is furnished as a material structure organized around a break (a girdle, by definition, can only be built
around an imperfect knot, whose provisionality holds open the possibility of continued use) that the object so aptly lends itself to a
demonstration of the properties of the linguistic signifier. For the
infrastructural detail that accommodates the girdle to repeated use
also accommodates it to the accumulation of diverse referents as it
moves across the levels of the text, unknotting from within one discursive modality to be remade within another, in a progression that
attests, perhaps invites, continual attempts at rescripting its signification. After a time, something very like an allegory of language or a
narrative of the sign is collected, a signifier for language, for the
operation and play of linguistic difference, a signifier for the signifier, no less. Yet something further takes place with this staging of
the sign, this putting-into-effect of the girdle-as-sign within the
poem. Etymologically, Shoshana Felman remarks in an extraordinary aside, "analysis" (a word we may identify as coextensive with
the reading process, and for which, perhaps, it may do service)
means "the undoing of a knot" ("Postal Survival" 71). That is to say,
the specter of a knot coalesces at the precise moment and location
in the text where analysis reading is to occur; and our performance
of that twin activity takes on, or mimes, the activity of the open,
imperfect knot, the knot of the girdle, in that we constantly repeat
the gestures of unraveling and reconstitution that are conditioned—
indeed, demanded—by the character of the knot itself.[2]

For a polemicized afterword to this never-ending story of the sign,
it would be timely to recapitulate that it is by the agency and operation of the sign that Gawain is marked over twice in pivotal

---

2. The cutting of a knot, Felman observes (an act whose prototypical example leaves the
navel scar), performs again the unloosening of the tie with the mother: a "cut" knot is
thus the witness of a necessary separation and rebeginning. Interestingly, the description
of the pentangle also recalls, in its vulnerability, Lacan's "Borromean knot": everything
comes apart once a crucial cut is introduced (Clément 184).
    R. A. Shoaf's close readings of the pentangle and girdle come to this conclusion: "The
knots people tie in or with the green girdle . . . are signs of the human and human signs:
they will submit to analysis, and life will go on. Unlike such geometrically perfect knots as
the pentangle, transcendental in the universality of their form, these knots, knots like the
knot of the green girdle, are not the termination of signification. They are rather terms of
signification, leading to more terms, more signification, the endless finitude of interpretation" ("'Syngne'" 165; italics mine).

sequences in the poem, first by the pentangle, and then by the girdle—he is re-marked, re-signed—in a kind of double writing, or writing double, by the feminine, in the style and signature of the feminine text.[3]

Works Cited

Arthur, Ross Gilbert. *Medieval Sign Theory and* Sir Gawain and the Green Knight. Toronto: U of Toronto P, 1987.

———. "The Signs of Sir Gawain: A Study in Fourteenth-Century Modes of Meaning." Diss. York U, 1982.

Baswell, Christopher, and William Sharpe, eds. *The Passing of Arthur: Essays in Arthurian Tradition*. New York: Garland, 1988.

Baughan, Denver Ewing. "The Role of Morgan le Fay in *Sir Gawain and the Green Knight.*" *English Literary History* 17 (1950): 241–51.

Benson, Larry D[ean]. *Art and Tradition in* Sir Gawain and the Green Knight. New Brunswick: Rutgers UP, 1965.

Bersani, Leo. *The Freudian Body: Psychoanalysis and Art*. New York: Columbia UP, 1986.

Blanch, Robert. "Games Poets Play: The Ambiguous Use of Color Symbolism in *Sir Gawain and the Green Knight.*" *Nottingham Medieval Studies* 20 (1976): 64–85.

———. Sir Gawain and the Green Knight: *A Reference Guide*. Troy: Whitston, 1983.

Bloomfield, Morton W. *Essays and Explorations: Studies in Ideas, Language, and Literature*. Cambridge: Harvard UP, 1970.

Brewer, D[erek] S. "Courtesy and the *Gawain*-Poet." *Patterns of Love and Courtesy: Essays in Memory of C. S. Lewis*. Ed. John Lawlor. London: Arnold, 1966. 54–85.

———. "The Interpretation of Dream, Folktale and Romance with Special Reference to *Sir Gawain and the Green Knight.*" *Neuphilologische Mitteilungen* 77 (1976): 569–81.

Brooks, Peter. "The Idea of a Psychoanalytic Literary Criticism." *Discourse in Psychoanalysis and Literature*. Ed. Shlomith Rimmon-Kenan. London: Methuen, 1987. 1–18.

Burrow, J[ohn] A[nthony]. *A Reading of* Sir Gawain and the Green Knight. London: Routledge, 1965.

Carson, Angela. "Morgain la Fée as the Principle of Unity in *Gawain and the Green Knight.*" *Modern Language Quarterly* 23 (1962): 3–16.

---

3. I would like to thank Eugene Vance, Ann C. Watts, and Jane Chance for their careful attention to this paper and for their helpful comments. A special group of readers—Janadas Devan, Sam Otter, Suvir Kaul, Alison Case, Paul Sawyer, Dorothy Mermin, Sandra Siegel, and Carol V. Kaske—constituted an indispensable community at all stages of writing.

Clark, S. L., and Julian N. Wasserman. "Gawain's 'Antifeminism' Reconsidered." *Journal of the Rocky Mountain Medieval and Renaissance Association* 6 (1985): 57–70.

Clément, Catherine. *The Lives and Legends of Jacques Lacan.* Trans. Arthur Goldhammer. New York: Columbia UP, 1983.

Coomaraswamy, Ananda K. "*Sir Gawain and the Green Knight*: Indra and Namuci." *Speculum* 14 (1944): 104–25.

Dove, Mary. "Gawain and the 'Blasme des Femmes' Tradition." *Medium Aevum* 41 (1972): 20–26.

Eadie, John. "Morgain la Fée and the Conclusion of *Sir Gawain and the Green Knight.*" *Neophilologus* 52 (1968): 299–304.

———. "Sir Gawain and the Ladies of Ill-Repute." *Annuale mediaevale* 20 (1981): 52–66.

Eagan, Joseph F. "The Import of Color Symbolism in *Gawain and the Green Knight.*" *Saint Louis University Studies* ser. A, Humanities, 1.2 (1949): 11–86.

Englehardt, George J. "The Predicament of Gawain." *Modern Language Quarterly* 16 (1955): 218–25.

Felman, Shoshana. "Postal Survival: Or, The Question of the Navel." *Yale French Studies* 69 (1985): 49–72.

———. "Rereading Femininity." *Yale French Studies* 62 (1981): 19–44.

———. "To Open the Question." *Literature and Psychoanalysis: The Question of Reading: Otherwise.* Ed. Felman. Baltimore: Johns Hopkins UP, 1982. 5–10.

Finlayson, J. "The Expectations of Romance in *Sir Gawain and the Green Knight.*" *Genre* 12 (1979): 1–24.

Fisher, Sheila. "Leaving Morgan Aside: Women, History, and Revisionism in *Sir Gawain and the Green Knight.*" Baswell and Sharpe 129–51.

———. "Taken Men and Token Women in *Sir Gawain and the Green Knight.*" *Seeking the Woman in Late Medieval and Renaissance Writings: Essays in Feminist Contextual Criticism.* Ed. Fisher and Janet E. Halley. Knoxville: U of Tennessee P, 1989. 71–105.

Freud, Sigmund. "Fetishism." Trans. Joan Riviere. *Sexuality and the Psychology of Love.* Ed. Philip Rieff. New York: Macmillan, 1963. 214–19.

Friedman, Albert B. "Morgan le Fay in *Sir Gawain and the Green Knight.*" *Speculum* 35 (1960): 260–74.

Friedman, Albert B., and Richard H. Osberg. "Gawain's Girdle as Traditional Symbol." *Journal of American Folklore* 90 (1977): 301–15.

Gallop, Jane. *The Daughter's Seduction: Feminism and Psychoanalysis.* Ithaca: Cornell UP, 1982.

Gold, Penny Schine. *The Lady and the Virgin: Image, Attitude, and Experience in Twelfth-Century France*. Chicago: U of Chicago P, 1985.

Griffith, Richard R. "Bertilak's Lady: The French Background of *Sir Gawain and the Green Knight*." *Machaut's World: Science and Art in the Fourteenth Century*. Ed. Madelaine Pelner Cosman and Bruce Chandler. Annals of the New York Academy of Sciences 314. New York: New York Acad. of Sciences, 1978. 249–66.

Hamel, Mary, ed. Morte Arthure: *A Critical Edition*. Garland Medieval Texts 9. New York: Garland, 1984.

Hanning, Robert W. "Sir Gawain and the Red Herring: The Perils of Interpretation." *Acts of Interpretation: The Text in Its Contexts, 700–1600. Essays on Medieval and Renaissance Literature in Honor of E. Talbot Donaldson*. Ed. Mary J. Carruthers and Elizabeth D. Kirk. Norman: Pilgrim, 1982. 5–23.

Heng, Geraldine. "Enchanted Ground: The Feminine Subtext in Malory." *Courtly Literature: Culture and Context*. Ed. Keith Busby and Erik Kooper. Amsterdam: Benjamins, 1990. 283–300.

Hieatt, A. Kent. "*Sir Gawain*: Pentangle, Luf-Lace, Numerical Structure." *Papers on Language and Literature* 4 (1968): 339–59.

Hulbert, J. R. "*Syr Gawayn and the Grene Knyȝt*." *Modern Philology* 13 (1915–16): 433–62, 689–730.

Johnson, Barbara. *The Critical Difference: Essays in the Contemporary Rhetoric of Reading*. Baltimore: Johns Hopkins UP, 1980.

Kane, George. "Some Reflections on Critical Method." *Essays and Studies, 1976*. English Association ns 29. London: Murray, 1976. 23–38.

Kiteley, John F. "'The Endless Knot': Magical Aspects of the Pentangle in *Sir Gawain and the Green Knight*." *Studies in the Literary Imagination* 4.2 (1971): 41–50.

Kittredge, G[eorge] L[yman]. *A Study of* Sir Gawain and the Green Knight. Cambridge: Harvard UP, 1916.

Krishna, Valerie, ed. *The Alliterative* Morte Arthure: *A Critical Edition*. New York: Franklin, 1976.

Kristeva, Julia. "Stabat Mater." Trans. Arthur Goldhammer. *The Female Body in Western Culture: Contemporary Perspectives*. Ed. Susan Rubin Suleiman. Cambridge: Harvard UP, 1986. 99–118.

Lewis, C[live] S[taples]. *The Allegory of Love: A Study in Medieval Tradition*. New York: Oxford UP, 1958.

Loomis, Laura Hibbard. "*Gawain and the Green Knight*." *Arthurian Literature in the Middle Ages: A Collaborative History*. Ed. Roger Sherman Loomis. Oxford: Clarendon-Oxford UP, 1959. 528–40.

Loomis, Roger Sherman. *Wales and the Arthurian Legend*. Cardiff: U of Wales P, 1956.

216   GERALDINE HENG

Malarkey, Stoddard, and J. Barre Toelken. "Gawain and the Green
   Girdle." *Journal of English and Germanic Philology* 63 (1964):
   14–20.
McAlindon, T[homas Edward]. "Magic, Fate, and Providence in
   Medieval Narrative and *Sir Gawain and the Green Knight*." *Review
   of English Studies* ns 16 (1965): 121–39.
Mertens-Fonck, Paule. "Morgan, fée et déesse." *Mélanges offerts à
   Rita Lejeune, Professeur à Université de Liège*. Vol. 2. Gembloux:
   Duculot, 1969, 1067–76.
Mills, David. "The Rhetorical Function of Gawain's Antifeminism."
   Neuphilologische Mitteilungen 71 (1970): 635–40.
Montrelay, Michèle. "Inquiry into Femininity." Trans. Parveen
   Adams. *M/F* 1 (1978): 83–101.
Moon, Douglas M. "The Role of Morgain la Fée in *Sir Gawain and
   the Green Knight*." *Neuphilologische Mitteilungen* 67 (1966):
   31–57.
Morris, John, ed. *Nennius: British History and the Welsh Annals*.
   Arthurian Period Sources 8. London: Phillimore; Totowa: Rowman,
   1980.
Novak, James Ballaz. "Magic as Theme in *Sir Gawain and the Green
   Knight*." Diss. Syracuse U, 1979.
Olstead, Myra. "Morgan le Fay in Malory's *Morte Darthur*." *Biblio-
   graphical Bulletin of the International Arthurian Society* 19 (1967):
   128–38.
Paton, Lucy Allen. *Studies in the Fairy Mythology of Arthurian
   Romance*. Boston: Athenæum, 1903.
Robertson, D. W. "Why the Devil Wears Green." *Modern Language
   Notes* 69 (1954): 470–72.
Rose, Jacqueline. *Sexuality in the Field of Vision*. London: Verso,
   1986.
Schor, Naomi. *Breaking the Chain: Women, Theory, and French
   Realist Fiction*. New York: Columbia UP, 1985.
———. *Reading in Detail: Aesthetics and the Feminine*. New York:
   Methuen, 1987.
Shoaf, R[ichard] A[llen]. *The Poem as Green Girdle: "Commercium"
   in Sir Gawain and the Green Knight*. Gainesville: UP of Florida,
   1984.
———. "The 'Syngne of Surfet' and the Surfeit of Signs in *Sir
   Gawain and the Green Knight*." Baswell and Sharpe 152–69.
Silverstein, Theodore, ed. Sir Gawain and the Green Knight: *A New
   Critical Edition*. Chicago: U of Chicago P, 1984.
Spearing, A. C. "Central and Displaced Sovereignty in Three
   Medieval Poems." *Review of English Studies* 33 (1982): 247–61.
———. *The Gawain-Poet: A Critical Study*. Cambridge: Cambridge
   UP, 1970.

Spivak, Gayatri Chakravorty. "Feminism and Critical Theory." *For Alma Mater: Theory and Practice in Feminist Scholarship.* Ed. Paula A. Treichler, Cheris Kamarae, and Beth Stafford. Urbana: U of Illinois P, 1985. 119–42.

Taylor, Paul Beekman. "Gawain's Garland of Girdle and Name." *English Studies* 55 (1974): 6–14.

Tolkien, J. R. R., E. V. Gordon, and Norman Davis, eds. *Sir Gawain and the Green Knight.* Oxford: Clarendon-Oxford UP, 1967.

Warner, Marina. *Alone of All Her Sex: The Myth and the Cult of the Virgin Mary.* New York: Random, 1983.

Williams, Edith Whitehurst. "Morgan le Fay as Trickster in *Sir Gawain and the Green Knight.*" *Folklore* 96 (1985): 38–56.

Zimmer, Heinrich. *The King and the Corpse: Tales of the Soul's Conquest of Evil.* Bollingen Series 11. New York: Pantheon, 1956.

LEO CARRUTHERS

The Duke of Clarence and the Earls of March: Garter Knights and *Sir Gawain and the Green Knight*[†]

'*Hony soit qui mal pence*': this slightly altered version of the motto of the Order of the Garter appears at the end of the Middle English alliterative poem *Sir Gawain and the Green Knight (SGGK),* the only extant copy of which is to be found in London, British Library, MS Cotton Nero A.x.[1] The motto appears to have been added in 'a somewhat later hand';[2] and it has been said that there is no clear evidence that the *Gawain*-poet himself, or even the original copyist, intended such a direct allusion to the Garter.[3] Much discussion has already been generated for and against the supposed connections between *SGGK* and the Garter.[4] To my mind, the indications are decidedly in favour of, rather than against, such an interpretation; any English poet writing in the Arthurian mode at this date would

---

† From *Medium Ævum* 70.1 (2001):66–79. Reprinted by permission.
1. *Sir Gawain and the Green Knight,* ed. J. R. R. Tolkien and E. V. Gordon (1925), 2nd edn rev. Norman Davis (Oxford, 1967). Line numbers of quotations from *SGGK* refer to this edition.
2. *Pearl, Cleanness, Patience and Sir Gawain: Facsimile of BM MS. Cotton Nero A.x,* ed. I. Gollancz, EETS, os 162 (Oxford, 1923), p. 8.
3. See *SGGK* ed. Tolkien and Gordon, p. 131; also *Sir Gawain and the Green Knight,* ed. and trans. W. R. J. Barron (Manchester, 1974), p. 179.
4. For a survey of Garter theories, see W. G. Cooke and D'A. J. D. Boulton, '*Sir Gawain and the Green Knight*: a poem for Henry of Grosmont?', *Medium Ævum,* 68 (1999), 42–54; Hugh Collins, *The Order of the Garter, 1348–1461: Chivalry and Politics in Later Medieval England* (Oxford, 2000), pp. 256–8.

necessarily see, and know that an aristocratic audience would also see, a parallel between the Round Table and the Order of the Garter. The motto, whenever added, is important as evidence of how an early reader—possibly a contemporary of the author's, or at least the copyist's—reacted to the poem. Whoever added the motto certainly intended to draw attention to the parallel between the real-life order of chivalry and the imaginary knights of the Round Table, perhaps even between the prestigious garter itself, symbol of the order, and the girdle of *SGGK*, which is adopted and worn as a sash by King Arthur's court. But it may well be the case, as I hope to show by pointing to certain clues within the text, that the anonymous poet himself intended the parallel, for there is a real connection between the Garter motto and the poem's inner dynamic. If someone other than the poet was responsible for adding the motto at the end of *SGGK*, that person was only making explicit what the author himself had left implicit. Furthermore, I would suggest that the poet intended by this reference to flatter a noble patron, one who desired to gain admission into the highly exclusive Order of the Garter—a mark of royal favour which would (if the proposed identification is correct) have increased his chances of being taken seriously as heir to the throne.

The presence of the Garter motto at the very end of the poem is the parting shot in a series of leave-takings through which the poet takes us, as the literary illusion recedes into the distance and the author draws us back to concrete reality. He takes leave firstly of Gawain's story, next of Arthurian romance in general, then of ancient British legend, and finally of salvation history. The perspective thus recedes into the ancient past before being telescoped into eternity, the Christian view of mankind. It is very striking that the symbolism of the green girdle is inverted in the final stanza, from a badge of shame to a badge of honour. Worn first by Sir Gawain as a talisman (at Hautdesert, where it must be hidden), it is elevated to the level of sign, on a par with the pentangle (on leaving the Green Chapel), then adopted as a chivalric emblem (at Camelot). Gawain returns home wearing it as a baldric, i.e. across his right shoulder and tied in a knot under his left arm. For the hero, the adventure has been one of progress from self-delusion to self-awareness, from pride to penitence. The 'endless knot' (line 630) of the pentangle has been undone along with the hero's 'trawþe', or fidelity (lines 626; 2470), and the new knot of the baldric is a sign of Gawain's remorse. The paradox of the baldric, seen in penitential terms, is the paradox of the crucifixion in St Paul's understanding of salvation: no cross, no crown. The humbling of Gawain leads to greater honour, but only when his sin is forgiven and he is reintegrated into the Christian community. His companions, in adopting the green baldric, reverse its meaning, now a sign of grace rather than disgrace.

At all events, the story ends at this point with the adoption of the baldric, and to remind us that it is indeed a story whose primary object is to entertain, the author recalls that it is recorded in 'þe best boke of romaunce' (line 2521). Bringing the story back round to its starting point, there is a final reminder of the Arthurian setting and, beyond that again, as in the introductory stanza, of the historical background of Brutus and the siege of Troy, which has the effect of distancing the events from the present. The final alliterative line, 'After þe segge and þe asaute watz sesed at Troye' (line 2525), is thus almost exactly the same as the poem's first line, 'Siþen þe sege and þe assaut watz sesed at Troye'. The meaning of the last two lines, 'Now þat bere þe croun of þorne, / He bryng vus to his blysse! Amen' (lines 2529–30), seems at first sight unrelated to what has gone before. The tone in this couplet is unabashedly pious, and scarcely in the style of romance. Although it is commonplace for romance authors to invoke a blessing on the audience they do not normally do so in the style of preachers, which is the convention followed here. This couplet is typical of medieval English sermons, such as in *Jacob's Well,* many of whose chapters end in a very similar way.[5] That the author was a religious man is undoubted; he may even have been a priest, perhaps a chaplain in a noble household, though there is no critical agreement on this point.[6] If such were indeed the case, as I think, one of his duties would be to preach regularly; and so the concluding couplet may be intended as a reminder of his role. This interpretation is in keeping with the analysis of Gawain's fault in penitential terms and throws the three scenes of confession (made first to the priest, then to the Green Knight, and finally to the Round Table) into sharper relief.

In just a few lines, therefore, the author goes through this series of conclusions or leave-takings. But there is one last line still to come, a parting shot which creates a new element of suspense, raising as it does further questions about the meaning and symbolism of the green girdle. That line is the motto of the Order of the Garter, '*Hony soit qui mal pence*', written in the manuscript just after the poem.[7] As said earlier, not everyone would agree that this is the *author's* parting shot: on the contrary, many commentators see it as a

---

5. See Leo Carruthers, "'And what schall be the ende": an edition of the final chapter of *Jacob's Well*', *Medium Ævum*, 61 (1992), 289–97 (p. 297 n. 24).
6. See Nicholas Watson, 'The *Gawain*-poet as a vernacular theologian', in *A Companion to the Gawain-Poet*, ed. Derek Brewer and Jonathan Gibson (Cambridge, 1997), pp. 293–313 (p. 299).
7. The spelling used in *SGGK* is Old French, the language of heraldry; the form used by the Order of the Garter today is 'Honi soit qui mal y pense', though *Honi* is still spelt in the medieval way, not with the double *n* of the modern French verb *honnir* (to shame, dishonour, disgrace). The shorter version in *SGGK*, without the French *y* ('of it'), gives the phrase a wider application to evil in general.

mere scribal addition, i.e. something added by the copyist—or even by someone else—for his own reasons, which are not necessarily those of the poet. I am not convinced that this dismissive attitude is justified. The similarities are obvious between the real-life garter and the poem's girdle or baldric: in both cases an item of dress—an accessory worn by both sexes—is adopted by a royal order of chivalry as a badge of honour. In reality the Knights of the Garter wear two emblems, a blue ribbon with a gold border below the left knee, and a dark blue sash; the Knights of the Round Table wear a green sash, baldric-wise. A sash may be worn as a belt or a baldric: Gawain does both with the lady's girdle. When he arms himself in the castle he puts it around his waist (line 2033), but when he leaves the Green Chapel he ties it as a baldric (line 2486), and it is thus that it is adopted at the Round Table (line 2516). In purely icono-graphic or heraldic terms the parallel is striking. Why a copyist working in the second half—perhaps the last quarter—of the four-teenth century would wish to draw attention to this fact requires some knowledge of the importance of the Order of the Garter and its direct relation to the Arthurian romance tradition.

The order of the Garter was England's first order of chivalry. The exact date of its foundation was once a matter of some doubt, even among contemporary writers, though there is now general agree-ment on the year 1348. The main reason for the confusion is that King Edward III first planned a Round Table, in 1344, which even-tually crystallized into the Order of the Garter four years later; and even fourteenth-century chroniclers are not always clear about the sequence. What is clear is the literary influence of chivalric romance: Edward III, attracted to pageantry and glamour, deliberately mod-elled his new order on the traditions of King Arthur and the knights of the Round Table. The young King had succeeded to the throne in 1327 at the age of 14—one thinks inevitably of the youthful Arthur of *SGGK* (lines 86; 105), surrounded by 'beardless boys' (line 280), as the Green Knight calls the knights of the Round Table—and reigned for fifty years, until his death in 1377—During his lifetime the English language was once again emerging as a literary force; many Arthurian romances were translated from French, and new English ones were composed. Edward and his companions were inspired by a wish to revive the traditions of the golden age of chivalry. In January 1544, at a splendid feast in Windsor Castle, the King announced his intention of refounding the Round Table, the formal initiation to take place, following the pattern of Arthurian romance, the following Pentecost.[8] He then planned a grand joust-

8. Juliet Vale, 'Arthur in English society', in *The Arthur of the English*, ed. W. R. J. Barton (Cardiff, 1999), pp. 185–96 (pp. 192–3).

ing tournament to take place at Windsor on St George's Day (23 April); a table 200 feet long was set up for the entertainment of the knights and their ladies. Edward's original idea was to recreate a very large chivalric fellowship of 300 knights, and construction even began at Windsor on a building designed to house the Round Table. This ambitious plan was modified at some point during the next few years, to be replaced by the much smaller, more exclusive Order of the Garter, limited to twenty-six members: the sovereign, the Prince of Wales, and twenty-four companions, most of whom had accompanied Edward III on the Crecy campaign of 1346.[9] It was still a chivalric fellowship but also one having an explicitly religious function, with its own collegiate church; and the completion in 1349 of the new chapel of St George in Windsor Castle, where the coats of arms of the Knights of the Garter were to remain on display, gave the order a permanent home.

As for Edward III's choice of the Order of the Garter's curious motto, which means 'Shame be to him who thinks evil of it', the reference is far from obvious and has been the object of much speculation. What would the English King wish the founding companions, or indeed the nobility at large, not to think evil of? In all likelihood, it was his claim to the French throne, and his consequent military engagements in France, that Edward had in mind. It is clear from the outset, at the foundation of the Order in 1348, that he gave priority, as far as Garter membership was concerned, to those who had campaigned at his side in France; and this priority (service in France rather than, say, Ireland or Scotland) was upheld throughout his reign.[1] The Garter motto, although mysterious, is not therefore totally opaque, while lending itself to more than one interpretation. Appearances, the words also seem to mean, are not what we think: let us not jump to hasty conclusions, especially when that involves making moral judgements about our neighbours. And this is precisely the case in *SGGK*—hence the relevance of the real-life motto to the poem.

Whatever the truth about the motto, the founding of the Order of the Garter was an event of European importance which struck the imagination of princes and poets everywhere.[2] From the middle of

9. For a full list of the founding companions and subsequent members in the fourteenth century, see *The Complete Peerage*, by G.E.C., vol. II, rev. and ed. The Hon. Vicary Gibbs (London, 1912), appendix B (pp. 534ff.); Grace Holmes, *The Order of the Garter: Its Knights and Stall Plates 1348 to 1984* (Windsor, 1984), pp. 12off.; and Collins, *The Order of the Garter*, pp. 288–99.

1. Collins, *The Order of the Garter*, pp. 39–41, 280.

2. For European connections see D'A. J. D. Boulton, *The Knights of the Crown: The Monarchical Orders of Knighthood in Later Medieval Europe, 1325–1520* (Woodbridge, 1986). On links between the fourteenth-century orders of knighthood and the knights of the Round Table, see further: *The Book of Chivalry of Geoffroi de Charny*, ed. Richard W. Kaeuper and Elspeth Kennedy (Philadelphia, Pa, 1996), and *Froissart across the Genres*, ed. Donald Maddox and Sara Sturm-Maddox (Gainesville, Fla, 1998), pp. 179–94.

the fourteenth century onwards, anyone writing in the Arthurian mode, especially in England, could hardly fail to be conscious of the parallel between the chivalric and overtly religious values of the Round Table and those of the Order of the Garter. For the copyist of *SGGK* to draw attention to this would thus seem to be very natural. I would go further, however, and suggest that it would be just as natural for the author, and not merely the copyist, to have thought along the same lines. For the entire poem is about appearances, about being deceived by illusion, about learning to see things as they really are, about learning to accept oneself as one really is. The motto of the Order of the Garter is very aptly related to the poet's moral meaning, going far beyond any similarity between the garter and the girdle, quite in keeping with this moralist's wish to make us think about what lies beneath the surface. It might be objected that the difference in colour between the green girdle and the blue garter makes any allusion unlikely; but an allusion is not a description. The poet is not describing the real garter but alluding to its moral significance, drawing a parallel between its real-life symbolism and its deeper meaning in his poem. He would not thereby feel obliged to labour the point by making Sir Gawain's sash blue like the Garter's: the reference is indirect, an allusion to the garter, not a description of it.

One may point, furthermore, to a later parallel between literature, real-life chivalry, and the wearing of a sash or 'lace' in *The Grene Knight* (c. 1500), a late tail-rhyme romance based on *SGGK*, which it abbreviates drastically.[3] In this poem the Lady gives Gawain a white 'lace' (a word *SGGK* sometimes uses for the girdle, cf. line 1830 etc.) which saves him from death; the story explains, says the poet, why the knights of the Bath wear a similar lace until they have proved their worth. Attention has also been drawn to the similarity of the oath sworn by the knights of the Bath and Malory's knights of the Round Table.[4] The knights of the Bath went through a ceremonial form of knighting traditionally said to have been initiated by Henry IV in 1399, to honour those who had assisted him at his bath the night before the coronation; and while this knightly fellowship did not constitute an order of chivalry like the Garter (the modern Order of the Bath was not, in fact, created until 1725), the distinction may not

3. *The Grene Knight*, in *Bishop Percy's Folio Manuscript: Ballads and Romances*, 3 vols, ed. J. W. Hales and F. J. Furnivall (London, 1867–8; Detroit, 1968), II, 56–77; also in *Sir Gawain: Eleven Romances and Tales* ed. Thomas Hahn (Kalamazoo, Mich., 1995), pp. 309–36.
4. See *SGGK*, ed. Tolkien and Gordon, p. 131; Richard Barber, 'Malory's *Le Morte Darthur* and court culture', in *Arthurian Literature* XII, ed. James P. Carley and Felicity Riddy (Cambridge, 1993), pp. 133–55 (p. 149); Sir Thomas Malory, *Le Morte Darthur: The Winchester Manuscript*, ed. Helen Cooper, Oxford World's Classics (Oxford, 1998), pp. xi, 536 n. 57.

have been apparent to those who did not regularly move in royal circles, as was probably the case of the author of *The Grene Knight*. It is of interest for our present purpose that even at the end of the fifteenth century it still seemed natural for an English poet, writing in the Arthurian tradition, to explain a real knightly ceremony in terms of a literary precedent, and vice versa. It is thus far from incongruous to suppose that a hundred years or more before, the author of *SGGK* would have seen and intended a similar connection between his poem and the Order of the Garter.

The analogy between Sir Gawain's girdle and the Order of the Garter may be confirmed by a previously unnoticed historical allusion within the romance itself, connecting the poem with one of Edward III's sons. This is the reference to the Duke of Clarence, mentioned as one of the knights gathered around Gawain on All Saints Day to offer him support and advice before his quest begins:

> þenne þe best of þe burȝ boȝed togeder,
> Aywan, and Errik, and oþer ful mony,
> Sir Doddinaul de Sauage, þe duk of Clarence,
> Launcelot, and Lyonel, and Lucan þe gode,
> Sir Boos, and Sir Byduer, big men boþe,
> And mony oþer menskful, with Mador de la Port.
> (lines 550–55)

These are all characters well known in the French romances of the previous century, but there are several odd features about the Duke's presence in this list. To begin with, he is the only one who is mentioned by title alone, without a Christian name, whereas in the French romances he is usually named Galeschin (or Galescalain), who is either Sir Dodinel's cousin (in *Merlin*) or his brother (in *Lancelot*).[5] Secondly, the fact that he is a duke is remarkable, for in the real world this was a very high and rare title, limited in France to a small number of hereditary provinces (Normandy, Brittany, Burgundy, Aquitaine) and unknown in the English peerage before 1337 (Cornwall). This makes the suggestion by the knights of the Round Table, that King Arthur would have done well to make Sir Gawain a duke (line 678)—of which more below—all the more surprising. Thirdly,

---

5. See *Lancelot: roman en prose du XIIIe siècle*, vols I-IX, ed. Alexandre Micha (Paris, 1978–83): 'Galescalains qui estoit dux de Clarence et cosins germains mon seignor Gauvain de par le roi Lot son pere . . . si estoit freres Dodinel le Salvage' (vol. I, X. 2, p. 176). In the index of proper names, under 'Claranz, Clarence, duc de', Micha refers the reader to 'Galescalain, Galechalain, Galeschin, duc de Clarence, fils du roi d'Escavalon, frère de Dodineaus, neveu d'Arthur et cousin germain de Gauvain', listing 141 entries for this character, whose name and/or title occur in the text both separately and together (IX, 72–3). There is another knight in the French *Lancelot*, Bertholai or Berthelai, the traitor behind the False Guinevere episode, who has been seen as an antecedent of SGGK's Sir Bertilak: see W. R. J. Barton, *Trawthe and Treason: The Sin of Gawain Reconsidered* (Manchester, 1980).

the Duke of Clarence is the only one in this list whose name could possibly refer to a real person, an English prince whom the poet might even have known: for, while the title is purely fictitious in the French romances, there being no Duke of Clarence in the thirteenth century, there was one, and only one, in the fourteenth. He was Lionel of Antwerp (1338–68), Edward III's second surviving son.

In the entire fourteenth century, there were very few dukes in England, and most of those were royal princes. The first time the title was used was for Edward III's eldest son Edward of Woodstock (1330–76), Prince of Wales, created Duke of Cornwall in 1337. The second time was in 1351, in favour of Henry of Grosmont, Earl and Duke of Lancaster, a great-grandson of Henry III and a founding companion of the Garter. The third dukedom was created for Lionel of Antwerp (1338–68), Edward III's second surviving son (the infant William of Hatfield had died in 1336): already Earl of Ulster through his marriage to an heiress in 1347, he was created Duke of Clarence in 1362. The King's fourth son was John of Gaunt (1340–99), Earl of Richmond, who became the second Duke of Lancaster, also in 1362 (his father-in-law, Henry of Grosmont, died in 1361; John of Gaunt first became Earl of Lancaster in right of his wife Blanche, but was elevated to the dukedom the following year, after the death of Blanche's sister Maud). The King's younger sons did not become dukes until the reign of their nephew Richard II in 1385: Edmund of Langley (1342–1402) became Duke of York and Thomas of Woodstock (1355–97) Duke of Gloucester. The year after that (1386), the first non-royal dukedoms were created for Richard II's favourites, Robert de Vere, Duke of Ireland, and Thomas Mowbray, Duke of Norfolk.

Lionel, Duke of Clarence's title died with him, in 1368. He and his wife Elizabeth, Countess of Ulster (1332–63), had an only daughter, Philippa (1355–81), who inherited her mother's title, an earldom in tail general, but not her father's, a dukedom in tail male. Philippa was married to Edmund Mortimer, third Earl of March (1352–81), and was the mother of Roger Mortimer, fourth Earl of March (1374–98); and as a first cousin to the childless Richard II and the first in order of succession after him, Philippa became heir presumptive to the throne, a right she passed on to her son. Despite Philippa's importance, her father's dukedom was not recreated in favour of her husband Edmund Mortimer, so the Clarence title reverted to the Crown, not to be revived until Henry IV granted it to his second son, Thomas.[6] At the date of composition of *SGGK*,

6. Thomas, made a duke in 1412, died childless in 1421; the Clarence title again reverted to the Crown and was not revived until 1461, by Edward IV, in favour of his brother George (1449–78).

whether in the reign of Edward III or that of Richard II, an aristocratic audience would be likely to see the reference to the Duke of
Clarence as a compliment to Prince Lionel, even a generation after
his death, since he was the first (and, until 1412, only) duke of this
name. If so, then this is the only identifiable point at which the poet
makes a direct reference to a contemporary person or event and it
thus constitutes a valuable historical clue, hitherto unremarked.

Nor has it been noticed that Lionel's Christian name as well as his
ducal tide, both unusual in England at the time, were inspired by
Arthurian romance. In the French Prose *Lancelot*, Lionel is King
Bors's first son, elder brother of Bors de Ganis, and cousin to
Lancelot; he is so named ('little lion') because of a lion-shaped birth-
mark on his chest.[7] Edward III, fond of games and jousts in which
he sometimes took part incognito, is known to have used the name
'Monseigneur Lyonel' on at least one occasion, a few years before
his son Lionel's birth, at a tournament held at Dunstable in 1354.[8]
His numerous children, girls as well as boys—with the single exception of Lionel of Antwerp—were all given traditional Plantagenet
names: Edward, Isabella, Joan, William, John, Blanche, Edmund,
Mary, Margaret, and Thomas. Lionel, born in 1338, the fifth child
and third son, stands out, in this large family, as the only one whose
name was not traditional, but seems to have been directly inspired
by the character in romance; and one can hardly doubt that the King
himself made the choice of this rather original, literary name.

Lionel's ducal tide, Clarence, very probably came from a similar
inspiration, notwithstanding the explanation given in the reference
books. According to *The Complete Peerage*, the dukedom of Clarence
(*dux de Clarentia*) derives from Clare in Suffolk, 'as it were of the
country about the town, Castle and honour of Clare',[9] because it was
part of the inheritance of Lionel's first wife; but the hesitant tone
adopted in this passage indicates that the etymology remains uncertain, though repeated by Onions.[1] It is far, indeed, from being an
entirely satisfactory account. Elizabeth, sole heiress of William de
Burgh, third Earl of Ulster, was a countess in her own right; she and
Lionel were married in 1347, when the young lady was 15 and the
Prince was still a child of 9. Many years passed before she inherited
the Clare estate from her grandmother Elizabeth de Clare, who died
in 1360; and though an important addition to her property, it was by

7. *Lancelot do Lac: The Non-Cyclic Old French Prose Romance*, 2 vols, ed. Elspeth Kennedy
   (Oxford, 1980), p. 358. I am grateful to Dr Kennedy for kindly drawing my attention to
   the passage explaining the origin of Lionel's name.
8. Vale, 'Arthur in English society', p. 190.
9. *The Complete Peerage*, vol. III, ed. The Hon. Vicary Gibbs and H. A. Doubleday (London,
   1913), P. 258.
1. C. T. Onions et al., *The Oxford Dictionary of English Etymology* (Oxford, 1966, corr.
   1969), s.v. 'Clarenc(i)eux king-of-arms'.

no means the source of her wealth. Two years later, when Lionel was made a duke, the logical thing to do would have been to raise the Irish earldom of Ulster to a dukedom. This was what had happened in the case of the two earlier dukedoms: Cornwall (1337) was originally an earldom held by King John's second son Richard, which had reverted to the Crown in 1300, and likewise Lancaster (1351) was previously an earldom created for Henry III's son Edmund in 1296. The two later royal dukedoms, York and Gloucester (1385), took their names from county towns; and the first non-royal dukedoms, Ireland and Norfolk (1386), were likewise place names. In this entire list, Clarence is the only title not to be that of a royal demesne, or of an important territory granted to loyal servants of the Crown; it is not even a real place name.[2] It is improbable that Prince Lionel would have seen fit to take a title based merely on one of his wife's English holdings, and that the most recent, rather than her earldom of Ulster, particularly since he spent most of the 1360s in Ireland as the King's envoy; and even supposing Lionel to have had a fondness for the manor of Clare (he was in fact buried there), it is unlikely, given the territorial titles in use in the family, that he would have wished the simple Clare to be transformed into the fanciful Clarence. Unlikely, that is, unless his father pointed out the pun; it is not improbable that the King, who had given his son a name taken from Arthurian romance, enjoyed the coincidental similarity between the manorial name of Clare and the literary Duke of Clarence. Should any of the court heralds object that Clarence was not a place name, an excuse could easily be found by attaching it, through a process of back-formation, to the manor of Clare; but this would appear to be an after-thought, a *post factum* explanation.

The year of Clarence's death (1368) has a bearing on my suggestion as to patronage, as does the date of composition of the poem; how-ever, *SGGK* cannot be placed more precisely than the second half (perhaps the final quarter) of the fourteenth century. The manuscript, a copy of a lost exemplar, is usually dated on linguistic and palaeo-graphical grounds to the years 1375–1400, some critics favouring an early date in that period, others a late one.[3] The original poem must have been composed some time—not necessarily a long time—before,

2. In the French tradition, Clarence is said to be the name of a city on the border of 'Sor-gales', or 'Sowailes', i.e. somewhere in the Welsh Marches, where Arthur defeated the Saxons; the victorious King used it as a war-cry and made his nephew Galeschin Duke of Clarence. There is of course no such place name; attempts to link it with St Clears in Car-marthen (which is too far removed from the border area) remain unconvincing. See fur-ther G. D. West, *An Index of Proper Names in French Arthurian Prose Romances* (Toronto, 1978), s.v. 'Clarence'; *Lancelot do Lac*, ed. Kennedy, 'Clarance' (vol. II, index); *Lancelot*, ed. Micha, 'Clarence' (vol. IX, index).

3. See A. S. G. Edwards, 'The manuscript: British Library MS Cotton Nero A.x', in *A Com-panion to the Gawain-Poet*, pp. 197–219 (p. 199).

but no certainty in the matter has been established; nor is there any
way of telling how many stages of copying were involved in the trans-
mission process. A date of composition any time between 1350 and
1399 would thus be acceptable and in harmony not only with the language but with the internal evidence provided by references to such
things as arms, armour, costume, and architecture. While Bennett
places the author at the court of Richard II himself, in the last years of
the King's reign,[4] Cooke and Boulton situate the poem's composition
much earlier, in the years 1352–61, and probably late in that period,
i.e. *circa* 1360; but their dating is at least partly influenced by the
desire to prove that Henry of Grosmont (who died in 1361) was the
poet's patron.[5] But nothing in the poem would exclude a date after
1362, the year Prince Lionel became a duke, which would therefore
be a *terminus ante quem* if the reference in the poem to the Duke of
Clarence at line 552 has any relevance, as I believe. Indeed, should
the later dating prove to be correct, nothing in the poem would preclude the patronage of any of Lionel's descendants down to the end of
the century. This means we should look closely at his heirs, who had
an interest in seeking the revival of the dukedom: his only daughter
Philippa (1355–81) and her husband Edmund Mortimer, third Earl of
March (1352–81), followed by their son Roger, fourth Earl of March
(1374–98).

The territorial holdings of the Mortimers would certainly place
them within easy range of the right dialect area to enable them to be
considered as patrons of the *Gawain*-poet. The author of *SGGK* is
believed, on linguistic grounds, to have come from the north-west
Midlands, the copyist's dialect (and most probably the author's too)
having been narrowed down to north-west Staffordshire and the
adjoining part of Cheshire.[6] It is generally accepted that the poet must
have been employed by a noble landowner having political and eco-
nomic interests in or near this rather small area. Though the principal
Mortimer estates lay somewhat further to the south and west, the first
Earl of March had been appointed, among many other honours, chief
keeper of the peace in the county of Staffordshire.[7] The March title
refers to the border counties of the March of Wales (*Comes Marchia
Walliae*), but the Mortimers were in possession of territories extending far beyond the region; they were, in fact, among the greatest
landowners of the kingdom, holding baronies and manors in many

---

4. Michael J. Bennett, '*Sir Gawain and the Green Knight* and the literary achievement of the
   north-west Midlands: the historical background', *Journal of Medieval History*, 5 (1979),
   63–88 (pp. 78–80).
5. Cooke and Boulton, 'A poem for Henry of Grosmont?', pp. 42–54.
6. Angus McIntosh, 'A new approach to Middle English dialectology', *English Studies*, 44
   (1963), I–II (pp. 5–6).
7. See *The Complete Peerage*, by G. E. C., vol. VIII, rev. and ed. The Hon. Vicary Gibbs, H.
   A. Doubleday, and Lord Howard de Walden (London, 1932), p. 438.

parts of England, Ireland, and Wales. Edmund, third Earl of March, was the owner of a great estate surpassed in extent and value only by those of his wife's uncles, the Prince of Wales and the Duke of Lancaster.[8] The Mortimers' prestige, fuelled by their close relationship with the royal family, as well as their almost unequalled wealth and property, would certainly be likely to attract the services of an author such as the *Gawain*-poet.

Originally of Norman origin, the Mortimers had steadily advanced in power and influence over many generations. They were known for their pride of ancestry, which they believed, on the Welsh side, to go back to the legendary King Arthur himself.[9] This sometimes took the form of colourful display in the Arthurian romance tradition: in 1279 Roger Mortimer, sixth Lord Wigmore (1231–82), invited 100 knights and 100 ladies to attend the Round Table feast at Kenilworth Castle.[1] His grandson, also Roger Mortimer (1287–1330), Queen Isabella's lover, was responsible for the murder of Edward II in 1327, in spite of which he was advanced to the earldom of March in 1328 by the young Edward III, no doubt acting under his mother's instructions. In the same year Mortimer organized an Arthurian Round Table, a sign of pride for which later chroniclers criticized him.[2] Two years later, however, on Edward's assumption of royal authority, at the age of 18, Mortimer was attained and executed (1350). Despite this tragedy, Edward III did not disdain the friendship of his enemy's grandson, also named Roger Mortimer; one of the King's intimate circle, he was a founding companion of the Order of the Garter in 1348 and was restored to his grandfather's title as second Earl of March in 1354.[3] Edward III even went so far as to allow this man's son, Edmund, third Earl of March (1352–81), to marry his eldest granddaughter Philippa, one of England's richest heiresses, in 1368. When Lionel, Duke of Clarence, died some months later, Edmund must have hoped to succeed to his father-in-law's title; but Edward III does not seem to have been anxious to give this ambitious man any more power.

When Richard II came to the throne in 1377, it was, as we have seen, his first cousin Philippa, nearest in the order of succession, who was his heir presumptive; at this point in time there was no

---

8. G. A. Holmes, *The Estates of the Higher Nobility in Fourteenth-Century England* (Cambridge, 1957), pp. 10–19, gives a detailed account of the extent of his landholdings; his son Roger, the fourth Earl, likewise held one of 'the greatest inheritances at the end of the century' (p. 40).

9. Vale, 'Arthur in English society', p. x95; also Holmes, *The Estates of the Higher Nobility*, p. 18.

1. Vale, 'Arthur in English society', p. 186.

2. Ibid., p. 187, citing the English prose *Brut* (c. 1400); the *Brut* reference is also quoted by W. R. J. Barton on p. 34 of the same volume. Vale places this Round Table in Wales, but it was at Bedford according to *The Complete Peerage*, VIII, 439.

3. *The Complete Peerage*, VIII, 443–4.

question of their mutual cousin Henry of Bolingbroke, Earl of Derby, claiming the crown. Philippa's husband was a member of the Regency Council in 1377, and from 1379 served as Richard II's lieutenant in Ireland.[4] But Philippa was dead by 1381, and Edmund Mortimer died on campaign in Ireland the same year, leaving a young son Roger, fourth Earl of March, who automatically inherited his mother's claim. Whether or not the King ever formally acknowledged the situation—Richard II was still young, not long married, and hoping for a son—some contemporary sources, such as the Wigmore Chronicler writing in 1385, speak of Roger as the King's heir.[5] In that very year Richard II began creating dukedoms, firstly for his two uncles Edmund of Langley and Thomas of Woodstock (York and Gloucester), then, the following year, for his close friends Robert de Vere and Thomas Mowbray (Ireland and Norfolk). This can only have aroused the envy of the young Earl of March, now old enough to understand that he was a royal heir, who might well have hoped for the revival of his grandfather's title.

In the light of these facts, one may attribute a new significance to the lamentation in *SGGK* surrounding Sir Gawain's departure from Camelot, together with the expressed opinion that the King would have been wiser to have made him a duke instead of listening to the hasty advice of others (see lines 674–83). Why is it suggested that Gawain should have been made a duke? This may well be intended as a hint to Richard II in favour of his heir Roger Mortimer, fourth Earl of March, who could claim the dukedom of Clarence. The Wigmore Chronicler has left a colourful portrait of Roger, who was 'very lustful and remiss in his duty to God', but otherwise splendid and popular; 'of approved honesty, active in knightly exercises, glorious in pleasantry (*in facescia gloriosus*), affable, and merry in conversation, excelling his contemporaries in beauty of appearance, sumptuous in his feastings, and liberal in his gifts'.[6] Unfortunately, he was killed fighting in Ireland in 1398, leaving a son, Edmund, fifth Earl of March, now heir presumptive to the throne—but too young and weak to act as a bulwark against Bolingbroke, who deposed Richard II in 1399 and seized the throne as Henry IV.

It may also be supposed that Roger Mortimer had probably hoped to become a member of the Order of the Garter in reward for his services to the Crown. It is a fact that although his grandfather Roger, second Earl of March, had been a founding companion of the Order in 1348, no other member of this family ever became a Garter knight. All the adult sons of Edward III, and several of his sons-in-law, were

---

4. *The Oxford Companion to British History*, ed. John Cannon (Oxford, 1997), p. 657.
5. See *The Complete Peerage*, VIII, 448; also Collins, 'The Order of the Garter', p. 59.
6. Quoted in *The Complete Peerage*, VIII, 449–50 n. (m).

companions of the Order; yet the Garter was never granted to
Edmund, third Earl of March, despite his marriage to Edward III's
own granddaughter Philippa, nor to their son Roger, fourth Earl, who
married a niece of Richard II. Even the women of the family were
pointedly excluded from the parallel Garter sorority, at a period when
many female members of the royal family, as well as other high-born
ladies, received Garter livery: for example Richard II issued Garter
robes to Alice, Countess of Kent, wife of his uterine half-brother
Thomas Holland, in 1388, and similarly in 1399 to two of his Holland
nieces, Joan, Duchess of York, and Margaret, Marchioness of
Dorset—but not to their sister Eleanor, Roger Mortimer's wife.[7] One
has the impression that the Mortimers, following the marriage of the
third Earl to Prince Lionel's daughter, were seen as something of
a threat, pretenders who might eventually prove dangerous. Both
Edmund, the Duke of Clarence's son-in-law, and Roger, heir presumptive to Richard II, had good grounds for hoping to see the Clarence
title revived in their favour. Equally, both of these men, father and
son, could legitimately aspire to the Garter, not indeed as a right, but
as close kin of the royal family who displayed military courage in the
field. But membership of the Order was a rare privilege, limited to the
King's inner circle and entirely depending on royal favour. The Mortimers must have felt frustrated at their exclusion, just as they must
have resented not succeeding to the Clarence title.

One may therefore explain the poet's reference to the Duke of
Clarence, and the opinion, voiced at Camelot, that Gawain should
have been made a duke, as a flattering reference to the late Prince
Lionel and his grandson Roger Mortimer; and I would conjecture
that in the course of the next few years (Roger lived until 1398), the
fourth Earl of March was the literary patron for whom the Gawain-
poet wrote. He, like his father before him, was a loyal subject and
when older fought for the King's interests, both against the rebel-
lious barons (headed by Richard's uncle Thomas, Duke of Gloucester) and in Ireland, where he fell. Does the poem contain a veiled
panegyric in his honour, or possibly in honour of his father? The precise date of the poem would obviously have a bearing on this question, since Edmund Mortimer died in 1381, but the allusions could
be applied equally to father or son. Either could claim that he should
have been made a duke (line 678), both were fine military leaders
(line 679), both died in battle, brought to naught (line 680), and
both were affected by the unwise decisions of kings (lines 682–3). It
is interesting to note that in the next generation, too, the last of the
Mortimers, the fifth Earl of March, was kept firmly under heel by

7. See list of ladies of the Garter in Holmes, *The Order of the Garter*, pp. 168–73, and
Collins, *The Order of the Garter*, appendix IV, pp. 301–3.

the usurping Lancastrian monarch; in a pointed snub, Henry IV gave the dukedom of Clarence to his own son Thomas in 1412.[8] Nevertheless, it was on the Mortimers' claim to the throne that the Yorkists—descended from the fifth Earl's sister Anne, Countess of Cambridge, grandmother of the future Edward IV—would base their war against Henry VI later in the century.

The poem we call *Sir Gawain and the Green Knight* is a rich and many-layered work of art defying any attempt to reduce it to mere propaganda. The theory put forward here is offered, not as an 'explanation' of the whole text, but only as an interpretation of some of the historical facts that may be gleaned from it. My conjectures are all based on references within the poem. Many attempts have been made to identify the anonymous poet of MS Cotton Nero A.x, or at least, failing all else, to situate him in relation to one of the great families of the north-west Midlands who would be likely patrons of this type of aristocratic literature.[9] Several members of the royal family have at various times been suggested, from John of Gaunt to his father-in-law Henry of Grosmont (supposing an early dating), not excluding the King himself in the person of Richard II, if a late date of composition be accepted; but no theory has met with wide critical acceptance. The poet's reference to the Duke of Clarence has not previously attracted any attention, nor have the real-life Duke's heirs been proposed as possible patrons. The Garter motto tends to be dismissed as a scribal afterthought and again, no link is usually suggested between an heir to the throne and the fact that the motto appears at the end of the poem. But the evidence is there in the text, and my application of the Garter motto is fully in keeping with both the moral tenor of the poem and its discernible historical situation.

8. *The Complete Peerage*, III, 259. The editors do not seem conscious of the nature or significance of the snub, commenting: 'It is difficult to conjecture why this title was selected, as the honour of Clare was in the hands of the York line of the Royal family.'
9. See Malcolm Andrew, 'Theories of authorship', in *A Companion to the Gawain-Poet*, pp. 23–33.

Chronology

ca. 1125	William of Malmesbury, *Gesta Regum Anglorum*, [Deeds of the English Kings], includes narrative of King Arthur
ca. 1137	Geoffrey of Monmouth, *Historia Regum Britanniae* [History of the Kings of Britain], relates the founding of Britain, including an expansive treatment of Arthur's conquests
1154–1189	Henry II, king of England, with extensive holdings in France
ca. 1155	Wace, *Roman de Brut*, Anglo-Norman poem based on Geoffrey of Monmouth's Latin history of England
ca. 1160–1180	Chrétien de Troyes (ca. 1140–1200), author of Arthurian romances, associated with the court of Marie de Champagne
ca. 1180–1200	"The Knight with the Sword," and "The Mule without a Bridle" (anon.)
ca. 1200–1225	Layamon, *Brut*, an English alliterative version of Wace's *Roman de Brut*
ca. 1220–1235	Prose Vulgate Cycle of Arthurian romance, in French
ca. 1235	Guillaume de Lorris, *Roman de la Rose*
ca. 1275	Jean de Meun's continuation of *Roman de la Rose*
1327–1377	Edward III, king of England
1339–1453	The Hundred Years' War, between England and France
1348	Order of the Garter established
1348–1350	Plague, known as "Black Death" in Britain, killing 25 to 50 percent of the population
ca. 1357–1371	*The Travels of Sir John Mandeville* (anon.), in Anglo-Norman French
ca. 1360–1400	*Alliterative Morte Arthure* (anon.)
1361	Plague returns to Britain
ca. 1362–1368	William Langland, *Piers Plowman* (A-text), with subsequent revisions in ca. 1377 (B-text) and in ca. 1390 (C-text)

ca. 1375–1400	Manuscript Cotton Nero A.x, which contains *Sir Gawain and the Green Knight*, copied from a previous copy or a lost original
1376	Earliest extant record of York Corpus Christi plays
1377–1399	Richard II, king of England
ca. 1381–1385	*Troilus and Criseyde*, by Geoffrey Chaucer (ca. 1342–1400)
ca. 1386–1390	*Confessio amantis* by John Gower (ca. 1330–1408), in English
1378–1417	The Great Schism, with rival popes in Avignon and Rome
1381	The Peasants' Revolt (The English Rising)
ca. 1387–1400	*The Canterbury Tales*, by Geoffrey Chaucer (ca. 1342–1400)
ca. 1390	*St. Erkenwald* (anon.)
1399–1413	Henry IV, king of England
1400	Murder of Richard II

Selected Bibliography

• indicates items included or excerpted in this Norton Critical Edition.

Editions

Andrew, Malcolm and Ronald Waldron, eds. *The Poems of the Pearl Manuscript.* York Medieval Texts. 2nd ser. Berkeley: University of California press, 1979. Rpt. Exeter: University of Exeter Press, 2002.
Tolkien, J. R. R. and E. V. Gordon, eds. *Sir Gawain and the Green Knight.* Oxford: Clarendon Press, 1925. 2nd ed. rev. Norman Davis (Oxford, 1967).

Reference Works

Brewer, Elizabeth, ed. *Sir Gawain and the Green Knight: Sources and Analogues.* Woodbridge, Suffolk, UK: D. S. Brewer, 1992.
Gollancz, I. *Pearl, Cleanness, Patience and Sir Gawain: Reproduced in Facsimile from the Unique MS. Cotton Nero A.x in the British Museum.* Early English Text Society O. S. 162. London: Oxford University Press, 1923.
Johnston, R. C. and D. D. R. Owen, eds. *Two Old French Gauvain Romances.* Edinburgh: Scottish Academic Press, 1972.
Kottler, Barnet and Alan M. Markman. *A Concordance to Five Middle English Poems: Cleanness, St. Erkenwald, Sir Gawain and the Green Knight, Patience and Pearl.* Pittsburgh: University of Pittsburgh Press, 1966.

Essay Collections

Blanch, Robert J., ed. *Sir Gawain* and *Pearl: Critical Essays.* Bloomington: Indiana University Press, 1966.
Brewer, D. S., ed. *Studies in Medieval English Romances: Some New Approaches.* Cambridge: D. S. Brewer, 1988.
Brewer, Derek and Jonathan Gibson, eds. *A Companion to the Gawain-Poet.* Cambridge: D. S. Brewer, 1997.
Fox, Denton, ed. *Twentieth Century Interpretations of Sir Gawain and the Green Knight: A Collection of Critical Essays.* Englewood Cliffs, N.J.: Prentice-Hall, 1968.
Howard, Donald and Christian Zacher, eds. *Critical Studies of Sir Gawain and the Green Knight.* Notre Dame, Ind.: University of Notre Dame Press, 1968.

Studies

Aers, David. " 'In Arthurus day': Community, Virtue, and Individual Identity in *Sir Gawain and the Green Knight.*" In *Community, Gender and Individual Identity: English Writing, 1360–1430* (153–178). London: Routledge, 1988.

Anderson, J. J. *Language and Imagination in the* Gawain-*Poems*. Manchester, UK: Manchester University Press, 2005.

Arthur, Ross G. *Medieval Sign Theory and Sir Gawain and the Green Knight*. Toronto: University of Toronto Press, 1987.

Bennett, Michael J. *Community, Class, and Careerism: Cheshire and Lancashire Society in the Age of Sir Gawain and the Green Knight*. Cambridge: Cambridge University Press, 1983.

Benson, Larry D. *Art and Tradition in Sir Gawain and the Green Knight*. New Brunswick, N.J.: Rutgers University Press, 1965.

Boitani, Piero. *English Medieval Narrative in the Thirteenth and Fourteenth Centuries*. Trans. Joan Krakover Hall. Cambridge: Cambridge University Press, 1982.

• Borroff, Marie. *Sir Gawain and the Green Knight: A Stylistic and Metrical Study*. Yale Studies in English, Vol. 152. New Haven, Conn.: Yale University Press, 1962.

———. "*Sir Gawain and the Green Knight*: The Passing of Judgment." In *Traditions and Renewals: Chaucer, the Gawain-Poet, and Beyond* (97–113). New Haven, Conn.: Yale University Press, 2003.

• Burrow, J. A. *A Reading of Sir Gawain and the Green Knight*. London: Routledge and Kegan Paul, 1965.

• Carruthers, Leo. "The Duke of Clarence and the Earls of March: Garter Knights and *Sir Gawain and the Green Knight*." *Medium Ævum* 70.1 (2001): 66–79.

Condron, Edward I. *The Numerical Universe of the Gawain-Pearl Poet: Beyond Phi*. Gainesville: University Press of Florida, 2002.

• Davenport, W. A. *The Art of the Gawain Poet*. London: Athlone Press, 1978.

Everett, Dorothy. "The Alliterative Revival." In *Essays on Middle English Literature* (74–85). Ed. Patricia Kean. Oxford: Clarendon Press, 1955.

Field, P. J. C. "A Rereading of *Sir Gawain and the Green Knight*." *University of Toronto Quarterly* 40 (1970–71): 255–269.

Fisher, Sheila. "Leaving Morgan Aside: Women, History, and Revisionism." In *Sir Gawain and the Green Knight. Arthurian Women* (129–151). Ed. Thelma Fenster. New York: Garland 1988.

Ganim, John M. "Disorientation, Style, and Consciousness in *Sir Gawain and the Green Knight*." *PMLA* 91 (1976): 376–84.

Green, Richard Firth. *A Crisis of Truth: Literature and Law in Ricardian England*. Philadelphia: University of Pennsylvania Press, 1999.

Hanna, Ralph. "Alliterative Poetry." In *The Cambridge History of Medieval English Literature* (488–512). Ed. David Wallace. Cambridge: Cambridge University Press, 1999.

• ———. "Unlocking What's Locked: Gawain's Green Girdle." *Viator* 14 (1983): 289–301.

Hanning, Robert W. "Sir Gawain and the Red Herring: The Perils of Interpretation." In *Acts of Interpretation: The Text in Its Contexts, 700–1600: Essays on Medieval and Renaissance Literature in Honor of E. Talbot Donaldson* (5–23). Ed. Mary Carruthers and Elizabeth D. Kirk. Norman, Okla.: Pilgrim Books, 1982.

Heng, Geraldine. "A Woman Wants: The Lady, *Gawain*, and the Forms of Seduction." *Yale Journal of Criticism* 5 (1992): 110–15.

• ———. "Feminine Knots and the Other *Sir Gawain and the Green Knight*. *PMLA* 106 (1991): 500–514.

• Hieatt, A Kent. "*Sir Gawain*: Pentangle, *Luf-Lace*, Numerical Structure." In *Silent Poetry: Essays in Numerological Analysis* (116–40). Ed. Alistair Fowler. New York: Barnes & Noble, 1970.

Hughes, Derek W. "The Problem of Reality in *Sir Gawain and the Green Knight*." *Studies in Philology* 68 (1971): 217–35.

• Johnson, Lynn Staley. *The Voice of the Gawain Poet*. Madison: University of Wisconsin Press, 1984.

Knight, Rhonda. "All Dressed Up with Someplace to Go: Regional Identity in *Sir Gawain and the Green Knight*." *Studies in the Age of Chaucer* 25 (2003): 259–84.

Mann, Jill. "Price and Value in *Sir Gawain and the Green Knight*." *Essays in Criticism* 36 (1986): 294–318.

Marvin, William Perry. *Hunting Law and Ritual in Medieval English Literature*. Cambridge: D. S. Brewer, 2006.

• Nicholls, Jonathan. *The Matter of Courtesy: Medieval Courtesy Books and the Gawain-Poet*. Woodbridge, Suffolk, UK: D. S. Brewer, 1985.

Pearsall, Derek. "The Origins of the Alliterative Revival." In *The Alliterative Tradition in the Fourteenth Century* (1–17). Ed. Barnard S. Levy and Paul E. Szarmach. Kent, Ohio: Kent State University Press, 1981.

———. "Rhetorical 'Descriptio' in Sir *Gawain and the Green Knight*." *Modern Language Review* 50 (1955): 129–34.

Prior, Sandra Pierson. *The Pearl Poet Revisited*. New York: Twayne, 1994.

Putter, Ad. *An Introduction to the Gawain-Poet*. London: Longman Press, 1996.

———. *Sir Gawain and the Green Knight and French Arthurian Romance*. Oxford: Clarendon Press, 1995.

• Renoir, Alain. "Descriptive Technique in Sir Gawain and the Green Knight." *Orbis Litterarum* 13 (1958): 126–32.

Rooney, Anne. *Hunting in Middle English Literature*. Cambridge: Boydell Press, 1993.

Spearing, A. C. *The Gawain-Poet: A Critical Study*. Cambridge: Cambridge University Press, 1970.

Stanbury, Sarah. *Seeing the Gawain-Poet: Description and the Act of Perception*. Philadelphia: University of Pennsylvania Press, 1991.

Whiteford, Peter. "Rereading Gawain's Five Wits." *Medium Ævum* 73 (2004): 225–34.

Wilson, Edward. *The Gawain-Poet*. Medieval and Renaissance Authors Series. Leiden: E. J. Brill, 1976.